THE SOHO BIBLIOGRAPHIES

I

W. B. YEATS

THE SOHO BIBLIOGRAPHIES

RUPERT BROOKE
GEOFFREY KEYNES

HENRY JAMES
EDEL & LAWRENCE

SIEGFRIED SASSOON
GEOFFREY KEYNES

D. H. LAWRENCE
WARREN ROBERTS

EDITH, OSBERT and
SACHEVERELL SITWELL
RICHARD FIFOOT

LUCRETIUS
COSMO GORDON

THE FOULIS PRESS
PHILIP GASKELL

RONALD FIRBANK
MIRIAM J. BENKOVITZ

EDMUND BURKE
WILLIAM B. TODD

W. B. YEATS

From the drawing by J. B. Yeats in 1898

W. B. YEATS

From the drawing by J. B. Yeats in *Mosada*.

A BIBLIOGRAPHY
OF THE WRITINGS OF
W. B. YEATS

ALLAN WADE

THIRD EDITION
REVISED AND EDITED BY
RUSSELL K. ALSPACH

RUPERT HART-DAVIS
1968

First published 1951
Second edition, revised, 1958
Third edition, revised, 1968

SBN 246·64138·X

Printed in Great Britain by Richard Clay (The Chaucer Press), Limited,
Bungay, Suffolk

CONTENTS

ILLUSTRATIONS

PREFACE TO THE FIRST EDITION

IT is now more than fifty years since I first began to make a list of the writings of W. B. Yeats, and my earlier attempt towards a bibliography appeared in 1908 in an edition of sixty copies; it also formed part of the eighth volume of the Yeats Collected Edition of that year, both published by A. H. Bullen at the Shakespeare Head Press, Stratford-on-Avon. Notes on American editions were then supplied by John Quinn of New York, who sold his important library, including a fine collection of Yeats's books, in 1924. I have thus been able to make use of Quinn's original notes on early American editions, and also those he contributed to his sale catalogue. In 1924 the First Edition Club published *A Bibliography of the First Editions of Books by William Butler Yeats*, compiled by A. J. A. Symons. This did not go beyond a description of the physical make-up of the various volumes, and adhered so rigorously to its title that enlarged or revised editions were left unrecorded; nor was any attempt made to detail the contents of the books. Within its narrow limits, however, it is fairly accurate. In 1939, on the occasion of an exhibition of Yeats's books held in the Yale University Library, Mr. W. M. Roth compiled and published at New Haven a *Catalogue of English and American First Editions of W. B. Yeats* (referred to in this book as Roth). Giving fuller measure than its title promised, Mr. Roth's book also mentioned many later editions and briefly noted the contents of the volumes described; a second part of the book included a list of contributions to periodicals, though this latter had numerous mistakes both of exclusion and inclusion. In 1939–1940 Mr. P. S. O'Hegarty contributed some valuable "Notes on the Bibliography of W. B. Yeats" to two successive numbers of the *Dublin Magazine*. These different authorities are quoted by name wherever I have been unable to check their findings by my own research.

In the present work I give full description of first editions with mention of any subsequent edition in which alteration and revision may be found. Yeats, it is well known, was an inveterate reviser of his work; he was tireless in his search for improvement, and there is scarcely a new edition of any book of his, either verse or prose, without alteration in the text, sometimes slight, often considerable. Hence no collector of Yeats's work could easily be content to possess only his first editions. I once asked him, at the time of its first publication, whether he was pleased with the Shakespeare Head Press Collected Edition, and he replied, "Oh yes; but if a publisher were to offer me another collecte edition in ten years' time I should accept as it would give me opportunity for further revision." This opportunity came to him when the six volumes, containing his work to that time, were issued by Macmillan & Co. between 1922 and 1926, and again with the two volumes of *Collected Poems*, 1933, and *Collected Plays*, 1935; and when a new "de luxe" collected edition was proposed to him in 1930 he wrote to a friend, "Six months of rewriting—what happiness!"

An Irish and an American scholar, Mr. Peter Allt and Lieut.-Colonel R. K. Alspach, have been for some years preparing a variorum edition of the lyrical poems; in time, doubtless, the plays and the prose works also will be studied with equal care; and in this bibliography I have aimed at making it possible for readers to trace the progress of Yeats's writing from its earliest appearance in newspaper or periodical, through the various editions and collections published in his lifetime, to its culmination, for the poems, in the two-volume Definitive Edition of 1949, the text of which Yeats carefully corrected in 1937.

Anthologies are only mentioned here when work by Yeats appeared there before being collected into one of his own books; and I have not attempted to note the very many musical settings of lyrics, with the single exception of Edward Elgar's setting of a song from *Diarmuid and Grania*, the play by Yeats and George Moore, which does not appear in the text of the play as published in 1951.

In listing Yeats's contributions to periodicals, both those collected later into volumes and those uncollected, I have not felt it necessary to enumerate all the reprintings of each item in later editions; if a poem has been included in *The Wind Among the Reeds*, for instance, it is not difficult to trace its subsequent appearances by referring to Part I.

Although I have tried to make my researches as far-reaching as possible there are, I am aware, still some contributions to periodicals to be discovered. In spite of widespread enquiries I have been unable to trace any copies of *The Gael*, the organ of the Gaelic Athletic Association, issued weekly in Dublin from the Spring of 1887; it is evident from letters, published and unpublished, that Yeats contributed both verse and prose to its literary department; probably some of the poems in *The Wanderings of Oisin*, possibly the short story *Dhoya* appeared there. Yeats is known, also, to have contributed some notes on literary matters to the *Manchester Courier* in the early part of 1889. The file of this paper in the British Museum not being at present available, Mr. Patrick Monkhouse kindly undertook to examine a file in Manchester; he reports that a column headed "Literary Notes" was a weekly feature of the paper for many years and that it consisted of a series of short book-reviews varying in length from 100 to 500 words. As none of these was signed, either by name or initials, identification of Yeats's contributions could only be a matter of guess-work.

I owe a deep debt of gratitude to Mrs. W. B. Yeats who has kindly allowed me free access not only to Yeats's own library but to her collection of his books which includes most of the later American editions; she also gave me permission to quote the various notes written by Yeats in copies of his books and elsewhere. Mr. P. S. O'Hegarty's great knowledge of Irish bibliography and of Yeats's books has been generously available to me at all times; for this and for reading the proofs of this book I offer him my thanks. Mr. Peter Allt has, with great kindness, helped me in the search, through dusty and crumbling files of old newspapers, for Yeats's early contributions to the Press in Ireland. I am also much indebted to Dr. R. J. Hayes, Librarian of the National Library of Ireland, and to Mr. John Bebbington, Librarian of the Central Library, Belfast, especially for their aid in attempting to discover the elusive *Gael*. I wish also to acknowledge the help I have received from Mr. Edmund Dulac, Mr. M. J. Macmanus and Mr. Frederic Prokosch, and, in America, from Lt.-Col. Russell K. Alspach, Mr. Leon Edel, Mr. Richard Ellmann, Mr. D. C. Gallup and Miss Barbara D. Simison of Yale University Library, Mr. Edwin Gilcher, Mr. James A. Healy, Mr. Horace Reynolds and Mr. G. Brandon Saul.

I am very grateful to Messrs Macmillan and Co. Ltd, for information concerning the editions they published, and to them and to the Macmillan Company of New York for supplying the actual dates of publication. Other publishers who have kindly and willingly given me information are Messrs Ernest Benn Ltd, Messrs Chapman and Hall, Ltd, The Clarendon Press, Mr. John Murray and Messrs Bernard Quaritch Ltd, in London; Messrs M. H. Gill and Son Ltd, of Dublin; Messrs Dodd Mead and Co, Messrs Charles Scribner's Sons, and Random House, in New York; and the Walter H. Baker Co. of Boston.

I acknowledge gratefully the loan of books from Mr. William Becker, Mr. Rupert Hart-Davis, Mr. T. R. Henn, Mr. W. S. Kennedy and Mr. Simon Nowell-Smith.

The section devoted to translations is as complete as I have been able to make it in present conditions, but there are probably other translations which I have not yet discovered. I wish to thank the Librarian of the Nobel Library, Stockholm, Dr. Ragnar Svanstrom of P. A. Norstedt & Söner, Stockholm, and Mrs. Birgit Bjersby of Uppsala for their help in compiling a list of Swedish translations, Mrs. R. Pennink of the Koninklijke Bibliotheek, The Hague, and Mr. Johan Van Delden in connection with the Dutch translations, Mr. E. E. Stein who kindly checked the entries of the German translations and lent me some books from his collection, and Professor Makoto Sangu of Hosei University, Tokyo, who sent me descriptions of the Japanese translations.

My sincere thanks are due to Mr. Richard Garnett who has taken infinite trouble to check my work and has saved me from many mistakes.

Probably no bibliography has ever been compiled without some errors; it remains for me now to ask pardon for any which may be found in this one, and to thank, in advance, those critics who will point them out.

ALLAN WADE

Boscastle, Cornwall
June, 1951

PREFACE TO THE SECOND EDITION

WHEN Allan Wade died suddenly on 12 July 1955, at the age of seventy-four, he was busily engaged in revising this bibliography for a new edition. Since his death I have to the best of my ability completed the task as I believe he would have liked it done. I have been greatly helped by the temporary use of his extensive Yeats collection, which is now in the University of Indiana.

Besides the new publications of the last six years, many minor corrections and a few additions have been incorporated in the text. Since the bibliography is already widely quoted as an authority, it seemed best not to alter any of Allan Wade's numberings, but rather to give an intermediate number (such as 313A) to any interpolated item. I have also taken the opportunity of providing a full index, which the original edition lacked.

I have received generous help from many experts; in particular, Professor Marion Witt, Dr. Hayes, Mr. Ellmann, Professor Sangu, Mr. Bertram Rota, and above all Colonel Alspach, whose relentless eye and unfailing kindness are responsible for much of the new material. I am particularly happy to be able to include here a description of the great variorum edition of Yeats's lyrical poems, on which he and the late Peter Allt have laboured so long. Professor George Whalley, besides devoting many patient hours to the laborious business of checking and transcription, has contributed a valuable new appendix on Yeats and Broadcasting. I feel sure that between 1951 and 1955 many other people sent in comments and queries, but I found no list of their names among Allan Wade's papers and must ask them to accept this anonymous acknowledgement.

RUPERT HART-DAVIS

November 1957

PREFACE TO THE THIRD EDITION

In revising the bibliography for the third edition I have tried to make a complete listing of all publications dealing primarily with Yeats that appeared between 1957 and early 1966. In the text of the second edition I have inserted newly discovered items and have added details to a number of old items.

The large increase in Japanese material was made possible by Professor Shotaro Oshima's generously giving me permission to make full use of the bibliography in his excellent W. B. YEATS AND JAPAN (No. 359).

I owe thanks to Rupert Hart-Davis, who waited patiently for the typescript and was helpful with suggestions; to Liam Miller, editor of *The Irish Book*, who published in the Autumn, 1963, issue my "Additions to Allan Wade's Bibliography of W. B. Yeats"; to Ronald Ayling, of Dublin; E. C. Beer, of the Douglas Library, Queen's College, Ontario; Professor Gustav Cross, of Sydney, Australia; Alan Denson, of Kendal, Westmorland; James F. Gallagher, of New York; Shirley Kaye, of the Walter H. Baker Company, Boston; Alexandra Mason, of the University of Kansas Library; David A. Randall, Librarian of The University Libraries, Indiana University; the children of the late T. B. Rogers, of Birmingham, England; Professor Ann Saddlemyer, of the University of Victoria; Michael Walsh, of Dublin; Geneva Warren, Curator of Special Collections, Indiana University; and Marion Witt, Professor Emeritus of Hunter College.

RUSSELL K. ALSPACH

University of Massachusetts,
October, 1966

BOOKS BY W. B. YEATS

MOSADA.

A Dramatic Poem.

BY

W. B. YEATS.

WITH A

Frontispiece Portrait of the Author

By J. B. YEATS.

Reprinted from the DUBLIN UNIVERSITY REVIEW.

DUBLIN:
PRINTED BY SEALY, BRYERS, AND WALKER,
94, 95 AND 96 MIDDLE ABBEY STREET.
1886.

BOOKS BY W. B. YEATS

I

MOSADA. | A DRAMATIC POEM. | BY | W. B. YEATS. | WITH A | FRONTISPIECE PORTRAIT OF THE AUTHOR | BY J. B. YEATS. | [rule] | REPRINTED FROM THE DUBLIN UNIVERSITY REVIEW. | [rule] | DUBLIN: | PRINTED BY SEALY, BRYERS, AND WALKER, | 94, 95 AND 96 MIDDLE ABBEY STREET. | [rule] | 1886. [*The whole enclosed in a decorative border composed of medallions at top and bottom and a device of shamrocks at the sides, inside double rules.*]

$8\frac{1}{2} \times 5\frac{1}{4}$; pp. 12: comprising text, pp. 1–11; imprint, Printed by Sealy, Bryers and Walker, 94, 95, and 96 Middle Abbey Street, Dublin. on p. [12].

An off-print from *The Dublin University Review*, June 1886.

Issued in light brown paper covers, lined white; stitched; all edges trimmed. There is no title-page, the above description being taken from the front cover. The frontispiece, reverse blank, is tipped in before the first leaf of text.

Miss E. C. Yeats told Mr. P. S. O'Hegarty that the edition consisted of 100 copies; the book probably appeared about October, as the following note was published in the November number of *The Dublin University Review*: "We are glad to note the publication by Messrs. Sealy Bryers & Walker of the powerful and pathetic poem 'Mosada' contributed to a recent number of this Review by Mr. W. B. Yeats. The reprint contains a pen-and-ink portrait of the author by Mr. J. B. Yeats—a very beautiful and characteristic piece of work admirably reproduced on zinc by a Dublin engraver, Mr. Lewis." Beneath the portrait in Quinn's copy, Yeats wrote in March 1904, "There was to have been a picture of some incident in the play but my father was too much of a portrait painter not to do this instead. I was alarmed at the impudence of putting a portrait in my first book, but my father was full of ancient and modern instances." In another copy, sold at the Anderson Galleries, New York, in 1926, he wrote, "The first copy that I have seen in many years. The play was published in the Dublin University Review and from that reprinted in the present form and had of course no success of any kind. It was my father who insisted on the portrait, as he refused to consider anybody's diffidence where a portrait was concerned, it was also his insistence that kept me bearded. W. B. Yeats, Nov. 10, 1923." He added, on the last page, "I read this through for the first time since it was first published. I wrote it when I was twenty-one & think rather sadly that when young men of that age send in like work I am not able to foresee his future or his talent. W. B. Yeats."

Mosada in this form is exceedingly rare. Between 1913 and 1946 only fourteen copies are recorded in *Book Prices Current*, ten appearing in English sale-rooms, four in American; and these probably include cases of the same copy reappearing. There were two copies in Quinn's sale catalogue, one a presentation copy inscribed "Mr. J. O'Leary from his disciple and friend the Author. W. B. Yeats", the other a review copy. The first of these now forms part of the Berg Collection in the New York Public Library. The American collector Paul Lemperly possessed a copy which was sold in January 1940 after his death, and another figured in the C. Walter Buhler sale in May 1941; this was a presentation copy inscribed "Miss Veasey with good wishes for the New Year from her friend the author." There was a copy in the Esher sale in November 1946; this was acquired by Lord Berwick who lent it for exhibition at the National Book League in 1947; it is now in the possession of Lady Berwick. Katharine Tynan mentions the possession of a copy in her *Twenty-Five Years*; this was sold at Sotheby's in March 1914, and was inscribed "Miss K. Tynan from her friend and fellow worker in Irish Poetry the Author." It is now in the Sterling Memorial Library at Yale University. The late T. W. Rolleston owned a copy which he lent me for examination when I was compiling my earlier Yeats bibliography in 1908. One copy is known to exist, in a private collection, in Dublin. Yeats himself seems to have kept no copy, and there is none in the British Museum, at Trinity College, Dublin, or in the National Library of Ireland. A copy in the Bodleian, another, inscribed to H. A. Pollexfen and now in the William Andrews Clark Memorial Library, University of California, and another owned by Mr. Cyril I. Nelson of New York, are bound in thicker paper, unlined.

A few facsimile copies of *Mosada*, omitting p. 12, made up from photostats printed on Vandyke paper and stitched inside plain light brown kraft paper covers were discovered by Mr. Pádraig Ó Broin of

Toronto, Canada. They were taken from a copy inscribed below the portrait: "To F Gregg from his friend the Author."
See also No. 206.

2

THE | WANDERINGS OF OISIN | AND OTHER POEMS | BY | W. B. YEATS | LONDON | KEGAN PAUL, TRENCH & CO., I, PATERNOSTER SQUARE | 1889

7 × 4½; pp. 2, vi, 156: comprising one blank leaf not included in pagination; half-title, verso blank, pp. [i–ii]; title, with note reserving rights on verso, pp. [iii–iv]; contents, pp. [v]–vi; text, pp. [1]–156; imprint, Printed by William Clowes and Sons, Limited, London and Beccles, beneath rule at foot of p. 156.

Issued in dark blue cloth, lettered in gold on front cover THE WANDER-INGS OF OISIN | AND OTHER POEMS. and on spine, THE | WANDERINGS | OF | OISIN | [short rule] | W. B. YEATS | KEGAN PAUL TRENCH & CO. with publisher's monogram stamped blind on back cover; black end-papers, lined white; all edges untrimmed.

500 copies were published in January 1889.

Contents

The Wanderings of Oisin
Time and the Witch Vivien
The Stolen Child
    First appeared in The Irish Monthly, December 1886.
Girl's Song
Ephemera
An Indian Song
    First appeared in The Dublin University Review, December 1886.
Kanva, the Indian, on God
    First appeared, under the title From the Book of Kauri, the Indian. Section V., On the Nature of God, in The Dublin University Review, October 1886.
Kanva on himself
Jealousy
Song of the Last Arcadian
    First appeared, under the title An Epilogue. To "The Island of Statues" and "The Seeker", in The Dublin University Review, October 1885.
King Goll
    First appeared, under the title King Goll. An Irish Legend, in The Leisure Hour, September 1887. An illustration by J. B. Yeats accompanied it.

The Meditation of the Old Fisherman
    First appeared in *The Irish Monthly*, October 1886.

The Ballad of Moll Magee
    Katharine Tynan wrote to me in 1908 saying that she thought
    this poem appeared in *The Gael*, a Dublin paper, in the late
    'eighties or very early 'nineties. This paper actually was
    published in 1887, but I have not yet succeeded in finding it.

The Phantom Ship
    First appeared, under the title *The Legend of the Phantom Ship*,
    in *The Providence Sunday Journal*, May 27, 1888.

A Lover's Quarrel among the Fairies

Mosada
    First appeared in *The Dublin University Review*, June 1886.

How Ferencz Renyi kept Silent
    First appeared in *The Boston Pilot*, August 6, 1887.

The Fairy Doctor
    First appeared in *The Irish Fireside*, September 10, 1887.

Falling of the Leaves

Miserrimus
    First appeared in *The Dublin University Review*, October 1886.

The Priest and the Fairy
    Also appeared in *The All Ireland Review*, August 11, 1900.

The Fairy Pedant
    First appeared in *The Irish Monthly*, March 1887.

She who dwelt among the Sycamores
    First appeared in *The Irish Monthly*, September 1887.

On Mr. Nettleship's Picture at the Royal Hibernian Academy, 1885.
    First appeared in *The Dublin University Review*, April 1886.

A Legend
    First appeared, hand-lettered and illustrated by Jack B. Yeats,
    in *The Vegetarian*, December 22, 1888.

An Old Song re-sung

Street Dancers
    Also appeared in *The Leisure Hour*, March 1890.

To an Isle in the Water

Quatrains and Aphorisms
    The first and fifth quatrains first appeared in *The Dublin Uni-*
    versity Review, February 1886, under the title *Life*; the second and
    sixth in January 1886, unsigned, under the title *In a Drawing Room*.

The Seeker
    First appeared under the title, *The Seeker. A Dramatic Poem.*
    In Two Scenes, in *The Dublin University Review*, September 1885.

Island of Statues

The whole poem first appeared, under the title *The Island of Statues. An Arcadian Faery Tale. In Two Acts*, in *The Dublin University Review*, April, May, June and July 1885; but only Act II, scene iii, which appeared in the July number, is reprinted here. It is described as *A Fragment* and is preceded by a "Summary of Previous Scenes" in prose.

Roth records a binding variant: the cloth is smoother and slightly darker; there is no publishers' monogram on the back; and T H E on the spine is more widely spaced.

Another binding variant appeared in a sale at Sotheby's on January 22, 1951. The cloth was light blue and the words *AND OTHER POEMS* on front cover and *W. B. YEATS* on spine were in italics; the end-papers were yellow; and the fore-edge and foot were lightly trimmed. It bore an inscription dated 11 Aug. 1889, and is presumably a later issue. Now in the collection of Mr. Cyril I. Nelson.

Another binding variant has Paul, Trench, Trübner & Co. at foot of spine; and there is no publishers' monogram on the back.

In his last published essay, *I Became an Author*, in *The Listener*, August 4, 1938, Yeats wrote that *The Wanderings of Oisin* "was published by subscription, John O'Leary finding almost all the subscribers."

3

In May 1892, Fisher Unwin published a second issue consisting of the original sheets with a cancel title and a frontispiece, representing Niam, Oisin and S. Patrick, by Edwin John Ellis:

THE | WANDERINGS OF OISIN | DRAMATIC SKETCHES | BALLADS | & | LYRICS | BY W. B. YEATS | T. FISHER UNWIN PATERNOSTER SQ. | LONDON E.C. MDCCCXCII. [small gargoyled ornament]

Bound in green paper boards, parchment spine, top edges gilt, others trimmed; spine blocked in gold; publisher's device in black on front cover.

On verso of title is a list of books BY THE SAME AUTHOR of which the first is THE COUNTESS KATHLEEN, AND CURIOUS (*sic*) LEGENDS AND LYRICS.

O'Hegarty notes: "This issue is scarcer than the original, and I have seen a statement somewhere that 100 copies were so done." This figure is confirmed in a letter from Yeats to John O'Leary (*Letters*, p. 198).

4

GANCONAGH | [rule] | JOHN SHERMAN | AND | DHOYA | [leaf ornament] | LONDON | T. FISHER UNWIN | PATERNOSTER SQUARE | [rule] | M DCCC XCI

$7 \times 3\frac{1}{2}$; pp. iv, 196: comprising half-title with publisher's monogram and the words Pseudonym Library at foot, list of volumes of the Pseudonym Library on verso, pp. [i–ii]; title, verso blank, pp. [iii–iv]; text, pp. [1]–195; imprint, The Gresham Press, Unwin Brothers Chilworth and London, p. [196]. There are fly-titles, versos blank, at pp. [3], [43], [83], [101], [143] and [171].

Issued in yellow paper covers, lettered in black on front cover and spine, with publisher's monogram on back cover. The paper covers are folded over white end-papers. All edges untrimmed.

Also issued in buff cloth, lettered in blue on front cover and spine, publisher's monogram in blue on back cover; blue lines at top and bottom carried over front cover across spine and over back cover. The pages of the cloth-bound copies measure $6\frac{4}{5} \times 3\frac{1}{2}$; white end-papers; top edges gilt, others untrimmed.

No. 10 of The Pseudonym Library. Symons states that the edition consisted of 1644 copies in paper and 356 in cloth. Published in November 1891.

Contents

Ganconagh's Apology
John Sherman
Dhoya

The poem on p. 187 had already appeared as "Girl's Song" in *The Wanderings of Oisin*, 1889. (No. 2.)

In Paul Lemperly's copy (now in the collection of Mr. Cyril I. Nelson) Yeats wrote, under date October 1904: "Written when I was very young & knew no better. Ballah is the town of Sligo where I lived as a child—a vague impression of it but I think a true one."

There was a second edition in 1891 and a third edition in 1892.

5

AMERICAN EDITION

THE "UNKNOWN" LIBRARY | [rule] | JOHN SHERMAN, | AND DHOYA | BY | GANCONAGH | NEW YORK | CASSELL PUBLISHING COMPANY | 104 & 106 FOURTH AVENUE

$7 \times 3\frac{1}{2}$; pp. viii, 182. Printed by The Mershon Company Press, Rahway, N.J.

Issued in lavender cloth, lettering and design on front cover and on spine. Entered for copyright at the Library of Congress on October 2, 1891; two copies received there on November 10, 1891.

The style of the Unknown Library was similar to that of the Pseudonym Library and the same designs for chapter headings and initial letters were used.

6

THE | COUNTESS KATHLEEN | AND VARIOUS LEGENDS AND LYRICS. | BY | W. B. YEATS. | "HE WHO TASTES A CRUST OF BREAD | TASTES ALL THE STARS AND ALL | THE HEAVENS" | PARACELSUS AB HOHENHEIM. | CAMEO SERIES | T. FISHER UNWIN PATERNOSTER SQ. | LONDON E.C. MDCCCXCII [ornament]

$7\frac{2}{5} \times 4\frac{1}{2}$; pp. 144: comprising half-title also bearing design of the Cameo Series, list of volumes in the series on verso, pp. [1–2]; title, with words Frontispiece by J. T. Nettleship on verso, pp. [3–4]; dedication, verso blank, pp. [5–6]; Preface, pp. [7]–8; contents, pp. [9]–10; fly-title, with quotation, verso blank, pp. [11–12]; text, pp. [13]–89; p. [90] blank; fly-title, with quotation, verso blank, pp. [91–92]; text, pp. 93–137; p. [138] blank; text of notes, pp. 139–141; p. [142] blank; imprint, The Gresham Press, Unwin Brothers, Chilworth and London, p. [143]; p. [144] blank.

Issued in dark green paper boards with parchment spine, the front and back covers folded over. Design of the Cameo Series printed in black on front cover, lettering in black on spine, publisher's device in black on back cover; white end-papers; top edges gilt, others untrimmed. The frontispiece represents Cuchullin fighting the waves.

500 copies were published in September 1892. There was also an edition of 30 copies in Japan vellum boards, signed by the publisher.

Contents

Preface

The Countess Kathleen

> The song in scene v. (p. 86) first appeared, under the title *Kathleen*, in *The National Observer*, October 31, 1891.

To the Rose upon the Rood of Time

Fergus and the Druid

> First appeared in *The National Observer*, May 21, 1892.

The Rose of the World
> First appeared, under the title *Rosa Mundi*, in *The National Observer*, January 2, 1892.

The Peace of the Rose
> First appeared in *The National Observer*, February 13, 1892.

The Death of Cuchullin
> First appeared in *United Ireland*, June 11, 1892.

The White Birds
> First appeared in *The National Observer*, May 7, 1892.

Father Gilligan
> First appeared, under the title *Father Gilligan. (A Legend told by the People of Castleisland, Kerry.)* in *The Scots Observer*, July 5, 1890.

Father O'Hart
> First appeared, under the title *The Priest of Coloony*, in *Irish Minstrelsy*, 1888, (No. 290); and in *Fairy and Folk Tales of the Irish Peasantry*, edited by W. B. Yeats, 1888. (No. 212.)

When You are Old

The Sorrow of Love

The Ballad of the Old Foxhunter
> First appeared in *East and West*, November 1889.

A Fairy Song
> First appeared in *The National Observer*, September 12, 1891.

The Pity of Love

The Lake Isle of Innisfree
> First appeared in *The National Observer*, December 13, 1890.

A Cradle Song
> First appeared in *The Scots Observer*, April 19, 1890.

The Man who Dreamed of Fairy Land
> First appeared, under the title *A Man who dreamed of Fairyland*, in *The National Observer*, February 7, 1891.

Dedication of "Irish Tales"
> First appeared in *Representative Irish Tales*, compiled by W. B. Yeats, 1891. (No. 215.)

The Lamentation of the Old Pensioner
> First appeared, under the title *The Old Pensioner*, in *The Scots Observer*, November 15, 1890.

When You are Sad

The Two Trees

They went forth to the Battle, but they always Fell

An Epitaph
> First appeared in *The National Observer*, December 12, 1891.

Apologia Addressed to Ireland in the Coming Days

Notes

In an inscribed copy of this book in the Buhler sale Yeats wrote:

> God loves dim ways of glint & gleam
> To please him well my rhyme must be
> A dyed & figured mystery,
> Thought hid in thought, dream hid in dream.
>   W. B. Yeats May 27th 1893

And in Quinn's copy he wrote, in March 1904, about the frontispiece: "Nettleship who made this rather disappointing picture might have been a great imaginative artist. Browning once in a fit of enthusiasm said a design of his of 'God creating Evil' was 'the most sublime conception of ancient or modern art.' "

Quinn's copy now forms part of the Henry W. and Albert A. Berg Collection in the New York Public Library, and the quotation above is given with the Library's consent.

7

AMERICAN EDITION

THE | COUNTESS KATHLEEN | AND VARIOUS LEGENDS AND LYRICS. | BY | W. B. YEATS. | [quotation, 4 lines] | CAMEO SERIES | BOSTON: ROBERTS BROS. | LONDON: T. FISHER UNWIN

7⅜ × 4⅜; pp. 142: comprising half-title, title, dedication, Preface and contents, pp. [1]–10; fly-title, text and notes, pp. [11]–141; p. [142] blank.

Issued in grey boards, white paper back, lettered.

Identical with English edition except for title, altered publisher's name on spine, and absence of publisher's device on back cover.   Published in 1892. In some copies only the title-page differs from the English edition.

8

THE CELTIC TWILIGHT. [*in red*] | MEN AND WOMEN, DHOULS AND | FAERIES. | BY | W. B. YEATS. | WITH A FRONTIS-PIECE BY J. B. YEATS. | [publishers' device] | LONDON: | LAWRENCE AND BULLEN, [*in red*] | 16, HENRIETTA ST., COVENT GARDEN. | 1893.

6½ × 3¾; pp. xii, 212: comprising list of books By the same Author, verso blank, pp.[i–ii]; half-title, verso blank, pp. [iii–iv]; title, note of acknowledgment on verso, pp. [v–vi]; poem *Time drops in decay,* poem, *The Host*, on verso, pp. [vii–viii]; *This Book*, pp. [ix]–x; contents, pp. [xi]–xii; fly-title, verso blank, pp. [1–2]; text, pp. [3]–212, with fly-titles, versos blank, before each essay; imprint, Richard Clay & Sons, Limited, London & Bungay, at foot of p. 212. Frontispiece, *The Last Gleeman*, faces title-page.

Issued in olive-green ribbed cloth, lettered CELTIC TWILIGHT | [rule] | W. B. YEATS | LAWRENCE AND BULLEN in gold on spine, with publisher's device stamped blind on back cover; white end-papers; all edges untrimmed. Published in December 1893.

Contents

[*Time drops in decay* (Poem)]
> First appeared, under the title *The Moods*, in *The Bookman*, August, 1893. Printed also, without title, in *United Ireland*, November 11, 1893.

The Host (Poem)
> First appeared, under the title *The Faery Host*, in *The National Observer*, October 7, 1893.

This Book
> First appeared, under the title *Preface to the Celtic Twilight*, in *United Ireland*, November 11, 1893.

A Teller of Tales
> A part of this essay first appeared in the introduction to *Fairy and Folk Tales of the Irish Peasantry*, 1888. (No. 212.)

Belief and Unbelief
> A part of this essay first appeared in an essay, *Irish Fairies*, in *The Leisure Hour*, October 1890.

A Visionary
> First appeared, under the title *An Irish Visionary*, in *The National Observer*, October 3, 1891.

Village Ghosts
> First appeared in *The Scots Observer*, May 11, 1889.

A Knight of the Sheep
> First appeared, under the title *An Impression*, in *The Speaker*, October 21, 1893.

The Sorcerers
The Last Gleeman
> First appeared in *The National Observer*, May 6, 1893.

Regina, Regina Pigmeorum, Veni
> This also appeared in *The Irish Home Reading Magazine*, May 1894.

Kidnappers
> First appeared in *The Scots Observer*, June 15, 1889.

The Untiring Ones

The Man and his Boots

A Coward

The Three O'Byrnes and the Evil Faeries
> First appeared as part of an essay *Irish Fairies*, in *The Leisure Hour*, October 1890.

Drumcliff and Rosses
> First appeared, under the title *Columkille and Rosses*, in *The Scots Observer*, October 5, 1889. A part of it also appeared as *A Fairy Enchantment*, in *Irish Fairy Tales* edited by W. B. Yeats, 1892. (No. 216.)

The Thick Skull of the Fortunate

The Religion of a Sailor

Concerning the Nearness Together of Heaven, Earth, and Purgatory

The Eaters of Precious Stones

Our Lady of the Hills
> First appeared in *The Speaker*, November 11, 1893.

The Golden Age

A Remonstrance with Scotsmen for having soured the disposition of their Ghosts and Faeries
> First appeared, under the title *Scots and Irish Fairies*, in *The Scots Observer*, March 2, 1889.

The Four Winds of Desire
> First appeared, under the title *Irish Folk-Tales*, in *The National Observer*, February 28, 1891.

Into the Twilight (Poem)
> First appeared, under the title *The Celtic Twilight*, in *The National Observer*, July 29, 1893.

There are two variants of the binding: in one the publisher's name at foot of spine appears in capitals, in the other it appears in capital and lower-case letters. Symons suggested that copies lettered in capitals may be the earlier because the British Museum copy (now rebound) was lettered thus; though this copy was received on April 26, 1894, some months after publication. However, a presentation copy from Yeats to Lionel Johnson, dated December 1893, is lettered in capitals, while copies with lower-case lettering, bound in somewhat lighter green, were being remaindered in 1903; it appears therefore almost certain that the copies with capital lettering are in fact the earlier. Dr. James S. Starkey of Dublin possesses a copy in a variant second-issue binding; this is without the publishers' device in blind on the back cover.

In Quinn's copy Yeats wrote in 1904: "All real stories heard among the people or real incidents with but a little disguise in names & places."

For the enlarged edition of *The Celtic Twilight* see No. 35.

9

THE CELTIC TWILIGHT. | MEN AND WOMEN, DHOULS AND | FAERIES. | BY | W. B. YEATS. | WITH A FRONTISPIECE BY J. B. YEATS. | NEW YORK: | MACMILLAN AND CO. | AND LONDON. | 1894

English sheets with new title-page, and differing otherwise only by the absence of the leaf of advertisement preceding half-title.

Issued in similar ribbed cloth but brighter green, with "Macmillan & Co." at foot of spine, and without stamp on back cover. (Quinn.)

10

[Fleuron] THE LAND | OF HEART'S | DESIRE [three fleurons] | BY | W. B. YEATS. | LONDON: T. FISHER | UNWIN, PATERNOSTER | SQUARE. MDCCCXCIV [*The above is printed on the right-hand half of the title-page, the left-hand half having a reproduction of Aubrey Beardsley's design for the Avenue Theatre poster.*]

7 × 5; pp. 48: comprising pp. [1–2] blank; half-title with publisher's monogram on verso, pp. [3–4]; title, cast of play at first performance on verso, pp. [5–6]; fly-title, Persons on verso, pp. [7–8]; text, pp. 9–43; p. 44 blank; list of books By the same Author, verso blank, pp. [45–46]; imprint, The Gresham Press, Unwin Brothers, Chilworth and London, p. [47]; p. [48] blank.

Issued in purple-pink paper covers folded over end-papers, lettered in black on front cover, and with Beardsley's design on left-hand side; the lettering follows that of the title-page but the three fleurons after the word DESIRE are omitted; all edges untrimmed. A printed slip stating: This Book is published at 1/- nett, | and the terms on which it is supplied to | Booksellers do not admit of any discount. is attached to the first leaf in some copies. Published in April 1894. The copy here described belongs to Mrs. Yeats and may possibly have been Yeats's own copy. If so, it would be earlier than other copies which are found with two fleurons on the cover after the word DESIRE. The copy in the British Museum has half its cover torn away, so cannot be cited in evidence.

❀THE LAND OF HEART'S DESIRE❀❀❀

BY

W. B. YEATS

LONDON: T. FISHER
UNWIN, PATERNOSTER
SQUARE. MDCCCXCIV

Symons states that the edition consisted of 500 copies and 60 in loose wrappers. I have never seen or heard of a copy in loose wrappers. Unfortunately the records of the firm of T. Fisher Unwin are no longer available.

II

FIRST AMERICAN EDITION

THE | LAND OF HEART'S DESIRE | BY | W. B. YEATS | [publisher's device, *in red*] | CHICAGO | STONE & KIMBALL | CAXTON BUILDING | MDCCCXIV [*sic*]

$6\frac{4}{5} \times 4\frac{1}{4}$; pp. iv, 48: comprising half-title, note, The frontispiece is designed by Mr. Aubrey Beardsley, on verso, pp. [i–ii]; recto blank, frontispiece on verso, pp. [iii–iv]; title, verso blank, pp. [1–2]; note, This first edition on small paper is limited to four hundred and fifty copies Stone & Kimball, verso blank, pp. [3–4]; fly-title, date of first performance and cast on verso, pp. [5–6]; Persons, verso blank, pp. [7–8]; text, pp. 9–43; p. [44] blank; colophon, "Here endeth this Poem entitled The Land of Heart's Desire, which same was printed in August, 1894, for Stone & Kimball, Publishers, Caxton Building: Chicago." Device of John Wilson & Son, University Press, p. [45]; pp. [46–48] blank.

Issued in grey paper boards with label, printed in black, on spine; white end-papers; all edges untrimmed.

450 copies published in 1894.

In Quinn's copy Yeats wrote: "This is the American edition of my first acted play. Wylde [Wilde] came late to the theatre & so missed the play, & to make amends he came up and was full of extravagant enthusiasm over a story of mine later, 'The Crucifixion of the Outcast.' This was the last time I had any conversation with him, though I saw him for a moment in the same theatre a few weeks later. He was an unfinished sketch of a great man and showed great courage and manhood amid the collapse of his fortunes. W. B. Yeats. New York, 1904."

The Land of Heart's Desire was produced at the Avenue Theatre on March 29, 1894 in front of *A Comedy of Sighs* by John Todhunter; this continued until April 14; the theatre was then closed for rehearsals of Bernard Shaw's *Arms and the Man*, which was produced on April 21, *The Land of Heart's Desire* being retained as the first piece until May 12, after which its place was taken by Louis N. Parker's *The Man in the Street*. *The Crucifixion of the Outcast* had been published in *The National Observer* on March 24, 1894. Yeats refers to the first of these two meetings with Wilde in *The Trembling of the Veil* and says it took place a few days after the production of his play; the second meeting may well have been at the first night of *Arms and the Man*.

12

AMERICAN EDITION, REVISED VERSION

THE LAND OF HEART'S | DESIRE | BY W. B. YEATS |
[ornament]] PORTLAND MAINE | PRIVATELY PRINTED |
MDCCCCIII

$6\frac{1}{16} \times 4\frac{5}{8}$; pp. xvi, 32: comprising p. [i] blank; notice of limitation,
p. [ii]; title, verso blank, pp. [iii–iv]; dedication, verso blank, pp.
[v–vi]; Foreword, pp. [vii–x]; fly-title, quotation on verso, pp.
[xi–xii]; list of characters, verso blank, pp. [xiii–xiv]; statement where
acted, verso blank, pp. [xv–xvi]; text, pp. 1–[29]; p. [30] blank;
Bibliographical Note, verso blank, pp. [31–32].

Issued in white Japan paper covers lettered THE LAND OF : : : | HEART'S
DESIRE on front cover, THE LAND OF HEART'S DESIRE on spine.

32 copies were printed on Japan vellum, for presentation, in July, 1903.
This revised version of the play first appeared in *The Bibelot*, Volume
IX, No. 6, June, 1903. Each number of *The Bibelot* was issued
separately and the copies were afterwards obtainable bound in annual
volumes.

13

PUBLISHED EDITION OF REVISED VERSION

THE LAND OF HEART'S | DESIRE BY WILLIAM |
BUTLER YEATS | [publisher's monogram, *in red*] | PORTLAND
MAINE | THOMAS B. MOSHER | MDCCCCIII

$7 \times 4\frac{3}{8}$; pp. vi, 36: comprising half-title, quotation on verso, pp.
[i–ii]; title, verso blank, pp. [iii–iv]; dedication, verso blank, pp.
[v–vi]; fly-title, cast of play and date of first performance on verso,
pp. [1–2]; Dramatis Personae, verso blank, pp. [3–4]; text, pp. 5–
[33]; p. [34] blank; limitation notice in black and publisher's monogram in red, p. [35]; p. [36] blank.

Of the first edition 950 copies were printed on Van Gelder paper, 100
on Japan paper and 10 on pure vellum. White parchment paper
boards, lettered THE | LAND | OF | HEART'S | DESIRE | YEATS on front
cover. Published in October 1903.

Later editions were issued in grey paper boards, lettered in red and
c

black on front cover and in black with red ornaments on spine; white end-papers; all edges untrimmed. Each edition consisted of 950 copies on Van Gelder paper. The thirteenth edition was issued in November 1925.

13A

THE LAND OF HEART'S | DESIRE by William | Butler Yeats || [publisher's device, *in red*] || Portland Maine : Printed for Thomas B Mosher | and published by him at *45 Exchange Street* | MDCCCCIX [*The whole enclosed inside panels.*]

$7\frac{1}{4} \times 5\frac{3}{8}$; pp. xx, 46: comprising pp. [i–xiv] blank; half-title, quotation on verso, pp. [xv–xvi]; title, verso blank, pp. [xvii–xviii]; dedication, verso blank, pp. [xix–xx]; fly-title, verso blank, pp. [1–2]; cast of play and date of first performance, Dramatis Personae on verso, pp. [3–4]; text, pp. 5–[32]; colophon, "Five hundred copies of this book printed on Japan vellum small quarto and the type distributed in the month of July MDCCCCIX," with publisher's device in red, underneath, verso blank, pp. [33–34]; pp. [35–46] blank.

Issued in cream-coloured cardboard covers, lettered in green on front cover and spine, with publisher's device in green on front cover. The cardboard covers are folded over cream-coloured endpapers. All edges untrimmed.

14

AMERICAN PRESENTATION EDITION

THE LAND | OF HEART'S | DESIRE | BY | W. B. YEATS | [ornament] | DODD, MEAD | & COMPANY | NEW YORK [*The whole printed in red inside panels of a light green decorative design.*]

$5\frac{11}{16} \times 3\frac{1}{8}$; pp. 56: comprising half-title, verso blank, pp. [1–2]; To . . . With the Season's Greetings From . . . [in red within green decorated panel], pp. [3–4]; title, verso blank, pp. [5–6]; fly-title, Persons on verso, pp. [7–8]; text, pp. 9–55; p. [56] blank.

Issued in ivory parchment covers folded over cardboard end-papers, lettering in red with panel surrounded by design in gold on front cover; top edges gilt, others untrimmed. Published on October 30, 1909.

14A

(Deleted)

The editor has not been able to substantiate Allan Wade's No. 14A:
THE LAND OF HEART'S DESIRE | BY W. B. YEATS | BOSTON |
WALTER H. BAKER & CO. Wade dated this edition as "probably
1918 or later, as evidenced by advertisement of 'A Drama of American
Patriotism' entitled *Over Here*." But a letter dated May 18, 1961, from
the Baker Co. to the editor reads in part "According to copyright
records which we have here . . . we made editions of the play in 1922,
1925 and 1928." And it is not until 1928 that *The United States
Catalog of Books in Print* mentions a Baker edition. No date is given.

See No. 96, which has been corrected to agree with the information
from the Baker Co.

15

· POEMS · | · BY · W · B · YEATS · | LONDON: PVBLISHED BY
T FISHER VNWIN · | Nº XI: PATERNOSTER BVILDINGS:
MDCCCXCV · [*The whole forms part of a decorative design by
H. G[ranville] F[ell].*]

7½ × 5; pp. xii, 288: comprising half-title, verso blank, pp. [i–ii];
title, quotation on verso, pp. [iii–iv]; preface, pp. v–vi; poem, "To
some I have talked with by the fire," verso blank, pp. vii–[viii]; contents, pp. ix–xi; p. [xii] blank; fly-title, bearing dedication, quotation
on verso, pp. [1–2]; fly-title, verso blank, pp. [3–4]; text, pp. 5–193;
p. [194] blank; fly-title, with dedication, quotation on verso, pp. [195–
196]; text, pp. 197–236; fly-title with dedication, quotation on verso,
pp. [237–238]; text, pp. 239–278; fly-title, verso blank, pp. [279–280];
text of Glossary, pp. 281–285, [286]; imprint, Printed by T. and A.
Constable, Printers to Her Majesty at the Edinburgh University Press,
below rule at foot of p. [286]; list of books By the same Writer, p.
[287]; p. [288] blank.

Issued in light brown cloth with design and lettering in gold on front
cover, spine, and back cover; off-white end-papers; all edges untrimmed.   Published in October 1895.

Contents
Preface
Dated Sligo, March 24th, 1895.

To some I have talked with by the fire
First appeared in *The Bookman*, May 1895.

The Wanderings of Usheen
The Countess Cathleen
The Land of Heart's Desire
The Rose:
    To the Rose upon the Rood of Time
    Fergus and the Druid
    The Death of Cuhoollin
    The Rose of the World
    The Rose of Peace
    The Rose of Battle
    A Faery Song
    The Lake Isle of Innisfree
    A Cradle Song
    The Pity of Love
    The Sorrow of Love
    When You are Old
    The White Birds
    A Dream of Death
    A Dream of a Blessed Spirit
        From the version of *The Countess Kathleen*, 1882
    The Man who dreamed of Faeryland
    The Dedication to a Book of Stories selected from the Irish Novelists
    The Lamentation of the Old Pensioner
    The Ballad of Father Gilligan
    The Two Trees
    To Ireland in the Coming Times
        All these poems are from *The Countess Kathleen*, 1892.
        (No. 6.)
Crossways:
    The Song of the Happy Shepherd. Dated 1885
    The Sad Shepherd. Dated 1885
    The Cloak, the Boat and the Shoes
        A rewriting of the first lines of *The Island of Statues*, Act II,
        scene iii.
    Anashuya and Vijaya. Dated 1887
    The Indian upon God. Dated 1886
    The Indian to his Love. Dated 1886
    The Falling of the Leaves
    Ephemera

The Madness of King Goll
The Stolen Child
To an Isle in the Water
Down by the Salley Gardens
The Meditation of the Old Fisherman
The Ballad of Father O'Hart
The Ballad of Moll Magee
The Ballad of the Old Foxhunter

All these poems are from *The Wanderings of Oisin*, 1889 (No. 2), except *The Ballad of Father O'Hart* and *The Ballad of the Foxhunter*, which are from *The Countess Kathleen*, 1892 (No. 6).

Glossary

The edition consisted of 750 copies, in addition to which 25 copies were printed on Japan vellum and signed by the author.

On Quinn's copy on vellum Yeats wrote: "The man who made this cover made a beautiful design, which I saw at an exhibition, but after I saw it Dent had spoilt him, with all kinds of odd jobs & when he did this the spirit had gone out of him. I hate this expressionless angel of his. W. B. Yeats, 1904."

16

AMERICAN EDITION

· POEMS · | · BY W. B. YEATS · | LONDON: PUBLISHED BY T. FISHER UNWIN · | BOSTON: COPELAND AND DAY: MDCCCXCV [*Description as given by Roth.*]

In 1908 Quinn wrote that "copies of the English edition were imported by Copeland & Day of Boston, whose name appears on the title-page and on the spine of all copies." This statement is repeated by Roth. O'Hegarty corrects this and notes that he has seen two copies, identical, of the American book, the only difference from the English edition being the addition of Copeland & Day *on the spine only*, not on the title. At the foot of the spine, instead of T. FISHER UNWIN, appeared T. FISHER UNWIN | COPELAND & DAY. In the Paul Lemperly sale, however, there was a copy of the book, described as being First edition, second issue, with the American publisher's name on the title-page as well as at the foot of the spine, and with the top edges gilt.

17

SECOND ENGLISH EDITION, REVISED

POEMS | BY W. B. YEATS | LONDON: T. FISHER | UNWIN, PATERNOSTER | SQUARE . . MDCCCXCIX

$7\frac{1}{2} \times 5$; pp. xii, 298; p. [299] containing list of books by the same Author; p. [300] blank, followed by 8 pp. of advertisements. Frontispiece portrait of the author by J. B. Yeats.

Issued in dark blue cloth, design (by Althea Gyles) stamped in gold on front cover, spine and back cover; white end-papers; all edges untrimmed. Published in May 1899.

In this edition the preface is rewritten, and the contents are rearranged thus:

Preface
        Dated February 24, 1899.
To some I have talked with by the fire
The Countess Cathleen
The Rose
The Land of Heart's Desire
Crossways
The Wanderings of Oisin
Glossary

The imprint, Unwin Brothers, The Gresham Press, Woking and London., at foot of p. [298].

Mr. O'Hegarty possesses a copy of *The Countess Cathleen*, which appears to be printed from the type of this edition of *Poems*. It consists of 96 pages, printed on good smooth paper different from that used in the complete volume, bound in plain brown wrappers, with top and lower edges trimmed down and fore edges roughtrimmed. The copy contains stage directions written in, and textual alterations, mostly in Act II., some of which are in Yeats's handwriting, some in another hand, and some typewritten; on the outside cover is the name Aleel, written in ink, but this has been struck through and another name, possibly Maire, written in pencil. It seems evident that this is one of the copies used for rehearsal in the production of the play by the Irish Literary Theatre; and as this production took place on May 8, 1899, and rehearsals, the earliest of which were held in London, would have occupied some two or three weeks at the least, it is likely that this copy, and any other which may have survived, was printed off specially after the volume of *Poems* was in page-proof, and before its publication early in May.

It may be noted that some of the textual alterations were adopted in the next edition of *Poems*, published in 1901.

18

THIRD ENGLISH EDITION, REVISED

POEMS | BY W. B. YEATS | LONDON: T. FISHER | UNWIN, PATERNOSTER | SQUARE + + + MCMI

$7\frac{1}{2} \times 5$; pp. 2, xiv (in some copies pp. xi–xii are both marked xi), 304; list of books By the same Writer at bottom of page and imprint, Unwin Brothers, The Gresham Press, Woking and London., below rule at foot of p. 304. No advertisements at end. Frontispiece as in No. 17.

Issued in dark blue cloth with design (by Althea Gyles) as in second edition. Published in April 1901.

This edition has a new preface, dated January 1901, and the note in the glossary on *The Countess Cathleen* is much enlarged.

There is an Errata slip facing p. 184; this makes three corrections to the text of *The Land of Heart's Desire*.

19

FOURTH ENGLISH EDITION

POEMS | BY W. B. YEATS | LONDON: T. FISHER | UNWIN, PATERNOSTER | SQUARE + + + MCMIV

$8\frac{1}{5} \times 5\frac{2}{5}$; pp. 2, xiv, 304.

Issued in dark blue cloth with design in gold, as before, on front cover, back cover and spine; white end-papers; all edges untrimmed. Frontispiece as in No. 17. Published in June 1904.

On p. [ii]: Copies of this volume may now be obtained bound in full parchment, price 10s. 6d. net.

On p. ix the bibliographical note is dated May 1904.

On p. [302]: Printed by Morrison and Gibb Limited Edinburgh.

20

POEMS [*in red*] | BY | W. B. YEATS | LONDON | T. FISHER
UNWIN [*in red*] | ADELPHI TERRACE | 1908

The contents and order of pagination, and the binding style are
similar to those of the fourth edition, 1904. (No. 19.)

The note on p. [ii] does not appear.

The bibliographical note is dated June 1908.

The book is printed by Morrison and Gibb Limited Edinburgh.

For the sixth English edition, much revised, see No. 99.

21

THE SECRET ROSE: [*in red*] | BY W. B. YEATS, WITH |
ILLUSTRATIONS BY J. B. | YEATS. | [publisher's device] |
LAWRENCE & BULLEN, LIMITED, [*in red*] | 16 HENRIETTA
STREET, COVENT GARDEN, | LONDON, MDCCCXCVII.

$7\frac{1}{2} \times 5$; pp. xii, 268: comprising blank page, list of books by the same
Writer on verso, pp. [i–ii]; half-title, verso blank, pp. [iii–iv]; title,
with two quotations on verso, pp. [v–vi]; dedication, verso blank,
pp. vii–[viii]; poem "To the Secret Rose", pp. ix–x; contents, verso
blank, pp. xi–[xii]; text, pp. 1–265; acknowledgement, p. [266];
imprint, Richard Clay & Sons, Limited, London & Bungay, p. [267];
p. [268] blank. Frontispiece facing title-page, six other illustrations
facing pp. 36, 53, 67, 80, 142 and 201.

Issued in dark blue cloth, with design (by Althea Gyles) stamped in
gold on front cover, spine and back cover; white end-papers; all edges
untrimmed. Published in April 1897.

Contents

Dedication to A.E.

To the Secret Rose (Poem)
> First appeared, under the title O'*Sullivan Rua to the Secret Rose*,
> in *The Savoy*, September 1896.

The Binding of the Hair
> First appeared in *The Savoy*, January 1896.

The Wisdom of the King
> First appeared, under the title *Wisdom*, in *The New Review*,
> September 1895.

Where there is Nothing, there is God
  First appeared in *The Sketch*, October 21, 1896.
The Crucifixion of the Outcast
  First appeared, under the title *A Crucifixion*, in *The National Observer*, March 24, 1894.
Out of the Rose
  First appeared in *The National Observer*, May 27, 1893.
The Curse of the Fires and of the Shadows
  First appeared in *The National Observer*, August 5, 1893.
The Heart of the Spring
  First appeared in *The National Observer*, April 15, 1893.
Of Costello the Proud, of Oona the Daughter of Dermott and of the Bitter Tongue
  First appeared, under the title *Costello the Proud, Oona Mac-Dermott and the Bitter Tongue*, in *The Pageant*, 1896. (No. 295.)
The Book of the Great Dhoul and Hanrahan the Red
  First appeared, under the title *The Devil's Book*, in *The National Observer*, November 26, 1892.
The Twisting of the Rope and Hanrahan the Red
  First appeared, under the title *The Twisting of the Rope*, in *The National Observer*, December 24, 1892.
Kathleen the Daughter of Hoolihan and Hanrahan the Red
  First appeared, under the title *Kathleen-ny-Houlihan*, in *The National Observer*, August 4, 1894.
The Curse of Hanrahan the Red
  First appeared, under the title *The Curse of O'Sullivan the Red upon Old Age*, in *The National Observer*, September 29, 1894.
The Vision of Hanrahan the Red
  First appeared, under the title *The Vision of O'Sullivan the Red*, in *The New Review*, April 1896.
The Death of Hanrahan the Red
  First appeared, under the title *The Death of O'Sullivan the Red*, in *The New Review*, December 1896.
The Rose of Shadow
  First appeared, under the title *Those Who Live in the Storm* in *The Speaker*, July 21, 1894.
The Old Men of the Twilight
  First appeared, under the title *St. Patrick and the Pedants*, in *The Weekly Sun Literary Supplement*, December 1, 1895. The story also appeared under the same title in *The Chap Book* (Chicago), June 1, 1896.
Rosa Alchemica
  First appeared in *The Savoy*, April 1896.

After the firm of Lawrence & Bullen had ceased to exist copies of this book were issued with the name of A. H. Bullen substituted at the foot of spine.

22

AMERICAN EDITION

THE SECRET ROSE: [*in red*] | BY W. B. YEATS, WITH | ILLUS-TRATIONS BY J. B. | YEATS. | [publisher's device] | NEW YORK: [*in black*] DODD, MEAD & COMPANY [*in red*] | LONDON: [*in black*] LAWRENCE & BULLEN, LTD. [*in red*] | MDCCCXCVII.

These copies for the American market are copies of the first English edition, with the original title torn out, after the book was bound, and the above new title pasted in on the stub. (Quinn.)

23

DUBLIN EDITION

THE SECRET ROSE: | BY W. B. YEATS, WITH | ILLUSTRA-TIONS BY J. B. | YEATS. | DUBLIN: MAUNSEL AND CO., LTD. 60 DAWSON STREET. 1905.

Sheets of the English edition, with title as above, two quotations on verso, substituted for the original title-leaf and pasted in. 200 cancel titles for this edition were printed by Richard Clay & Sons, Ltd in August 1905, and a further 200 later in the same month.

Issued in dark blue-green cloth, and also in green paper boards with yellow linen spine, lettered on spine THE SECRET | ROSE. | W. B. YEATS| MAUNSEL

These copies were for sale, at a reduced price, in Ireland only.

24

THE TABLES OF THE LAW. | THE ADORATION OF THE MAGI. | BY W. B. YEATS. | [publisher's device] | PRIVATELY PRINTED | MDCCCXCVII

$7\frac{1}{2} \times 5$; pp. 48: comprising half-title, with note concerning limitation of edition on verso, pp. [1-2]; title, with note on verso, pp. [3-4]; fly-title, verso blank, pp. [5-6]; text of The Tables of the Law, pp. 7-32; fly-title, verso blank, pp. [33-34]; text of The Adoration of the Magi, pp. 35-[48]; imprint, R. Clay & Sons, Ltd., London & Bungay, at foot of p. [48]. Frontispiece portrait of the author by J. B. Yeats facing title-page.

110 copies, numbered, issued in red buckram, lettered in gold on spine THE | TABLES | OF THE | LAW | ETC. | W. B. | YEATS; white end-papers; all edges untrimmed. Issued in June 1897.

Contents

The Tables of the Law
    First appeared in *The Savoy*, November 1896.
The Adoration of the Magi

Although described as "privately printed," copies of this book were advertised in some of Lawrence and Bullen's catalogues for sale at five shillings each.

In Quinn's copy Yeats wrote: "The portrait which is by my father, & the Latin which is by Lionel Johnson, are the only things which are worth anything in this little book. W. B. Yeats. Oct., 1901."

25

FIRST PUBLISHED EDITION

THE TABLES OF THE LAW | AND | THE ADORA-TION OF THE MAGI | BY | W. B. YEATS | LONDON | ELKIN MATHEWS, VIGO STREET | 1904

$6\frac{3}{10} \times 5$; pp. 60: comprising half-title, verso blank, pp. [1–2]; title with Prefatory Note on verso, pp. [3–4]; fly-title, verso blank, pp. [5–6]; text of The Tables of the Law, pp. 7–39; p. [40] blank; fly-title, verso blank, pp. [41–42]; text of The Adoration of the Magi, pp. 43–60. At the end are inserted i–iv pages of advertisements. Imprint, R. Folkard & Son, 22, Devonshire Street, Bloomsbury, W.C., at foot of p. iv.

Issued in blue paper covers, lettered in black on front with design of Elkin Mathews's shop, publisher's device on back. No lettering on spine. List of Vigo Cabinet Series printed inside covers. This book is No. 17 of the Series. Published in June 1904.

Contents

Prefatory Note
The Tables of the Law
The Adoration of the Magi

An unspecified number of copies were also issued as a "de luxe" edition. These were printed on slightly thicker paper than the above-described issue, and were issued in blue-grey paper boards with buff linen spine, lettered in black on front cover THE TABLES OF THE LAW AND | THE ADORATION OF THE MAGI | BY W. B. YEATS and on the spine THE TABLES OF THE LAW [short rule] W. B. YEATS | upward ELKIN | MATHEWS across foot.

These copies contain the same 4 pp. of advertisements at end but bear no mention of belonging to the Vigo Cabinet Series.

Copies of this edition were issued later in green cloth, lettered in gold on front cover THE TABLES OF THE LAW | [short rule] | THE ADORATION OF THE MAGI | W. B. YEATS, all in black-letter, the author's name in bottom right-hand corner; on spine in gold ELKIN MATHEWS THE TABLES OF THE LAW W. B. YEATS, title being in black-letter. 8 pp. of advertisements containing Elkin Mathews's list for 1909 are bound in at the end.

There was a reissue in 1905, in brown paper covers.

26

SECOND PUBLISHED EDITION

THE TABLES OF THE LAW; & | THE ADORATION OF THE MAGI | BY WILLIAM BUTLER YEATS | THE SHAKES-PEARE HEAD PRESS | STRATFORD-UPON-AVON MCMXIV

$7\frac{1}{10} \times 4\frac{3}{4}$; pp. vi, 38: comprising half-title, note Five hundred and ten copies printed; type distributed. No. . . . on verso, pp. [i–ii]; title, verso blank, pp. [iii–iv]; fly-title, verso blank, pp. [v–vi]; text, pp. [1]–22; fly-title, verso blank, pp. [23–24]; text, pp. [25]–35; imprint, Printed by A. H. Bullen, at the Shakespeare Head Press, Stratford-upon-Avon., p. [36]; pp. [37–38] blank.

Issued in grey paper boards with green linen spine, label printed in black within red ornamental border on front cover, no label on spine; light brown end-papers; all edges untrimmed. Published in 1914.

Contents

The Tables of the Law
The Adoration of the Magi

On or about June 28, 1916 the remainder of this edition was transferred to Messrs. Macmillan and Co., Ltd. These copies were bound in grey-green cloth, lettered in black on front cover.

27

THE WIND | AMONG THE REEDS | BY | W. B. YEATS | [ornament] | LONDON: ELKIN MATHEWS | VIGO STREET, W., 1899

$7\frac{3}{5} \times 4\frac{3}{4}$; pp. 2, viii, 108: comprising one leaf not included in pagination; half-title, with list of books By the Same Author inside panel on verso, pp. [i–ii]; title, verso blank, pp. [iii–iv]; contents, pp. v–vii; p. [viii] blank; text, pp. 1–108.

Issued in dark blue cloth with design (by Althea Gyles) stamped in gold on front cover, spine and back cover; white end-papers; all edges untrimmed. Published in April 1899.

Contents

The Hosting of the Sidhe
    First appeared, under the title *The Faery Host,* in *The National Observer,* October 7, 1893, and already printed, under the title *The Host,* in *The Celtic Twilight,* 1893.
The Everlasting Voices
    First appeared, under the title *Everlasting Voices,* in *The New Review,* January 1896.
The Moods
    First appeared in *The Bookman,* August 1893, and already printed, without title, in *The Celtic Twilight,* 1893.
Aedh tells of the Rose in his Heart
    First appeared, under the title *The Rose in my Heart,* in *The National Observer,* November 12, 1892.
The Host of the Air
    First appeared, under the title *The Stolen Bride,* in *The Bookman,* November 1893.
Breasal the Fisherman
    First appeared, under the title *Bressel the Fisherman,* in *The Cornish Magazine,* December 1898.
A Cradle Song
    First appeared as the first of *Two Poems concerning Peasant Visionaries,* in *The Savoy,* April 1896.

Into the Twilight
> First appeared, under the title *The Celtic Twilight,* in *The National Observer*, July 29, 1893, and already printed in *The Celtic Twilight*, 1893.

The Song of Wandering Aengus
> First appeared, under the title *A Mad Song*, in *The Sketch*, August 4, 1897.

The Song of the Old Mother
> First appeared in *The Bookman*, April 1894.

The Fiddler of Dooney
> First appeared in *The Bookman*, December 1892.

The Heart of the Woman
> First appeared, without title, in the story *Those Who Live in the Storm*, in *The Speaker*, July 21, 1894, and already printed in *The Secret Rose*, 1897.

Aedh laments the Loss of Love
> First appeared as the second of *Aodh to Dectora. Three Songs*, in *The Dome*, May 1898.

Mongan laments the Change that has come upon him and his Beloved.
> First appeared, under the title *The Desire of Man and of Woman*, in *The Dome*, June 1897.

Michael Robartes bids his Beloved be at Peace
> First appeared, under the title *The Shadowy Horses*, in *The Savoy*, January 1896.

Hanrahan reproves the Curlew
> First appeared, under the title *Windlestraws. I. O'Sullivan Rua to the Curlew*, in *The Savoy*, November 1896.

Michael Robartes remembers forgotten Beauty
> First appeared, under the title *O'Sullivan Rua to Mary Lavell*, in *The Savoy*, July 1896.

A Poet to his Beloved
> First appeared, under the title *O'Sullivan the Red to Mary Lavell*, in *The Senate*, March 1896.

Aedh gives his Beloved certain Rhymes
> First appeared, without title, in the story *The Binding of the Hair*, in *The Savoy*, January 1896, and already printed in *The Secret Rose*, 1897.

To my Heart, bidding it have no Fear
> First appeared, under the title *Windlestraws. II. Out of the Old Days*, in *The Savoy*, November 1896.

The Cap and Bells
> First appeared, under the title *Cap and Bell*, in *The National Observer*, March 17, 1894.

The Valley of the Black Pig
> First appeared, as the second of *Two Poems concerning Peasant Visionaries*, in *The Savoy*, April 1896.

Michael Robartes asks Forgiveness because of his many Moods
> First appeared, under the title *The Twilight of Forgiveness*, in *The Saturday Review*, November 2, 1895.

Aedh tells of a Valley full of Lovers
> First appeared, under the title *The Valley of Lovers*, in *The Saturday Review*, January 9, 1897.

Aedh tells of the perfect Beauty
> First appeared, under the title *O'Sullivan the Red to Mary Lavell*, in *The Senate*, March 1896.

Aedh hears the Cry of the Sedge
> First appeared, as the first of *Aodh to Dectora. Three Songs*, in *The Dome*, May 1898.

Aedh thinks of those who have spoken Evil of his Beloved
> First appeared, as the third of *Aodh to Dectora. Three Songs*, in *The Dome*, May 1898.

The Blessed
> First appeared in *The Yellow Book*, April 1897.

The Secret Rose
> First appeared, under the title *O'Sullivan Rua to the Secret Rose*, in *The Savoy*, September 1896, and already printed, under the title *To The Secret Rose*, in *The Secret Rose*, 1897.

Hanrahan laments because of his Wanderings
> First appeared, under the title *O'Sullivan the Red upon his Wanderings*, in *The New Review*, August 1897.

The Travail of Passion
> First appeared in *The Savoy*, January 1896.

The Poet pleads with his Friend for old Friends
> First appeared, under the title *Song*, in *The Saturday Review*, July 24, 1897.

Hanrahan speaks to the Lovers of his Songs in coming Days
> First appeared, without title, in the story *The Vision of O'Sullivan the Red*, in *The New Review*, April 1896, and already printed in *The Secret Rose*, 1897.

Aedh pleads with the Elemental Powers
> This revised version of a poem first appeared, under the title *Aodh Pleads with the Elemental Powers*, in *The Dome*, December 1898. The first version of the poem appeared, under the title *A Mystical Prayer to the Masters of the Elements, Michael, Gabriel, and Raphael*, in *The Bookman*, October 1892, and was reprinted under the title *A Mystical Prayer to the Masters of the*

Elements—Finvarra, Feacra, and Caolte, in *The Second Book of the Rhymers' Club,* 1894. (No. 294.)

Aedh wishes his Beloved were dead
    First appeared, under the title *Aodh to Dectora,* in *The Sketch,* February 9, 1898.

Aedh wishes for the Cloths of Heaven
Mongan thinks of his past Greatness
    First appeared, under the title *Song of Mongan,* in *The Dome,* October 1898.

Notes

In Quinn's copy Yeats wrote: "Elkin Mathews without consulting me printed 'editions' 1 and 2 together and then to my great joy sent out some copies of the 'second edition' first. He was not found out, however, but had a bad moment when he found out what he had done. March, 1904."

Some copies, but not the earliest issued, of the first edition contain a slip, printed on smooth paper and headed ERRORS. It sets out the following seven errors:

Page 13 line 5 for "Erie" read "Eire"
    18   6 for "prayers" read "prayer"
    31   3 for "He" read "him"
    43   9 for "head" read "breast"
                 for "on" read "by"
    49 after line 4 insert "by a gray shore where the wind never blew"
    93 line 12 for "night" read "light"
    96   18 take out comma after misroide, and for "son" read "sow"

These errors also appear in the second edition, but if Yeats's recollection is correct it is possible that some copies of the second edition may have been sent out before the errors had been discovered; these would also lack the ERRORS slip.

Concerning the Notes, Yeats wrote in a letter addressed, I believe, to M. Henry D. Davray, the French man of letters who had translated some of his work: "The notes are really elaborate essays in the manner of *The Celtic Twilight.* They deal with Irish fairy lore and mythology, and are in most cases made out of quite new material. They have given me a good deal of trouble, and will probably make most of the critics spend half of every review in complaining that I have written very long notes about very short poems. I am in hopes, however, that others will forgive me the poems for the sake of the valuable information in the notes. It is a way of getting the forgiveness of the Philistines which may serve as a useful model."

An unspecified number of copies of *The Wind Among the Reeds* were issued in full vellum binding with the design stamped in gold. That this course was under consideration before the book was published seems clear from a letter from Yeats to Elkin Mathews, dated Galway, Sept. 20, [n.y.] which appeared in the C. Walter Buhler sale, in which Yeats suggests that the design be printed on the vellum copies only. It is possible, therefore, that copies in vellum may belong to the first, second, third or fourth editions; they were still advertised in Elkin Mathews's list in the 1904 edition of *The Tables of the Law*. Quinn's library possessed a fourth edition (1903) so bound, and inscribed "The binding of this book pleases me well. W. B. Yeats. March, 1904."

28

FIRST AMERICAN EDITION

THE WIND | AMONG THE REEDS | BY | W. B. YEATS | [ornament] | JOHN LANE: THE BODLEY HEAD | NEW YORK AND LONDON | 1899

$7\frac{3}{5} \times 4\frac{3}{4}$; pp. 4, viii, 112: comprising 2 leaves not included in pagination; half-title, with list of books By the Same Author inside panel on verso, pp. [i–ii]; title, copyright notice and imprint, The University Press, Cambridge, U.S.A., on verso, pp. [iii–iv]; contents, pp. v–vii; p. [viii] blank; text, pp. 1–108; imprint, Printed at the University Press Cambridge, U.S.A., MDCCCXCIX, p. [109]; pp. [110–112] blank.

Similar in binding to the English edition and printed from duplicate plates that repeat the errors of the English edition. No errata slip.

Filed for copyright at the Library of Congress on April 13, 1899.

A later American edition is dated 1902 on the title and MDCCCCII in the imprint on p. [109]; the errors are corrected and ten pages of advertisements, pp. [111–120], are added. Top edges gilt, others untrimmed. A still later edition is dated MCMV on the title, there is an additional copyright notice dated 1905 on the verso of title, and there is no imprint on p. [109]. The ten pages of advertisements remain. Some copies of this edition were issued in green cloth with lettering in gold on front cover and spine and a different design stamped blind on the front cover; all edges untrimmed. Another American edition has Elkin Mathews on the title and is dated MCMXI; on the verso of title are John Lane's copyright notices of 1899 and 1905 and beneath them Sixth edition, 1911. At bottom of page is imprint, The University Press, Cambridge, U.S.A. Top edges trimmed, others untrimmed.

D

29

THE WIND AMONG | THE REEDS [ornament] BY |
WILLIAM BUTLER YEATS | [ornament] | LONDON · ELKIN
MATHEWS | VIGO STREET · W · MDCCCC

7½ × 5; pp. 2, viii, 108, with 4 unnumbered pages added at end of book:
comprising 2 pp. not included in pagination; half-title, with list of
books By the Same Writer, not enclosed in panel, on verso, pp.
[i–ii]; title, the words Third Edition on verso, pp. [iii–iv]; contents,
pp. v–vii; p. [viii] blank; text, pp. 1–108. The errors in first and second
editions have all been corrected, causing one line to be transferred from
the bottom of p. 49 to the top of p. 50. The first of the additional pages
at end bears advertisement of the third edition, with press notices, the
second and third pages advertisements of other books published by
Elkin Mathews, and the fourth page Elkin Mathews's device.

This edition was issued in two different styles of binding: one in dark
blue cloth with the design (by Althea Gyles) in gold, as in the first
and second editions; and other in blue-grey boards, the same design
stamped in black on front cover, spine and back cover; white end-
papers; all edges untrimmed.

The Buhler sale contained Yeats's autograph transcripts of excerpts
from the reviews, 2 pp., about 250 words, and a note saying that he
had prepared this to be used by Elkin Mathews in advertising the
third edition.

There were further editions in 1903, 1907 and 1911, the 1903 edition
being issued in light mottled blue paper boards with buff linen spine,
lettered in black on front cover, with a label, printed in black, pasted
on the spine. The edition of 1907 is similar but in dark blue paper
boards; that of 1911 is similar but in light blue.

30

THE SHADOWY WATERS | BY W. B. YEATS | LONDON:
HODDER AND | STOUGHTON | 27 PATERNOSTER ROW: MCM

9½ × 6¾; pp. 60: comprising half-title, verso blank, pp. [1–2]; title,
imprint, Edinburgh: T. and A. Constable, Printers to Her Majesty,
on verso, pp. [3–4]; dedication, verso blank, pp. [5–6]; poem, "I

walked among the seven woods of Coole," pp. 7–9; p. [10] blank; fly-title, with list of dramatis personae on verso, pp. [11–12]; text of play, pp. 13–57; p. [58] blank; imprint, Printed by T. and A. Constable, Printers to Her Majesty at the Edinburgh University Press, verso blank, pp. [59–60].

Issued in dark blue ribbed cloth with design in gold on front cover, lettering in gold on spine; white end-papers; top edge gilt, others untrimmed. Published in December 1900.

Contents

I walked among the seven woods of Coole
> Dated September 1900. First appeared, under the title *Introduction to a Dramatic Poem*, in *The Speaker*, December 1, 1900.

The Shadowy Waters
> First appeared in *The North American Review*, May 1900.

There was a second edition in 1901.

31

AMERICAN EDITION

THE SHADOWY WATERS | BY | W. B. YEATS | [ornament] | NEW YORK | DODD, MEAD AND COMPANY | 1901

$9\frac{3}{4} \times 6\frac{3}{8}$; pp. 64: comprising half-title, title, copyright notice, dedication and preliminary poem, pp. [1–6], 7–9; p. [10] blank; fly-title, with list of dramatis personae on verso, pp. [11–12]; text of play pp. [13]–62; pp. [63–64] blank.

Issued in grey boards with white paper label measuring $4\frac{3}{8} \times 3\frac{1}{10}$ printed THE | SHADOWY WATERS | BY W. B. YEATS, the title in red and the author's name in black, on front cover; no label on spine.

Entered for copyright at the Library of Congress, February 25, 1901; two copies received there on April 25, 1901.

Second edition. Identical with the first except that the date on title is 1905 and the cover is of paler colour of paper. (Quinn.)

32

AMERICAN PRESENTATION EDITION

THE | SHADOWY | WATERS | W. B. YEATS | [design] | DODD, MEAD | & COMPANY | NEW YORK [*The whole printed in red, the title and author's name framed in an elaborate leaf and vase design of green and white.*]

$5\frac{13}{16} \times 3\frac{1}{8}$; pp. ii, 68: comprising half-title, verso blank, pp. [i–ii]; Christmas card, framed in green and lettered in red: To | With the Season's Greetings | From | verso blank, pp. [1–2]; title, on verso Copyright, 1901 by Dodd, Mead & Company, pp. [3–4]; dedication "To Lady Gregory", verso blank, pp. [5–6]; text, pp. 7–67; p. [68] blank.

Issued in wrappers, the front cover having the same elaborate design as the title-page but in gold and white with title in red; top edges gilt, others untrimmed. Published in the autumn of 1901.

33

IS THE ORDER OF R.R. & A.C. | TO REMAIN A MAGICAL ORDER? | WRITTEN IN MARCH, 1901, AND GIVEN TO THE | ADEPTI OF THE ORDER OF R.R. & A.C. IN | APRIL, 1901.

$7\frac{1}{2} \times 5$; pp. 32: comprising title, verso blank, pp. [1–2]; text, pp. 3–30; pp. [31–32] blank.

Issued in brown paper covers, title printed in black at head of front cover, and at foot "This Essay must not be given to any but Adepti of the Order of R.R. & A.C."

The essay is signed, on p. 30, D.E.D.I. *In the Mountain of Abiegnos.*

The Order Rubidae Rosae & Aureae Crucis was apparently a section of the Order of the Golden Dawn, the mystical society to which Yeats belonged. Each member adopted a motto, usually in Latin, and was known in the Order by the initials of the motto; Yeats was D aemon E st D eus I nversus.

34

A POSTSCRIPT TO ESSAY CALLED "IS | THE ORDER OF R.R. & A.C. TO | REMAIN A MAGICAL ORDER?" | WRITTEN ON MAY 4TH, 1901.

$7\frac{1}{2} \times 5$; pp. 8: comprising title, verso blank, pp. [1–2]; text, pp. 3–7; p. [8] blank.

Issued in brown paper covers, title printed in black at head of front cover, and at foot "The Postscript is not to be given to any but Adepti of the Order of R.R. & A.C."

A Postscript to Essay called "Is the Order of R. R. & A. C. to remain a Magical Order?"

WRITTEN ON MAY 4TH, 1901.

Is the Order of R.R. & A.C. to remain a Magical Order?

WRITTEN IN MARCH, 1901, AND GIVEN TO THE ADEPTI OF THE ORDER OF R.R. & A.C. IN APRIL, 1901.

The Postscript is signed, on p. 7, D.E.D.I.

The first of the two items, No. 33, appeared in the Quinn sale catalogue with the following note: "[Yeats] has never acknowledged the authorship of this article. It was written as a member of a magical society in London, and when there was a split in the society, this copy was bought by Mr. Quinn from Miss Florence Farr, the actress-author, also a member of the society, against Mr. Yeats' rather strenuous opposition. No copy of this brochure has ever been offered at public sale, and it is one of the rarest of Yeats' writings in existence."

There is no mention of the Postscript in the Quinn sale catalogue, and it is first recorded in Roth. Since the Quinn sale copies of the two pamphlets have only appeared twice in the auction room: on February 21, 1950, a set was sold at the Parke-Bernet Galleries, New York, for $320, and at Hodgson's, London, on November 30, 1950, a set was bought by a London bookseller for £65.

35

REVISED AND ENLARGED EDITION

THE CELTIC TWILIGHT [*in red*] | BY W. B. YEATS | A. H. BULLEN, [*in red*] 18 CECIL COURT | ST. MARTIN'S LANE, LONDON, W.C. | MCMII

$7\frac{1}{2} \times 5$; pp. 2, x, 236: comprising one leaf not included in pagination, blank page with list of Books by the Same Writer on verso, pp. [i–ii]; half-title, with note "Printed 1893 Reprinted with additions 1902" on verso, pp. [iii–iv]; title, with poem *Time drops in decay* on verso, pp. [v–vi]; poem *The Hosting of the Sidhe*, verso blank, pp. vii–[viii]; contents, pp. ix–x; text, pp. 1–[235]; imprint, Richard Clay & Sons, Limited, London & Bungay, p. [236].

Issued in dark blue cloth with lettering and design in gold on front cover, lettering and design (as in No. 21) in gold on spine; white end-papers; all edges untrimmed. The frontispiece, facing title-page, is the portrait of the author by J. B. Yeats already used in *The Tables of the Law*. 2000 copies were printed. Published in July 1902.

Contents

Time drops in decay (Poem)
The Hosting of the Sidhe (Poem)
This Book. I. 1893. II. 1902

A Teller of Tales
Belief and Unbelief
Mortal Help
    First appeared in *The Speaker*, April 19, 1902.
A Visionary. (With a new footnote.)
Village Ghosts
'Dust hath closed Helen's Eye'. I. 1900. II. 1902.
    Part I first appeared in *The Dome*, October 1899.
A Knight of the Sheep
An Enduring Heart
    First appeared in *The Speaker*, April 26, 1902.
The Sorcerers. (With a new footnote.)
The Devil
    First appeared in *The Speaker*, April 19, 1902.
Happy and Unhappy Theologians
    First appeared in *The Speaker*, February 15, 1902.
The Last Gleeman
Regina, Regina Pigmeorum, Veni. (With a new footnote.)
'And Fair, Fierce Women'
    First appeared in *The Speaker*, April 19, 1902.
Enchanted Woods
    First appeared in *The Speaker*, January 18, 1902.
Miraculous Creatures
    First appeared in *The Speaker*, April 26, 1902.
Aristotle of the Books
    First appeared in *The Speaker*, April 19, 1902.
The Swine of the Gods
    First appeared in *The Speaker*, April 19, 1902.
A Voice
    First appeared in *The Speaker*, April 19, 1902.
Kidnappers. (With a new footnote.)
The Untiring Ones. (With a new footnote.)
Earth, Fire and Water
    First appeared in *The Speaker*, March 15, 1902.
The Old Town
    First appeared in *The Speaker*, March 15, 1902.
The Man and his Boots
A Coward
The Three O'Byrnes and the Evil Faeries
Drumcliff and Rosses
The Thick Skull of the Fortunate. I. 1893. II. 1902.

The Religion of a Sailor
Concerning the nearness together of *Heaven, Earth, and Purgatory.*
    1892 and 1902.
The Eaters of Precious Stones
Our Lady of the Hills
The Golden Age
A Remonstrance with Scotsmen for having soured the disposition of their
    Ghosts and Faeries
War
    First appeared in *The Speaker*, March 15, 1902.
The Queen and the Fool
    First appeared, under the title *The Fool of Faery*, in *The Kensing-*
    ton, June 1901.
The Friends of the People of Faery
    First appeared, as part of an essay, *The Tribes of Danu*, in *The*
    New Review, November 1897.
Dreams that have no moral
By the Roadside
    First appeared in *An Claideamh Soluis*, July 13, 1901.
Into the Twilight (Poem).

One essay from the edition of 1893, "The Four Winds of Desire," is
omitted from this edition.

36

THE CELTIC TWILIGHT

The English sheets were imported and bound in America in ribbed
blue cloth, without side or spine stamp, front of cover lettered in
gold THE CELTIC TWILIGHT and spine lettered in gold THE CELTIC |
TWILIGHT | W. B. YEATS | THE MACMILLAN COMPANY (Quinn). Some
copies are without the gold lettering on the front cover and the foot
of spine is lettered The Macmillan | Company. Top edges gilt.

37

THE CELTIC TWILIGHT: | BY W. B. YEATS. | DUBLIN: MAUNSEL AND CO., LTD. | 60 DAWSON STREET. 1905.

Sheets of the English edition, with title-leaf as above pasted in on the
stub. 200 cancel titles for this edition were printed by Richard Clay

& Sons, Ltd. in August 1905, and a further 200 later in the same month.

Issued in dark blue-green cloth, and also in green paper boards with yellow linen spine, lettered on spine THE CELTIC | TWILIGHT. | W. B. YEATS | MAUNSEL

These copies were for sale, at a reduced price, in Ireland only.

38

THE CELTIC TWILIGHT | BY | W. B. YEATS | [fleuron] | A. H. BULLEN | LONDON & STRATFORD-UPON-AVON | MCMXII

$7\frac{3}{5} \times 5$; pp. 2, xii, 224: comprising two blank pages not included in pagination; p. [i] blank; list of books By the same Author, p. [ii]; half-title, on verso, Printed 1893; Reprinted with additions 1902; Included in The Collected Works of W. B. Yeats, Vol. V., 1908; Reprinted 1912, pp. [iii–iv]; title, poem on verso, pp. [v–vi]; poem, verso blank, pp. vii–[viii]; contents, pp. ix–x; fly-title, verso blank, pp. [xi–xii]; text, pp. 1–[222]; p. [223] blank; imprint, Printed by A. H. Bullen, at the Shakespeare Head Press, Stratford-upon-Avon, p. [224].

Issued in light brown paper boards with grey-green linen spine, lettered in black on spine; white end-papers; all edges untrimmed. Published in December 1911.

Contents

The same as those of the edition of 1902. (No. 35.)

Copies of this edition were issued in America by the Macmillan Company, the words THE MACMILLAN COMPANY appearing at the foot of the spine.

On or about June 28, 1916, the remainder of this edition was transferred to Messrs. Macmillan and Co., Ltd.

In the Henry W. and Albert A. Berg Collection in the New York Public Library there is a copy of this edition of 1912 corrected by Yeats in 1914 for a new edition. It does not appear, however, that this proposed edition ever appeared; the copies transferred to Messrs. Macmillan and Co. were of 1912.

39

THERE ARE | SEVEN THAT PULL | THE THREAD |
SONG IN ACT I. | "GRANIA AND DIARMID" | THE VERSE
WRITTEN BY | W. B. YEATS | THE MUSIC COMPOSED BY |
EDWARD ELGAR. | [rule] | PRICE | TWO SHILLINGS | NET. |
LONDON | NOVELLO & CO., LTD. | [*All the above contained in
an ornamental frame*] | COPYRIGHT, 1902, BY NOVELLO AND
COMPANY, LIMITED. | [rule] | ORCHESTRAL PARTS CAN BE
OBTAINED FROM THE PUBLISHERS.

$12\frac{1}{10} \times 9\frac{2}{5}$; pp. ii, 6; comprising title, verso blank, pp. [i–ii]; text
and music, pp. [1]–3; p. [4] blank; advertisements, pp. [5–6].

Issued in grey paper covers, printed in black inside ornamental design,
advertisements on inside covers and on back cover.

The words first appeared under the title "Spinning Song" in *A Broad
Sheet*, January 1902. The text of the play, by George Moore and
W. B. Yeats, as printed in *The Dublin Magazine*, April–June 1951,
and in a small edition of 25 copies (No. 211B), does not contain this
song.

The British Museum copy bears the date stamp July 18, 1902.

40

CATHLEEN NI HOOLIHAN | A PLAY IN ONE ACT AND |
IN PROSE BY W B YEATS | [ornament, *in red*] | PRINTED AT
THE CARADOC | PRESS CHISWICK FOR A H | BULLEN 18 CECIL
COURT LON | DON MDCCCCII

$6\frac{3}{10} \times 4\frac{3}{10}$; pp. ii, 30: comprising 1 blank leaf unnumbered; title,
quotation on verso, pp. [1–2]; dedication, list of dramatis personae in
red on verso, pp. [3–4]; text, pp. 5–29, the title of play and scenic
description on p. 5 being in red; colophon in red on p. [30].

Issued in cream paper boards with leather spine; lettered in brown on
front cover; 4 extra blank leaves are bound in at each end, the outer
leaf being pasted down to the board; all edges untrimmed. Published
in October 1902.

Contents

Cathleen ni Hoolihan

This play was first printed in *Samhain*, 1902. The lyrics had
previously appeared in *The United Irishman*, May 5, 1902.

Symons states that the edition on paper consisted of 500 copies, but I have seen this statement definitely corrected in a bookseller's catalogue and the number printed said to have been 300. This latter figure seems to be more likely for the product of a small hand-press, and copies of the book are not often found.

One copy, possibly a trial one, exists in grey boards with dark olive leather spine. To the bookseller who reported it Allan Wade wrote: "I despair of ever keeping track of the variant bindings of Yeats's earlier books. His publishers, apart from Unwin, were not in a big way of business and almost certainly printed their editions of 500 or 1000 or whatever it might be, bound up sufficient for immediate sales and some to go on with, and then had further small batches bound up as and when required. It is improbable that the binders could always match the previous binding, and they might substitute dark blue boards for light blue, grey for buff, and so on. Then somebody proudly announces the discovery of a 'variant'. This is, strictly speaking, correct; but I feel it is generally of very small bibliographical importance."

There was also an edition of 8 copies printed on Japanese vellum and bound in full vellum with silk ties.

The book was transferred to Elkin Mathews in 1903 and figures in his list as late as 1906.

In a letter to Sir Sydney Cockerell, dated Oct 17 [1902], Yeats wrote: "Bullen has published a little play of mine, *Kathleen ni Hoolihan*, at the Caradoc Press—and though it is better than mechanical printing it is bad enough. I am sorry I agreed to it. It is not worth the price and I am ashamed to hear of anybody buying it."

41

SUPPLEMENT TO THE UNITED IRISHMAN. SAMHAIN, 1902. | WHERE THERE IS NOTHING: | A PLAY IN FIVE ACTS BY W. B. YEATS. | (ALL RIGHTS RESERVED BY THE AUTHOR.)

Issued as a special supplement to *The United Irishman*, November 1, 1902. The supplement is the same size as the newspaper and measures 32½ × 13½, but is paginated separately, pp. 1–4. The text is printed in three columns to the page.

Although dated November 1, a Saturday, the *United Irishman* and its Supplement were, Mr. P. S. O'Hegarty tells me, on sale in London on the previous Thursday, October 30; Yeats recounts in *Dramatis Personae*: "Boys were shouting the supplement in the streets as he [George Moore] came out of the Antient Concert Rooms, where he had seen Fay's company." These performances by the Irish National Dramatic Company were given on October 29, 30 and 31. It seems certain therefore that the Irish edition of *Where There is Nothing* appeared possibly a day before or at any rate on the same day as that on which copies of the American printing were deposited for copyright at the Library of Congress in Washington.

In *Dramatis Personae* Yeats has told the story of the writing of this play, in which, at one time, there had been an idea that George Moore might collaborate. In conversation Yeats was even more explicit, and told me with much amusement that his reason for publishing the play as a supplement to *The United Irishman* was that he knew Moore would not dare to issue an injunction against a Nationalist newspaper for fear of getting his windows broken.

In a postscript to an article on *The Freedom of the Theatre*, not re-printed, which he published in *The United Irishman* on the same date, November 1, 1902, Yeats wrote:

"*Where There is Nothing* is founded upon a subject which I suggested to George Moore when there seemed to be a sudden need of a play for the Irish Literary Theatre; we talked of collaboration, but this did not go beyond some rambling talks. Then the need went past, and I gradually put so much of myself into the fable that I felt I must write on it alone, and took it back into my own hands with his consent. Should he publish a story upon it some day, I shall rejoice that the excellent old custom of two writers taking the one fable has been revived in a new form. If he does I cannot think that my play and his story will resemble each other. I have used nothing of his, and if he uses anything of mine he will have so changed it, doubtless, as to have made it his own."

42

FIRST AMERICAN EDITION

WHERE THERE IS | NOTHING | A DRAMA | IN FIVE ACTS | BY | W. B. YEATS | JOHN LANE | MCMII

$7\frac{1}{16} \times 4\frac{11}{16}$; pp. viii, 100: comprising half-title, verso blank, pp. [i–ii]; title, copyright notice and imprint, The Knickerbocker Press New Rochelle, N.Y., U.S.A. beneath rule at foot of page, on verso, pp. [iii–iv]; dedication, verso blank, pp. v–[vi]; Dramatis Personae, verso blank, pp. vii–[viii]; fly-title, Act I., verso blank, pp. [1–2]; text, pp. [3]–24; fly-title, Act II., verso blank, pp. [25–26]; text, pp. [27]–45; p. [46] blank; fly-title, Act III., verso blank, pp. [47–48]; text, pp. [49]–64; fly-title, Act IV., verso blank, pp. [65–66]; text, pp. [67]–82; fly-title, Act V., verso blank, pp. [83–84]; text, pp. [85]–99; p. [100] blank.

Issued in grey paper covers, the front cover printed from types of the title-page.

15 copies printed for copyright of which not over eight are now known. (Quinn, 1908.)

Printed for Mr. John Quinn from the author's first draft and containing some errors corrected in the large paper edition. (Quinn, 1908.)

Contents

Dedication
Where there is Nothing

In his Sale Catalogue (1924) Quinn gives the number of copies printed as 10. I take this to be an error of memory, in view of his definite statement above that the number was 15, the earlier statement being made comparatively soon after the date of the printing.

This edition was entered for copyright at the Library of Congress on October 24, 1902; two copies were received there on October 30, 1902.

43

AMERICAN PRIVATELY PRINTED LARGE PAPER EDITION

WHERE THERE IS | NOTHING | A DRAMA | IN FIVE ACTS | BY | W. B. YEATS | M · CM · II

$9\frac{9}{16} \times 6\frac{7}{16}$; pp. 2, viii, 102.

Issued in pale green paper boards with white labels printed in black on front cover and spine; duplicate labels inserted loose at end; white end-papers; all edges untrimmed.

Thirty copies printed for Quinn from the same types as the preceding, but without the publisher's name on title and without imprint on verso of title below copyright, and with some errors corrected.

These two editions contain a dedication to Lady Gregory, dated September 19, 1902, which does not appear in any subsequent edition. It was, however, reprinted, not quite complete, by Lady Gregory in *Our Irish Theatre*, 1914. (No. 307.)

44

FIRST ENGLISH EDITION

WHERE THERE IS NOTHING: | BEING VOLUME ONE OF
PLAYS | FOR AN IRISH THEATRE: BY | W. B. YEATS | LONDON:
A. H. BULLEN, 47, GREAT | RUSSELL STREET, W.C. 1903

$7\frac{1}{2} \times 5$; pp. xii, 132: comprising blank page, list of books By the Same
Writer on verso, pp. [i–ii]; half-title, verso blank, pp. [iii–iv]; title,
imprint, Chiswick Press: Charles Whittingham and Co. Tooks
Court, Chancery Lane, London, on verso, pp. [v–vi]; dedication,
pp. vii–x; list of dramatis personae, verso blank, pp. [xi–xii]; text,
pp. 1—[130]; imprint, Chiswick Press: Printed by Charles Whittingham and Co. Tooks Court, Chancery Lane, London, below rule, at
foot of p. [130]; pp. [131–132] blank.

Issued in grey paper boards with green linen spine, white label printed
in black inside green rule border on spine; white end-papers; all edges
untrimmed. Published in May 1903.

Contents

Dedication of Volumes One and Two of Plays for an Irish Theatre.
    Dated February 1903.
Where There is Nothing

45

FIRST AMERICAN PUBLIC EDITION

WHERE THERE IS | NOTHING | BEING VOLUME ONE
OF PLAYS FOR | AN IRISH THEATRE | BY | W. B. YEATS | NEW
YORK | THE MACMILLAN COMPANY | LONDON: MACMILLAN
& CO., LTD. | 1903 | ALL RIGHTS RESERVED

$7 \times 4\frac{3}{4}$; pp. 216: comprising half-title, Macmillan's monogram on
verso, pp. [1–2]; title, copyright notice and imprint, Norwood Press
J. S. Cushing & Co.—Berwick & Smith Co. Norwood, Mass., U.S.A.
on verso, pp. [3–4]; list of books By the same Writer, verso blank,
pp. [5–6]; dedication, pp. 7–11; list of characters, p. 12; text, pp.
13–212; advertisements, pp. [213–215]; p. [216] blank.

Issued in dark blue ribbed cloth, lettered in gold on spine; white end-papers; top edges gilt, others untrimmed. Published on May 13, 1903.

The contents are the same as those of the English edition of 1903.

LARGE PAPER EDITION

Printed on Japan paper from the same types and differing only in not containing advertisements at end and in having on verso of half-title (p. 2), the notice "Of this book One Hundred Copies have been printed | on Japanese vellum, of which this is | No. . .

Size $8\frac{13}{16} \times 5\frac{3}{4}$; edges untrimmed.

Issued in parchment paper binding, lettered on front cover and on spine.

46

IDEAS OF GOOD AND [*in red*] | EVIL. [*in red*] | BY W. B. YEATS | A. H. BULLEN, [*in red*] 47 GREAT RUSSELL | STREET, LONDON, W. C. MCMIII

$7\frac{1}{2} \times 5$; pp. viii, 344: comprising blank page, list of books By the Same Writer on verso, pp. [i–ii]; half-title, verso blank, pp. [iii–iv]; title, verso blank, pp. [v–vi]; contents, verso blank, pp. vii–[viii]; text, pp. 1–341; imprint, Richard Clay & Sons, Limited, London & Bungay. p. [342]; pp. [343–344] blank.

Issued in green paper boards with dark green cloth spine; white label printed in black inside green rule border; white end-papers; all edges untrimmed. 1490 copies were printed in April 1903, this figure including 520 with American imprint. Published in May 1903.

Contents

What is 'Popular Poetry'?
　　First appeared in *The Cornhill Magazine*, March 1902.
Speaking to the Psaltery
　　First appeared in *The Monthly Review*, May 1902.
Magic
　　First appeared in *The Monthly Review*, September 1901.
The Happiest of the Poets
　　First appeared in *The Fortnightly Review*, March 1903.

The Philosophy of Shelley's Poetry
    I. *His Ruling Ideas.*
    First appeared in *The Dome*, July 1900.
    II. *His Ruling Symbols.*
At Stratford-on-Avon
    First appeared in *The Speaker*, May 11 and 18, 1901.
William Blake and the Imagination
    First appeared, under the title *William Blake*, in *The Academy*,
    June 19, 1897.
William Blake and his Illustrations to "The Divine Comedy"
    I. *His Opinions upon Art*
    First appeared in *The Savoy*, July 1896.
    II. *His Opinions on Dante*
    First appeared in *The Savoy*, August 1896.
    III. *The Illustrations of Dante*
    First appeared in *The Savoy*, September 1896.
Symbolism in Painting
    First appeared as part of the introduction to *A Book of Images*,
    1898. (No. 255.)
The Symbolism of Poetry
    First appeared in *The Dome*, April 1900.
The Theatre
    The first section of this essay originally appeared in *The Dome*,
    April 1899; the second originally appeared, as part of an essay,
    The Irish Literary Theatre, 1900, in *The Dome*, January 1900.
The Celtic Element in Literature
    The first section of this essay originally appeared in *Cosmopolis*,
    June 1898.
The Autumn of the Body
    First appeared, under the title *The Autumn of the Flesh*, in *The
    Dublin Daily Express*, December 3, 1898, and already reprinted
    in *Literary Ideals in Ireland*, 1899. (No. 297.)
The Moods
    First appeared, as part of one of a series of articles on Irish
    National Literature, in *The Bookman*, August 1895.
The Body of the Father Christian Rosencrux
    First appeared, as part of one of a series of articles on Irish
    National Literature, in *The Bookman*, September 1895.
"The Return of Ulysses"
    First appeared, under the title *Mr. Robert Bridges*, in *The Book-
    man*, June 1897.
Ireland and the Arts
    First appeared in *The United Irishman*, August 31, 1901.

The Galway Plains
>   First appeared, under the title *Poets and Dreamers*, in *The New
>   Liberal Review*, March 1903.

Emotion of Multitude
>   First appeared in *The All Ireland Review*, April 11, 1903.

There were further editions in 1903 (1090 copies), 1907 and 1914.
The title-page of the third edition (1907) bore at foot:

LONDON: [in black] A. H. BULLEN [in red] | DUBLIN: [in black] MAUNSEL
& CO., LTD. [in red] | MCMVII

Some copies of the second and third editions were shipped to
America and bound as No. 47.

On or about June 28, 1916 the remainder of the edition of 1914 was
transferred to Messrs. Macmillan and Co., Ltd. These copies were
bound in grey-green paper boards with grey-green linen spine,
lettered in black on spine.

47

AMERICAN EDITION

IDEAS OF GOOD AND [*in red*] | EVIL. [*in red*] BY W. B.
YEATS | THE MACMILLAN COMPANY [*in red*] | NEW YORK.
MCMIII

Bound from English sheets but with new title as above; 520 copies
were printed in England with title for America in April 1903. Issued in
ribbed blue cloth, lettered in gold on front cover and on spine.

The second edition was issued in 1903.

The third edition has the unaltered title of the English third edition
but is bound as the first edition described above. (Quinn.)

In Quinn's copy of the first American edition Yeats wrote: "I got
the title of this book out of one of Blake's MSS. works if I remember
rightly. He made a title-page with these words on it but I do not think
—no, I know—he never printed the sections. W. B. Yeats. March 8,
1904."

48

DUBLIN EDITION

IDEAS OF GOOD AND | EVIL. BY W. B. YEATS. |
DUBLIN: MAUNSEL AND CO., LTD. | 60 DAWSON STREET. 1905.

Sheets of the English second edition with title as above pasted in. The
words SECOND EDITION appear on the verso of half-title; on the verso

E

of title is the imprint Richard Clay & Sons, Limited, Bread Street Hill, E.C., and Bungay, Suffolk. 200 cancel titles for this edition were printed in August 1905, and a further 200 later in the same month.

Issued in dark blue-green cloth, and also in green paper boards with yellow linen spine, lettered on spine IDEAS | OF | GOOD AND EVIL | W. B. YEATS | MAUNSEL. Some copies are lettered on spine Ideas | of | Good | and | Evil.

At the end is a list of Maunsel & Co.'s new and forthcoming books, 4 pp. unnumbered. Some copies are without the list of books at the end.

These copies were for sale, at a reduced price, in Ireland only.

49

IN THE SEVEN WOODS: BEING POEMS | CHIEFLY OF THE IRISH HEROIC AGE | BY WILLIAM BUTLER YEATS | THE DUN EMER PRESS | DUNDRUM | MCMIII

8⅕ × 5¾; pp. viii, 68: comprising pp. [i–iv] blank; title, verso blank, pp. [v–vi]; p. [vii] blank; table of contents, p. [viii]; text, pp. [1]–[64]; colophon, in red, on p. [64]; pp. [65–68] blank. The heading to p. [1], verses on pp. 7, 8, 9, 11, 12 and 15, a note on p. 25, and the preliminaries to the play on p. 26 are all in red. An additional title-slip, in red, for the cover is tipped in at head of title-page.

Issued in off-white linen, white label in red IN THE SEVEN WOODS. WILLIAM BUTLER YEATS pasted on front cover; no label on spine; white end-papers; all edges untrimmed.

Printed on paper made in Ireland and published by Elizabeth Corbet Yeats at the Dun Emer Press, Dundrum. Finished on July 16, 1903. Published in August 1903.

The edition consisted of 325 copies. This is not stated in the colophon, but the information is to be found in the earliest prospectus of the Dun Emer Press.

Contents

In the Seven Woods. Dated August 1902.
The Old Age of Queen Maeve
> First appeared in *The Fortnightly Review*, April 1903; printed also in *The Gael* (New York), June 1903.
Baile and Aillinn
> First appeared in *The Monthly Review*, July 1902.

The Arrow

The Folly of being Comforted
   First appeared in *The Speaker*, January 11, 1902.

The Withering of the Boughs
   First appeared, under the title *Echtge of Streams*, in *The Speaker*,
   August 25, 1900.

Adam's Curse
   First appeared in *The Monthly Review*, December 1902; printed
   also in *The Gael* (New York), February 1903.

The Song of Red Hanrahan
   This revised version of a poem which appeared, without title, in
   the story *Kathleen the Daughter of Hoolihan and Hanrahan the
   Red* in *The Secret Rose* first appeared, without title, in *A Broad
   Sheet*, April 1903.

The Old Men admiring themselves in the Water
   First appeared in *The Pall Mall Magazine*, January 1903;
   printed also in *The Gael* (New York), September 1903.

Under the Moon
   First appeared in *The Speaker*, June 15, 1901.

The Players ask for a Blessing on the Psalteries and themselves

The Rider from the North. From the play *The Country of the Young.**
   First appeared, under the title *The Happy Townland*, in *The
   Weekly Critical Review* (Paris), June 4, 1903.

Note, without heading.

On Baile's Strand, a Play

The note which separates the lyrics from the play reads as follows:
"I made some of these poems walking about among the Seven Woods,
before the big wind of nineteen hundred and three blew down so many
trees, & troubled the wild creatures, & changed the look of things;
and I thought out there a good part of the play which follows. The
first shape of it came to me in a dream, but it changed much in the
making, foreshadowing, it may be, a change that may bring a less
dream-burdened will into my verses. I never re-wrote anything so
many times; for at first I could not make these wills that stream into
mere life poetical. But now I hope to do easily much more of the
kind, and that our new Irish players will find the buskin and the sock."

Yeats wrote in Quinn's copy: "This is the first book of mine that it
is a pleasure to look at—a pleasure whether open or shut. W. B.
Yeats. March, 1904."

   * I asked Yeats in 1908 why he had changed the title of the poem *The Happy
Townland* to *The Rider from the North* and subsequently back to the original
title; he said that he had completely forgotten doing so.

50

AMERICAN EDITION

IN THE SEVEN WOODS | BEING POEMS CHIEFLY OF THE |
IRISH HEROIC AGE | BY | W. B. YEATS | NEW YORK | THE
MACMILLAN COMPANY | LONDON: MACMILLAN & CO., LTD. |
1903 | ALL RIGHTS RESERVED

$7\frac{1}{2} \times 5$; pp. vi, 90: comprising half-title, list of books By the same
Writer, in panel, on verso, pp. [i–ii]; title, copyright notice and im-
print, Norwood Press J. S. Cushing & Co.—Berwick & Smith Co.
Norwood, Mass. U.S.A. on verso, pp. [iii–iv]; fly-title, verso blank,
pp. v–[vi]; text, pp. 1–87; p. [88] blank; list of Essays, etc. by William
Butler Yeats, p. [89]; p. [90] blank. There are headings or passages
printed in red on pp. 1, 10, 11, 14, 15, 19, 33 and 34, following the
Dun Emer Press edition.

Issued in dark blue ribbed cloth, lettered in gold on spine; white
end-papers; top edges gilt, others untrimmed. Published on August
25, 1903.

The contents are the same as those of the Dun Emer Press edition.
(No. 49.)

In Quinn's copy Yeats wrote: "The printer followed my sister's
edition in this book without consulting me, & spoilt in copying.
W. B. Yeats, 1904."

51

THE | HOUR-GLASS | A MORALITY | BY | W. B. YEATS |
LONDON | WM. HEINEMANN, 21 BEDFORD ST., W.C. | 1903

$9\frac{1}{2} \times 6\frac{1}{2}$; pp. 16: comprising title, copyright notice on verso, pp.
[1–2]; text, pp. [3]–14; pp. [15–16] blank. The title-leaf forms the
cover. All edges trimmed.

The Hour-Glass first appeared in *The North American Review*,
September 1903

This edition, made for copyright purposes, was an off-print in the
Review type. Quinn stated in 1908 that "there were twelve copies
only, of which six went for English copyright; two others were lost

in the mail; the printer kept one; one belongs to Mr. W. B. Yeats, one to Lady Gregory and one to Mr. John Quinn." In the Quinn sale catalogue he adds to this "The author lost or mislaid his copy; the printer years ago lost or gave away his copy. This copy and the one in possession of Lady Gregory are therefore in all probability the only copies in existence, and may rank perhaps as the rarest of all Yeats items."

In July 1909, that is after the publication of Quinn's first note, Lady Gregory wrote to me that her copy also had been lost by the binders and that she had mentioned this to Quinn when my 1908 bibliography reached her, saying that now his copy was the only one extant. She had just received from him, she wrote, his copy "in a beautiful case." Nevertheless a copy appears in his sale catalogue, and there was one also in Edmund Gosse's library, inscribed by Yeats: "Never heard of this edition before. Oct. 13, 1914"; this copy appeared again in the Buhler sale. A copy was also sold at Messrs. Hodgson's on November 30, 1950.

Quinn was mistaken in saying that the author had lost or mislaid his copy; it remained in his library and is now in the possession of Mrs. Yeats. But Yeats cared little for his own first editions and was, no doubt, sincere in saying, on the Edmund Gosse copy, that he had never heard of this edition.

The copy in the British Museum bears the date stamp August 29, 1903.

52

AMERICAN EDITION

THE HOUR-GLASS | AND OTHER PLAYS | BEING VOLUME TWO OF PLAYS FOR | AN IRISH THEATRE | BY | W. B. YEATS | NEW YORK | THE MACMILLAN COMPANY | LONDON: MAC- MILLAN & CO., LTD. | 1904 | ALL RIGHTS RESERVED

$7 \times 4\frac{3}{4}$; pp. viii, 116: comprising p. [i] blank; list of books By the same Writer, p. [ii]; half-title, Macmillan's monogram on verso, pp. [iii–iv]; title, copyright notice and imprint, Norwood Press J. S. Cushing & Co.—Berwick & Smith Co. Norwood, Mass., U.S.A. on verso, pp. [v–vi]; contents and notes as to first performances, verso blank, pp. vii–[viii]; fly-title, Dramatis Personae on verso, pp. [1–2]; text, pp. 3–113; p. [114] blank; advertisements, p. [115]; p. [116] blank.

Issued in blue cloth, lettered in gold on spine; white end-papers; top edges gilt, others untrimmed. Published on January 13, 1904.

Contents

The Hour-Glass: A Morality
> First appeared in *The North American Review*, September 1903, and issued in a small edition for copyright purposes in 1903. (No. 51.)

Cathleen ni Hoolihan
> First appeared in *Samhain*, October 1902, and printed in a separate edition in 1902. (No. 40.)

The Pot of Broth
> First appeared in *The Gael* (New York), September 1903.

There were further impressions in December 1904; April 1906; September 1909; October 1911; November 1912; February 1914; March 1915; and 1919.

LARGE PAPER EDITION

Printed on Japan paper from the same type. Does not contain advertisement leaf at end and has limitation notice on verso of half-title. Size of page, untrimmed, $8\frac{13}{16} \times 5\frac{3}{4}$.

Issued in parchment paper binding, lettered on front cover and on spine. Edition limited to 100 copies.

These American editions do not contain the bars of music (p. 65 of English edition) or the *Note on the Music* at the end.

It may be noted that these editions retain the original spelling "Cathleen ni Hoolihan" instead of "Houlihan".

53

ENGLISH EDITION

THE HOUR-GLASS, CATHLEEN | NI HOULIHAN, THE POT OF | BROTH: BEING VOLUME TWO OF | PLAYS FOR AN IRISH THEATRE: | BY W. B. YEATS | LONDON: A. H. BULLEN, 47, GREAT | RUSSELL STREET, W.C. 1904

$7\frac{1}{2} \times 5$; pp. viii, 84: comprising blank page, list of Books by the Same Author on verso, pp. [i–ii]; half-title, verso blank, pp. [iii–iv]; title-page, imprint, Chiswick Press: Charles Whittingham and Co. Tooks Court, Chancery Lane, London, on verso, pp. [v–vi]; contents, verso blank, pp. vii–[viii]; fly-title, verso blank, pp. [1–2]; text, pp. 3–[83]; printers' emblem and imprint as above, p. [84].

Issued in grey paper boards with green cloth spine; white label printed in black inside green rule border on spine; white end-papers; all edges untrimmed. Published in March 1904.

Contents

The Hour-Glass: A Morality
Cathleen ni Houlihan
The Pot of Broth
> For previous appearances of these plays see the American edition. (No. 52.)

Note on the Music

54

DUBLIN EDITION

THE HOUR-GLASS, CATHLEEN | NI HOULIHAN, THE POT OF | BROTH: BY W. B. YEATS | DUBLIN: MAUNSEL AND CO., LTD. | 60, DAWSON STREET. 1905

$7\frac{1}{2} \times 5$; pp. ii, 84: comprising title, verso blank, pp. [i–ii]; followed by sheets of Bullen's edition (No. 53), pp. 1–84. At the end is a 4-page list of Maunsel & Co.'s new and forthcoming books; this is printed by Hely's, Limited, Printers Dublin.

Issued in purple paper covers with design of girl and wolf-hound by Elinor Monsell in black and lettered in black THE HOUR GLASS, CATH- | LEEN NI HOULIHAN, THE | POT OF BROTH, BY W. B. | YEATS, BEING VOLUME IV. | OF THE ABBEY THEATRE | SERIES. No lettering on spine; all edges trimmed. Published in 1905.

These copies were for sale in Ireland only.

55

THE KING'S THRESHOLD [*in red*] | A PLAY IN VERSE | BY | W. B. YEATS | NEW YORK | PRINTED FOR PRIVATE CIRCULATION [*in red*] | 1904

$9 \times 6\frac{1}{4}$; pp. 6, x, 58: comprising 3 leaves not included in pagination; half-title, note of limitation with initial letter in red and number of copy written in red ink, on verso, pp. [i–ii]; title, copyright notice on verso and imprint, below rule, The University Press Cambridge, U.S.A. at foot of verso, pp. [iii–iv]; Prologue, pp. v–viii; cast of characters, verso blank, pp. [ix–x]; fly-title, verso blank, pp. [1–2]; text, pp. 3–58.

Issued in grey paper boards, title stamped in gold on spine; cream end-papers; top edges gilt, others untrimmed. Enclosed in grey cardboard slip case.

One hundred copies printed on cream-coloured old hand-made Italian paper, for Quinn.

This edition was entered for copyright at the Library of Congress on March 18, 1904; two copies were received there on March 19, 1904.

Roth notes that the Library of Congress has an advance proof of this edition, and gives the following description:

THE KING'S THRESHOLD | A PLAY IN VERSE | BY | W. B. YEATS | NEW YORK | PRINTED FOR PRIVATE CIRCULATION | 1904

The page numbering is identical with the above, the plates being with one exception the same; there are, however, two sheets for every one of the finished book, the printing appearing on the front of the first sheet, and on the back of the second.

Apparently it was later decided to enlarge the edition, as p. [4] reads: "Of this edition seventy-five copies have been printed, of which this is No.   "

56

THE KING'S THRESHOLD: AND | ON BAILE'S STRAND: BEING | VOLUME THREE OF PLAYS | FOR AN IRISH THEATRE: BY | W. B. YEATS | LONDON: A. H. BULLEN, 47, GREAT | RUSSELL STREET, W.C. 1904

$7\frac{1}{2} \times 5$; pp. viii, 120: comprising blank page with list of books By the same Author on verso, pp. [i–ii]; half-title, verso blank, pp. [iii–iv]; title, with imprint, Chiswick Press: Charles Whittingham and Co. Tooks Court, Chancery Lane, London, on verso, pp. [v–vi]; note, contents on verso, pp. vii–[viii]; fly-title, verso blank, pp. [1–2]; List of Characters, verso blank, pp. 3–[4]; Prologue, pp. 5–9; p. [10] blank; text, pp. 11–117; printer's emblem and imprint as above, p. [118], pp. [119–120] blank.

Issued in grey paper boards with green linen spine; white label printed in black within green rule border on spine; white end-papers; all edges untrimmed. Published in March 1904.

Contents

Note
A Prologue
 First appeared in *The United Irishman*, September 9, 1903.
The King's Threshold
On Baile's Strand
 First appeared in *In the Seven Woods*, 1903. (No. 49.)

57

DUBLIN EDITION

THE KING'S THRESHOLD: | BY W. B. YEATS | DUBLIN:
MAUNSEL AND CO., LTD. | 60, DAWSON STREET. 1905

$7\frac{1}{2} \times 5$; pp. ii, 66 followed by 4 pp. of advertisements: comprising
title, verso blank, pp. [i–ii]; followed by sheets of Bullen's edition
(No. 56), pp. [1]–66; Maunsel & Co.'s List of New and Forthcoming
Books, 4 pp., unnumbered, at end.

Issued in grey paper covers, design of girl and wolf-hound and
lettering THE KING'S THRESHOLD, BY | W. B. YEATS, BEING VOL. V. |
OF THE ABBEY THEATRE | SERIES. in dark green on front cover; no
lettering on spine; all edges untrimmed. Published in 1905.

These copies were for sale in Ireland only.

58

DUBLIN EDITION

ON BAILE'S STRAND: BY | W. B. YEATS | DUBLIN:
MAUNSEL AND CO., LTD. | 60, DAWSON STREET. 1905

$7\frac{1}{2} \times 5$; pp. ii, 67 to 120: comprising title, verso blank, pp. [i–ii];
followed by sheets of Bullen's edition (No. 56), pp. 67–120. At the
end is a 4-page list of Maunsel & Co.'s New and Forthcoming Books,
printed by Hely's.

Issued in light brown paper covers with design of girl and wolf-
hound and lettering ON BAILE'S STRAND, BY | W. B. YEATS, BEING VOL.
VI. | OF THE ABBEY THEATRE | SERIES in red on front cover; no lettering
on spine; all edges untrimmed. Published in 1905.

These copies were for sale in Ireland only.

59

STORIES OF RED HANRAHAN BY | WILLIAM BUTLER
YEATS | THE DUN EMER PRESS | DUNDRUM MCMIV

$8\frac{2}{5} \times 5\frac{3}{4}$; pp. viii, 64: comprising pp. [i–ii] blank; note of limitation of
edition [in red], verso blank, pp. [iii–iv]; title, verso blank, pp. [v–
vi]; acknowledgement [in red], table of contents and woodcut [by
Robert Gregory] on verso, pp. [vii–viii]; text, pp. [1]–[57]; colophon,
in red, on p. [57]; pp. [58–64] blank.

Issued in blue paper boards with buff linen spine; label, printed in
black, carrying title and author's name, pasted on front cover; label,
printed in black, carrying title only, pasted on spine; blue end-papers
matching binding; all edges untrimmed.

500 copies printed on paper made in Ireland and published by
Elizabeth Corbet Yeats at the Dun Emer Press, Dundrum. Finished
on Lady Day in August 1904. Published on May 16, 1905.

Contents

Red Hanrahan
> First appeared in *The Independent Review*, December 1903.
The Twisting of the Rope
Hanrahan and Cathleen the daughter of Hoolihan
Red Hanrahan's Curse
Hanrahan's Vision
> First appeared, under the title *Red Hanrahan's Vision*, in
> *McClure's Magazine*, March 1905.
The Death of Hanrahan

Most of these stories are rewritten versions of stories from *The Secret
Rose* (No. 21).

In Quinn's copy Yeats wrote "Red Hanrahan is an imaginary name—
I saw it over a shop, or rather part of it over a shop in a Galway
village—but there were many poets like him in the eighteenth century
in Ireland. I wrote these stories first in literary English but I could not
get any sense of the village life with the words. Now, however, Lady
Gregory has helped me, & I think the stories have the emotion of
folklore. They are but half mine now, & often her beautiful idiom is
the better half. W. B. Yeats, June 1905."

60

THE POT OF BROTH | BY W. B. YEATS | A. H. BULLEN |
47 GREAT RUSSELL STREET, LONDON, W.C. | PRICE SIXPENCE
NET | 1905

$7\frac{1}{10} \times 4\frac{3}{4}$; pp. 16: comprising text, pp. 1–15; imprint, Strangeways,
Tower Street, Cambridge Circus, London, W.C. p. [16]. There is no
title-page.

Issued in grey paper covers, lettered in black on front cover as above.
The words PRICE SIXPENCE NET are printed on a separate slip and
pasted on. Advertisements of W. B. Yeats's works on back cover.
All edges trimmed.

The first separate edition of this play.

61

THE POT OF BROTH | BY | W. B. YEATS | LONDON:
A. H. BULLEN | 1911

$7\frac{1}{2} \times 5$; pp. 16: comprising title, verso blank, pp. [1–2]; text, pp. 3–
15; imprint of The Shakespeare Head Press, Stratford-on-Avon,
p. [16].

Issued in brown paper covers, lettered in black on front cover THE POT
OF BROTH | BY | W. B. YEATS | LONDON: A. H. BULLEN | MCMXI | PRICE
SIXPENCE NET. All edges untrimmed. Published in November 1911.

On or about June 28, 1916, the remainder of this edition was transferred to Messrs. Macmillan and Co., Ltd. The firm thinks it likely
that new paper covers were substituted bearing their imprint.

62

CATHLEEN NI HOULIHAN | BY W. B. YEATS | A. H.
BULLEN | 47 GREAT RUSSELL STREET, LONDON, | W.C. | PRICE
SIXPENCE NET | 1906

$6\frac{4}{5} \times 4\frac{1}{5}$; pp. 16: comprising text, pp. 1–16. There is no title-page and
no printer's name.

Issued in dark green paper covers, lettered in black on front cover as
above. Advertisements of W. B. Yeats's works on back cover. All
edges trimmed.

63

CATHLEEN NI HOULIHAN: | BY | W. B. YEATS |
LONDON: A. H. BULLEN, | MCMIX | PRICE SIXPENCE NET.

$7\frac{1}{2} \times 5$; pp. 16: comprising text, pp. 1–14; list of works By the same
Writer, p. [15]; imprint of The Shakespeare Head Press, Stratford-on-
Avon, p. [16]. There is no title-page.

Issued in dark grey paper covers, lettered in black on front cover as
above. All edges untrimmed.

CATHLEEN NI HOULIHAN | BY | W. B. YEATS | SHAKE-
SPEARE HEAD PRESS | STRATFORD-UPON-AVON | MCMXI

$7\frac{1}{2} \times 4\frac{3}{4}$; pp. 16: comprising title, imprint Printed by A. H. Bullen at
The Shakespeare Head Press, Stratford-on-Avon, on verso, pp.
[1–2]; text, pp. 3–15; list of The Works of W. B. Yeats, p. [16].

Issued in dark grey paper covers, lettered in black on front cover
CATHLEEN NI HOULIHAN | BY | W. B. YEATS | SHAKESPEARE HEAD
PRESS | STRATFORD-UPON-AVON | SIXPENCE NET. All edges untrimmed.

On or about June 28, 1916 the remainder of this latter edition was
transferred to Messrs. Macmillan and Co., Ltd. The firm thinks it
likely that new paper covers were substituted bearing their imprint.

64

POEMS, 1899–1905 [*in red*] | BY W. B. YEATS | LONDON:
A. H. BULLEN | DUBLIN: MAUNSEL & CO., LTD. | 1906

$7\frac{1}{2} \times 5$; pp. xvi, 280: comprising pp. [i–iii] blank, list of books By the
Same Writer, p. [iv]; half-title, verso blank, pp. [v–vi]; title, verso
blank, pp. [vii–viii]; contents, verso blank, pp. ix–[x]; Preface,
pp. xi–xv; p. [xvi] blank; fly-title, dedication on verso, pp. [1–2];
introductory poem, pp. 3–5; p. [6] blank; poem, The Harp of Aengus,
list of Persons of the Play on verso, pp. 7–[8]; text, pp. 9–68; fly-title,
dedication on verso, pp. [69–70]; Persons of the Play, verso blank,
pp. [71–72]; text, pp. 73–138; fly-title, dedication on verso, pp. [139–
140]; text, pp. 141–185; p. [186] blank; fly-title, dedication on verso,
pp. [187–188]; Persons in the Play, verso blank, pp. [189–190]; text,
pp. 191–270; fly-title, verso blank, pp. [271–272]; text, pp. 273–
[280]; imprint, Plymouth William Brendon and Son, Ltd, Printers,
at foot of p. [280].

Issued in dark blue cloth, lettered in gold on front cover and on spine,
the design on spine being that used on *The Secret Rose*; white end-
papers; all edges untrimmed. Published in October 1906.

Contents

Preface. Dated 18 May, 1906.

I walked among the seven woods of Coole. Dated September 1900.

The Harp of Aengus
>This poem is a passage taken from the first version of *The
Shadowy Waters*, 1900. (No. 30.)

The Shadowy Waters. (A new version)

On Baile's Strand. (A new version)
>*The Song of the Women* (pp. 102–104) first appeared, under the
title *Against Witchcraft*, in *The Shanachie*, No. I, Spring 1906.

In the Seven Woods
>This section contains the twelve poems published in the Dun
Emer Press edition of 1903 (No. 49), and also
>*Old Memory*
>>First appeared in *Wayfarer's Love*, 1904. (No. 302.)
>*Never Give all the Heart*
>>First appeared in *McClure's Magazine*, December 1905.

The Entrance of Deirdre
> Two verses of this poem first appeared, under the title *Queen Edaine*, in *McClure's Magazine*, September 1905; and the whole poem was printed, under the title *The Praise of Deirdre*, in *The Shanachie*, Spring 1906.

The King's Threshold. (A new version.)

Notes

65

THE POETICAL WORKS | OF | WILLIAM B. YEATS | IN TWO VOLUMES | VOLUME I | LYRICAL POEMS | NEW YORK | THE MACMILLAN COMPANY | LONDON: MACMILLAN & CO., LTD. | 1906 | ALL RIGHTS RESERVED

$7\frac{1}{2} \times 5$; pp. 2, xiv, 340: comprising 2 pp. not included in pagination; half-title, Macmillan's monogram on verso, pp. [i–ii]; title, copyright notice and imprint, Norwood Press, J. S. Cushing & Co.— Berwick & Smith Co. Norwood, Mass., U.S.A. on verso, pp. [iii–iv]; Preface, pp. v–viii; contents, pp. ix–xiii; p. [xiv] blank; fly-title, quotation on verso, pp. [1–2]; dedication, verso blank, pp. [3–4]; text, pp. 5–338; list of books By the same Author, p. [339]; advertisements, p. [340].

Issued in dark blue cloth, lettering and design in gold on spine, the design being that used on *Poems*, 1899 (No. 17); white end-papers; top edges gilt, others untrimmed. Published on November 27, 1906.

Contents

Preface. Dated July 1906.

Early Poems: I. Ballads and Lyrics
> 16 poems from *Crossways*, preceded by *To some I have talked with by the fire.*

Early Poems: II. The Wanderings of Oisin.

Early Poems: III. The Rose
> 21 poems.

The Wind among the Reeds
> 37 poems.

In the Seven Woods
> 13 poems.

The Old Age of Queen Maeve

Baile and Aillinn

There were further impressions in October 1908; December 1911;
December 1913; August 1914; August 1915; August 1916; December
1917; June 1920; and August 1922.

66

THE SHADOWY WATERS, | BY W. B. YEATS. | ACTING
VERSION, | AS FIRST PLAYED AT THE ABBEY THEATRE,
DECEMBER 8TH, 1906. | A. H. BULLEN, | 47 GREAT RUSSELL
STREET, LONDON, W. C. | 1907

7×5; pp. 28: comprising title, verso blank, pp. [1–2]; text, pp.
[3]–28.

Issued in green paper covers, front cover printed in black, with
advertisements on verso; all edges untrimmed.

Written partly in verse, partly in prose; the prose seems to be largely
the work of Lady Gregory.

67

THE HOUR-GLASS: | A MORALITY | BY | W. B. YEATS |
LONDON: A. H. BULLEN, | MCMVII | PRICE SIXPENCE.

$7 \times 4\frac{4}{8}$; pp. 16: comprising text, pp. 1–16. There is no title-page and
no printer's name.

Issued in dark brown paper covers, lettered in black on front cover as
above; all edges trimmed.

A. H. Bullen appears to have reprinted this play twice at Stratford-on-
Avon at dates unknown. Messrs. Macmillan and Co. Ltd. to whom
the play was transferred on or about June 28, 1916 have two copies
in their files. The first:

THE HOUR-GLASS | BY | W. B. YEATS | [ornament] |
SHAKESPEARE HEAD PRESS | STRATFORD-UPON-AVON |
SIXPENCE NET

$7\frac{1}{2} \times 5$; pp. 16: comprising text, pp. 1–16. No title-page.

Issued in dark grey paper covers, lettered in black on front cover as above; all edges trimmed.

The second is similar but measures $7\frac{3}{10} \times 4\frac{4}{5}$, and is bound in greenish brown paper covers.

In the Berg Collection in the New York Public Library there is a copy of the 1907 edition of *The Hour-Glass* containing Yeats's corrections for a new edition. I do not know whether these were carried out in the reprints here mentioned.

68

THEATRE EDITION

ON BAILE'S STRAND | BY | W. B. YEATS | LONDON: A. H. BULLEN, | MCMVII

$7\frac{1}{2} \times 4\frac{3}{4}$; pp. 36: comprising title, verso blank, pp. [1–2]; text, pp. 3–35; imprint of The Shakespeare Head Press, Stratford-on-Avon on p. [36].

Issued in brown paper covers, lettered in black on front cover ON BAILE'S STRAND | BY | W. B. YEATS | PRICE SIXPENCE. All edges untrimmed.

The first separate edition of this play, in the revised version.

On or about June 28, 1916, the remainder of this edition was transferred to Messrs. Macmillan and Co., Ltd. The firm thinks that it is probable that new paper covers were substituted bearing their imprint.

69

DEIRDRE BY W. B. YEATS | BEING VOLUME FIVE OF PLAYS | FOR AN IRISH THEATRE | LONDON: A. H. BULLEN | DUBLIN: MAUNSEL & CO., LTD | 1907

$7\frac{1}{2} \times 5$; pp. viii, 48: comprising blank page, list of books By the same Writer on verso, pp. [i–ii]; half-title, verso blank, pp. [iii–iv]; title, verso blank, pp. [v–vi]; dedication, list of Persons and Players at first performance on verso, pp. [vii–viii]; text, pp. 1–[48]; imprint, London: Strangeways, Printers, at foot of p. [48].

Issued in grey paper boards with green cloth spine; white label printed in black within green rule border on spine; white end-papers; all edges untrimmed. Published in August 1907.

Contents

Deirdre

    For first appearance of the song *Why is it, Queen Edaine said*
(p. 9), see *The Entrance of Deirdre* in *Poems, 1899–1905.* (No. 64.)

Note

The British Museum has what is evidently an advance copy; this copy
is probably made up of page-proofs. The title-page and description
are as follows:

DEIRDRE | BY W. B. YEATS | BEING VOLUME FIVE OF PLAYS |
FOR AN IRISH THEATRE | LONDON: A. H. BULLEN, 47 GREAT |
RUSSELL STREET, W.C. 1907

Blank page with list of books By the same Writer on verso, pp. [i–
ii]; half-title, with dedication on the same page, verso blank, pp.
[iii–iv]; title, with Persons and Players at first performance on verso,
pp. [v–vi]; text, pp. 1–48; no imprint on p. 48.

This copy bears the British Museum date stamp 8 July, 1907; the
book was not published until late in August.

70

ALTERATIONS IN 'DEIRDRE.'

In November 1908 a four-page leaflet, Alterations in 'Deirdre',
$7\frac{1}{2} \times 5$; pp. 1–4, was printed for insertion in the published copies of
the play. The text follows that printed in *Samhain*, November 1908
with slight alteration and with the punctuation revised.

I give this date on the authority of a letter to myself from A. H.
Bullen, the publisher. The leaflet was printed for Mrs. Patrick
Campbell's production of the play in London on November 27, 1908.

71

THE POETICAL WORKS | OF | WILLIAM B. YEATS |
IN TWO VOLUMES | VOLUME II | DRAMATICAL POEMS | NEW
YORK | THE MACMILLAN COMPANY | LONDON: MACMILLAN &
CO., LTD. | 1907 | ALL RIGHTS RESERVED

$7\frac{1}{2} \times 5$; pp. x, 530: comprising half-title, Macmillan's monogram on
verso, pp. [i–ii]; title, copyright notice and imprint, Norwood Press

F

J. S. Cushing & Co.—Berwick & Smith Co. Norwood, Mass., U.S.A. on verso, pp. [iii–iv]; Preface, pp. v–viii; contents, verso blank, pp. ix–[x]; fly-title, verso blank, pp. [1–2]; list of characters, verso blank, pp. [3–4]; fly-title, verso blank, pp. [5–6]; text, pp. 7–524; advertisements, pp. [525–528]; pp. [529–530] blank.

Issued in similar style to Volume I.   (No. 65.)

Published on July 8, 1907.

Contents

Preface. Dated December 1906.
The Countess Cathleen
The Land of Heart's Desire
The Shadowy Waters
On Baile's Strand
The King's Threshold
Deirdre
Appendix I. The Legendary and Mythological Foundation of the Plays and Poems.
Appendix II. The Dates and Places of Performance of the Plays.
Appendix III. Acting Version of "The Shadowy Waters".
Appendix IV. The Work of the National Theatre Society at the Abbey Theatre, Dublin: A Statement of Principles.
   This corresponds to sections III, IV and V of the essay *Literature and the Living Voice*, first published in *The Contemporary Review*, October 1906.

This volume was reprinted in June 1909, and again in August 1911.

For a revised edition see No. 98.

72

DISCOVERIES; A VOLUME OF ESSAYS | BY WILLIAM BUTLER YEATS. | [woodcut of unicorn by Robert Gregory] | DUN EMER PRESS | DUNDRUM | MCMVII

$8\frac{1}{5} \times 5\frac{1}{2}$; pp. xvi, 56: comprising pp. [i–xi] blank; notice of limitation, printed in red, p. [xii]; title, verso blank, pp. [xiii–xiv]; p. [xv] blank; contents, p. [xvi]; text, pp. [1]–43, the word Discoveries in red on p. [1]; p. [44] blank; colophon in red on p. [45]; pp. [46–56] blank.

Issued in blue-grey paper boards with white linen spine; lettered in black on front cover; no label on spine; blue-grey end-papers matching binding; all edges untrimmed.

200 copies printed on paper made in Ireland. Finished on 12th September, 1907. Published December 15, 1907.

Contents

Prophet, Priest and King
Personality and the Intellectual Essences
The Musician and the Orator
A Banjo Player
The Looking-glass
> These five chapters first appeared, unsigned, under the general title *My Thoughts and my Second Thoughts* in *The Gentleman's Magazine*, September 1906.

The Tree of Life
The Praise of Old Wives' Tales
The Play of Modern Manners
Has the Drama of Contemporary Life a Root of its Own?
Why the Blind Man in Ancient Times was made a Poet
> These five chapters first appeared, unsigned, under the general title *My Thoughts and my Second Thoughts*, in *The Gentleman's Magazine*, October 1906.

Concerning Saints and Artists
The Subject Matter of Drama
The Two Kinds of Asceticism
In the Serpent's Mouth
The Black and the White Arrows
His Mistress's Eyebrows
The Tresses of the Hair
> These seven chapters appeared, unsigned, under the general title *My Thoughts and my Second Thoughts* in *The Gentleman's Magazine*, November 1906.

A Tower on the Apennine
The Thinking of the Body
Religious Belief necessary to symbolic Art
The Holy Places
> These four chapters appeared, under the general title *Discoveries*, in *The Shanachie*, Autumn, 1907.

72A

THE UNICORN FROM | THE STARS | by | William
B. Yeats | and | Lady Gregory | New York | The Macmillan
Company | 1908 | All rights reserved

$6\frac{3}{4} \times 4\frac{3}{8}$; pp. iv, 132: comprising half-title, Macmillan's monogram
and addresses on verso, pp. [i–ii]; title, copyright notice and imprint,
Norwood Press J. S. Cushing & Co.—Berwick & Smith Co. Norwood, Mass., U.S.A. on verso, pp. [iii–iv]; fly-title, verso blank, pp.
[1–2]; list of characters, verso blank, pp. [3–4]; fly-title, verso blank,
pp. [5–6]; text, pp. 7–132.

Issued in blue paper covers; title page repeated in black lettering on
front cover; no end-papers; all edges trimmed. Published in 1908.

This edition, apparently of very small quantity, was obviously for
copyright purposes only. The Library of Congress single copy (a
second copy has been lost) is stamped Two copies Received January 15
1908 Copyright entry Jan 15 1908. The Library of Congress copy,
three copies in other libraries, and my copy are all I know of.

73

THE UNICORN FROM | THE STARS | AND OTHER
PLAYS | BY | WILLIAM B. YEATS | AND | LADY GREGORY | NEW
YORK | THE MACMILLAN COMPANY | 1908 | ALL RIGHTS
RESERVED

$7\frac{1}{2} \times 5$; pp. xiv, 210: comprising half-title, Macmillan's monogram and
addresses on verso, pp. [i–ii]; title, copyright notice and imprint,
Norwood Press J. S. Cushing & Co.—Berwick & Smith Co. Norwood,
Mass., U.S.A. on verso, pp. [iii–iv]; Preface, pp. v–ix; p. [x] blank;
Notes, pp. xi–xii; contents, pp. xiii–[xiv]; fly-title, verso blank,
pp. [1–2]; Characters, verso blank, pp. 3–[4]; fly-title, verso blank,
pp. [5–6]; text, pp. 7–210.

Issued in dark blue cloth, lettered in gold on spine THE | UNICORN
| FROM THE | STARS ETC | W. B. YEATS | THE MACMILLAN CO. and with
design in gold on spine, the design being that used on *Poems*, 1899
(No. 17); white end-papers; top edges trimmed, others untrimmed.
Published on May 13, 1908. May 13, 1908; the edition consisted of
1200 copies.

Contents

Preface
Notes
The Unicorn from the Stars. By Lady Gregory and W. B. Yeats.
Cathleen ni Houlihan
The Hour-Glass

The volume was reprinted in August 1915.

74

THE GOLDEN HELMET | BY | WILLIAM BUTLER YEATS |
PUBLISHED | BY | JOHN QUINN | NEW YORK 1908

$6\frac{3}{4} \times 4\frac{3}{8}$; pp. 36: comprising limitation notice, verso blank, pp. [1–2];
half-title, verso blank, pp. [3–4]; title, copyright notice and reservation
on verso, pp. [5–6]; half-title, verso blank, pp. [7–8]; Persons in the
Play, p. 9; text, pp. 10–[33]; pp. [34–36] blank.

Issued in grey paper boards with white label lettered in black on front
cover; grey end-papers; top edges trimmed, others uncut.

Fifty copies were printed, numbered in red ink.

This edition was entered for copyright at the Library of Congress on
June 9, 1908, two copies being received there on the same date.

75

THE COLLECTED EDITION OF 1908

POEMS LYRICAL AND NARRATIVE | BEING THE
FIRST VOLUME OF [*in black*] THE [*in red*] | COLLECTED WORKS
IN VERSE AND [*in red*] | PROSE OF WILLIAM BUTLER YEATS [*in
red*] | IMPRINTED AT THE SHAKESPEARE | HEAD PRESS STRAT-
FORD-ON-AVON | MCMVIII

$8\frac{2}{5} \times 5\frac{1}{2}$; pp. 2, x, 248: comprising one blank leaf not included in
pagination; half-title: The Collected Works of William Butler Yeats,
verso blank, pp. [i–ii]; title, verso blank, pp. [iii–iv]; contents, pp.
[v]–ix; p. [x] blank; fly-title, verso blank, pp. [1–2]; text, pp. [3]–244;
imprint, Printed by A. H. Bullen, at The Shakespeare Head Press,
Stratford-on-Avon, p. [245]; pp. [246–248] blank. Frontispiece from
a charcoal drawing by John S. Sargent, R.A.

Issued in quarter vellum binding with grey linen sides, lettered in gold
on front cover and on spine; white end-papers; top edges gilt, others
untrimmed; a white silk marker is attached to head-band. Published
in September 1908.

Contents

The Wind Among the Reeds
> Many of the titles have been changed. *Hanrahan laments
> because of his Wanderings* is reduced from 12 lines to 8, and is
> now called *Maid Quiet*. *The Heart of the Woman* is now included
> in the section *The Rose*, and *The Fiddler of Dooney* in the section
> *Ballads and Lyrics*.

The Old Age of Queen Maeve

Baile and Aillinn

In the Seven Woods:
> Two poems are added:
> *The Hollow Wood*
>> First appeared, without title, in *The Twisting of the Rope* in
>> *Stories of Red Hanrahan*, 1904. (No. 59.)
> *O do not love too long*
>> First appeared, under the title *Do not love too long*, in *The
>> Acorn*, October 1905.

Early Poems:
> *Ballads and Lyrics*
> *The Rose*
> *The Wanderings of Oisin*

Notes
> Some of the notes to *The Wind Among the Reeds* have been
> omitted, and others revised and shortened. There is a new note
> to the *Early Poems*.

76

THE KING'S THRESHOLD. ON | BAILE'S STRAND.
DEIRDRE. | SHADOWY WATERS [fleuron] BEING |
THE SECOND VOLUME OF | THE COLLECTED WORKS IN [*in red*] |
VERSE & PROSE OF WILLIAM [*in red*] | BUTLER YEATS [*in red*]
[fleuron] IMPRINTED | AT THE SHAKESPEARE HEAD | PRESS
STRATFORD-ON-AVON | MCMVIII

$8\frac{2}{5} \times 5\frac{1}{2}$; pp. viii, 260: comprising pp. [i–ii] blank; half-title as in No.
75, verso blank, pp. [iii–iv]; title, verso blank, pp. [v–vi]; contents,

four-line poem, "The friends that have it I do wrong" on verso, pp. [vii–viii]; fly-title, verso blank, pp. [1–2]; dedication, verso blank, pp. [3–4]; Persons in the Play, verso blank, pp. [5–6]; text, pp. [7]–258; imprint, Printed by A. H. Bullen, at The Shakespeare Head Press, Stratford-on-Avon, p. [259]; p. [260] blank.

Issued in similar binding to that of Volume I (No. 75). Published in September 1908.

Contents

Preliminary poem: The friends that have it I do wrong.
The King's Threshold. (The version of 1906.)
On Baile's Strand. (The version of 1906.)
Deirdre
The Shadowy Waters. With the two preliminary poems. (The version of 1906.)
Appendix I. Acting version of *The Shadowy Waters.*
Appendix II. A different version of Deirdre's entrance.
Appendix III. The Legendary and Mythological Foundation of the Plays.
Appendix IV. The Dates and Places of Performance of Plays.

77

THE COUNTESS CATHLEEN. THE | LAND OF HEART'S DESIRE. THE | UNICORN FROM THE STARS [fleuron] BE- | ING THE THIRD VOLUME OF [*in black*] THE [*in red*] | COLLECTED WORKS IN VERSE [*in red*] | AND PROSE OF WILLIAM BUTLER [*in red*] | YEATS [*in red*] [fleuron] IMPRINTED AT THE SHAKESPEARE HEAD PRESS [fleuron] | STRATFORD-ON-AVON | MCMVIII

$8\frac{2}{5} \times 5\frac{1}{2}$; pp. viii, 240: comprising pp. [i–ii] blank; half-title as in No. 75, verso blank, pp. [iii–iv]; title, verso blank, pp. [v–vi]; contents, verso blank, pp. [vii–viii]; fly-title, quotation on verso, pp. [1–2]; dedication, verso blank, pp. [3–4]; Persons in the Play, verso blank, pp. [5–6]; text, pp. [7]–239; imprint, Printed by A. H. Bullen, at The Shakespeare Head Press, Stratford-on-Avon, p. [240]. Frontispiece portrait from a picture by Charles Shannon.

Issued in similar binding to that of Volume I (No. 75). Published in October 1908.

Contents

The Countess Cathleen
The Land of Heart's Desire
The Unicorn from the Stars. By Lady Gregory and W. B. Yeats.
Appendix: The Countess Cathleen. Preface to the Fourth Edition,
    dated January 1901.
    (This is actually the Preface to the Third Edition; a footnote has
    been added.)
Notes
    Those on *The Countess Cathleen* and *The Land of Heart's Desire*
    are from the edition of *Poems*, 1901, slightly lengthened and with
    a new footnote, dated March, 1908. The note on *The Unicorn
    from the Stars* is dated March 1908, and is new.
The Music for use in the Performance of these Plays. Dated March,
    1908.
Music by Florence Farr, Sara Allgood and Arthur Darley.
Music for Lyrics
Note by Florence Farr
Music by Florence Farr, W. B. Yeats, and A. H. Bullen.

It may be noted that the text of *The Land of Heart's Desire* in this
volume does not make the corrections called for by the Errata slip in
Poems, 1901. (No. 18.)

78

THE HOUR-GLASS. CATHLEEN NI | HOULIHAN. THE GOLDEN HELMET. | THE IRISH DRAMATIC MOVEMENT | [fleuron] BEING THE FOURTH VOLUME OF | THE COLLECTED WORKS IN VERSE & [in red] | PROSE OF WILLIAM BUTLER YEATS [in red] | IMPRINTED AT THE SHAKE-SPEARE | HEAD PRESS STRATFORD-ON-AVON | MCMVIII

$8\frac{2}{5} \times 5\frac{1}{2}$; pp. viii, 248: comprising pp. [i–ii] blank; half-title as in No.
75, verso blank, pp. [iii–iv]; title, verso blank, pp. [v–vi]; contents,
verso blank, pp. [vii–viii]; fly-title, Persons in the Play on verso, pp.
[1–2]; text, pp. [3]–247; imprint, Printed by A. H. Bullen, at The
Shakespeare Head Press, Stratford-on-Avon, p. [248].

Issued in similar binding to that of Volume I (No. 75). Published in
October 1908.

Contents

The Hour-Glass
Cathleen ni Houlihan
The Golden Helmet
The Irish Dramatic Movement
> Under this title are printed the greater part of Yeats's contri-
> butions to *Samhain*, 1901–1906, and to *The Arrow*, 1906–1907,
> and two essays, *An Irish National Theatre* and *The Theatre, the
> Pulpit and the Newspapers*, which first appeared in *The United
> Irishman*, October 10 and 17, 1903.

Appendix I. The Hour-Glass
Appendix II. Cathleen ni Houlihan
> This includes the dedication to Lady Gregory which first
> appeared in *Where There is Nothing*, 1903. (No. 44.)

Appendix III. The Golden Helmet
*Appendix IV. Dates and Places of the First Performance of New Plays
Produced by the National Theatre Society and its Predecessors.*

There are two lines of *Corrigenda* on p. 247.

79

THE CELTIC TWILIGHT AND | STORIES OF RED
HANRAHAN | BEING THE FIFTH VOLUME OF | THE COL-
LECTED WORKS IN [*in red*] | VERSE & PROSE OF WILLIAM
[*in red*] | BUTLER YEATS [*in red*] [fleuron] IMPRINTED | AT
THE SHAKESPEARE HEAD | PRESS STRATFORD-ON-AVON |
MCMVIII

$8\frac{2}{5} \times 5\frac{1}{2}$; pp. xvi, 264: comprising pp. [i–vi] blank; half-title as in No.
75, verso blank, pp. [vii–viii]; title, verso blank, pp. [ix–x]; contents,
pp. [xi–xii]; fly-title, poem "Time drops in decay" on verso, pp.
[xiii–xiv]; "The Hosting of the Sidhe", verso blank, pp. [xv–xvi];
text, pp. [1]–261; imprint, Printed by A. H. Bullen at the Shakespeare
Head Press, Stratford-on-Avon, p. [262]; pp. [263–264] blank.
Frontispiece portrait from a drawing by A. Mancini.

Issued in similar binding to that of Volume I (No. 75). Published in
November 1908.

Contents

The Celtic Twilight
Stories of Red Hanrahan
> In *The Twisting of the Rope* a variant of the first verse of *The
> Happy Townland*, beginning "O Death's old bony finger", is

now substituted for the poem called *The Hollow Wood*. The same variant and most of the remainder of *The Happy Townland* are substituted for *The Song of Wandering Aengus* in *Hanrahan's Vision*.

Quinn's copy is inscribed: "And if I only looked like the Manchini portrait I should have defeated all my enemies here in Dublin. Manchini did it in an hour or so working at the last with great vehemence and constant cries, 'Cristo, O', and so on. W. B. Yeats."

80

IDEAS OF GOOD AND EVIL | BEING THE SIXTH VOLUME OF | THE COLLECTED WORKS IN [*in red*] | VERSE & PROSE OF WILLIAM BUTLER YEATS [*in red*] [fleuron] IMPRINTED | AT THE SHAKESPEARE HEAD | PRESS STRATFORD-ON-AVON | MCMVIII

$8\frac{2}{5} \times 5\frac{1}{2}$; pp. viii, 268: comprising pp. [i–ii] blank; half-title as in No. 75, verso blank, pp. [iii–iv]; title, verso blank, pp. [v–vi]; contents, verso blank, pp. [vii–viii]; text, pp. [1]–266; imprint, Printed by A. H. Bullen, at The Shakespeare Head Press, Stratford-on-Avon, p. [267]; p. [268] blank.

Issued in similar binding to that of Volume I (No. 75). Published in November 1908.

Quinn's copy is inscribed: "I think the best of these Essays is that on Shakespeare. It is a family exasperation with the Dowden point of view, which rather filled Dublin in my youth. There is a good deal of my father in it, though nothing is just as he would have put it. W. B. Yeats."

81

THE SECRET ROSE. ROSA ALCHEM- | ICA. THE TABLES OF THE LAW. THE | ADORATION OF THE MAGI. JOHN | SHERMAN AND DHOYA [fleuron] BEING THE | SEVENTH VOLUME OF [*in black*] THE COL- [*in red*] | LECTED WORKS IN VERSE & PROSE [*in red*] | OF WILLIAM BUTLER YEATS [*in red*] [fleuron] IM- | PRINTED AT THE SHAKE- SPEARE | HEAD PRESS STRATFORD-ON-AVON | MCMVIII

$8\frac{2}{5} \times 5\frac{1}{2}$; pp. viii, 304: comprising pp. [i–ii] blank; half-title as in No. 75, verso blank, pp. [iii–iv]; title, verso blank, pp. [v–vi]; contents, verso blank, pp. [vii–viii]; fly-title, two quotations on verso, pp. [1–2]; dedication, verso blank, pp. [3–4]; text, pp. [5]–299; imprint, Printed by A. H. Bullen, at The Shakespeare Head Press, Stratford-on-Avon, p. [300]; pp. [301–304] blank. Frontispiece portrait from a drawing by J. B. Yeats. (This is the same as that in *The Tables of the Law*, 1897, and *The Celtic Twilight*, 1902.)

Issued in similar binding to that of Volume I (No. 75). Published in December 1908.

Contents

Dedication to A.E.
To the Secret Rose (Poem)
The Secret Rose
>The six Red Hanrahan stories of the 1897 volume are omitted as the rewritten versions of them appear in Volume V of this edition (No. 79). Two other stories are omitted also: *The Binding of the Hair* and *The Rose of Shadow*.

The Tables of the Law
The Adoration of the Magi
John Sherman. With a new preface, dated November 14, 1907.
Dhoya

Quinn's copy is inscribed: "Early stories, of which 'The Crucifixion of the Outcast' is nearest my heart. W. B. Yeats."

82

DISCOVERIES. EDMUND SPENSER. | POETRY AND TRADITION; & OTHER | ESSAYS [fleuron] BEING THE EIGHTH VOLUME | OF [*in black*] THE COLLECTED WORKS IN VERSE [*in red*] | & PROSE OF WILLIAM BUTLER YEATS [*in red*] | [fleuron] IMPRINTED AT THE SHAKESPEARE | HEAD PRESS STRATFORD-ON-AVON | MCMVIII

$8\frac{2}{5} \times 5\frac{1}{2}$; pp. 2, vi, 288: comprising one leaf not included in pagination; half-title as in No. 75, verso blank, pp. [i–ii]; title, verso blank, pp. [iii–iv]; contents, pp. [v]–vi; fly-title, verso blank, pp. [1–2]; text, pp. [3]–196; fly-title, note on verso, pp. [197–198]; poem, p. [199]; text of bibliography, pp. [199]–287; imprint, Printed by A. H. Bullen, at The Shakespeare Head Press, Stratford-on-Avon, p. [288].

Issued in similar binding to that of Volume I (No. 75) Published in December 1908.

Contents

Discoveries

Edmund Spenser

First appeared as introduction to *Poems of Spenser*, 1906. (No. 235.)

Poetry and Tradition

Appeared also, under the title *Poetry and Patriotism* in *Poetry and Ireland*: Essays by W. B. Yeats and Lionel Johnson, Cuala Press, published December 1, 1908. (No. 242.)

Modern Irish Poetry

First appeared as the introduction to *A Book of Irish Verse*, 1895 (No. 225); revised in 1900 and here printed with a postscript dated April 1908.

Note

This refers to the *Stories of Red Hanrahan* and is dated April 14, 1908.

Lady Gregory's "Cuchulain of Muirthemne"

First appeared as the preface to *Cuchulain of Muirthemne*, 1902. (No. 256.)

Lady Gregory's "Gods and Fighting Men"

First appeared as the preface to *Gods and Fighting Men*, 1904. (No. 258.)

Mr. Synge and his Plays

First appeared as the preface to *The Well of the Saints* by J. M. Synge, 1905. (No. 262.)

Lionel Johnson

First appeared in *The Dublin Daily Express*, August 27, 1898 and printed also in *A Treasury of Irish Poetry*, 1900. (No. 298.)

The Pathway

First appeared, under the title *The Way of Wisdom*, in *The Speaker*, April 14, 1900.

A Bibliography of the Writings of William Butler Yeats by Allan Wade

This contains a poem for the bibliography *Accursed who brings to light of day*, and the Prologue to *The King's Threshold* which was accidentally omitted from Volume II.

American Editions. Compiled by John Quinn.

Of this Collected Edition Bullen printed 1060 copies. He arranged with Messrs. Chapman and Hall, Ltd., to take over 250 copies, his reason being that, as he did not employ a traveller and Chapman and Hall did, they would be able to interest booksellers whom he would not be able to reach. The volumes taken over had special titles with LONDON: | CHAPMAN & HALL | LIMITED at foot, and the binding bore CHAPMAN & HALL at foot of spine; otherwise they were identical with

Letter from Yeats to Allan Wade postmarked 15/1/1909, referring to the first bibliography (No. 303).

those issued from the Shakespeare Head Press. Messrs. Chapman and Hall's records show that the volumes were delivered to them, at the rate of two volumes a month, from September to December 1908; their issue therefore must have been simultaneous, or almost simultaneous, with Bullen's own.

A number of copies were also similarly prepared for Messrs. Maunsel & Co. Ltd., of Dublin and the title-page of the volumes bore their name. From a letter written to me by A. H. Bullen I gather that he expected Maunsel to be able to take 50 sets, but it seems probable that the number was considerably less; Mr. P. S. O'Hegarty puts it at a maximum of 20. The volumes were at first advertised by Maunsel & Co. in the vellum and grey cloth binding, but Mr. O'Hegarty has seen a set bound in dark green buckram.

Later Bullen issued a "remainder" of the unsold copies. These were bound in light brown paper boards with grey-green linen spine; all edges were untrimmed and there were no silk markers. The sets were sold at a lower price.

Bullen at one time intended to add a ninth volume to the Collected Edition. This was announced in *Plays for an Irish Theatre*, 1911. "A little later a new volume of the Collected Edition will be published, containing *The Green Helmet*; a stage version of the *Countess Cathleen*; a new play in three acts; notes and alterations made for stage purposes in various plays of Mr. Yeats; a good deal of criticism arising out of the work of the Abbey Theatre. This volume will contain stage designs by Gordon Craig and Robert Gregory." The volume never appeared.

82A

ADVICE TO PLAYWRIGHTS WHO ARE SENDING | PLAYS TO THE ABBEY THEATRE, DUBLIN.

$10\frac{1}{8} \times 8\frac{1}{8}$; a single sheet, printed on one side only. No date, but probably published in 1908 or 1909.

Reprinted in Lady Gregory's *Our Irish Theatre* (No. 307).

83

WILLIAM BUTLER YEATS | POEMS: | SECOND SERIES | THE WIND AMONG THE REEDS | THE OLD AGE OF QUEEN MAEVE | BAILE AND AILLINN | IN THE SEVEN WOODS | SONGS FROM DEIRDRE | THE SHADOWY WATERS | [ornament] | A. H. BULLEN | LONDON & STRATFORD-ON-AVON | MCMIX

$7\frac{1}{2} \times 5$; pp. viii, 164: comprising half-title, list of books By the same Writer on verso, pp. [i–ii]; title, verso blank, pp. [iii–iv]; contents, pp. [v]–vii; p. [viii] blank; fly-title, verso blank, pp. [1–2]; text, pp. [3]–162; imprint, Printed by A. H. Bullen, at The Shakespeare Head Press, Stratford-on-Avon, p. [163]; p. [164] blank. Frontispiece portrait of the author from a photograph by Alvin Langdon Coburn, 1908.

Issued in dark blue cloth with design in gold, as used in *The Secret Rose*, stamped on spine; white end-papers; all edges untrimmed. Published in March 1910.

Contents

The Wind Among the Reeds
> 37 poems, following the arrangement of the *Collected Edition*, 1908, Volume I (No. 75), with the addition of *The Song of the Old Mother* and *The Fiddler of Dooney*.

The Old Age of Queen Maeve
Baile and Aillinn
In the Seven Woods
> 14 poems.

The Musicians' Songs from Deirdre
> I, II and III.

The Shadowy Waters
> The version of 1906 with the two preliminary poems.

Notes
> The notes to *The Wind Among the Reeds* are printed from the Collected Works, 1908, Volume I, and the note to *The Shadowy Waters* from Volume II.

In Quinn's library was a rare copy of this edition. It was bound in suede calf and had a misprint on p. 8, line 6, "host of the hair" for "host of the air." Bullen wrote to Quinn on February 1, 1910, saying that this was an advance copy sent as a trial to a new binder, and that after the book had been sent to Quinn the misprint was discovered and every copy of the edition had to be sent back to the press for rectification.

Signs of erasure of the letter "h" may be seen in copies of the first edition.

Later copies of the first edition were issued in brown paper boards with yellow linen spine, white label printed in black pasted on spine and reading POEMS | SECOND | SERIES | [*rule*] | W. B. YEATS | [*rule*] | SHAKESPEARE | HEAD PRESS | STRATFORD- | ON-AVON. There is a duplicate label inside the back cover. Bullen had only a very limited amount of type at the Shakespeare Head Press and would not keep any book set up for long. He usually printed enough copies to last some years and bound them up as required. It seems probable that some copies issued in this second binding escaped the obliteration of the "h" on p. 8 as they were still in sheets when the first issue in blue cloth was made; from my own recollection I feel certain that the book was not issued simultaneously in two different styles of binding.

There was a reissue in 1913 bound in grey paper boards with grey-green canvas spine, label, printed in black, on spine.

The second edition is also found in brown paper boards with grey-green linen spine lettered in black. A copy in my possession has the portrait by J. B. Yeats, as in No. 24, substituted for the Coburn photograph.

On or about June 28, 1916, the remainder of this latter edition was transferred to Messrs. Macmillan and Co., Ltd.

84

THE GREEN HELMET AND OTHER | POEMS BY WILLIAM BUTLER YEATS | [woodcut of girl and tree, by Elinor Monsell] | THE CUALA PRESS | CHURCHTOWN | DUNDRUM | MCMX

$8\frac{1}{8} \times 5\frac{1}{2}$; pp. xvi, 48: comprising pp. [i–ix] blank; notice of limitation on p. [x]; title, verso blank, pp. [xi–xii]; pp. [xiii–xiv] blank; contents, verso blank, pp. [xv–xvi]; text, pp. [1]–[33]; colophon [in red] on p. [33]; pp. [34–48] blank. An erratum slip is inserted loose: this is headed AN ERROR and reads "By a slip of the pen when I was writing out the heading for the first group of poems, I put Raymond Lully's name in the room of the later Alchemist, Nicolas Flamel. W. B. Yeats. These poems have been copyrighted in America."

Issued in grey paper boards with linen spine; lettered in black on front cover THE GREEN HELMET AND OTHER POEMS BY WILLIAM BUTLER YEATS, and having a white label printed in black POEMS BY W. B. YEATS pasted on spine; grey end-papers matching binding; all edges untrimmed.

400 copies printed and published by Elizabeth Corbet Yeats at the Cuala Press. Finished on the last day of September 1910. Published in December 1910.

Contents

Raymond Lully and his wife Pernella:
    His Dream
        First appeared, with a note in prose, in *The Nation* July 11, 1908.
    A Woman Homer Sung
    The Consolation

No Second Troy
Reconciliation
King and No King
Peace
Against Unworthy Praise
Momentary Thoughts:
    The Fascination of What's Difficult
    A Drinking Song
    The Coming of Wisdom with Time
        Printed, under the title *Youth and Age*, in *McClure's Magazine*, December 1910.
    To a Poet, Who would have Me Praise certain bad Poets, Imitators of His and of Mine
    A Lyric from an Unpublished Play
    Upon a Threatened House
        Printed, under the title *To a Certain Country House in Time of Change*, in *McClure's Magazine*, December 1910.
    These are the Clouds
    At Galway Races
        First appeared, under the title *Galway Races*, in *The English Review*, February 1909.
    A Friend's Illness
    All Things can Tempt Me
        First appeared, under the title *Distraction*, in *The English Review*, February 1909.
The Young Man's Song
The Green Helmet, An Heroic Farce
    The song beginning "Nothing that he has done" was printed in the programme when the play was first produced at the Abbey Theatre, Dublin, on February 10, 1910.

    The play was subsequently printed in *The Forum*, September 1911.

85

AMERICAN EDITION

THE GREEN HELMET AND | OTHER POEMS | BY | WILLIAM BUTLER YEATS | NEW YORK | R. HAROLD PAGET | 1911

$7\frac{1}{2} \times 5$; pp. ii, 42: comprising pp. [i–ii] blank; title, Copyright, 1911, by William Butler Yeats on verso, pp. [1–2]; text, pp. [3]–[40]; pp. [41–42] blank. There is no list of contents.

G

Issued in green paper covers, lettering in black on front cover; no end-papers; all edges trimmed. Entered at the Library of Congress, following publication, on January 16, 1911.

The contents are the same as those of the Cuala Press edition. (No. 84.)

86

FIRST THEATRE EDITION

DEIRDRE | BY | WILLIAM BUTLER YEATS | [fleuron] | SHAKESPEARE HEAD PRESS | STRATFORD-UPON-AVON | MCMXI

$7\frac{3}{10} \times 4\frac{4}{8}$; pp. 32: comprising title, imprint of The Shakespeare Head Press on verso, pp. [1–2]; text, pp. 3–32.

Issued in dark grey paper covers, lettered in black on front cover as title-page except that the words ONE SHILLING NET replace the date. Advertisements of The Works of W. B. Yeats on back cover. All edges trimmed. Published in July 1911.

The text has been slightly revised. On the back cover the announcement of *Plays for an Irish Theatre* has the mistake "illustrations by Norman Craig" instead of "by Gordon Craig".

87

SECOND THEATRE EDITION

DEIRDRE | BY | WILLIAM BUTLER YEATS | [fleuron] | SHAKESPEARE HEAD PRESS | STRATFORD-UPON-AVON | MCMXIV

$7\frac{3}{8} \times 5$; pp. 32: comprising title, imprint, Printed by A. H. Bullen, at The Shakespeare Head Press, Stratford-upon-Avon. on verso, pp. [1–2]; text, pp. 3–32.

Issued in grey-green paper covers, lettered in black on front cover, as on title-page except that the words ONE SHILLING NET replace the date; list of The Works of W. B. Yeats on back cover. Published in 1914.

On or about June 28, 1916, the remainder of this edition was transferred to Messrs. Macmillan and Co., Ltd. The firm informs me that the covers were probably replaced by others bearing their imprint.

88

SYNGE AND THE IRELAND OF HIS | TIME BY
WILLIAM BUTLER YEATS | WITH A NOTE CONCERNING A WALK |
THROUGH CONNEMARA WITH HIM | BY JACK BUTLER YEATS. |
[woodcut as in No. 84] | THE CUALA PRESS | CHURCHTOWN |
DUNDRUM | MCMXI

$8\frac{1}{5} \times 5\frac{1}{2}$; pp. xvi, 56: comprising pp. [i–ix] blank; notice of limitation,
p. [x]; title, with note on verso of copyright in America, pp. [xi–xii];
Preface, pp. [xiii–xv]; p. [xvi] blank; text, pp. [1]–[43]; p. [44] blank;
colophon [in red], p. [45]; pp. [46–56] blank.

Issued in grey paper boards with white linen spine; title printed in
black on front cover; no label on spine; grey end-papers matching
binding; all edges untrimmed.

350 copies printed and published by Elizabeth Corbet Yeats at the
Cuala Press, Churchtown, Dundrum, in the County of Dublin, Ireland.
Finished on May Eve, 1911. Published on July 26, 1911.

Contents

Preface
J. M. Synge and the Ireland of his Time. Dated September 14th,
1910.
    This also appeared in *The Forum*, August 1911.
With Synge in Connemara. By Jack B. Yeats.

The essay had been intended to appear as Preface to the Collected
Edition of Synge's works, in four volumes, published by Maunsel and
Co., Ltd. in 1910. Yeats withdrew it because he considered that the
fourth volume reprinted some work insufficiently revised to be worthy
of Synge's reputation.

89

THEATRE EDITION

THE GREEN HELMET | AN HEROIC FARCE | BY | W. B.
YEATS | SHAKESPEARE HEAD PRESS | STRATFORD-UPON-
AVON | MCMXI

$7\frac{4}{5} \times 5$; pp. 16: comprising title, imprint, Printed by A. H. Bullen at
The Shakespeare Head Press, Stratford-upon-Avon on verso, pp.
[1–2]; text, pp. [3]–16.

Issued in dark grey paper covers, lettered in black on front cover as title-page except that the words Price Sixpence Net replace the date; all edges untrimmed. Published in November 1911.

This is the only separate edition of the play.

On or about June 28, 1916, the remainder of this edition was transferred to Messrs. Macmillan and Co., Ltd. The firm thinks it likely that new paper covers were substituted bearing their imprint.

90

THEATRE EDITION

THE KING'S THRESHOLD | BY | W. B. YEATS | [ornament] | SHAKESPEARE HEAD PRESS | STRATFORD-UPON-AVON | MCMXI

7×5; pp. 40: comprising title, imprint, Printed by A. H. Bullen, at The Shakespeare Head Press, Stratford-on-Avon, on verso, pp. [1–2]; Persons in the Play, verso blank, pp. [3–4]; text, pp. [5]–40.

Issued in dark grey paper covers, lettered in black on front cover, as title-page except that the words ONE SHILLING NET take the place of the date. Published in November 1911.

91

SECOND THEATRE EDITION

THE KING'S THRESHOLD | BY | W. B. YEATS | [ornament] | SHAKESPEARE HEAD PRESS | STRATFORD-UPON-AVON | MCMXV

$7\frac{1}{2} \times 5$; pp. 40: comprising title, imprint, Printed by A. H. Bullen, at The Shakespeare Head Press, Stratford-upon-Avon. on verso, pp. [1–2]; Persons in the Play, verso blank, pp. [3–4]; text, pp. [5]–40.

Issued in paper covers, lettered in black on front cover; all edges untrimmed. Published in 1915.

On or about June 28, 1916, the remainder of this edition was transferred to Messrs. Macmillan and Co., Ltd. Copies were re-issued in light brown paper covers, lettered in black at foot of front cover MACMILLAN AND CO., LIMITED | ST. MARTIN'S STREET, LONDON | ONE SHILLING NET.

92

PLAYS FOR AN IRISH THEATRE | BY | W. B. YEATS |
WITH DESIGNS BY GORDON CRAIG | DEIRDRE | THE GREEN
HELMET | ON BAILE'S STRAND | THE KING'S THRESHOLD |
THE SHADOWY WATERS | THE HOUR-GLASS | CATHLEEN NI
HOULIHAN | A. H. BULLEN | LONDON & STRATFORD-UPON-
AVON | MCMXI

$9\frac{1}{4} \times 6$; pp. 6, xvi, 230: comprising 6 pp. not included in pagination;
half-title, list of books By the same Author on verso, pp. [i–ii]; title,
imprint, Printed by A. H. Bullen, at the Shakespeare Head Press, Stratford-on-Avon on verso, pp. [iii–iv]; Preface, pp. [v]–xiv; contents,
verso blank, pp. [xv–xvi]; fly-title, dedication on verso, pp. [1–2];
Persons in the Play, verso blank, pp. [3–4]; text, pp. [5]–224; pp.
[225–230] blank. There are four drawings by Gordon Craig: one as
frontispiece, the others facing pp. 33, 65 and 169.

Issued in brown paper boards with yellow linen spine; white label
printed in black pasted on spine; dark brown end-papers, lined with
white; all edges untrimmed; duplicate label tipped inside back cover; a
brown silk marker is attached to headband. Published in December
1911. Copies are also found with white end-papers. I believe them to
be later than the first issued.

Contents

Preface, with postscript
> The preface first appeared, under the title *The Tragic Theatre*, in
> *The Mask* (Florence), October 1910.

Deirdre
The Green Helmet
On Baile's Strand
The King's Threshold
The Shadowy Waters
The Hour-Glass
Cathleen ni Houlihan
Appendix. Acting version of *The Shadowy Waters*
Notes
> The notes to *Deirdre, The Green Helmet* and *The Hour-Glass* are
> new; the others are taken, with slight modification, from the
> *Collected Works*, 1908.

There was a second impression in 1913.

On or about June 28, 1916, the remainder of this edition was transferred to Messrs. Macmillan and Co., Ltd. These copies were bound
in brown paper boards with either yellow linen or yellow buckram
spine, and were lettered in black on the spine; they had no silk marker.

93

REVISED VERSION

THE COUNTESS | CATHLEEN | BY | W. B. YEATS |
LONDON | T. FISHER UNWIN | ADELPHI TERRACE | 1912

$7\frac{7}{10} \times 5$; pp. 128: comprising half-title, list of The Works of W. B.
Yeats on verso, pp. [1–2]; title, bibliographical note and rights
reservation on verso, pp. [3–4]; dedication, quotation on verso, pp.
[5–6]; list of characters, verso blank, pp. [7–8]; fly-title, verso blank,
pp. [9–10]; text, pp. 11–128; imprint, Unwin Brothers, Limited, The
Gresham Press, Woking and London, at foot of p. 128.

Issued in stiff grey paper covers, lettered in black THE COUNTESS |
CATHLEEN | BY W. B. YEATS | [design of girl and wolf-hound by Elinor
Monsell] | VOLUME I. OF DUBLIN PLAYS | PRICE ONE SHILLING NET and
lettered in black on spine; white end-papers; all edges trimmed.
Published in June 1912.

Contents

The Countess Cathleen
Notes. Dated Abbey Theatre, Dublin.

There were further impressions in 1916 (2), 1920 and 1922. The
last was issued in parchment covers, lettered in green inside rules on
front cover, lettered in green on spine. It was thus uniform in style
with Macmillan's edition of *The Player Queen*, 1922. (No. 138.)

These impressions were all revised from the 1912 edition to make them
almost identical to the version of *The Countess Cathleen* in No. 103.
The revisions were followed in general in No. 95 and No. 100 and
their successive impressions.

An edition issued by Ernest Benn, Ltd. is mentioned in the latest issue
of No. 94, but I have never seen a copy.

See No. 103.

94

THE LAND OF | HEART'S DESIRE | BY | W. B. YEATS |
LONDON | T. FISHER UNWIN | ADELPHI TERRACE | 1912

$7\frac{7}{10} \times 5$; pp. 48: comprising half-title, The Works of W. B. Yeats
[in panel] and notice to amateurs on verso, pp. [1–2]; title, list of
editions and notice of reservation of rights on verso, pp. [3–4]; dedication, quotation on verso, pp. [5–6]; list of characters, etc., verso
blank, pp. [7–8]; text, pp. 9–45; p. [46] blank; note on p. 47, imprint,
Unwin Brothers Limited, on p. [48].

Issued in grey paper covers, lettered in black on front cover THE LAND
OF | HEART'S DESIRE | BY W. B. YEATS | [Design of girl and wolf-hound
as on No. 93] | VOLUME II. OF DUBLIN PLAYS | PRICE ONE SHILLING.;
white end-papers; all edges trimmed. Published in June 1912.

Contents

The Land of Heart's Desire
Note. Dated Abbey Theatre, Dublin. March 1912.

There were further impressions in 1913, 1916, 1919, 1922 (2), 1923,
1924 (5), and 1925. Some of the later impressions were issued in
parchment covers, title on front cover THE LAND OF | HEART'S DESIRE |
BY | W. B. YEATS in green within green rules, and at foot, outside rules,
PRICE TWO SHILLINGS NET; green lettering on spine. Uniform in style
with Macmillan's edition of *The Player Queen*, 1922. (No. 138.) A
new edition, printed by Purnell and Sons, Ltd., Paulton (Somerset)
and London, and issued in the later style of binding, was published by
Ernest Benn Ltd. and is dated 1937. As Messrs. Benn relinquished
their rights to Yeats's *Poems* in 1933 I am inclined to think this should
have been dated 1927.

See also No. 95.

95

In 1924 *The Countess Cathleen* and *The Land of Heart's Desire* were
issued bound together in one volume in dark red ribbed cloth,
lettered in gold on spine THE | COUNTESS | CATHLEEN | W. B. YEATS |
T. FISHER UNWIN; red marbled end-papers; top edges gilt, others
trimmed. Each play is paged separately. The volume contained the
sixth impression of the revised *Countess Cathleen* and the tenth
impression of the revised *Land of Heart's Desire*.

THE LAND OF HEART'S | DESIRE | · · · · · | THE
COUNTESS | CATHLEEN · BY W. B. YEATS | T. FISHER
UNWIN LTD | LONDON: ADELPHI TERRACE

$6 \times 4\frac{1}{4}$; pp. 168. The pagination is continuous.

Issued in green ribbed cloth, the author's signature in facsimile
on front cover, lettering in gold on spine; green marbled end-papers;
top edges gilt, others untrimmed. A volume of The Cabinet Library,
published in 1925. The volume was also issued in a leather binding.

Here the usual order of the plays is reversed, *The Land of Heart's
Desire* being printed before *The Countess Cathleen*. Each play is
followed by its appropriate note.

In July 1929, after the transfer to the firm of Ernest Benn, Ltd. of the
publications of T. Fisher Unwin, the two plays were re-issued as a
volume of Benn's Essex Library.

96

THE LAND OF HEART'S DESIRE | BY W. B. YEATS |
BOSTON | WALTER H. BAKER & CO.

$6\frac{3}{4} \times 4\frac{1}{2}$; pp. 24: comprising title, p. [1]; characters, p. [2]; text, pp.
3–21; p. [22] blank; advertisements, pp. [23–24].

Issued in brown paper covers lettered in black on front cover W. B.
YEATS [in panel] | THE LAND OF HEART'S DESIRE | [publisher's device] |
BAKER'S EDITION OF PLAYS | WALTER H. BAKER COMPANY, BOSTON [in
panel].

The text is that printed in Mosher's edition of 1903. (No. 12.)

This edition was printed in 1922.

There were further printings in 1925 and 1928. These vary in make-
up, but not in text, from the printing of 1922.

97

THE LAND OF HEART'S | DESIRE | BY | WILLIAM
BUTLER YEATS | WITH A FOREWORD | BY | JAMES S. JOHNSON |
[design] | SAN FRANCISCO | THE WINDSOR PRESS | MCMXXVI

$6\frac{1}{2} \times 4\frac{3}{8}$; pp. viii, 30: comprising half-title, verso blank, pp. [i–ii];
title, verso blank, pp. [iii–iv]; Foreword, pp. v–vii; p. [viii] blank;

fly-title, Persons in the Play on verso, pp. [1–2]; text, pp. 3–27; p. [28] blank; colophon on p. [29]; p. [30] blank.

The colophon reads: This book printed for C. F. Benoit by the | Brothers Johnson at The Windsor Press: | 750 copies printed on Rye Mill hand-made | paper and the type distributed. | [ornament] | In the year MCMXXVI.

Signed by James S. Johnson, C. F. Benoit

Issued in grey paper wrapper over cardboard, with title in black: THE LAND OF HEART'S | DESIRE | BY | WILLIAM BUTLER YEATS | [floral decoration] |. Enclosed in slip case. Published in 1926.

This edition prints the revised text of 1903.

98

AMERICAN EDITION, REVISED

THE POETICAL WORKS | OF | WILLIAM B. YEATS | IN TWO VOLUMES | VOLUME II | DRAMATIC POEMS | NEW AND REVISED EDITION | NEW YORK | THE MACMILLAN COMPANY | LONDON: MACMILLAN & CO., LTD. | 1912 | ALL RIGHTS RESERVED

$7\frac{2}{5} \times 5$; pp. x, 534: comprising half-title, Macmillan's monogram and addresses on verso, pp. [i–ii]; title, copyright notice and imprint, Norwood Press J. S. Cushing Co.—Berwick & Smith Co. Norwood, Mass., U.S.A. on verso, pp. [iii–iv]; Preface, pp. v–viii; contents, p. ix; p. [x] blank; fly-title, quotation on verso, pp. [1–2]; dedication, list of characters on verso, pp. [3–4]; fly-title, verso blank, pp. [5–6]; text, pp. 7–533; p. [534] blank.

Issued in dark blue cloth, design and lettering in gold on spine, the space between PLAYS and W. B. YEATS, formerly part of the design, now carries the words REVISED AND ENLARGED; white end-papers; top edges gilt, others trimmed. Published on August 7, 1912.

Contents

Preface. Dated December 1906, with a short paragraph added at end and dated February 1912.
The Countess Cathleen. (Revised version of 1912.)
The Land of Heart's Desire. (Revised version of 1912.)
The Shadowy Waters
On Baile's Strand

The King's Threshold

Deirdre

Appendix I: The Legendary and Mythological Foundation of the Plays and Poems

Appendix II: The Dates and Places of Performance of the Plays. Dated Abbey Theatre, March 1912.

> This contains the new notes to *The Countess Cathleen* and *The Land of Heart's Desire* from the separate editions of 1912 (Nos. 93 and 94) and notes on the other plays.

Anppedix III: Acting version of *The Shadowy Waters.*

Appendix IV: The Work of the National Theatre Society at the Abbey Theatre, Dublin: A Statement of Principles.

There were further issues of this book in February 1914; September 1916; October 1917; November 1919; and March 1921.

99

SIXTH ENGLISH EDITION, REVISED

POEMS [*in red*] | BY | W. B. YEATS [*in red*] | LONDON | T. FISHER UNWIN [*in red*] | ADELPHI TERRACE | 1912

8 × 5; pp. xvi, 324. Printed at The Gresham Press, Unwin Brothers, Limited, Woking and London.

Issued in a somewhat brighter blue cloth than that used for the previous editions, design and lettering in gold on front cover, spine, and back cover, as before; white end-papers; all edges untrimmed. Published in September 1912.

Some copies have a slip pasted to back of frontispiece reading: This book is supplied to the Booksellers on the understanding that it will not be sold to the Public at less than the published price.

Contents

Bibliographical note

Preface. Dated June 1912.

Preface to the Third Edition. Dated January 1901.

To some I have talked with by the fire

The Countess Cathleen

> Revised version, published separately in 1912. (No. 93.)

The Rose

> The song beginning "Who will go drive with Fergus now?" which is discarded from the new version of *The Countess Cathleen*

is now included as a separate poem, under the title *Who goes with Fergus?*, in this section. It is omitted by error from the list of Contents.

The Land of Heart's Desire
Revised version, published separately in 1912. (No. 94.)

Crossways

The Wanderings of Usheen

Glossary and Notes
The notes to *The Countess Cathleen* and *The Land of Heart's Desire* are from the separate editions.

100

SEVENTH ENGLISH EDITION, REVISED

POEMS [*in red*] | BY | W. B. YEATS [*in red*] | LONDON | T. FISHER UNWIN [*in red*] | ADELPHI TERRACE

$8 \times 5\frac{1}{4}$; pp. xvi, 316.

Issued in dark blue-green cloth, design (by Althea Gyles) in gold on front cover, spine and back cover; white end-papers; all edges untrimmed. Published in 1913.

Printed at The Gresham Press, Unwin Brothers, Limited. Woking and London.

Copies of this edition are also to be found with the design in gold on spine, but stamped blind on front and back covers. As there was no further printing of this volume until 1919 it seems probable that these copies were bound during the war of 1914–1918 when materials were scarce. But the later editions never had the full gold binding restored to them.

There were further impressions, each slightly revised, of this book in 1919, 1920, 1922 (2), 1923 and 1924.

For a new revised edition see No. 153.

101

THE GREEN HELMET AND | OTHER POEMS | BY | WILLIAM BUTLER YEATS | NEW YORK | THE MACMILLAN COMPANY | LONDON: MACMILLAN & CO., LTD. | 1912 | ALL RIGHTS RESERVED

$7\frac{1}{2} \times 5$; pp. viii, 92: comprising pp. [i–ii]; blank; half-title, verso blank, pp. [iii–iv]; title, copyright notice on verso, pp. [v–vi]; fly-title, verso blank, pp. [vii–viii]; text, pp. 1–37; p. [38] blank; fly-title, The Persons of the Play on verso, pp. [39–40]; text, pp. 41–91; emblem of The De Vinne Press, p. [92]. There is no list of contents.

Issued in tan paper boards, with ornamental design in green enclosing title on front cover, no lettering on spine; white end-papers; top edges trimmed, others untrimmed. Published on October 23, 1912.

Contents

In addition to *The Green Helmet* and the nineteen poems printed in the Cuala Press edition (No. 84), the following poems have been added:

That the Night Come

Friends

The Cold Heaven

On hearing that the students of our new University have joined the Ancient Order of Hibernians and the Agitation against Immoral Literature

The Attack on the "Play Boy"
    First appeared, under the title *On those who Dislike the Playboy* in *The Irish Review*, December 1911.

At the Abbey Theatre
    This poem appeared in *The Irish Review*, December 1912.

In a copy which Yeats gave me he wrote: "The cover of this book is the unaided work of the American publisher. He says he believes it the kind of cover I like."

102

THE CUTTING | OF AN AGATE | BY | WILLIAM BUTLER YEATS | AUTHOR OF "IDEAS OF GOOD AND | EVIL," ETC. | NEW YORK | THE MACMILLAN COMPANY | 1912 | ALL RIGHTS RESERVED

$7\frac{1}{2} \times 5$; pp. x, 262: comprising half-title, Macmillan's monogram and addresses on verso, pp. [i–ii]; title, copyright notice on verso, pp. [iii–iv]; Preface, pp. v–vi; contents, pp. vii–viii; fly-title, verso blank, pp. [ix–x]; text, pp. 1–255; p. [256] blank; notice of advertisements, verso blank, pp. [257–258]; advertisements, pp. [259–262].

Issued in green paper boards, white label printed in red and green with decorated initial "T" and ornamental frame on front cover, label printed in green on spine; white end-papers; top edges trimmed, others uncut. Published on November 13, 1912.

Contents

Preface. Dated August 1912.

Thoughts on Lady Gregory's Translations
    I. *Cuchulain and his Cycle.*
    II. *Fion and his Cycle.* Dated 1903.

Preface to the First Edition of the Well of the Saints. Dated Abbey Theatre, January 27, 1905.

Discoveries. Dated 1906.

Poetry and Tradition. Dated August 1907.

Preface to the First Edition of John M. Synge's Poems and Translations. Dated April 4, 1909.

J. M. Synge and the Ireland of his Time. Dated September 14th, 1910.

The Tragic Theatre. Dated August 1910.
    This contains passages not printed in the Preface to *Plays for an Irish Theatre*, 1911 (No. 92), and omits some which appear there.

John Shawe-Taylor. Dated July 1, 1911.
    First appeared in *The Observer*, July 2, 1911.

Edmund Spenser. Dated October 1902.

103

A | SELECTION FROM THE POETRY | OF | W. B.
YEATS | COPYRIGHT EDITION | LEIPZIG | BERNHARD TAUCH-
NITZ | 1913

$6\frac{1}{2} \times 4\frac{3}{5}$; pp. 272. 32 pp. of advertisements: comprising half-title, verso blank, pp. [1–2]; title, verso blank, pp. [3–4]; Preface, pp. [5]–6; contents, pp. [7]–10; fly-title, verso blank, pp. [11–12]; text, pp. [13]–270; imprint, Printing Office of the Publisher, p. [271]; p. [272] blank. At end is a catalogue of the Tauchnitz Edition, dated January 1, 1913, filling 32 pp.

Issued in light buff paper covers, lettered in black on front cover and spine; advertisements of Latest Volumes—January 1913 printed inside front cover and on both sides of back cover. The book forms Volume 4384 of the Tauchnitz Edition. Published early in 1913. (My copy was bought in Paris on March 17 of that year.)

A later issue, lacking the 32 pp. catalogue, has on back cover a list of the latest Tauchnitz volumes dated July 1924.

Contents

Preface. Dated October 1912.

> The Preface states that the selection of poems was made by Yeats himself.

Early Poems (1885–1892)

> This section contains the following 13 lyrics from *Poems*:
>
> > *To Ireland in the Coming Times; The Lake Isle of Innisfree; The Meditation of the Old Fisherman; Down by the Salley Gardens; To an Isle in the Water; The Fiddler of Dooney; The Song of the Old Mother; The Man who dreamed of Faeryland; The Rose of the World; The Rose of Peace; The Rose of Battle; The Two Trees; The White Birds.*

The Wanderings of Usheen (1889)

> Book III.

The Countess Cathleen (1892–1912)

> A revised version of the 1912 edition of No. 93. This revision was followed in the 1916 and later impressions of No. 93, and in No. 95 and No. 100.

Lyrics (1892–1899)

> This section contains the following 22 lyrics from *The Wind Among the Reeds*:
>
> > *The Hosting of the Sidhe; The Everlasting Voices; The Moods; The Lover tells of the Rose in His Heart; Into the Twilight; The Song of Wandering Aengus; The Heart of the Woman; He mourns for the Change that has come upon him and his Beloved and longs for the End of the World; He bids his Beloved be at Peace; He reproves the Curlew; He remembers forgotten Beauty; He gives his Beloved certain Rhymes; To my Heart, bidding it have no Fear; The Cap and Bells; The Valley of the Black Pig; The Lover asks Forgiveness because of his many Moods; He tells of the Perfect Beauty; He hears the Cry of the Sedge; The Travail of Passion; The Lover pleads with his Friend for Old Friends; He wishes his Beloved were dead; He wishes for the Cloths of Heaven.*

The Old Age of Queen Maeve

Baile and Aillinn (1902)

Lyrics (1899–1904).

> This section contains the following 10 lyrics from *In the Seven Woods*:
>
> > *The Folly of being Comforted; Old Memory; Never give all the Heart; The Withering of the Boughs; The Ragged Wood; Under the Moon; Adam's Curse; Red Hanrahan's Song about Ireland; The Old Men admiring themselves in the Water; The Happy Townland.*

On Baile's Strand (1904)

Deirdre (1906)

Lyrics (1904–1912)

This section contains the following 11 lyrics from *The Green Helmet and other Poems*, American edition (No. 101):

His Dream; A Woman Homer sung; That the Night come; Friends; No Second Troy; Reconciliation; King and no King; Against Unworthy Praise; The Cold Heaven; These are the Clouds; At Galway Races; and the following poems:

Fallen Majesty

First appeared in *Poetry* (Chicago), December 1912.

To a Child dancing in the Wind

First appeared, under the title *To a Child dancing upon the Shore* in *Poetry* (Chicago), December 1912.

The Mountain Tomb

First appeared in *Poetry* (Chicago), December 1912. Also printed in *The Quest* (London), April 1913.

Notes

These are from *Poems*, 1912 edition, from the Collected Works, Volume I., 1908 (No. 75), and from *Plays for an Irish Theatre*, 1911 (No. 92).

In the New York Public Library a copy of this book, forming part of the Maloney Collection, contains a note inserted saying "This Tauchnitz copy of Yeats' poems was given today [24 Feb. '41] by Dr. Maloney with statement that Yeats had told him the entire edition of 1913, several thousands in number, had been destroyed at the outbreak of war in 1914." Copies in new condition are known, however, to have survived in Paris, and there would probably have been others remaining in European countries where the Tauchnitz volumes were circulated.

104

STORIES OF RED HANRAHAN: | THE SECRET ROSE: | ROSA ALCHEMICA | BY | W. B. YEATS | [fleuron] | A. H. BULLEN | LONDON & STRATFORD-UPON-AVON | MCMXIII

$7\frac{1}{2} \times 5$; pp. viii, 232: comprising half-title, list of books By the same Author on verso, pp. [i–ii]; title, bibliographical note "First edition 1897 (under the general title *The Secret Rose*). In the present volume the revised version (from Vol. VII. of W. B. Yeats's *Collected Works*, 1908) has been followed." on verso, pp. [iii–iv]; contents, verso blank, pp. [v–vi]; fly-title, acknowledgement on verso, pp. [vii–viii]; text, pp. 1–228; imprint, Printed by A. H. Bullen, at the Shakespeare Head Press, Stratford-upon-Avon. p. [229]; pp. [230–232] blank.

Issued in grey-brown paper boards with green linen spine, lettered in black on spine; white end-papers; all edges untrimmed. Published in March 1913.

Contents

Stories of Red Hanrahan
      Six stories
The Secret Rose
      Dedication to A. E., poem and eight stories.
Rosa Alchemica

On or about June 28, 1916, the remainder of this edition was transferred to Messrs. Macmillan and Co., Ltd.

105

AMERICAN EDITION

STORIES OF RED HANRAHAN | THE SECRET ROSE | ROSA ALCHEMICA | BY | W. B. YEATS | NEW YORK | THE MACMILLAN COMPANY | 1914 | ALL RIGHTS RESERVED

$7\frac{1}{2} \times 5$; pp. vi, 242: comprising half-title, Macmillan's monogram and addresses on verso, pp. [i–ii]; title, copyright notice and imprint, Norwood Press J. S. Cushing Co.—Berwick & Smith Co. Norwood, Mass., U.S.A. on verso, pp. [iii–iv]; contents, pp. v–[vi]; fly-title, acknowledgement on verso, pp. [1–2]; text, pp. 3–231; p. [232] blank; advertisements, pp. [233–242].

Issued in green paper boards, labels, lettered in green within double rule in red, on front cover and on spine; white end-papers; top edges trimmed, others untrimmed. Published on April 1, 1914.

Contents

Stories of Red Hanrahan
Dedication to A.E.
      This is erroneously printed in the list of Contents at the end of *Stories of Red Hanrahan* instead of at the beginning of the next section.
The Secret Rose
      Poem and eight stories.
Rosa Alchemica

106

A SELECTION FROM THE LOVE POETRY | OF
WILLIAM BUTLER YEATS | [woodcut as in No. 84] | THE
CUALA PRESS | CHURCHTOWN | DUNDRUM | MCMXIII

$8\frac{3}{10} \times 5\frac{3}{4}$; pp. xvi, 40: comprising pp. [i–ix] blank; limitation notice,
p. [x]; acknowledgement, verso blank, pp. [xi–xii]; title, verso blank,
pp. [xiii–xiv]; contents, pp. [xv–xvi]; text, pp. [1]–[30]; colophon, in
red, on p. [30]; pp. [31–40] blank.

Issued in grey paper boards with white linen spine, lettered in black,
as title-page, on front cover, white paper label printed in black reading
POEMS OF LOVE BY W. B. YEATS. on spine; grey end-papers matching
binding; all edges untrimmed.

300 copies printed and published by Elizabeth C. Yeats at The Cuala
Press, Churchtown, Dundrum. Finished in the last week of May 1913.
Published on July 25, 1913.

Contents

Early Poems 1890–1892
> The Pity of Love; The Rose of Battle; When You are Old; The
> Rose of the World.

The Wind Among the Reeds 1892–1897
> The Lover Tells of the Rose in his Heart; The Lover Mourns for
> the Loss of Love; He Mourns for the Change that has come upon
> Him and His Beloved; He Tells of a Valley full of Lovers; He
> Remembers Forgotten Beauty; He Bids his Beloved be at Peace;
> He Gives his Beloved Certain Rhymes; He Tells of the Perfect
> Beauty; He Reproves the Curlew; The Travail of Passion; The
> Lover asks Forgiveness; The Lover Pleads with his Friends; He
> wishes His Beloved were Dead; A Poet to his Beloved; He Wishes
> for the Cloths of Heaven.

In the Seven Woods 1897–1904
> Adam's Curse; The Folly of Being Comforted; Old Memory;
> Under the Moon; Baile and Aillinn.

The Green Helmet 1904–1911
> The Mask; His Dream; A Woman Homer Sung; Peace; The Con-
> solation; No Second Troy; Reconciliation; King and No King;
> Against Unworthy Praise.

H

107

POEMS WRITTEN IN DISCOURAGE- | MENT, by
w. b. yeats | 1912–1913 | cuala press | dundrum | 1913

$6\frac{2}{5} \times 5\frac{3}{5}$; pp. 8: comprising text, pp. [1–8]. There is no title-page, but
p. [1] is headed poems written in discourage- | ment, 1912–1913.
The pages are unnumbered.

Issued in dark grey paper covers, lettered in black on front cover as
above; stitched with red silk cord.

50 copies were printed, not for sale, in October 1913.

Contents

*To a Wealthy Man, who promised a second subscription if it were proved
the people wanted pictures.* Dated December 1912.
First appeared, under the title *The Gift*, in *The Irish Times*,
January 8, 1913.

September, 1913
First appeared, under the title *Romance in Ireland* and dated
Dublin, September 7th, 1913, in *The Irish Times*, September 8,
1913.

To a Friend whose Work has come to Nothing
This appeared later in *Poetry* (Chicago), May 1914.

Paudeen
This appeared later in *Poetry* (Chicago), May 1914, and in *The
New Statesman*, May 9, 1914.

To a Shade
This appeared later in *Poetry* (Chicago), May 1914, and in *The
New Statesman*, May 9, 1914.

108

THE HOUR GLASS | by | w. b. yeats | (privately
printed) | 50 copies only

$8\frac{1}{5} \times 5\frac{7}{10}$; pp. iii, 37: comprising title, verso blank, pp. [i–ii]; p. [iii]
blank; text, pp. 1–[35]; pp. [36–37] blank.

Issued in dark grey paper covers lettered in black on front cover the
hour glass | by | w. b. yeats | cuala press and fastened together by
a purple ribbon passed through two holes punched in covers and
sheets; all edges untrimmed.

This is a new version of the play, partly in verse, partly in prose. These copies were printed in January 1914.

This new version first appeared in *The Mask* (Florence), April 1913.

109

NINE POEMS | CHOSEN FROM THE WORKS OF | WILLIAM BUTLER YEATS | PRIVATELY PRINTED | FOR JOHN QUINN AND HIS FRIENDS | APRIL FIRST | MCMXIV

$7\frac{7}{10} \times 5$; pp. 36, unnumbered: the text is printed on alternate openings. P. [i] is blank, a photograph of Yeats by Arnold Genthe is mounted on p. [2] facing title-page, p. [3]; list of contents on p. [7]; text of poems on pp. [11], [14], [15], [18], [19], [22], [23], [26–27], [30–31]; the other pages are blank.

Issued in stiff blue paper covers, a white label printed in red on front cover bearing the words Mr. W. B. Yeats; stitched with a blue silk cord; no end-papers; all edges untrimmed.

25 copies were printed by Mitchell Kennerley for presentation at a farewell dinner to Yeats given by John Quinn. Set by Bertha Goudy [at the Village Press, Forest Hills Gardens, N.Y.] and printed by Publishers' Printing Co. [according to M. B. Cary, *A Bibliography of the Village Press*, New York, 1938, p. 117].

Contents

The Song of Wandering Aengus; The Young Man's Song; The Mask; A Drinking Song; Against Unworthy Praise; A Woman Homer Sung; That the Night Come; The Three Hermits; Romantic Ireland (September, 1913).

The above description is taken from Yeats's own copy. Roth states that each guest at the dinner had his name pasted on the cover. I have seen a copy, also in Yeats's library, with no label on the front cover.

110

RESPONSIBILITIES: POEMS AND A | PLAY BY WILLIAM BUTLER YEATS | [woodcut as in No. 84] | THE CUALA PRESS | CHURCHTOWN | DUNDRUM | MCMXIV

$8\frac{2}{5} \times 5\frac{4}{5}$; pp. xvi, 88: comprising pp. [i–viii] blank; title, verso blank, pp. [ix–x]; two quotations, verso blank, pp. [xi–xii]; table of contents, pp. [xiii–xiv]; limitation notice, p. [xiv]; p. [xv] blank; poem, in red,

p. [xvi]; text, pp. [1]–[75]; poem, in red, p. [76]; Notes, pp. [77–81]; p. [82] blank; colophon in red, p. [83]; pp. [84–88] blank.

Issued in grey paper boards with white linen spine, lettered in black on front cover, no label on spine; grey end-papers matching binding; all edges untrimmed.

400 copies printed by Elizabeth Corbet Yeats at the Cuala Press, Churchtown, Dundrum. Finished on May Eve, 1914. Published on May 25, 1914.

A copy, now in the Lockwood Memorial Library at the University of Buffalo, N.Y., has an errata slip loosely inserted. This reads

ERRORS

> Page 25, line 23, for "we" read "he."
> Page 39, line 15, for "balls" read "bawls."
> Page 76, line 9, instead of a full stop there should be a comma.
> Page 76, line 13, instead of "of" read "my."

On the bottom of the slip in ink there is the following note: "These are alterations my brother made after the book was printed—so are not our misprints   E. C. Yeats"

My own copy, bought on publication direct from Miss Yeats, had no slip, and no other collectors I have asked have seen it; I think, therefore, that it was only inserted in copies which remained after subscribers' demands had been met.

Contents

Preliminary Poem: Pardon, old fathers, if you still remain, printed in red, without title.

The Grey Rock
> First appeared in *The British Review*, April 1913 and in *Poetry* (Chicago), April 1913.

The Two Kings
> First appeared in *The British Review*, October 1913 and in *Poetry*, October 1913.

To a Wealthy Man who promised a second subscription to the Dublin Municipal Gallery if it were proved the people wanted pictures. Dated December 1912
> First appeared, under the title *The Gift*, in *The Irish Times*, January 8, 1913, and previously reprinted in *Poems Written in Discouragement*, 1913. (No. 107.)

September, 1913
> First appeared, under the title *Romance in Ireland*, in *The Irish Times*, September 8, 1913, and previously reprinted in *Poems*

Written in Discouragement, 1913 (No. 107) and, under the title *Romantic Ireland* (*September*, *1913*), in *Nine Poems*, 1914. (No. 109.)

To a Friend whose Work has come to Nothing
First appeared in *Poems Written in Discouragement*, 1913 (No. 107), and printed in *Poetry*, May 1914.

Paudeen
First appeared in *Poems Written in Discouragement*, 1913 (No. 107), and printed in *The New Statesman*, May 9, 1914, and in *Poetry*, May 1914.

To a Shade. Dated September 29th. 1913.
First appeared in *Poems Written in Discouragement*, 1913 (No. 107), and printed in *The New Statesman*, May 9, 1914, and in *Poetry*, May 1914.

When Helen Lived
First appeared in *Poetry*, May 1914.

The Attack on 'The Playboy of the Western World' 1907
First appeared, under the title *On those who Dislike the Playboy*, in *The Irish Review*, December 1911, and printed in *The Green Helmet and other Poems*, New York, 1912. (No. 101.)

The Three Beggars
First appeared in *Harper's Weekly*, November 15, 1913.

The Three Hermits
First appeared in *The Smart Set*, September 1913.

Beggar to Beggar Cried
First appeared in *Poetry*, May 1914.

Running to Paradise
First appeared in *Poetry*, May 1914.

The Hour Before Dawn

The Player Queen. (Song from an Unfinished Play.)
First appeared in *Poetry*, May 1914.

The Realists
First appeared in *Poetry*, December 1912.

The Witch
First appeared in *Poetry*, May 1914.

The Peacock
First appeared in *Poetry*, May 1914.

The Mountain Tomb
First appeared in *Poetry*, December 1912, and printed in *A Selection from the Poetry of W. B. Yeats*, Tauchnitz Edition, 1913 (No. 103), and in *The Quest* (London), April 1913.

To a Child Dancing in the Wind
> The first stanza first appeared, under the title *To a Child Dancing upon the Shore*, in *Poetry* (Chicago), December 1912, and was printed under its present title in *A Selection from the Poetry of W. B. Yeats*, Tauchnitz Edition, 1913 (No. 103). The second stanza first appeared, under the title *To a Child Dancing in the Wind*, in *Poetry* (Chicago), May 1914.

A Memory of Youth
> First appeared, under the title *Love and the Bird*, in *Poetry*, December 1912.

Fallen Majesty
> First appeared in *Poetry*, December 1912, and printed in *A Selection from the Poetry of W. B. Yeats*, Tauchnitz Edition, 1913. (No. 103.)

Friends
> Previously printed in *The Green Helmet and other Poems*, New York, 1912. (No. 101.)

The Cold Heaven
> Previously printed in *The Green Helmet and other Poems*, New York, 1912. (No. 101.)

That the Night Come
> Previously printed in *The Green Helmet and other Poems*, New York, 1912. (No. 101.)

An Appointment
> First appeared, under the title *On a Recent Government Appointment in Ireland*, in *The English Review*, February 1909.

The Magi
> First appeared in *The New Statesman*, May 9, 1914; printed also in *Poetry*, May 1914.

The Dolls

A Coat
> First appeared in *Poetry*, May 1914.

The Hour-Glass. New Version.
> First appeared in *The Mask* (Florence), April 1913, and privately printed by the Cuala Press in January 1914. (No. 108.)

Valedictory poem: While I, from that reed-throated whisperer, printed in red, without title.
> First appeared, under the title *Notoriety*, in *The New Statesman*, February 7, 1914.

Notes

III

REVERIES OVER CHILDHOOD AND | YOUTH BY
WILLIAM BUTLER YEATS | [woodcut of leaping unicorn,
Monoceros de Astris, by Sturge Moore] | THE CUALA PRESS |
CHURCHTOWN | DUNDRUM | MCMXV

$8\frac{3}{10} \times 5\frac{4}{5}$; pp. xii, 132: comprising pp. [i–v] blank; dedication, in red,
p. [vi]; woodcut, in red, of candle among waves [by Sturge Moore],
verso blank, pp. [vii–viii]; p. [ix] blank; Preface, and notice of
limitation, the latter in red, p. [x]; title, verso blank, pp. [xi–xii];
text, pp. [1]–[128]; colophon, in red, p. [128]; pp. [129–132] blank.

Issued in grey paper boards with white linen spine; lettered in black
on front cover; no label on spine; grey end-papers matching binding;
all edges untrimmed.

425 copies, numbered in ink, printed on paper made in Ireland and
published by Elizabeth C. Yeats at the Cuala Press. Finished on All
Hallows' Eve, 1915. Published March 20, 1916.

Contents

Preface. Dated Christmas Day, 1914.
A Reverie over Childhood and Youth

The book was accompanied by a portfolio measuring $8\frac{1}{2} \times 5\frac{7}{10}$, blue
paper boards lined blue with white linen spine, lettered in black on
front cover PLATES TO ACCOMPANY | REVERIES OVER CHILDHOOD AND
YOUTH | BY W. B. YEATS | CUALA PRESS | CHURCHTOWN DUNDRUM CO.
DUBLIN IRELAND | 1915 | and containing portraits of John Butler Yeats
from a water-colour drawing by himself, of Mrs. Yeats from a drawing
by J. B. Yeats made in 1867, and *Memory Harbour* by Jack B. Yeats, a
print in colours on a black mount; and a note, *Memory Harbour*,
printed on one side of a single sheet, $8\frac{1}{8} \times 5\frac{1}{2}$, signed W.B.Y.

The book was first announced by the Cuala Press under the title
Memory Harbour: A Revery on my Childhood and Youth.

112

AMERICAN EDITION

REVERIES OVER CHILDHOOD AND | YOUTH BY
WILLIAM BUTLER YEATS | THE MACMILLAN COMPANY | NEW
YORK | MCMXVI

$8\frac{1}{4} \times 5\frac{7}{16}$; pp. viii, 136: comprising half-title, Macmillan's monogram and addresses on verso, pp. [i–ii]; title, copyright notice and, at foot, imprint, Norwood Press, J. S. Cushing Co.—Berwick & Smith Co. Norwood, Mass., U.S.A. on verso, pp. [iii–iv]; dedication, verso blank, pp. [v–vi]; Preface, verso blank, pp. vii–viii; text, pp. 1–131; pp. [132–136] blank. Coloured frontispiece mounted on black page *Memory Harbour* by Jack B. Yeats; portraits facing pp. 32 and 48. The title appears at the top of p. 1 *"Reveries Over Childhood and Youth"* with initial letter at the beginning of first paragraph, but there are no running headlines.

Issued in buff cloth, design by Sturge Moore printed in black on blue-grey paper and pasted on front cover and on spine; white end-papers; top and bottom edges trimmed. Published on April 26, 1916.

The contents are the same as those of the Cuala Press edition. (No. 111.)

113

ENGLISH EDITION

REVERIES OVER | CHILDHOOD & YOUTH | BY | WILLIAM BUTLER YEATS | MACMILLAN AND CO., LIMITED | ST. MARTIN'S STREET, LONDON | 1916

$7\frac{4}{5} \times 5$; pp. 2, x, 216: comprising one leaf not included in pagination; half-title, Macmillan's monogram and addresses on verso, pp. [i–ii]; title, copyright notice on verso, pp. [iii–iv]; dedication, verso blank, pp. [v–vi]; Preface, pp. vii–viii; list of Illustrations, verso blank, pp. ix–[x]; text, pp. 1–213; imprint, Printed by R. & R. Clark, Limited, Edinburgh, at foot of p. 213; p. [214] blank; list of The Works of William Butler Yeats, p. [215]; p. [216] blank. Coloured frontispiece mounted on black page, *Memory Harbour* by Jack B. Yeats; portraits facing pp. 54 and 80.

Issued in dark blue cloth with design in gold, signed Sturge Moore, on front cover and on spine; white end-papers; all edges untrimmed. Published on October 10, 1916; the edition consisted of 1000 copies.

Contents

Preface. Dated Christmas Day, 1914.
Note on "Memory Harbour"
> This, which formed a separate sheet in the portfolio accompanying the Cuala Press Edition, is now printed in the list of illustrations.
A Reverie over Childhood and Youth

There was a second impression in March 1917.

114

EIGHT | POEMS | BY | W B YEATS | TRANSCRIBED BY |
EDWARD PAY | PUBLISHED BY | "FORM" | AT THE MORLAND
PRESS LTD. | 190 EBURY STREET LONDON S.W. [*The whole
title-page is printed in red.*]

Vellum copies, $11\frac{3}{10} \times 7\frac{2}{5}$; Dutch hand-made paper copies, $12 \times 8\frac{1}{5}$;
Italian hand-made copies, $11\frac{2}{5} \times 8\frac{1}{2}$; pp. 24, unnumbered: comprising
silhouette of nude figure in red (by Austin Spare), verso blank, pp.
[1–2]; title in red, verso blank, pp. [3–4]; text, the titles of the poems
and the initial letters to each stanza in red, the rest black, pp. [5–21];
the words London | January | 1916 | E. P., in red on p. [22]; p. [23] blank;
design and imprint of F. J. Head & Co. 21 Gt. Russell St. London
W.C. p. [24].

At the bottom of title-page a typewritten slip is attached which states
"This edition is an exact facsimile of certain pages in the quarterly
periodical, FORM.

The responsibility for the caligraphy and design rests entirely with the
proprietors of FORM."

Copies are also found with a printed slip attached to the title-page
containing the same announcement but with the word "exact" omitted
and a capital letter to Proprietors. I believe the copies with typewritten
slips to be the earlier issued.

Issued in cream card covers, lettered in black on front cover POEMS |
BY | W B YEATS | [design of ten dots arranged to form an inverted
triangle].

On the inside of front cover is printed in black notice of limitation of
issue and address of the sole agents; on the inside of back cover are
printed in black 5 lines of errata.

The edition comprised 200 copies, numbered by hand, of which 8
copies were on Dutch hand-made paper, 122 copies on Italian hand-
made paper and 70 copies on Japanese vellum.

Some copies on Italian hand-made paper are without the statement of
limitation and agents' address on verso of front cover; these are said
to be the earlier state, and I believe them to be advance copies. The
copies on Japanese vellum are without the illustration.

Published in April 1916.

Contents

The Dawn; On Woman; The Fisherman; The Hawk; Memory; The Thorn Tree; The Phoenix; There is a Queen in China.

These poems first appeared in *Poetry* (Chicago), February 1916; they appeared in *Form*, April 1916.

The British Museum copy is evidently an advance copy; it was received on February 15, 1916, presumably to synchronize with the magazine publication of the poems in America. It is on Japanese vellum and does not have the Austin Spare figure or any note of limitation or the errata. The insides of the covers are blank. There are 20 unnumbered pages instead of 24.

In a similar copy in his own library Yeats wrote "This pamphlet was brought out by a magazine called 'Form' to save my copyright as the poems were being published in America & the magazine was delayed."

In Quinn's copy, on Dutch hand-made paper, Yeats wrote:

"I think this picture vulgar. I had no responsibility for the pamphlet, which was issued by 'Form' to whom I gave eight poems free. These delays made 'technical publication' necessary to secure my copyright and 200 pamphlets like this are what they call 'technical publication.' If you want to reproduce a poem you should print it not WRITE it, and if you do write it you should not break your lines. W. B. Yeats. April 2, 1916."

In the Buhler sale there was a copy on Italian hand-made paper, also inscribed by Yeats on the front cover:

"I gave these poems to the designer at the request of Charles Ricketts, R.A., W. B. Yeats June 1935. I don't like the work. The red woman is a brute."

In another copy in his own library Yeats wrote that he had taken steps to stop the publication, but was persuaded by a friend to let it go on. It seems probable that the friend was Charles Ricketts, and perhaps the slip was added to the title-page in order to disassociate Yeats from the style of production, of which he obviously disapproved.

115

RESPONSIBILITIES | AND OTHER POEMS | BY | WILLIAM BUTLER YEATS | MACMILLAN AND CO., LIMITED | ST. MARTIN'S STREET, LONDON | 1916

$7\frac{3}{8} \times 5$; pp. xii, 188: comprising half-title, Macmillan's monogram and addresses on verso, pp. [i–ii]; title, copyright notice on verso, pp. [iii–iv]; contents, pp. v–vii; p. [viii] blank; fly-title, verso blank, pp. [ix–x]; two quotations, p. [xi]; p. [xii] blank; text, pp. 1–188; imprint, Printed by R. & R. Clark, Limited, Edinburgh, beneath rule at foot of p. 188.

Issued in dark blue cloth with design in gold stamped on front cover and on spine, signed Sturge Moore; off-white end-papers; all edges untrimmed. Published on October 10, 1916; the edition consisted of 1,000 copies.

Contents

Responsibilities, 1912–1914
> This section includes the thirty-one poems printed in the Cuala Press volume of 1914 (No. 110), and also
> *The Well and the Tree.*

From the Green Helmet and other Poems, 1909–1912
> This section includes the nineteen poems printed in the Cuala Press volume of 1910 (No. 84) and two poems printed in the New York edition of 1912 (No. 101).

The Hour-Glass—1912

Notes
> The note to the *Prefatory Poem* is new; the notes to the group of poems on the Municipal Gallery controversy have a new postscript, dated July, 1916; the remainder are from the Cuala Press volume of 1914 (No. 110).

There was a second impression in March 1917.

116

AMERICAN EDITION

RESPONSIBILITIES | AND OTHER POEMS | BY | WILLIAM BUTLER YEATS | NEW YORK | THE MACMILLAN COMPANY | 1916 | ALL RIGHTS RESERVED

$7\frac{1}{2} \times 5$; pp. xii, 196.

Issued in grey paper boards with buff linen spine, design by Sturge Moore in black on front cover; white end-papers; top edges trimmed, others untrimmed. Published on November 1, 1916.

The contents are the same as those of the English edition. (No. 115.)

117

EASTER, 1916 | BY | W. B. YEATS | [*The whole enclosed within rules*]

$10 \times 7\frac{1}{2}$; pp. vi, 10: comprising pp. [i–ii] blank; half-title, verso blank, pp. [iii–iv]; title-page, verso blank, pp. [v–vi]; text, pp. 1–[6]; note on p. [7] Of this poem twenty-five copies only have been privately printed by Clement Shorter for distribution among his friends; pp. 8–10] blank.

Issued in green paper covers lettered in black, as title-page, on front cover, within black rules; stitched with green silk cord; white end-papers; all edges untrimmed.

Contents

Easter, 1916. Dated Sept. 25, 1916.

118

THE WILD SWANS AT COOLE, | OTHER VERSES AND A PLAY | IN VERSE, BY W. B. YEATS. | THE CUALA PRESS | CHURCHTOWN | DUNDRUM | MCMXVII

$8\frac{3}{10} \times 5\frac{3}{4}$; pp. xii, 52: comprising pp. [i–iv] blank; woodcut, in red, as in No. 72, verso blank, pp. [v–vi]; title, verso blank, pp. [vii–viii]; contents, pp. [ix–x]; pp. [xi–xii] blank; text, pp. [1]–[47]; colophon, in red, p. [48]; pp. [49–52] blank.

Issued in dark blue paper boards with buff linen spine, lettered in black on front cover as on title-page, white label POEMS AND A PLAY printed in black on spine; dark blue end-papers matching binding; all edges untrimmed.

400 copies printed on paper made in Ireland and published by Elizabeth Corbet Yeats at The Cuala Press. Finished October 10, 1917. Published on November 17, 1917.

Contents

The Wild Swans at Coole
    First appeared in *The Little Review*, June 1917.
Men Improve with the Years
    First appeared in *The Little Review*, June 1917.
The Collar-Bone of a Hare
    First appeared in *The Little Review*, June 1917.

Lines Written in Dejection
> The eight poems from *Eight Poems*, 1916. (No. 114.) Three titles are changed: *The Thorn Tree* to *Her Praise*, *The Phoenix* to *The People*, and *There is a Queen in China* to *His Phoenix*.

A Thought from Propertius

Broken Dreams
> First appeared in *The Little Review*, June 1917.

A Deep-sworn Vow
> First appeared in *The Little Review*, June 1917.

Presences
> First appeared in *The Little Review*, June 1917.

The Balloon of the Mind
> First appeared in *The New Statesman*, September 29, 1917.

To a Squirrel at Kyle-na-gno
> First appeared in *The New Statesman*, September 29, 1917.

On being asked for a War Poem
> First appeared, under the title *A Reason for Keeping Silent*, in *The Book of the Homeless*, 1916. (No. 310.)

In Memory
> First appeared in *The Little Review*, June 1917.

Upon a Dying Lady
> *Her Courtesy; Certain Artists bring her Dolls and Drawings; She Turns the Dolls' Faces to the Wall; The End of Day; Her Race; Her Courage; Her Friends Bring Her a Christmas Tree.*
>> This group of poems first appeared in *The Little Review*, August 1917 and in *The New Statesman*, August 11, 1917.

Ego Dominus Tuus
> First appeared in *Poetry* (Chicago), October 1917; printed in *The New Statesman*, November 17, 1917.

The Scholars
> First appeared in *Catholic Anthology*, 1915 (No. 309); printed in *Poetry*, February 1916.

At the Hawk's Well: a Play
> First appeared, under the title *At the Hawk's Well* or *Waters of Immortality*, in *Harper's Bazaar*, March 1917; printed in *To-day* (London), June 1917. The final lyric beginning "The man that I praise" had appeared, under the title *The Well and the Tree*, in *Responsibilities*, 1916 (No. 115), and does not appear in *To-day*.

A Note on "At the Hawk's Well". Dated December 1916.
> First appeared, with a few alterations, as a preface to the play in *Harper's Bazaar*, March 1917; printed, under the title *Instead of a*

Theatre, in *To-day* (London), May 1917; reprinted, with some minor verbal alterations and the elimination of the note on the cast, in *Theatre Arts Magazine* (Detroit), January 1919; and again, cut almost by half, in *Theatre Arts Monthly* (New York), April 1939.

119
THE WELL OF IMMORTALITY

Lieut-Colonel Alspach of West Point, New York, has recently discovered in the New York Public Library, where it had been bound up with other plays, a 12-page pamphlet bearing the title *The Well of Immortality*; this was an earlier title of the play *At the Hawk's Well*.

THE WELL | OF | IMMORTALITY

$8\frac{1}{4} \times 5$; pp. 12: comprising p. [1] lettered in black as above and serving as cover, verso blank; text, pp. 3-11; p. [12], the outside back page, blank. P. 3 is headed THE WELL OF IMMORTALITY | BY WILLIAM B. YEATS | [dotted line] followed by text.

There is no printer's name and no date. The printing is careless and the text, incorrectly given, seems to have been taken from a rehearsal typescript; it embodies some, though not all, of the alterations which were made during the rehearsals of the play in London in April 1916.

Mr. Edmund Dulac tells me that an exhibition of his work, including the masks which he had made for the London performance of *At the Hawk's Well*, was held in New York in November 1916, at the Gallery of Messrs. Scott and Fowles, and that Mr. Martin Birnbaum, a partner in the firm, arranged to have the play given at the Greenwich Village Theatre, himself playing the Chorus, while the Guardian of the Well was played by Michio Ito, the Japanese dancer, who had already taken that part in London. It seems possible that the play was printed for rehearsal purposes from an incompletely revised typescript which Ito may have taken over with him to America. There seems to be no record of a copy appearing for sale; that in the New York Public Library bears the bookplate "From the Library of Alice and Irene Lewisohn" on the verso of the title.

120

PER AMICA | SILENTIA LUNAE | BY | WILLIAM BUTLER YEATS | MACMILLAN AND CO., LIMITED | ST. MARTIN'S STREET, LONDON | 1918

$7\frac{1}{2} \times 5$; pp. 2, vi, 96: comprising blank page, list of The Works of William Butler Yeats in panel on verso, not included in pagination; half-title, Macmillan's monogram and addresses on verso, pp. [i–ii]; title, copyright notice on verso, pp. [iii–iv]; Prologue, pp. v–vi; text, pp. 1–43; p. [44] blank; text, pp. 45–89; p. [90] blank; text, pp. 91–[95]; imprint, R. & R. Clark, Limited, Edinburgh, at foot of p. [95]; p. [96] blank.

Issued in dark blue cloth with design in gold, signed Sturge Moore, stamped on front cover and on spine; white end-papers; all edges untrimmed. Published on January 18, 1918. The edition consisted of 1,500 copies.

Some copies, though not the earliest issued, contain an errata slip, facing p. 8 and reading as follows:

ERRATA

Page 34, line 14, *for* "kingdom" *read* "kingdoms."
Page 72, line 13, *cross out* "the" *before* "woods."
Page 75, line 9, *for* "nor that Caesarea" *read* "nor Caesarion";
and in line 11, *for* "that so" *read* "the"; and in the footnote,
for "Caesarea" *read* "Caesarion."

Contents

Prologue. Dated May 11, 1917.
Ego Dominus Tuus. (From No. 118.) Dated December 1915.
Anima Hominis. Dated February 25, 1917.
Anima Mundi. Dated May 9, 1917.
Epilogue. Dated May 11, 1917.

121

AMERICAN EDITION

PER AMICA | SILENTIA LUNAE | BY | WILLIAM BUTLER YEATS | NEW YORK | THE MACMILLAN COMPANY | 1918 | ALL RIGHTS RESERVED

$8\frac{3}{10} \times 6$; pp. 98 followed by 6 pp. of advertisements: comprising p. [1] blank; list of Other works by William Butler Yeats, inside panel, p. [2]; half-title, on verso Special Limited Edition, pp. [3–4]; title, copyright notice and imprint, Norwood Press J. S. Cushing Co.— Berwick & Smith Co. Norwood, Mass., U.S.A. on verso, pp. [5–6]; Prologue, verso blank, pp. 7–[8]; text, pp. 9–15; p. [16] blank; text, pp. 17–98; at foot of p. 98 below rule, Printed in the United States of America; advertisements, [6] pp. unnumbered.

Issued in blue paper boards, lettering and design, signed Sturge Moore, on front cover and on spine; white end-papers; top edges trimmed, other untrimmed. Published on January 18, 1918.

The contents are the same as those of the English edition. (No. 120.)

122

NINE POEMS | BY | W. B. YEATS | LONDON | PRIVATELY PRINTED BY CLEMENT SHORTER | OCTOBER 1918 [*The whole enclosed within rules*]

10 × 7½; pp. ii, 18: comprising pp. [i–ii] blank; half-title, note on verso "This little collection of Mr. Yeats's Poems is privately printed here for the first time in an edition limited to twenty-five copies by kind permission of the Author, William Butler Yeats", pp. [1–2]; title, verso blank, pp. [3–4]; text, pp. 5–[16]; imprint, Printed by Eyre and Spottiswoode, Ltd., East Harding Street, E.C.4. below rule at foot of p. [16]; pp. [17–18] blank.

Issued in green stiff paper covers, lettered in black, as title-page, within black rules, on front cover; stitched with black silk cord; white end-papers; all edges untrimmed.

Contents

Solomon to Sheba; To a Young Beauty; To a Young Girl; Under the Round Tower; Tom O'Roughley; A Song; The Living Beauty; The Cat and the Moon; A Prayer on going into my House.

Seven of these poems—*To a Young Girl; A Song; Solomon to Sheba; The Living Beauty; Under the Round Tower; Tom O'Roughley;* and *A Prayer on going into my House*—were also printed in *The Little Review*, October 1918.

123

TWO PLAYS FOR DANCERS | BY W. B. YEATS | [woodcut *Monoceros de Astris* as in No. 111] | THE CUALA PRESS | MCMXIX

8$\frac{3}{10}$ × 5$\frac{4}{5}$; pp. viii, 44: comprising pp. [i–iv] blank; title, verso blank, pp. [v–vi]; Preface, p. [vii]; p. [viii] blank; text, pp. [1]–38; colophon [in red], p. [39]; pp. [40–44] blank. The title and scenic directions at the beginning of each play printed in red.

Issued in green paper boards with buff linen spine, lettered in black on front cover, white label printed in black on spine; green end-papers matching binding; all edges untrimmed.

400 copies on paper made in Ireland printed and published by Elizabeth Corbet Yeats at the Cuala Press, Churchtown, Dundrum. Finished January 10, 1919. Published in January 1919.

Contents

Preface. Dated October 11th. 1918, with a postscript.
The Dreaming of the Bones
    This play was also printed in *The Little Review*, January 1919.
The Only Jealousy of Emer
    This play was also printed in *Poetry* (Chicago), January 1919.

124

THE WILD SWANS | AT COOLE | BY | W. B. YEATS | MACMILLAN AND CO., LIMITED | ST. MARTIN'S STREET, LONDON | 1919

$7\frac{1}{2} \times 5$; pp. 2, x, 116: comprising blank page, on verso list of Works by W. B. Yeats, in a panel, not included in pagination; half-title, Macmillan's monogram and addresses on verso, pp. [i–ii]; title, copyright notice on verso, pp. [iii–iv]; Preface, pp. v–vi; contents, pp. vii–ix; p. [x] blank; text, pp. 1–[115]; imprint, Printed by R. & R. Clark, Limited [*sic*] Edinburgh, p. [116].

Issued in dark blue cloth with design in gold, signed Sturge Moore, on front cover and on spine; white end-papers; all edges untrimmed. Published on March 11, 1919; the edition consisted of 1500 copies.

Contents

Preface. Dated Ballylee, Co. Galway, September 1918.
The twenty-nine poems from the Cuala Press volume, *The Wild Swans at Coole*, 1917. (No. 118.)
In Memory of Major Robert Gregory
    First appeared, under the title *In Memory of Robert Gregory*, in *The English Review*, August 1918; printed, under the same title, in *The Little Review* (New York), September 1918.
An Irish Airman foresees his Death

I

Under the Round Tower; Solomon to Sheba; The Living Beauty; A Song.
 These four poems first appeared in *Nine Poems*, 1918 (No. 122),
 and in *The Little Review*, October 1918.

To a Young Beauty
 First appeared in *Nine Poems*, 1918. (No. 122.)

To a Young Girl; Tom O'Roughley
 These two poems first appeared in *Nine Poems*, 1918 (No. 122),
 and in *The Little Review*, October 1918.

The Sad Shepherd

A Prayer on going into my House
 First appeared in *Nine Poems*, 1918 (No. 122), and in *The Little
 Review*, October 1918.

The Phases of the Moon

The Cat and the Moon
 First appeared in *Nine Poems*, 1918 (No. 122).

The Saint and the Hunchback

Two Songs of a Fool

Another Song of a Fool

The Double Vision of Michael Robartes

Note

There was a second impression in January 1920.

125

AMERICAN EDITION

THE WILD SWANS | AT COOLE | BY | W. B. YEATS |
NEW YORK | THE MACMILLAN COMPANY | 1919 | ALL RIGHTS
RESERVED

$7\frac{1}{2} \times 5$; pp. x, 122: comprising half-title, Macmillan's monogram and
addresses on verso, pp. [i–ii]; title, copyright notices and imprint,
Norwood Press J. S. Cushing Co.—Berwick & Smith Co. Norwood,
Mass., U.S.A. on verso, pp. [iii–iv]; Preface, pp. v–vi; contents, pp.
vii–ix; p. [x] blank; text, pp. 1–[115]; imprint, Printed in the United
States of America, beneath rule at foot of p. [115]; p. [116] blank;
advertisements of Macmillan's books, pp. [117–122].

Issued in grey paper boards, design and lettering by Sturge Moore in
black on front cover and on spine; white end-papers; all edges trimmed.
Published on March 11, 1919.

The contents are the same as those of the English edition. (No. 124.)

126

ENGLISH EDITION

THE CUTTING OF | AN AGATE | BY | W. B. YEATS |
MACMILLAN AND CO., LIMITED | ST. MARTIN'S STREET,
LONDON | 1919

$7\frac{1}{2} \times 5$; p. viii, 224: comprising half-title, Macmillan's monogram and
addresses on verso, pp. [i–ii]; title, copyright notice on verso, pp.
[iii–iv]; Preface, pp. v–vi; contents, verso blank, pp. vii–[viii]; text,
pp. 1–223; imprint, Printed by R. & R. Clark, Limited, Edinburgh,
at foot of p. 223; p. [224] blank.

Issued in dark blue cloth with design in gold, signed T S[turge]
M[oore], stamped on front cover and on spine; white end-papers;
all edges untrimmed. Published on April 8, 1919.; the edition consisted
of 1500 copies.

Contents

Preface. Dated December 1918.   With a postscript.

Certain Noble Plays of Japan. Dated April 1916.
   First appeared as introduction to *Certain Noble Plays of Japan*,
   Cuala Press (No. 269), published September 16, 1916, and in
   Drama, November 1916.

The Tragic Theatre. Dated August 1910.
   First appeared in *The Mask* (Florence), October 1910, and
   printed, with alterations, as preface to *Plays for an Irish Theatre*,
   1911. (No. 92.)

Poetry and Tradition. Dated August 1907.

Discoveries. Dated 1906.

Preface to the First Edition of The Well of the Saints. Dated Abbey
   Theatre, January 27, 1905.

*Preface to the First Edition of John M. Synge's Poems and Transla-
tions.* Dated April 4, 1909.

J. M. Synge and the Ireland of his Time. Dated September 14, 1910.

John Shawe-Taylor. Dated July 1, 1911.

Edmund Spenser. Dated October 1902.
   For previous appearance of these latter essays see *The Cutting of
   an Agate*, New York, 1912. (No. 102.)

127

MICHAEL ROBARTES AND THE | DANCER, BY
WILLIAM BUTLER | YEATS. | [woodcut, in red, of candle among
waves by Sturge Moore] | THE CUALA PRESS | CHURCHTOWN |
DUNDRUM | MCMXX

$8\frac{2}{5} \times 5\frac{3}{4}$; pp. xii, 40: comprising pp. [i–iv] blank; title, verso blank,
pp. [v–vi]; half-title [in red], verso blank, pp. [vii–viii]; Preface, pp.
[ix–x]; p. [xi] blank; contents, p. [xii]; text, pp. [1]–[35]; colophon,
in red, on p. [35]; pp. [36–40] blank.

Issued in blue paper boards with buff linen spine; lettered in black on
front cover, paper label printed in black bearing the words MICHAEL
ROBARTES on spine; blue end-papers matching binding; all edges
untrimmed.

400 copies printed on paper made in Ireland and published by
Elizabeth Corbet Yeats at the Cuala Press, Churchtown, Dundrum.
Finished on All Souls' Day, 1920. Published in February 1921.

Contents

Preface
Michael Robartes and the Dancer
    First appeared in *The Dial* (New York), November 1920.
Solomon and the Witch
An Image from a Past Life
    First appeared in *The Nation*, November 6, 1920.
Under Saturn. Dated November, 1919.
    First appeared in *The Dial* (New York), November 1920.
Easter, 1916. Dated September 25th, 1916.
    Privately printed, 1916. (No. 117); printed in *The New Statesman*,
    October 23, 1920, and in *The Dial* (New York), November 1920.
Sixteen Dead Men
    First appeared in *The Dial* (New York), November 1920.
The Rose Tree
    First appeared in *The Dial* (New York), November 1920, and in
    The Nation, November 6, 1920.
On a Political Prisoner
    First appeared in *The Dial* (New York), November 1920, and in
    The Nation, November 13, 1920.

The Leaders of the Crowd
Towards Break of Day
> First appeared in *The Dial* (New York), November 1920, and in *The Nation*, November 13, 1920.

Demon and Beast
> First appeared in *The Dial* (New York), November 1920.

The Second Coming
> First appeared in *The Nation*, November 6, 1920, and in *The Dial*, November 1920.

A Prayer for my Daughter. Dated June, 1919.
> First appeared in *The Irish Statesman*, November 8, 1919, and in *Poetry* (Chicago), November 1919.

A Meditation in Time of War
> First appeared, under the title *A Mediation* [sic] *in Time of War*, in *The Dial* (New York), November 1920, and in *The Nation*, November 13, 1920.

To be Carved on a Stone at Ballylee
Notes: An Image from a Past Life; The Second Coming.

128

SELECTED POEMS | BY | WILLIAM BUTLER YEATS | NEW YORK | THE MACMILLAN COMPANY | 1921 | ALL RIGHTS RESERVED

$7\frac{1}{2} \times 5$; pp. viii, 310: comprising half-title, list of books By William Butler Yeats inside panel on verso, pp. [i–ii]; title, copyright notices and imprint, Printed in the United States of America Ferris Printing Company New York City on verso, pp. [iii–iv]; contents, pp. [v–viii]; fly-title, verso blank, pp. [1–2]; text, pp. 3–308; pp. [309–310] blank. Frontispiece portrait from a charcoal drawing by John S. Sargent, R.A.

Issued in grey-green cloth with design by Sturge Moore in black on front cover, lettering in black on spine; pale grey end-papers, lined white; all edges trimmed.

Also issued in grey paper boards, with design by Sturge Moore and lettering in black on front cover, design and lettering in black on spine. Published on June 28, 1921.

Contents

Early Poems (1885–1892) 13 poems.
The Land of Heart's Desire (1894, revised 1911).

The Countess Cathleen (1893, revised 1911).
Lyrics (1892–1899) 22 poems.
The Old Age of Queen Maeve (1903).
Baile and Aillinn (1903).
Lyrics (1899–1904) 9 poems.
On Baile's Strand (1904).
Deirdre
Lyrics (1904–1919) 37 poems.
Notes

Roth lists an edition of *Selected Poems*, 1904, of which he gives the collation, and adds that the book was reprinted with new material in 1919 and 1921. (Roth No. 89. An asterisk precedes the number, indicating that he was not able to see a copy of the book but had to rely on other sources.) The Macmillan Company of New York have been good enough to inform me that there was no edition of the book either in 1904 or in 1919, and that the edition of 1921, described above, is the only edition of the book that they have issued. They suggest that the mistake occurred through a misunderstanding of the copyright page where the earlier dates appear; these dates are those on which material included in *Selected Poems* had previously been published and copyrighted in some other form.

129

FOUR PLAYS | FOR DANCERS | BY | W. B. YEATS | MACMILLAN AND CO., LIMITED | ST. MARTIN'S STREET, LONDON | 1921

$8\frac{3}{5} \times 6\frac{3}{5}$; pp. xii, 140: comprising half-title, Macmillan's monogram and addresses on verso, pp. [i–ii]; title, copyright notice on verso, pp. [iii–iv]; Preface, pp. v–vii; p. [viii] blank; contents, verso blank, pp. ix–[x]; list of Illustrations, verso blank, pp. xi–[xii]; fly-title, verso blank, pp. 1–[2]; text, pp. 3–138; imprint, R. & R. Clark, Limited, Edinburgh, at foot of p. 138; list of Works by William Butler Yeats, in panel, p. [139]; p. [140] blank. Frontispiece and illustrations on pp. 4, 7, 9, 10, 12 and 15 by Edmund Dulac.

Issued in decorated grey paper boards printed in black with black cloth spine; design by Sturge Moore, signed T.S.M. Del[ineavit] on front cover, grey label with black lettering on spine; white end-papers; all edges trimmed. Published on October 28, 1921; the edition consisted of 1500 copies.

Contents

Preface. Dated July 1920
At the Hawk's Well
The Only Jealousy of Emer
The Dreaming of the Bones
Calvary
Note on the First Performance of "At the Hawk's Well." Dated 1916.
Music for "At the Hawk's Well." By Edmond [*sic*] Dulac.
   This is preceded by *A Note on the Instruments.*
Note on "The Only Jealousy of Emer"
Music for "The Dreaming of the Bones" by Walter Morse Rummel.
   This is preceded by a note signed W.M.R. The music is dated
   Paris, September 1917.
Note on "The Dreaming of the Bones"
Note on "Calvary"

130

AMERICAN EDITION

FOUR PLAYS | FOR DANCERS | BY | W. B. YEATS |
NEW YORK | THE MACMILLAN COMPANY | 1921 | ALL RIGHTS
RESERVED

$7\frac{11}{16} \times 5\frac{7}{16}$; pp. 2, xii, 142: comprising 2 pp. not included in pagination; half-title, Macmillan's monogram and addresses on verso, pp.
[i–ii]; title, copyright notice and, at foot of page, imprint, Ferris
Printing Company New York, on verso, pp. [iii–iv]; Preface, pp.
v–vii; p. [viii] blank; Contents, verso blank, pp. ix–[x]; list of Illustrations, verso blank, pp. xi–[xii]; fly-title, verso blank, p. [1–2]; text,
notes and music, pp. 3–138; pp. [139–142] blank. Frontispiece and
illustrations as in English edition.

Issued in grey cloth printed with black design, signed T.S.M. Del., on
front cover. Published on October 28, 1921.

The contents are the same as those of the English edition. (No. 129.)

131

FOUR YEARS | BY | WILLIAM BUTLER YEATS. | [woodcut,
in red, of eagle attacking small bird, by Sturge Moore] |
THE CUALA PRESS | CHURCHTOWN | DUNDRUM | MCMXXI

$8\frac{3}{8} \times 5\frac{7}{10}$; pp. viii, 96: comprising pp. [i–iv] blank; title, verso blank, pp. [v–vi]; pp. [vii–viii] blank; text, pp. [1]–[92]; colophon, in red, on p. [92]; pp. [93–96] blank.

Issued in blue paper boards with buff linen spine; lettered in black on front cover, white paper label, printed in black, on spine; blue end-papers matching binding; all edges untrimmed.

400 copies printed on paper made in Ireland and published by Elizabeth C. Yeats at the Cuala Press, Churchtown, Dundrum. Finished on All Hallows' Eve, 1921. Published in December 1921.

Contents

Four Years 1887–1891
> First appeared in *The London Mercury* and in *The Dial*, June, July and August 1921.

132

SEVEN POEMS AND A FRAGMENT | BY WILLIAM BUTLER YEATS. | [woodcut, *in red*, of candle among waves as in No. 127] | THE CUALA PRESS | DUNDRUM | MCMXXII

$8\frac{3}{8} \times 5\frac{7}{10}$; pp. xii, 32: comprising pp. [i–vi] blank; title, verso blank, pp. [vii–viii]; p. [ix] blank; table of contents, p. [x]; pp. [xi–xii] blank; text, pp. [1]–24; colophon, in red, p. [25]; pp. [26–32] blank. The general title is printed in red at top of p. [1].

Issued in grey paper boards with buff linen spine; lettered in black on front cover; no label on spine; grey end-papers matching binding; all edges untrimmed.

500 copies printed on paper made in Ireland and published by Elizabeth Corbet Yeats at the Cuala Press, Churchtown, Dundrum. Finished in the third week of April 1922. Published in June 1922.

Contents

All Souls' Night
> First appeared in *The London Mercury*, March 1921 and in *The New Republic*, March 9, 1921.

Suggested by a Picture of a Black Centaur
Thoughts upon the Present State of the World
> First appeared in *The Dial*, September 1921, and in *The London Mercury*, November 1921.

The New Faces

A Prayer for my Son
Cuchulain the Girl and the Fool
The Wheel
A New End for 'The King's Threshold'
Note on 'Thoughts upon the Present State of the World,' Section Six
Note on The New End to 'The King's Threshold'

133

THE TREMBLING | OF THE VEIL | BY | W. B. YEATS |
LONDON | PRIVATELY PRINTED FOR SUBSCRIBERS ONLY BY |
T. WERNER LAURIE, LTD. | 1922

$8\frac{7}{10} \times 5\frac{1}{2}$; pp. 2, viii, 248: comprising half-title with list of privately printed books on verso, not included in pagination; title, dedication and notice of printing on verso, pp. [i–ii]; fly-title and notice of limitation, number of copy marked by stamping machine, and signed by the author, verso blank, pp. [iii–iv]; Preface, verso blank, pp. v–[vi]; contents, verso blank, pp. vii–[viii]; fly-title, verso blank, pp. [1–2]; text, pp. 3–247; imprint, Printed in Great Britain by The Dunedin Press Limited, Edinburgh, p. [248]. Frontispiece portrait by Charles Shannon, the same as that in the Collected Works, 1908, Volume III, is protected by a thin paper guard bearing on verso the words William Butler Yeats from a picture by Charles Shannon, in green.

Issued in light blue paper boards with cream parchment half-binding; paper label, lettered in brown, on spine; blue end-papers matching binding; all edges untrimmed.

1000 copies on hand-made paper, signed by the author, issued to subscribers in October 1922.

Contents

Preface. Dated May 1922.
Book I. *Four Years 1887–1891*
     Previously published by the Cuala Press, 1921. (No. 131.)
Book II. *Ireland after the Fall of Parnell*
Book III. *Hodos Camelionis* [sic]
Book IV. *The Tragic Generation*
Book V. *The Stirring of the Bones*

> *Ireland after the Fall of Parnell* and parts of *Hodos Camelionis* and of *The Tragic Generation* first appeared, under the title *More Memories* in *The London Mercury*, May to August 1922, and in *The Dial*, May to October 1922. A passage in *The Tragic*

Generation is taken from the essay *Verlaine in 1894* which appeared in *The Savoy*, April 1896.

134

LATER POEMS | BY | W. B. YEATS | MACMILLAN AND CO., LIMITED | ST. MARTIN'S STREET, LONDON | 1922

$7\frac{3}{8} \times 5$; pp. 2, xiv, 368: comprising two blank pages not included in pagination; half-title, Macmillan's monogram and addresses on verso, pp. [i–ii]; title, copyright notice and place of printing on verso, pp. [iii–iv]; Preface, verso blank, pp. v–[vi]; contents, pp. vii–xiii; p. [xiv] blank; fly-title, verso blank, pp. 1–[2]; text, pp. 3–363; imprint, Printed in Great Britain by R. & R. Clark, Limited, Edinburgh, at foot of p. 363; p. [364] blank; list of Works by William Butler Yeats in panel, p. [365]; pp. [366–368] blank.

Issued in light green cloth with design (by Charles Ricketts) stamped blind on front cover and on spine, lettered in gold on spine; white end-papers with design of unicorn etc. in black inside front and back covers; all edges untrimmed.

1500 copies published on November 3, 1922.

Contents

Preface. Dated May 1922.

The Wind Among the Reeds (1899)
>   37 poems, including *The Fiddler of Dooney* and *The Song of the Old Mother*, which had been moved to another section in the *Collected Works*, 1908, but are now replaced.

The Old Age of Queen Maeve (1903)

Baile and Aillinn (1903)

In the Seven Woods (1904). 14 poems.

The Shadowy Waters (1906)
>   Including the two introductory poems; this is the poetical version of the play.

From *The Green Helmet and other Poems* (1912). 21 poems.

Responsibilities (1914). 32 poems.
>   *The Well and the Tree*, printed in *Responsibilities*, 1916 (No. 115) is omitted as it forms part of the play *At the Hawk's Well*.

The Wild Swans at Coole (1919). 46 poems.

Michael Robartes and the Dancer (1921). 15 poems.

Notes
>   The notes are taken from *The Wind Among the Reeds*, 1899; from *Poems, 1899–1905*, 1906; from *Responsibilities*, 1914, with

omissions and a new paragraph dated January 1917; from *The Wild Swans at Coole*, 1919. There are four new notes dated 1922.

This forms the first volume of Macmillan's *Collected Edition of the Works*.

This volume was also issued in the *Cardinal Series*, bound in crimson écrasé morocco.

There were further impressions in December 1922, February 1924, March 1926 and March 1931.

135

AMERICAN EDITION

LATER POEMS | BY | W. B. YEATS | NEW YORK | THE MACMILLAN COMPANY | 1924 | ALL RIGHTS RESERVED

$7\frac{3}{5} \times 5$; pp. xvi, 368: comprising half-title, Macmillan's monogram and addresses on verso, pp. [i–ii]; title, copyright notices and imprint, Printed in the United States of America on verso, pp. [iii–iv]; Preface, verso blank, pp. [v–vi]; contents, pp. vii–xiii; p. [xiv] blank; half-title, verso blank, pp. [xv–xvi]; fly-title, verso blank, pp. [1–2]; text, pp. 3–363; pp. [364–368] blank.

Issued in similar style and binding to the English edition except that lettering on spine is LATER POEMS | [*short rule*] | W. B. YEATS and the top and bottom edges are trimmed.

Published on April 8, 1924. Colonel Alspach's copy, however, reads "Published March, 1924."

There was a further impression in August 1928.

LIMITED EDITION

Issued in brown paper boards with blue cloth spine, labels, printed in black, on front cover and on spine.

"Of this edition of *Later Poems* 250 copies have been printed, of which this is Number . . ." Signed by the Author.

Published on September 16, 1924.

The contents of both volumes are the same as those of the English edition.

136

PLAYS IN | PROSE AND VERSE | WRITTEN FOR AN IRISH THEATRE, | AND GENERALLY WITH THE HELP OF A FRIEND | BY | W. B. YEATS | MACMILLAN AND CO., LIMITED | ST. MARTIN'S STREET, LONDON | 1922

$7\frac{3}{5} \times 5$; pp. 2, x, 452: comprising two pages not counted in pagination; half-title, Macmillan's monogram and addresses on verso, pp. [i–ii]; title, notice of copyright and place of printing on verso, pp. [iii–iv]; Preface, pp. v–vii; p. [viii] blank; contents, verso blank, pp. ix–[x]; fly-title, persons in the play on verso, pp. 1–2; text, pp. 3–435; p. [436] blank; music, pp. 437–447; imprint, Printed in Great Britain by R. & R. Clark, Limited, Edinburgh, at foot of p. 447; p. [448] blank; list of Works by William Butler Yeats, p. [449]; pp. [450–452] blank.

Issued in uniform binding with *Later Poems* (No. 134) and with uniform decorated end-papers; all edges untrimmed. Spine lettered PLAYS | BY | W. B. YEATS.

1500 copies published on November 3, 1922.

Contents

Preface. Dated May 1, 1922.
Cathleen ni Houlihan
The Pot of Broth
The Hour-Glass (in Prose)
The King's Threshold
On Baile's Strand
The Shadowy Waters (Acting version)
Deirdre
The Unicorn from the Stars (in collaboration with Lady Gregory)
The Green Helmet
The Hour-Glass (in Verse)
The Player Queen
Notes
> Some of the notes are taken from *Plays for an Irish Theatre*, 1911; others are new and are dated 1922.

The Music for Use in the Performance of these Plays. Dated May 1, 1922.
> Music by Florence Farr, Sara Allgood, and from Irish Traditional Airs.

This forms the second volume of Macmillan's *Collected Edition of the Works.*

The volume was also issued in the *Cardinal Series*, bound in crimson écrasé morocco.

There were further impressions in December 1922, October 1926 and December 1930.

137

PLAYS IN | PROSE AND VERSE | WRITTEN FOR AN
IRISH THEATRE, | AND GENERALLY WITH THE | HELP OF A
FRIEND | BY | W. B. YEATS | NEW YORK | THE MACMILLAN
COMPANY | 1924 | ALL RIGHTS RESERVED

$7\frac{3}{5} \times 5$; pp. x, 460: comprising half-title, Macmillan's monogram and
addresses on verso, pp. [i–ii]; title, copyright notices and imprint,
Printed in the United States of America on verso, pp. [iii–iv]; Preface,
pp. v–vii; p. [viii] blank; contents, verso blank, pp. [ix–x]; fly-title,
persons in the play on verso, pp. [1–2]; text, pp. 3–438; music for
plays, pp. [439]–455; pp. [456–460] blank.

Issued in similar style and binding to the English edition except that
lettering on spine is PLAYS | IN PROSE | AND | VERSE | [*short rule*] | W. B.
YEATS and the top and bottom edges are trimmed.

Published on April 8, 1924. A second impression in 1928 differs
slightly in pagination from the first impression.

Issued in brown paper boards with blue cloth spine, labels, printed in
black, on front cover and on spine.

"Of this edition of *Plays in Prose and Verse* two hundred fifty
copies have been printed, of which this is Number . . ." Signed by
the Author.

Published on September 16, 1924. Colonel Alspach's copy, however,
reads "Published March, 1924."

The contents of these volumes are the same as those of the English
edition (No. 136).

138

THE | PLAYER QUEEN | BY | W. B. YEATS | MACMILLAN
AND CO., LIMITED | ST. MARTIN'S STREET, LONDON | 1922

$7\frac{1}{5} \times 5$; pp. iv, 64: comprising pp. [i–iv] blank; half-title, notice to
amateurs on verso, pp. [1–2]; title, notice of copyright and place of
printing on verso, pp. [3–4]; fly-title, Persons in the Play on verso,
pp. [5]–6; text, pp. 7–57; p. [58] blank; note, p. 59; imprint, Printed
in Great Britain by R. & R. Clark, Limited, Edinburgh, on p. [60];
pp. [61–64] blank.

Issued in white paper covers; lettered in green on front cover, title and author's name inside panel formed by green rules, price printed outside panel at foot of cover, lettered also in green on spine; all edges trimmed. Published on November 21, 1922; the edition consisted of 1000 copies.

Contents

The Player Queen
> The play was also printed in *The Dial*, November 1922.

Note. Dated 1922.

139

PLAYS | AND | CONTROVERSIES | BY | W. B. YEATS | MACMILLAN AND CO., LIMITED | ST. MARTIN'S STREET, LONDON | 1923

$7\frac{3}{8} \times 5$; pp. 2, x, 464: comprising two pages not counted in pagination; half-title, Macmillan's monogram and addresses on verso, pp. [i–ii]; title, notice of copyright and place of printing on verso, pp. [iii–iv]; Preface, pp. v–vi; contents, verso blank, pp. vii–[viii]; Illustrations, verso blank, pp. ix–[x]; fly-title, verso blank, pp. 1–[2]; text, pp. 3–461; imprint, Printed in Great Britain by R. & R. Clark, Limited, Edinburgh, at foot of p. 461; p. [462] blank; list of Works by W. B. Yeats, p. [463]; p. [464] blank. The frontispiece portrait of the author from a charcoal drawing by John S. Sargent, R.A. is that used in Volume I. of the Collected Works, 1908 (No. 75). There are seven illustrations to *At the Hawk's Well* by Edmund Dulac; these face pp. 335, 338, 340, 342, 344, 346 and 348.

Issued in uniform binding with *Later Poems* (No. 134) and with uniform decorated end-papers; all edges untrimmed.

1960 copies published on November 27, 1923.

Contents

Preface. Dated February 1923.
The Irish Dramatic Movement
> There are new footnotes, dated 1923, on pp. 67, 73, 83 and 171.

> At the end of the essays follows:

A People's Theatre, A letter to Lady Gregory.
> First appeared in *The Irish Statesman*, November 29 and December 6, 1919, and later in *The Dial*, April 1920.

> There are new footnotes, dated 1923, on pp. 199 and 214.

The Countess Cathleen

Note on "The Countess Cathleen"
Preface to "The Land of Heart's Desire", dated March 10.
The Land of Heart's Desire
Note. Dated 1912 with an addition dated 1923.
Four Plays for Dancers: Preface.

> *At the Hawk's Well*
> *The Only Jealousy of Emer*
> *The Dreaming of the Bones*
> *Calvary*

Note on the first performance of "At the Hawk's Well"
Note and Music for "At the Hawk's Well" by Edmund Dulac
Note on "The Only Jealousy of Emer"
Note and Music for "The Dreaming of the Bones" by Walter Morse
Rummel.
Note on "The Dreaming of the Bones"
Note on "Calvary"

This forms the third volume of Macmillan's *Collected Edition of the Works*.

There was a further impression in January 1927.

140

AMERICAN EDITION

PLAYS | AND | CONTROVERSIES | BY | W. B. YEATS |
NEW YORK | THE MACMILLAN COMPANY | 1924 | ALL RIGHTS
RESERVED

Issued in similar style and binding to the English edition. On the
verso of title is copyright notice and Printed in the United States of
America.

Published on September 16, 1924.

LIMITED EDITION

Issued in brown paper boards with blue cloth spine, labels, printed in
black, on front cover and on spine.

"Of this edition of *Plays and Controversies* 250 copies have been
printed, of which this is Number . . ." Signed by the Author.

Published on September 16, 1924.

The contents of these volumes are the same as those of the English
edition (No. 139).

141

ESSAYS | BY | W. B. YEATS | MACMILLAN AND CO., LIMITED |
ST MARTIN'S STREET, LONDON | 1924

$7\frac{1}{2} \times 5$; pp. viii, 540: comprising half-title, Macmillan's monogram
and addresses on verso, pp. [i–ii]; title, copyright notice and place of
printing on verso, pp. [iii–iv]; dedication, verso blank, pp. [v–vi];
contents, pp. vii–[viii]; fly-title, verso blank, pp. 1–[2]; text, pp.
3–538; imprint, Printed in Great Britain by R. & R. Clark, Limited,
Edinburgh, at foot of p. 538; p. [539] blank; list of Works by W. B.
Yeats, p. [540].

Issued in uniform binding with *Later Poems* (No. 134) and with uniform decorated end-papers; all edges untrimmed. 2240 copies published on May 6, 1924.

Contents

Dedication "*To Lennox Robinson*". Dated November 26, 1923.

I. *Ideas of Good and Evil* (1896–1903)
   The essay *Speaking to the Psaltery* has two additional sections:
   iv. *Poems for the Psaltery.* Dated 1907.
      This is the note *Music for Lyrics* from the *Collected
      Edition* of 1908, Volume III (No. 77), rearranged and
      slightly abbreviated.
   v. *Note by Florence Farr upon her Settings*
      This appeared as *Note by Florence Farr* in the *Collected
      Edition* of 1908, Volume III.

   The essay is followed by five pages of music for lyrics.
   The essays on William Blake have a postscript, dated 1924.
   There are additional footnotes, dated 1924, on pp. 59, 114, 187,
   210, 223, 228 and 257.

II. *The Cutting of an Agate* (1903–1915)
   This section follows the English edition of 1919 (No. 126), but
   includes a new essay:
   Art and Ideas
      First appeared in *The New Weekly*, June 20 and 27, 1914.
   There are additional footnotes, dated 1924, on pp. 432 and 444.

III. *Per Amica Silentia Lunae* (1916–1917)
   There is an additional footnote, dated February 1924, on p. 498,
   and others, dated 1924, on pp. 514 and 523.

This forms the fourth volume of Macmillan's *Collected Edition of the Works*.

142

AMERICAN EDITION

ESSAYS | BY | W. B. YEATS | NEW YORK | THE MACMILLAN COMPANY | 1924 | ALL RIGHTS RESERVED

Issued in similar style and binding to the English edition. On the verso of title is Printed in the United States of America by the Berwick & Smith Co.

A variant binding is in light bluish-green cloth, lettering on spine in black, and no design stamped on the front cover or spine.

Published on October 14, 1924.

LIMITED EDITION

Issued in brown paper boards with blue cloth spine, labels, printed in black, on front cover and on spine.

"Of this edition of *Essays*, 250 copies have been printed, of which this is Number . . ." Signed by the Author.

Published on October 26, 1924.

The contents of these volumes are the same as those of the English edition.

143

THE LAKE ISLE OF INNISFREE | BY WILLIAM BUTLER YEATS, WITH A FACSIMILE | OF THE POEM IN THE POET'S HANDWRITING, ALSO | AN APPRECIATIVE NOTE BY GEORGE STERLING. | THE MANUSCRIPT IS IN THE BENDER COLLEC- | TION AT MILLS COLLEGE. THE PRINTING WAS | FINISHED IN THE MONTH OF MAY, MCMXXIV

$12\frac{3}{4} \times 9$; pp. 8, unnumbered: comprising title, facsimile of poem on a sheet of note-paper mounted on verso, pp. [1–2]; text of poem, copyright notice on verso, pp. [3–4]; text of note, pp. [5–7]; colophon on p. [8]. On pp. [2]–[7] the text is surrounded by a green ornamental border enclosed within gilt rules.

K

Issued in mottled green cloth, pink label printed in black on spine; white end-papers; top edges trimmed, others untrimmed. Issued in 1924.

The colophon reads:

The Lake Isle of Innisfree printed by John Henry Nash as an expression of his admiration for the Trustees and President of Mills College and presented by him to the members of the graduating class of MCMXXIV. A few additional copies were made for his friends.

144

LES PRIX NOBEL | EN 1923 | [long rule] | THE IRISH | DRAMATIC MOVEMENT | LECTURE DELIVERED TO THE ROYAL ACADEMY | OF SWEDEN | BY | W. B. YEATS | STOCK-HOLM 1924 | IMPRIMERIE ROYALE. P. A. NORSTEDT & FILS | 241553

$9\frac{7}{10} \times 6\frac{3}{5}$; pp. 12: comprising text, pp. 1–11; imprint, Stockholm 1924. P. A. Norstedt & Sönen 241553; p. [12] blank.

Issued in stiff white paper covers, lettered on front cover as above There is no title-page and no end-papers. The pages are fastened with two metal staples; all edges trimmed. Published in 1924.

Contents

The Irish Dramatic Movement
    First appeared, with the four notes, in *Les Prix Nobel en 1923* Stockholm, 1924. (No. 316.)
Notes
    These are numbered 1 to 4.

145

THE CAT AND THE MOON AND | CERTAIN POEMS: BY WILLIAM | BUTLER YEATS. | [woodcut as in No. 72] | THE CUALA PRESS | MERRION SQUARE | DUBLIN IRELAND | MCMXXIV

$8\frac{3}{10} \times 5\frac{7}{10}$; pp. xvi, 48: comprising pp. [i–viii] blank; title, verso blank, pp. [ix–x]; Preface, pp. [xi–xii]; contents [heading in red], verso blank, pp. [xiii–xiv]; pp. [xv–xvi] blank; text, pp. [1]–41; p. [42] blank; colophon, in red, p. [43]; pp. [44–48] blank.

THE ARROW.

~~All the livelong day~~ I thought of your beauty and this arrow.
Made out of a wild thought is in my marrow,
There's no man may look upon her, no man,
As when newly grown to be a woman
Blossom pale she pulled down the ~~full~~ blossom
At the moth hour and hid it in her bosom
This beauty's ~~tender~~ yet for a reason
I could weep that the old is out of season.

Proof of poem from *In The Seven Woods* 1903, (No 49) showing Yeats's corrections.

(*All find safety in the tomb*)
May call ~~a curse out of the sky~~ *down curses on his head*/
~~Ere the one or t'other die,~~ *Because of my dear Jack that's dead*/
~~None so old as he and I~~ *Cockscomb was the last he said:*
The solid man and the cockscomb.

~~Seyme by that oak, for she~~
~~That had my virginity,~~
(*All find safety in the tomb*)
Wanders out into the night
And there is shelter under it,
But should that other come, I spit:
The solid man and the cockscomb.

Proofs of two verses of *Crazy Jane and the Bishop* showing publisher's queries and Yeats's corrections (*circa* 1931).

Issued in blue paper boards with buff linen spine, lettered in black on front cover, white label, printed in black, on spine; blue end-papers matching binding; all edges untrimmed.

500 copies printed on paper made in Ireland and published by Elizabeth Corbet Yeats at the Cuala Press, Merrion Square, Dublin Finished on May 1, 1924. Published in July 1924.

Contents

Preface. To Lady Gregory. Dated 25th. February, 1924.

The Cat and the Moon. Dated 1917.
> First appeared in *The Criterion*, July 1924, and in *The Dial*, July 1924.
> The poem *The cat went here and there* had appeared in *Nine Poems*, 1918 (No. 122), and in *The Wild Swans at Coole*, 1919 (No. 124).

Youth and Age. Dated 1924.

Leda and the Swan. Dated 1923.
> First appeared in *The Dial*, June 1924, and in *To-Morrow* (Dublin), August 1924.

Meditations in time of Civil War
>   I. *Ancestral Houses*
>   II. *My House*
> III. *My Table*
> IV. *My Descendants*
>   V. *The Road at My Door*
> VI. *The Stare's Nest at My Window*
> VII. *I see Phantoms of Hatred and of the Heart's Fullness and of the Coming Emptiness*
> First appeared in *The London Mercury*, and in *The Dial*, January 1923. In *The Dial* the vith poem had the title *The Jay's Nest by my Window*.

The Gift of Harun-Al-Rashid. Dated 1923.
> First appeared, under the title *The Gift of Haroun El Rashid*, in *English Life and The Illustrated Review*, January 1924; then in *The Dial*, June 1924.

The Lover Speaks
> First appeared in *The Dial*, June 1924.

The Heart Replies
> First appeared in *The Dial*, June 1924.

Notes

146

THE BOUNTY OF SWEDEN: | A MEDITATION, AND A
LECTURE | DELIVERED BEFORE THE ROYAL | SWEDISH ACADEMY
AND CERTAIN | NOTES BY WILLIAM BUTLER YEATS. | [woodcut,
in red, as in No. 131] | THE CUALA PRESS | DUBLIN, IRELAND |
MCMXXV

$8\frac{3}{10} \times 5\frac{3}{4}$; pp. viii, 60: comprising pp. [i–iv] blank; title, verso blank,
pp. [v–vi]; Preface, verso blank, pp [vii–viii]; text, pp. [1]–[54];
colophon, in red, p. [55]; pp. [56–60] blank. The heading of the essay
on p. [1] printed in red.

Issued in blue paper boards with buff linen spine, lettered in black on
front cover, white paper label, printed in black, on spine; blue end-
papers matching binding; all edges untrimmed.

400 copies printed on paper made in Ireland and published by Elizabeth
Corbet Yeats at the Cuala Press, 133 Lower Baggot Street, Dublin.
Finished on the last day of May 1925. Published in July 1925.

Contents

Preface. Dated June 15th. 1924.
The Bounty of Sweden. A Meditation.
　　First appeared in *The London Mercury* and in *The Dial*, Septem-
　　ber 1924.
The Irish Dramatic Movement
　　First appeared in *Les Prix Nobel en 1923*, Stockholm, 1924 (No.
　　316); also issued separately in 1924. (No. 144.)
Notes
　　There are six notes. The first and sixth are new; the others
　　appeared in the Stockholm editions of the lecture. The sixth is
　　dated June 15th. 1924.

147

EARLY POEMS | AND | STORIES | BY | W. B. YEATS |
MACMILLAN AND CO., LIMITED | ST. MARTIN'S STREET, LON-
DON | 1925

$7\frac{1}{2} \times 5$; pp. 2, x, 532: comprising 2 pp. not included in pagination;
half-title, Macmillan's monogram and addresses on verso, pp. [i–ii];

title-page, notice of copyright and place of printing on verso, pp. [iii–iv]; Dedication, pp. v–vi; contents, pp. vii–x; fly-title, quotation on verso, pp. 1–2; dedication, verso blank, pp. 3–[4]; text, pp. 5–528; imprint, Printed in Great Britain by R. & R. Clark, Limited, Edinburgh, below rule at foot of p. 528; list of The Collected Works of W. B. Yeats, p. [529]; list of books By W. B. Yeats, p. [530]; pp. [531–532] blank.

Issued in uniform binding with *Later Poems* (No. 134) and with uniform decorated end-papers; all edges untrimmed. 2908 copies published on September 22, 1925.

Contents

Dedication (to Richard Ashe King). Dated May 1925.

The Wanderings of Usheen (1889)

Crossways (1889)

 16 poems. *The Ballad of Father Gilligan, The Lamentation of the Old Pensioner*, and *The Dedication to a Book of Stories* are now returned to the section *The Rose.*

The Rose (1893)

 22 poems. Of those mentioned above as returned to this section two have been largely rewritten and *The Dedication to a Book of Stories* first appeared, in its new version, under the title *An Old Poem Re-Written*, in *The Irish Statesman*, November 8, 1924.

 The Fiddler of Dooney and *The Song of the Old Mother* now appear in *Later Poems* (No. 134).

 The poem *To some I have talked with by the fire* is omitted.

The Celtic Twilight (1893)

 This section reprints the text of the edition of 1902; but the preliminary poems and the preface *This Book* are omitted. Also paragraphs or sentences have been left out of the following: *A Teller of Tales; Belief and Unbelief; A Visionary; Village Ghosts; A Knight of the Sheep; The Sorcerers; The Last Gleeman; Regina, Regina Pigmeorum, Veni; Miraculous Creatures; A Voice; Kidnappers; The Untiring Ones; A Coward; Drumcliffe and Rosses; Our Lady of the Hills; The Golden Age; A Remonstrance with Scotsmen.*

 There are new footnotes, dated 1924, on pp. 159, 201, 203, 228 and 293.

The Secret Rose (1897)

 Preliminary poem and 7 stories. *Where there is nothing there is God* is now omitted.

Stories of Red Hanrahan (1897, rewritten in 1907 with Lady Gregory's help).

Six stories.

Rosa Alchemica, The Tables of the Law and *The Adoration of the Magi.*
Note

This note is new, and mentions various alterations made in the text of the book.

This forms the fifth volume of Macmillan's *Collected Edition of the Works.*

148

AMERICAN EDITION

EARLY POEMS | AND | STORIES | BY | W. B. YEATS |
NEW YORK | THE MACMILLAN COMPANY | 1925 | ALL RIGHTS
RESERVED

Issued in similar style and binding to the English edition. On the verso of title is Printed in the United States of America by the Berwick & Smith Co. There is no list of books by W. B. Yeats at the end.

A variant binding is in light bluish-green cloth, lettering on the spine in black, and no design stamped on the front cover or spine.

Published on November 17, 1925.

LIMITED EDITION

Issued in brown paper boards with blue cloth spine, labels, printed in black, on front cover and on spine.

"Of this edition of *Early Poems and Stories* two hundred fifty copies have been printed, of which this is Number . . ." Signed by the Author.

Published on September 22, 1925.

The contents of these volumes are the same as those of the English edition.

149

A VISION | AN EXPLANATION OF LIFE | FOUNDED UPON THE
WRITINGS | OF GIRALDUS AND UPON CER- | TAIN DOCTRINES
ATTRIBUTED | TO KUSTA BEN LUKA | BY | WILLIAM | BUTLER |
YEATS | LONDON | PRIVATELY PRINTED FOR SUBSCRIBERS
ONLY BY | T. WERNER LAURIE, LTD. | 1925

$8\frac{7}{10} \times 5\frac{1}{2}$; pp. xxiv + ii, 256 + 2: comprising p. [i] blank; list of Privately Printed Books, p. [ii]; half-title, verso blank, pp. [iii–iv]; title, acknowledgement and, at foot of page, beneath rule, Printed in Great Britain by The Dunedin Press, Limited, Edinburgh, on verso, pp. [v–vi]; inserted leaf bearing notice of limitation, number of copy marked by stamping machine, and author's signature, verso blank, unnumbered; contents, verso blank, pp. vii–[viii]; Dedication, pp. ix–xiii; p. [xiv] blank; Introduction, pp. xv–xxiii; p. [xxiv] blank; fly-title, verso blank, pp. [1–2]; text, pp. 3–178; interpolated leaf, design in red and black on recto, verso blank, unnumbered; text, pp. 179–256.

Frontispiece, a woodcut portrait of Giraldus, printed on brown paper; woodcut design *The Great Wheel* printed on brown paper facing p. xv; small woodcut design of unicorn, printed on brown paper and pasted on at foot of p. 8. [These are by Edmund Dulac.]

Issued in pale blue paper boards with parchment half-binding; white paper label, printed in brown, on spine; pale blue end-papers matching binding; all edges untrimmed.

600 copies, numbered, and signed by the author, issued to subscribers on January 15, 1926.

Contents

Dedication. To Vestigia. Dated February 1925.
Introduction. By Owen Aherne. Dated May 1925.
Book I. *What the Caliph Partly Learned*
    1. Poem. *The Wheel and the Phases of the Moon.*
        Already printed as *The Phases of the Moon*, in *The Wild Swans at Coole*, 1919 (No. 124), and in *Later Poems*, 1922. (No. 134.)
    2. *The Dance of the Four Royal Personages.* By Owen Aherne. Dated May 1925.
    3. *The Great Wheel*
    4. *The Twenty-Eight Embodiments*
        "Finished at Thoor Ballylee, 1922, in a time of Civil War."
Book II. *What the Caliph Refused to Learn*
    1. Poem. *Desert Geometry or The Gift of Harun Al-Raschid.* Dated 1923.
        Previously printed, under the title *The Gift of Harun-al-Rashid*, in *The Cat and the Moon*, 1924 (No. 145).
    2. *The Geometrical Foundation of the Wheel*

Book III. *Dove or Swan*
  1. Poem. *Leda.*
      Previously printed in *The Cat and the Moon*, 1924. (No.
      145.)
  2. *The Great Wheel and History.*
      Finished at Capri, February 1925.
Book IV. *The Gates of Pluto*
  1. Poem. *The Fool by the Roadside.*
      First appeared as the final lyric in *Cuchulain the Girl and the
      Fool* in *Seven Poems and a Fragment*, 1922. (No. 132.)
  2. *The Great Wheel and From Death to Birth*
      Finished at Syracuse, January 1925.
  3. Poem. *All Souls' Night.* Dated Oxford, Autumn 1920.
      Reprinted from *Seven Poems and a Fragment*, 1922. (No.
      132.)

For the revised edition of *A Vision* see no. 191.

150

ESTRANGEMENT: BEING SOME FIFTY | THOUGHTS FROM
A DIARY KEPT BY | WILLIAM BUTLER YEATS IN THE YEAR |
NINETEEN HUNDRED AND NINE. | [woodcut, *in red*, as in No.
131] | THE CUALA PRESS | DUBLIN, IRELAND | MCMXXVI

$8\frac{3}{10} \times 5\frac{3}{4}$; pp. viii, 48: comprising pp. [i–iv] blank; title, verso blank,
pp. [v–vi]; pp. [vii–viii] blank; text, pp. [1]–[40]; colophon, in red,
on p. [40]; pp. [41–48] blank.

Issued in blue paper boards with buff linen spine; lettered in black on
front cover, white paper label, printed in black, on spine; blue end-
papers matching binding; all edges untrimmed.

300 copies printed on paper made in Ireland and published by Elizabeth
Corbet Yeats at the Cuala Press, 133 Lower Baggot Street, Dublin.
Finished in the second week of June 1926. Published in August 1926.

Contents

Estrangement
    Also appeared, under the title *Estrangement: Thoughts from a
    Diary kept in 1909*, in *The London Mercury*, October and
    November 1926, and under the title *Estrangement: Being some
    Fifty Thoughts from a Diary*, in *The Dial*, November 1926.

    Chapters I, II and V had previously appeared as Chapters II,
    I and III of *The Folly of Argument* in *The Manchester Playgoer*,
    June 1911.

151

AUTOBIOGRAPHIES: | REVERIES OVER CHILDHOOD | AND YOUTH AND THE | TREMBLING OF THE VEIL | BY | W. B. YEATS | MACMILLAN AND CO., LIMITED | ST. MARTIN'S STREET, LONDON | 1926

$7\frac{2}{5} \times 5$; pp. viii, 480: comprising half-title, Macmillan's monogram and addresses on verso, pp. [i–ii]; title, notice of copyright and imprint, Printed in Great Britain by R. & R. Clark, Limited, Edinburgh, on verso, pp. [iii–iv]; Contents, verso blank, pp. v–[vi]; list of Illustrations, verso blank, pp. vii–[viii]; fly-title, dedication on verso, pp. 1–2; Preface, verso blank, pp. 3–4; text, pp. 5–477; imprint, Printed in Great Britain by R. & R. Clark, Limited, Edinburgh, at foot of p. 477; p. [478] blank; list of The Collected Works of W. B. Yeats, p. [479]; list of books By W. B. Yeats, p. [480]. Frontispiece of the author, age 21, From a drawing by his Father; illustrations facing pp. 18, 38, 142 and 446.

Issued in similar binding to that of *Later Poems*, 1922 (No. 134), and with similar decorated end-papers; all edges untrimmed. 2820 copies published on November 5, 1926.

Contents

Note on "Memory Harbour"
Preface. Dated Christmas Day, 1914.
. *Reveries over Childhood and Youth* (1914)
Preface. Dated May 1922.
II. *The Trembling of the Veil* (1922)
    Book I. *Four Years: 1887–1891*
    Book II. *Ireland after Parnell*
    Book III. *Hodos Chameliontos*
        Chapter VI in this Book is new; the subsequent chapters are renumbered accordingly.
    Book IV. *The Tragic Generation*
    Book V. *The Stirring of the Bones*
        A new opening to Chapter VI of the last section of *The Trembling of the Veil* (p. 456 to half-way down p. 462), first appeared, under the title *A Biographical Fragment*, in *The Criterion*, and in *The Dial*, July 1923.
Notes
    I. *The Hermetic Students*

II. *The Vision of an Archer*

The notes in section II first appeared in *The Criterion*, and in *The Dial*, July 1923.

There are new footnotes, dated 1926, on pp. 101 and 324, and others, undated, on pp. 335 and 340.

This forms the sixth volume of Macmillan's *Collected Edition of the Works*.

152

AMERICAN EDITION

AUTOBIOGRAPHIES: | REVERIES OVER CHILDHOOD | AND YOUTH AND THE | TREMBLING OF THE VEIL | BY | W. B. YEATS | NEW YORK | THE MACMILLAN COMPANY | 1927 | ALL RIGHTS RESERVED

Issued in similar style and binding to the English edition (No. 151) except that lettering on spine is AUTOBIOGRAPHIES: | REVERIES | OVER | CHILDHOOD | AND YOUTH | AND | THE TREMBLING | OF THE VEIL | [*short rule*] | W. B. YEATS. On the verso of title is Printed in the United States of America by the Berwick & Smith Co.

Published on February 8, 1927.

There was a further impression in August 1927.

LIMITED EDITION

Issued in brown paper boards with blue cloth spine, labels, printed in black, on front cover and on spine.

"Of this edition of *Autobiographies* two hundred fifty copies have been printed, of which this is Number . . ." Signed by the Author.

Published on January 25, 1927.

The contents of these volumes are the same as those of the English edition.

153

NEW REVISED EDITION

POEMS | BY | W. B. YEATS | T. FISHER UNWIN LIMITED | (ERNEST BENN LIMITED) | BOUVERIE HOUSE, FLEET STREET, LONDON | 1927

$8 \times 5\frac{1}{4}$; pp. xii, 324.

Issued in blue-green cloth, design and lettering in gold on spine only; white end-papers; top edges stained dark green, other edges trimmed. Published in February 1927.

Contents

(in addition to the revised text of poems)

Preface. Dated January 1927.
Preface to the Seventh Edition. Dated 1912.
    (This is actually the Preface to the Sixth Edition; Yeats seems sometimes to consider the separate volumes of 1889 (No. 2), 1892 (No. 6), and 1894 (No. 10) as the first edition.)
Note on "Crossways." Dated 1925.
    From *Early Poems and Stories*, 1925. (No. 147.)
Note on revisions of some of the lyrics. Dated 1926.

Printed in Great Britain by Unwin Brothers, Limited. London and Woking.

In the Preface, Yeats writes: "The volume contains what is, I hope, the final text of the poems of my youth; and yet it may not be . . . One is always cutting out the dead wood." And again: "Whatever changes I have made are but an attempt to express better what I thought and felt when I was a young man."

154

NEW EDITION

POEMS | BY | W. B. YEATS | LONDON: | ERNEST BENN LIMITED

$8 \times 5\frac{1}{4}$; pp. xii, 324.

Issued in blue-green cloth, lettered in gold on spine; white end-papers; top edges stained green, others trimmed. (The design by Althea Gyles, hitherto used for this collection, is now discarded.) Published on May 10, 1929.

In a copy in his own library, Yeats wrote:

The poems in this book were all written before I was twenty-seven. For many years they were the only poems of mine known to the general public.

    This book for about thirty years brought me twenty or thirty times as much money as any other book of mine—no twenty or thirty times

as much as all my other books put together. This success was pure
accident. Five or six years ago "T. Fisher Unwin" ceased to exist
and it passed to the firm of "Benn" & within twelve months the sales
were halved, & another twelve months fallen to one tenth of what
they had been. Gradually my later work had however grown into a
little popularity. When the poems in this book were first written they
had the merit, hard to discover now, of a novel simplicity. Swinburne
was dominant; the blank verse of "The Countess Cathleen" was less
rhetorical than recent dramatic verse, and it was not yet clearly appar-
ent that, in avoiding rhetoric and complications, I had fallen into
sentimentality.

W. B. Yeats.

155

THE AUGUSTAN BOOKS OF | ENGLISH POETRY |
SECOND SERIES NUMBER FOUR | [rule] | W. B. YEATS | [rule] |
LONDON: ERNEST BENN LTD. | BOUVERIE HOUSE, FLEET
STREET [*The whole enclosed within decorative border*]

$8\frac{1}{2} \times 5\frac{1}{2}$; pp. 32, numbered [i]–iv, 5–[32]: comprising title-page on
cover, list of The Augustan Books in the Second Series and acknow-
ledgement on verso, pp. [i–ii]; Introductory note on W. B. Yeats by
Humbert Wolfe, contents on verso, pp. iii–iv; text, pp. 5–31; list
of authors included in the series and imprint, Printed in Great Britain
by Billing and Sons, Ltd, Guildford and Esher on p. [32].

Issued in white paper covers, stitched; all edges trimmed. Published
in April 1927.

Contents

*The Indian upon God; The Indian to His Love; To an Isle in the Water;
Down by the Salley Gardens; The Rose of the World; The Rose of
Battle; The Lake Isle of Innisfree; The Sorrow of Love; When You are
Old; The Hosting of the Sidhe; The Everlasting Voices; The Moods;
The Lover Tells of the Rose in His Heart; The Fisherman; The Heart of
the Woman; The Lover Mourns for the Loss of Love; He Mourns for
the Change that has come upon Him and His Beloved and Longs for the
End of the World; He Reproves the Curlew; He Remembers Forgotten
Beauty; A Poet to His Beloved; He gives His Beloved Certain Rhymes;
To His Heart, bidding it have no Fear; He Tells of the Perfect Beauty;
He Hears the Cry of the Sedge; He Wishes for the Cloths of Heaven;
The Fiddler of Dooney; In the Seven Woods; The Arrow; The Old Men*

Admiring Themselves in the Water; Dedication to the Shadowy Waters; A Woman Homer Sung; No Second Troy; All Things can Tempt Me; When Helen Lived; Fallen Majesty; The Cold Heaven; That the Night Come; The Wild Swans at Coole; Men Improve with the Years; The Collar-Bone of a Hare; A Song; To a Young Girl; Lines Written in Dejection; Memory; Her Praise; The Saint and the Hunchback; To be Carved on a Stone at Thoor Ballylee.

There were further impressions in January 1928, February 1931, August 1935 and November 1939.

The third and later impressions were issued in stiff red paper covers, imitating linen, lined white, a white label panel printed in black, reading W. B. YEATS on front cover. This cover is still included in the pagination, the text continuing to the inside of back cover; the outside of cover is blank. Messrs. Ernest Benn Ltd. inform me that the change of cover took place "approximately 1930."

156

OCTOBER BLAST | BY | WILLIAM BUTLER YEATS | [woodcut of candle among waves as in No. 127] | THE CUALA PRESS | DUBLIN IRELAND | MCMXXVII

$8\frac{3}{10} \times 5\frac{3}{4}$; pp. viii, 32: comprising pp. [i–iv] blank; title, verso blank, pp. [v–vi]; p. [vii] blank; contents, p. [viii]; text, pp. [1]–[25]; p. [26] blank; colophon, in red, p. [27]; pp. [28–32] blank.

Issued in light blue paper boards with buff linen spine, lettered in black on front cover, white paper label, printed in black, on spine; light blue end-papers matching binding; all edges untrimmed.

350 copies printed on paper made in Ireland and published by Elizabeth Corbet Yeats at the Cuala Press, 133 Lower Baggot Street, Dublin. Finished in the first week of June 1927. Published in August 1927.

Contents

Sailing to Byzantium
    This poem was also printed in *The Exile*, Spring 1928.
The Tower. Dated 1925.
    First appeared in *The Criterion*, June 1927, and in *The New Republic*, June 29, 1927.
Wisdom

Two Songs from a Play
> First appeared, as part of *The Resurrection*, in *The Adelphi*, June 1927.

Among School Children
> First appeared in *The London Mercury*, and in *The Dial*, August 1927.

The Young Countryman. I–IV
> First appeared, under the title *Four Songs from the Young Countryman*, in *The London Mercury*, May 1927.

The Old Countryman. I–VI
> Poems I and V first appeared, under the title *Two Songs from the Old Countryman*, in *The London Mercury*, May 1927; poems II, III, IV and VI first appeared, under the title *More Songs from an Old Countryman*, in *The London Mercury*, April 1926.

The Three Monuments
From "Oedipus at Colonus"
Notes

157

STORIES OF | RED HANRAHAN | AND | THE SECRET ROSE | BY | W · B · YEATS | ILLUSTRATED & DECORATED | BY NORAH McGUINNESS | [design] | MAC-MILLAN AND CO., LIMITED | ST. MARTIN'S STREET. LONDON | 1927

$8\frac{7}{10} \times 5\frac{7}{10}$; pp. viii, 184: comprising half-title, Macmillan's monogram and addresses on verso, pp. [i–ii]; title, copyright notice and imprint on verso, pp. [iii–iv]; contents, design at head, verso blank, pp. v–[vi]; list of Plates in Colour, verso blank, pp. vii–[viii]; fly-title, verso blank, pp. 1–[2]; text, pp. 3–182; imprint, Printed in Great Britain by R. & R. Clark, Limited, Edinburgh. beneath rule at foot of p. 182; design, verso blank, pp. [183–184]. There is a coloured frontispiece and a plate in colours facing p. 89.

Issued in dark blue cloth, design in gold on front cover, design and lettering in gold on spine; white end-papers; all edges trimmed. Published on November 11, 1927; the edition consisted of 1885 copies.

Colonel Alspach owns a copy bound in red cloth, design in blue on front cover, design and lettering in blue on spine.

Contents

Sailing to Byzantium. Dated 1927. (Dedicated to Norah McGuinness.)
> From *October Blast*, 1927. (No. 156.)

Stories of Red Hanrahan. (1897, rewritten in 1907 with Lady Gregory's help.)

Six stories.

The Secret Rose

Poem *To the Secret Rose* and seven stories.

158

THE TOWER | BY | W. B. YEATS | MACMILLAN AND CO., LIMITED | ST. MARTIN'S STREET, LONDON | 1928

$7\frac{1}{2} \times 5$; pp. 2, vi, 110, 2: comprising one leaf not included in pagination; half-title, Macmillan's monogram and addresses on verso, pp. [i–ii]; title, notice of copyright and imprint on verso, pp. [iii–iv]; contents, pp. v–vi; text, pp. 1–110; imprint, Printed in Great Britain by R. & R. Clark, Limited, Edinburgh, at foot of p. 110; lists of books By W. B. Yeats, pp. 1–2, these latter two pages numbered at foot.

Issued in olive green cloth with design and lettering in gold, signed T S[turge] M[oore] DEL, stamped on front cover and on spine; white end-papers; all edges untrimmed. Published on February 14, 1928; the edition consisted of 2000 copies.

Contents

Sailing to Byzantium. Dated 1927.
    From *October Blast*, 1927. (No. 156.)
The Tower. Dated 1926.
    From *October Blast*, 1927. (No. 156.)
Meditations in Time of Civil War. Dated 1923.
    From *The Cat and the Moon*, 1924. (No. 145.)
Nineteen Hundred and Nineteen. Dated 1919.
    This is the poem *Thoughts upon the Present State of the World* from *Seven Poems and a Fragment*, 1922. (No. 132.)
The Wheel
    From *Seven Poems and a Fragment*, 1922. (No. 132.)
Youth and Age. Dated 1924.
    From *The Cat and the Moon*, 1924. (No. 145.)
The New Faces
    From *Seven Poems and a Fragment*, 1922. (No. 132.)
A Prayer for my Son
    From *Seven Poems and a Fragment*, 1922. (No. 132.)
Two Songs from a Play
    From *October Blast*, 1927. (No. 156.)

Wisdom
> From *October Blast*, 1927. (No. 156.)

Leda and the Swan. Dated 1923.
> From *The Cat and the Moon*, 1924. (No. 145.)

On a Picture of a Black Centaur by Edmond Dulac
> From *Seven Poems and a Fragment*, 1922. (No. 132.)

Among School Children
> From *October Blast*, 1927. (No. 156.)

Colonus' Praise
The Hero, the Girl, and the Fool
> From *Seven Poems and a Fragment*, 1922. (No. 132.)

Owen Ahern and his Dancers
> This comprises the two poems *The Lover Speaks* and *The Heart Replies* from *The Cat and the Moon*, 1924. (No. 145.)

A Man Young and Old
> This comprises *The Young Countryman* and *The Old Countryman* from *October Blast*, 1927. (No. 156.)

The Three Monuments
> From *October Blast*, 1927. (No. 156.)

From 'Oedipus at Colonus'
> From *October Blast*, 1927. (No. 156.)

The Gift of Harun Al-Rashid. Dated 1923.
> From *The Cat and the Moon*, 1924. (No. 145.)

All Souls' Night. An Epilogue to 'A Vision.'
> From *Seven Poems and a Fragment*, 1922. (No. 132.)

Notes
> These are all taken from *Seven Poems and a Fragment*, *The Cat and the Moon* and *October Blast*, except the last, on *The Gift of Harun Al-Rashid*, which is new.

There were further impressions in March 1928 and in July 1929.

159

AMERICAN EDITION

THE TOWER | BY | W. B. YEATS | NEW YORK | THE MAC-
MILLAN COMPANY | 1928 | ALL RIGHTS RESERVED

$7\frac{3}{4} \times 5\frac{6}{16}$; pp. 2, viii, 120: comprising one leaf not included in pagination, half-title, Macmillan's monogram and addresses on verso, pp. [i–ii]; title, copyright notice and, at foot of page, imprint, Printed Norwood Press J. S. Cushing Co.—Berwick & Smith Co. Norwood,

L

Mass. U.S.A. on verso, pp. [iii–iv]; contents, pp. v–vi; fly-title verso blank, pp. [vii–viii]; text, pp. 1–110; pp. [111–120] blank.

Issued in green cloth with design in gold on front cover and on spine; green end-papers. Published on May 22, 1928.

The contents are the same as those of the English edition. (No. 158.)

There was a further impression in January 1929.

160

SOPHOCLES' | KING OEDIPUS | A VERSION FOR THE MODERN STAGE | BY | W. B. YEATS | MACMILLAN AND CO., LIMITED | ST. MARTIN'S STREET, LONDON | 1928

$7\frac{1}{8} \times 5$; pp. viii, 62 + 2: comprising half-title, Macmillan's monogram and addresses on verso, pp. [i–ii]; title, copyright notice and imprint of R. & R. Clark on verso, pp. [iii–iv]; Preface, pp. v–vi; Cast of First Production, verso blank, pp. [vii–viii]; text, pp. 1–51; p. [52] blank; fly-title, verso blank, pp. [53–54]; music, pp. 55–61; imprint, Printed in Great Britain by R. & R. Clark, Limited, Edinburgh, p. [62]; 2 pp. advertisements, pp. 1–2, numbered at foot, listing books By W. B. Yeats.

Issued in white paper covers folded over white end-papers, lettered in green, inside double rule panel, with fifteen-line quotation from *The New York Times* of 26th December 1926 on front cover; lettered in green on spine; all edges trimmed. Uniform with *The Player Queen* (No. 138). Published on March 27, 1928; the edition consisted of 2000 copies.

Contents

Preface. Dated June 1st.
King Oedipus
The Music for the Chorus. Preceded by a note signed L[ennox] R[obinson].

161

AMERICAN EDITION

SOPHOCLES' | KING OEDIPUS | A VERSION FOR THE MODERN | STAGE | BY | W. B. YEATS | NEW YORK | THE MACMILLAN COMPANY | 1928 | ALL RIGHTS RESERVED

$7\frac{1}{4} \times 5$; pp. viii, 64: comprising half-title, Macmillan's monogram and addresses on verso, pp. [i–ii]; title, copyright notice and imprint,

Set up by Brown Brothers Linotypers Printed in the United States of America by the Cornwall Press, Inc. on verso, pp. [iii–iv]; Preface, pp. [v–vi]; Cast of First production, verso blank, pp. [vii–viii]; text, pp. 1–51; p. [52] blank; fly-title, verso blank, pp. [53–54]; music, with prefatory note signed L.R. pp. 55–61; pp. [62–64] blank.

Issued in dark green cloth, stamped in gold on front cover and on spine; white end-papers. Published on July 3, 1928.

The contents are the same as those of the English edition. (No. 160.)

162

THE DEATH OF SYNGE, | AND OTHER PASSAGES FROM AN OLD | DIARY, BY WILLIAM BUTLER YEATS. | [woodcut of lone tree, by Elizabeth C. Yeats] | THE CUALA PRESS | DUBLIN, IRELAND. | MCMXXVIII

$8\frac{3}{10} \times 5\frac{1}{2}$; pp. viii, 48: comprising pp. [i–iv] blank; title, verso blank, pp. [v–vi]; p. [vii] blank; notice of limitation [in red], p. [viii]; text, pp. [1]–[35]; p. [36] blank; colophon, in red, p. [37]; pp. [38–48] blank.

Issued in grey paper boards with buff linen spine, lettered in black on front cover, white paper label, printed in black, on spine; grey end-papers matching binding; all edges untrimmed.

400 copies printed on paper made in Ireland and published by Elizabeth Corbet Yeats at the Cuala Press, 133 Lower Baggot Street, Dublin. Finished in the first week in May 1928. Published in June 1928.

Contents

The Death of Synge, and other Passages from an old Diary
First appeared in *The London Mercury*, April 1928, and, under the title *The Death of Synge, and other pages from an old Diary*, in *The Dial*, April 1928.

Section XVIII, *Detractions*, had already been quoted, almost in its entirety, in an essay *Synge* by Lady Gregory in *The English Review*, March 1913.

163

A PACKET FOR EZRA POUND, | BY WILLIAM BUTLER YEATS. | [woodcut of candle among waves as in No. 127] | THE CUALA PRESS | DUBLIN, IRELAND | MCMXXVIV [*sic*]

$8\frac{1}{8} \times 5\frac{7}{16}$; pp. viii, 48: comprising pp. [i–iv] blank; title, verso blank, pp. [v–vi]; pp. [vii–viii] blank; text, pp. [1]–[38]; colophon, in red, p. [39]; pp. [40–48] blank.

Issued in pale blue paper boards with buff linen spine, lettered in black on front cover, white paper label, with title only, printed in black, on spine; pale blue end-papers matching binding; all edges untrimmed.

425 copies printed on paper made in Ireland and published by Elizabeth Corbet Yeats at the Cuala Press, 133 Lower Baggot Street, Dublin. Finished in the first week of June 1929. Published in August 1929.

Contents

Rapallo. Dated March and October 1928.
Meditations upon Death:
     I. Dated February 4th. 1929.
     II. Dated February 9th. 1929.
Introduction to "The Great Wheel". Dated November 23rd. 1928.
To Ezra Pound.

164

THE | WINDING STAIR | BY | W. B. YEATS | NEW YORK | THE FOUNTAIN PRESS | MCMXXIX [*The last five lines are enclosed in a fountain device.*]

$8\frac{4}{8} \times 6$; pp. xii, 28: comprising pp. [i–vi] blank; half-title bearing author's signature, verso blank, pp. [vii–viii]; title, notice of copyright and place of printing on verso, pp. [ix–x]; contents, verso blank, pp. [xi–xii]; fly-title, verso blank, pp. [1–2]; text, pp. 3–[26]; colophon on p. [27]; p. [28] blank.

Issued in dark blue cloth, pattern in gold stamped on front cover, title stamped in gold on spine; two small red leather labels, lettered in gold YEATS and FOUNTAIN PRESS respectively pasted on spine at head and foot; purple end-papers, flecked with gold and lined white; top edges gilt, others untrimmed.

The colophon reads: "Of this edition of The Winding Stair, six hundred and forty-two copies were printed on Kalmar paper in the Printing House of William Edwin Rudge. Six hundred numbered copies, signed by the author, will be for sale. Distributed in America by Random House, and in Great Britain by Grant Richards and Humphrey Toulmin, at the Cayme Press Limited. Designed by Frederic Warde. This is copy number   ."

The copies are numbered in red ink. Entered for copyright at the Library of Congress following publication on October 1, 1929.

Contents

In Memory of Eva Gore Booth and Con Markiewicz
Death
A Dialogue of Self and Soul
Blood and the Moon
      First appeared in *The Exile*, Spring 1928.
Oil and Blood
A Woman Young and Old
      I *Father and Child*
    II *Before the World was Made*
   III *A First Confession*
   IV *Her Triumph*
    V *Consolation*
   VI *The Choice*
  VII *Parting*
 VIII *Her Vision in the Wood*
   IX *A Last Confession*
    X *Meeting*
   XI *From "The Antigone"*
Notes. Dated March, 1928.

Roth mentions a copy, printed on green paper, bound in black cloth, and numbered 72.

165

SELECTED POEMS | LYRICAL AND NARRATIVE | BY | W. B. YEATS | [portrait of the author by J. S. Sargent] | MACMILLAN AND CO., LIMITED | ST. MARTIN'S STREET, LONDON | 1929

$7\frac{1}{5} \times 4\frac{3}{4}$; pp. 2, x, 204: comprising pp. [i–ii] blank; half-title, Macmillan's monogram and addresses on verso, pp. [iii–iv]; title, notice of copyright and imprint, Printed in Great Britain by R. & R. Clark, Limited, Edinburgh, on verso, this is a leaf of thicker paper to take the impression of the portrait, 2 pp. unnumbered; Preface, verso blank, pp. v–[vi]; contents, pp. vii–x; fly-title, verso blank, pp. 1–[2]; text, pp. 3–199; p. [200] blank; Index to first lines, pp. 201–[203]; imprint at foot of p. [203]; p. [204] blank.

Issued in dark blue cloth, design (by Charles Ricketts) stamped blind on front cover, design and lettering in gold on spine; white end-papers; top edges gilt, others trimmed. Published on October 8, 1929; the edition consisted of 1500 copies.

Some copies, though not the earliest issued, have an erratum slip between p. x and p. 1 reading as follows:

ERRATUM

Page 186, line 7, *for* "ladies and lords" *read* "lords and ladies."

Contents

Preface. Dated May 1929.

The Wanderings of Usheen (1889)

From *Crossways* (1889)
> *The Indian upon God; The Stolen Child; To an Isle in the Water; Down by the Salley Gardens.*

From *The Rose* (1893) [Yeats's Dating]
> *The Rose of the World; A Faery Song; The Lake Isle of Innisfree; A Cradle Song; The Sorrow of Love; When You are Old; The Man who Dreamed of Faeryland; The Two Trees; To Ireland in the Coming Times.*

From *The Wind Among the Reeds* (1899)
> *The Hosting of the Sidhe; The Everlasting Voices; The Unappeasable Host* [new title of *A Cradle Song*]; *Into the Twilight; The Song of Wandering Aengus; The Song of the Old Mother; He bids his Beloved be at Peace; He reproves the Curlew; He remembers Forgotten Beauty; To his Heart bidding it have no Fear; The Cap and Bells; The Lover pleads with his Friend for Old Friends; He wishes for the Cloths of Heaven; The Fiddler of Dooney.*

Baile and Aillinn (1903)

From *In the Seven Woods* (1904)
> *The Folly of being Comforted; The Withering of the Boughs; Red Hanrahan's Song about Ireland; The Old Men Admiring Themselves in the Water; The Ragged Wood; The Happy Townland.*

From *The Green Helmet and other Poems* (1912)
> *The Mask; These are the Clouds.*

From *Responsibilities* (1914)
> *Introductory Rhymes; The Grey Rock; September 1913; To a Friend whose Work has come to Nothing; To a Shade; When*

Helen Lived; Running to Paradise; The Hour Before Dawn; The Mountain Tomb; I. To a Child Dancing in the Wind; II. Two Years Later; Friends; The Cold Heaven; That the Night Come; The Magi.

From *The Wild Swans at Coole* (1919)
The Wild Swans at Coole; In Memory of Major Robert Gregory; An Irish Airman Foresees his Death; Lines Written in Dejection; The Dawn; On Woman; The Fisherman; Memory; His Phoenix; Upon a Dying Lady (seven poems)*; Two Songs of a Fool; The Scholars; To a Young Girl.*

From *Four Plays for Dancers* (1921)
A Woman's Beauty is like a White Frail Bird; Why does Your Heart beat thus?; Why does my Heart beat so?; Why should the Heart take Fright?; At the Grey Round of the Hill.

From *Michael Robartes and the Dancer* (1921)
Easter, 1916; Sixteen Dead Men; The Rose Tree; On a Political Prisoner; Demon and Beast; A Prayer for my Daughter.

From *The Tower* (1928)
Sailing to Byzantium; Meditations in Time of Civil War (seven poems)*; The Wheel; A Prayer for my Son; Two Songs from a Play; From "Oedipus at Colonus."*

Index of First Lines.

There were further impressions in January 1930, September 1932, February 1936 and in August 1938.   See also No. 211c.

166

THREE THINGS | BY W. B. YEATS | [drawing] | DRAW-INGS BY GILBERT SPENCER

$7\frac{3}{16} \times 4\frac{3}{4}$; pp. 8, unnumbered: comprising pp. [1–2] blank, coloured drawing, verso blank, pp. [3–4]; text, verso blank, pp. [5–6]; pp. [7–8] blank.   There is no title-page, the above being taken from the front cover.

Issued in blue paper covers; stitched; all edges trimmed. On back cover: This is No. 18 of THE ARIEL POEMS Published by Faber & Faber Limited at 24 Russell Square, London, W.C.1 Printed at The Curwen Press, Plaistow.

Published on October 9, 1929.

First appeared in *The New Republic*, October 2, 1929.

THREE THINGS | BY W. B. YEATS | DRAWINGS BY GILBERT
SPENCER | [rule] | LONDON: FABER & FABER LTD | 1929

8½ × 5½; pp. 12: comprising limitation notice, This large-paper edition,
printed on English hand-made paper, is limited to five hundred copies.
This is Number . . . [Signed] W. B. Yeats, verso blank, pp. [1–2];
half-title with drawing, verso blank, pp. [3–4]; title, imprint, Printed
in England at the Curwen Press, on verso, pp. [5–6]; coloured drawing,
verso blank, pp. [7–8]; text, verso blank, pp. [9–10]; colophon, verso
blank, pp. [11–12].

Issued in light blue paper boards, lettered in gold w. b. yeats |
[three asterisks arranged in an inverted triangle] | THREE THINGS

167

STORIES OF MICHAEL ROBARTES AND | HIS
FRIENDS: AN EXTRACT FROM A | RECORD MADE BY HIS
PUPILS: AND | A PLAY IN PROSE BY W. B. YEATS. | [woodcut
of unicorn by Edmund Dulac] | THE CUALA PRESS | DUBLIN,
IRELAND | MCMXXXI

8⅛ × 5¾; pp. viii, 56: comprising pp. [i–iv] blank; title, verso blank,
pp. [v–vi]; p. [vii] blank; poem, in red, p. [viii]; text, pp. [1]–[46];
colophon, in red, on p. [46]; pp. [47–56] blank. Illustrations, on
grey paper, taken from *A Vision*, 1925, facing pp. 8 and 24.

Issued in dark blue paper boards with buff linen spine, lettered in
black on front cover, white paper label printed in black, STORIES OF
MICHAEL ROBARTES, on spine; dark blue end-papers matching binding:
all edges untrimmed.

450 copies printed on paper made in Ireland and published by Elizabeth
Corbet Yeats at the Cuala Press 133 Lower Baggot Street, Dublin.
Finished on All Hallows' Eve, 1931. Published in March 1932.

Contents

Huddon, Duddon and Daniel O'Leary. (Poem.)
*Stories of Michael Robartes and his Friends; an Extract from a Record
    made by his Pupils.* Signed John Duddon.
A letter beginning *Dear Mr. Yeats.* Signed John Aherne.

The Resurrection

An earlier version of this play appeared in *The Adelphi*, June 1927.

The songs for the opening and finish of the play previously appeared in *October Blast*, 1927. (No. 156.)

168

WORDS FOR MUSIC PERHAPS AND | OTHER POEMS: BY W. B. YEATS | THE CUALA PRESS | DUBLIN, IRELAND | MCMXXXII

$8\frac{3}{10} \times 5\frac{7}{10}$; pp. xvi, 48: comprising pp. [i–viii] blank; title, verso blank, pp. [ix–x]; woodcut of winged sword within circles [by A.E.], in red, p. [xi]; p. [xii] blank; contents, pp. [xiii–xiv]; pp. [xv–xvi] blank; text, pp. [1]–22; fly-title, p. [23]; text, pp. 24–[42]; colophon, in red, p. [43]; pp. [44–48] blank.

Issued in dark blue paper boards with buff linen spine, lettered in black on front cover, white paper label, printed in black, reading WORDS FOR MUSIC PERHAPS · W. B. YEATS on spine; dark blue end-papers matching binding; all edges untrimmed.

450 copies printed on paper made in Ireland and published by Elizabeth Corbet Yeats at The Cuala Press, 133 Lower Baggot Street, Dublin. Finished in the last week of September 1932. Published on November 14, 1932.

Contents

Byzantium. Dated 1929.
Vacillation:
    I. *What is Joy*
   II. *The Burning Tree*
  III. *Happiness*
  IV. *Conscience*
   V. *Conquerors*
  VI. *A Dialogue*
 VII. *Von Hügel*
The Mother of God
Coole Park 1929
    First appeared in *Coole* by Lady Gregory, 1931. (No. 319.)
Coole Park and Ballylee 1932

Anne Gregory
> Also appeared, under the title *For Anne Gregory*, in *The Spectator*, December 2, 1932.

A Meditation written during Sickness at Algeciras
> First appeared, under the title *Meditations upon Death*. I. in *A Packet for Ezra Pound*, 1929 (No. 163). Also printed in *The London Mercury*, November 1930, and in *The New Republic*, January 14, 1931.

Mohini Chatterji
> First appeared, under the title *Meditations upon Death*. II. in *A Packet for Ezra Pound*, 1929 (No. 163). Also printed in *The London Mercury*, November 1930, and in *The New Republic*, January 14, 1931.

Veronica's Napkin
Symbols
> Also appeared in *The Spectator*, December 2, 1932.

Swift's Epitaph
> Also appeared in *The Spectator*, December 2, 1932.

The Seven Sages
The Nineteenth Century and After
Spilt Milk
Statistics
Three Movements
The Crazed Moon
Quarrel in Old Age
The Results of Thought. Dated August 1931.
Gratitude to the Unknown Powers
Remorse for Intemperate Speech. Dated August 28th. 1931.
> Also appeared in *The Spectator*, November 18, 1932.

Stream and Sun at Glendalough. Dated June 1932.
Words for Music Perhaps:
> *Crazy Jane and the Bishop*
>> First appeared in *The London Mercury*, November 1930; also, under the title *Cracked Mary and the Bishop*, in *The New Republic*, November 12, 1930.
>
> *Crazy Jane Reproved*
>> First appeared in *The London Mercury*, November 1930; also, under the title *Cracked Mary Reproved*, in *The New Republic*, November 12, 1930.
>
> *Crazy Jane and Jack the Journeyman*
> *Crazy Jane on the Day of Judgement*
> *Crazy Jane on God*

Crazy Jane grown old looks at the Dancers
> First appeared, under the title *Crazy Jane and the Dancers*, in *The London Mercury*, November 1930; also, under the title *Cracked Mary and the Dancers*, in *The New Republic*, November 12, 1930.

Young Man's Song
> First appeared in *The New Republic*, October 22, 1930.

Girl's Song
> First appeared in *The New Republic*, October 22, 1930.

His Confidence
> First appeared in *The New Republic*, October 22, 1930.

Her Anxiety
> First appeared in *The New Republic*, October 22, 1930.

His Bargain
> First appeared in *The New Republic*, October 22, 1930; in *The London Mercury*, November 1930.

Her Dream
> First appeared in *The New Republic*, October 22, 1930; in *The London Mercury*, November 1930.

Love's Loneliness
> First appeared in *The New Republic*, October 22, 1930; in *The London Mercury*, November 1930.

Three Things
> First appeared in *The New Republic*, October 2, 1929; published separately in 1939. (No. 166.)

Lullaby
> First appeared in *The New Keepsake*, 1931. (No. 320.)

After Long Silence

Mad as the Mist and Snow

Those Dancing Days are Gone
> First appeared, under the title *A Song for Music*, in *The London Mercury*, November 1930; and in *The New Republic*, November 12, 1930.

I am of Ireland

The Dancer at Cruachan and Croagh Patrick

Tom the Lunatic

Old Tom at Cruachan

Old Tom again

The Delphic Oracle upon Plotinus. Dated August 19th. 1931.

169

THE | WINDING STAIR | AND OTHER POEMS | BY |
W. B. YEATS | MACMILLAN AND CO., LIMITED | ST. MARTIN'S
STREET, LONDON | 1933

$7\frac{1}{2} \times 5$; pp. 2, x 104: comprising one leaf not included in pagination;
half-title, Macmillan's monogram and addresses on verso, pp. [i–ii];
title, copyright notice and imprint on verso, pp. [iii–iv]; dedication
verso blank, pp. [v–vi]; contents, pp. vii–ix; p. [x] blank; text, pp.
1–101; imprint, Printed in Great Britain by R. & R. Clark, Limited,
Edinburgh, at foot of p. 101; pp. [102–104] blank.

Issued in olive green cloth, design, signed T S[turge] M[oore], stamped
blind on front cover and in gold on spine; white end-papers; all edges
untrimmed. Published on September 19, 1933; the edition consisted
of 2000 copies.

Contents

Dedication. To Edmund Dulac. Dated 1933.

In Memory of Eva Gore-Booth and Con Markiewicz, dated October
1927; *Death; A Dialogue of Self and Soul; Blood and the Moon;
Oil and Blood.*
These five poems from *The Winding Stair*, New York, 1929.
(No. 164.)

*Veronica's Napkin; Symbols; Spilt Milk; The Nineteenth Century and
After; Statistics; Three Movements; The Seven Sages; The Crazed
Moon; Coole Park, 1929; Coole and Ballylee, 1931; For Anne
Gregory; Swift's Epitaph; At Algeciras—a Meditation upon Death*,
dated November 1928.
These thirteen poems from *Words for Music Perhaps*, 1932.
(No. 168.)

The Choice
First appeared as the sixth stanza of *Coole and Ballylee* in *Words
for Music Perhaps*, 1932. (No. 168.)

Mohini Chatterjee, dated 1928; *Byzantium*, dated 1930; *The Mother of
God; Vacillation*, dated 1932; *Quarrel in Old Age; The Results
of Thought*, dated August 1931; *Gratitude to the Unknown
Instructors; Remorse for Intemperate Speech*, dated August 28,
1931; *Stream and Sun at Glendalough*, dated June, 1932.

These nine poems from *Words for Music Perhaps*, 1932. (No.
168.)

Words for Music Perhaps:

    I. *Crazy Jane and the Bishop;* II. *Crazy Jane Reproved;* III. *Crazy Jane on the Day of Judgement;* IV. *Crazy Jane and Jack the Journeyman;* V. *Crazy Jane on God.*

        These five poems from *Words for Music Perhaps*, 1932. (No. 168.)

    VI. *Crazy Jane Talks with the Bishop*

    VII. *Crazy Jane Grown Old Looks at the Dancers;* VIII. *Girl's Song;* IX. *Young Man's Song;* X. *Her Anxiety;* XI. *His Confidence;* XII. *Love's Loneliness;* XIII. *Her Dream;* XIV. *His Bargain;* XV. *Three Things;* XVI. *Lullaby;* XVII. *After Long Silence;* XVIII. *Mad as the Mist and Snow;* XIX. *Those Dancing Days are Gone;* XX. *'I am of Ireland';* XXI. *The Dancer at Cruachan and Cro-Patrick;* XXII. *Tom the Lunatic;* XXIII. *Tom at Cruachan;* XXIV. *Old Tom Again;* XXV. *The Delphic Oracle upon Plotinus*, dated August 19, 1931.

        These nineteen poems from *Words for Music Perhaps*, 1932. (No. 168.)

A Woman Young and Old

    These eleven poems from *The Winding Stair* (New York), 1929. (No. 164.)

Notes

There was a further impression in January 1934.

170

AMERICAN EDITION

THE | WINDING STAIR | AND OTHER POEMS | BY | W. B. YEATS | NEW YORK | THE MACMILLAN COMPANY | 1933

$7\frac{1}{2} \times 5$; pp. x, 102: comprising half-title, Macmillan's monogram and addresses on verso, pp. [i–ii]; title, imprint on verso, pp. [iii–iv]; Dedication, verso blank, pp. [v–vi]; contents, pp. vii–ix; p. [x] blank; text, pp. 1–101; p. [102] blank. The imprint reads Set up and printed. Published October 1933. Printed in the United States of America.

Issued in dark blue cloth, design by Sturge Moore stamped blind on front cover, design stamped blind, lettering in gold between gold bands on spine; white end-papers; all edges untrimmed.

The contents are the same as those of the English edition (No. 169).

There was a further impression in December 1933.

171

THE | COLLECTED POEMS | OF | W. B. YEATS | NEW
YORK | THE MACMILLAN COMPANY | 1933

$7\frac{4}{5} \times 5\frac{1}{2}$; pp. xviii, 478: comprising half-title, Macmillan's monogram
and addresses on verso, pp. [i–ii]; title, copyright notices and imprint,
Printed in the United States of America, on verso, pp. [iii–iv]; contents, pp. v–xvii; p. [xviii] blank; fly-title, verso blank, pp. [1–2];
fly-title, quotation on verso, pp. [3–4]; dedication, verso blank, pp.
[5–6]; text, pp. 7–456; Index to Titles, pp. 457–467; Index to First
lines, pp. 468–478. Frontispiece portrait of Yeats. 1907. From the
portrait by Augustus John, R.A.

Issued in dark blue cloth, design [by Charles Ricketts] stamped
blind on front cover, lettering in gold between gold bands on spine;
white end-papers; top and bottom edges trimmed, fore-edges untrimmed. Published on November 14, 1933.

Contents

Lyrical:

Crossways (1889)

16 poems, following the arrangement in *Early Poems and
Stories*, 1925 (No. 147).

The Rose (1893)

23 poems, following the arrangement in *Early Poems and
Stories*, 1925 (No. 147), with the addition of *To Some I
have Talked with by the Fire.*

The Wind Among the Reeds (1899)

37 poems, following the arrangement in *Later Poems*, 1922
(No. 134). The titles of two poems have been altered: *The
Fisherman* to *The Fish* and *A Lover Speaks* to *The Lover
Speaks.*

In the Seven Woods (1904)

14 poems, following the arrangement in *Later Poems*, 1922
(No. 134).

The Green Helmet and other Poems (1910)

21 poems, following the arrangement in *Later Poems*, 1922
(No. 134). The titles of two poems have been altered: *The
Consolation* to *Words* and *The Young Man's Song* to *Brown
Penny.*

Responsibilities (1914)

30 poems, following the arrangement in *Later Poems*, 1922
(No. 134). *The Two Kings* is transferred to the Narrative
and Dramatic section.

The Wild Swans at Coole (1919)
>   46 poems, following the arrangement in *Later Poems*, 1922
>   (No. 134). The title of *The Sad Shepherd* has been altered
>   to *Shepherd and Goatherd*.

Michael Robartes and the Dancer (1921)
>   15 poems, following the arrangement in *Later Poems*, 1922
>   (No. 134).

The Tower (1928)
>   36 poems, mainly following the arrangement in *The Tower*,
>   1928 (No. 158), but with the addition of *Fragments* of
>   which I. first appeared in the Introduction to *The Words
>   upon the Window Pane* in *The Dublin Magazine*, October–
>   December 1931.
>   The early dialogue portion of *The Hero, the Girl and the
>   Fool* is omitted, leaving only the final lyric, now called
>   *The Fool by the Roadside*.
>   From *"Oedipus at Colonus"* is omitted.
>   *The Gift of Harun-Al-Rashid* is transferred to the Narrative
>   and Dramatic section.

The Winding Stair and other Poems (1932)
>   64 poems, following the arrangement in *The Winding Stair*,
>   1933 (No. 169).

Narrative and Dramatic:

>   *The Wanderings of Oisin* (1889)

>   *The Old Age of Queen Maeve* (1903). With a new eight-line
>   introductory stanza.

>   *Baile and Aillinn* (1903)

>   *The Shadowy Waters* (1906)
>   >   Introductory Lines.
>   >   The Harp of Aengus.

>   *The Two Kings* (1914)

>   *The Gift of Harun-al-Raschid* (1923)

Notes
>   There is a preliminary note dated 1933. The other notes are
>   taken from *The Wind Among the Reeds*, 1899; *Collected Works*,
>   Vol. I., 1908; *Responsibilities*, 1916; *Later Poems*, 1922; *The
>   Tower*, 1928; *The Winding Stair*, 1933, the notes here including
>   the dedication to Edmund Dulac; and *Poems*, 1912.

Index to Titles
Index to First Lines

There was a reprint of this volume in January 1934; a reissue in April 1934; reprints in October 1935; April 1937; October 1938; January 1940; March 1941; July 1942; May 1944; September 1945; May 1946; March 1947; February 1948; January and December 1949.

172

ENGLISH EDITION

THE | COLLECTED POEMS | OF | W. B. YEATS | MAC-MILLAN AND CO., LIMITED | ST. MARTIN'S STREET, LONDON | 1933

$7\frac{7}{10} \times 5$; pp. xvi, 476. Frontispiece, W. B. Yeats, 1907. From the Portrait by Augustus John, R.A. in the possession of Dr. Oliver St. John Gogarty.

Issued in red-purple cloth, lettering stamped in gold, design stamped in gold and blind, on spine; white end-papers; all edges trimmed. Published on November 28, 1933; the edition consisted of 2040 copies. This book was also issued in a leather binding.

The contents are the same as the American edition (No. 171).

There were further impressions in March 1934 (top edges gilt, others trimmed), December 1935, October 1937 and November 1939.

173

LETTERS TO THE NEW ISLAND | BY | WILLIAM BUTLER YEATS | EDITED WITH AN INTRODUCTION | BY | HORACE REYNOLDS | [ornament] | CAMBRIDGE, MASSA-CHUSETTS | HARVARD UNIVERSITY PRESS | 1934

$7\frac{1}{2} \times 5$; pp. xvi, 224: comprising half-title, on verso LONDON: HUMPHREY MILFORD | OXFORD UNIVERSITY PRESS, pp. [i–ii]; title, copyright notice, acknowledgements and imprint, Printed at the Harvard University Press Cambridge, Mass, U.S.A., on verso, pp. [iii–iv]; quotation, verso blank, pp. [v–vi]; Preface, pp. [vii]–xiii; p. [xiv] blank; contents, verso blank, pp. [xv–xvi]; fly-title, verso blank, pp. [1–2]; text, pp. [3]–222; pp. [223–224] blank. Frontispiece portrait of W. B. Yeats by H. M. Paget.

Issued in light green cloth, design by T. S[turge] M[oore] printed in dark green on front cover, design and lettering printed in dark green on spine; white end-papers; top edges trimmed, others untrimmed. Published on January 24, 1934.

Contents

---

* Most of Yeats's contributions to *The Boston Pilot* appeared under the generic title *The Celt in Ireland* as well as their own title.

M

A Ballad Singer
> First appeared, under the title *The Celt in Ireland,* in *The Boston Pilot,* September 12, 1891.

The Rhymers' Club
> First appeared in *The Boston Pilot,* April 23, 1892.

Maude Gonne
> First appeared, under the title *The New "Speranȝa"*, in *The Boston Pilot,* July 30, 1892.

The Irish National Literary Society
> First appeared, under the titles *The New National Library—The National Literary Society—Mr. O'Grady's Stories—Dr. Hyde's Forthcoming Book—Themes for Irish Literateurs,* in *The Boston Pilot,* November 19, 1892.

The Poet of Ballyshannon
> First appeared in *The Providence Sunday Journal,* September 2, 1888.

The Children of Lir
> First appeared, under the title *Dr. Todhunter's Latest Volume of Poems,* in *The Providence Sunday Journal,* February 10, 1889.

Irish Wonders
> First appeared in *The Providence Sunday Journal,* July 7, 1889.

A Scholar Poet
> First appeared in *The Providence Sunday Journal,* June 15, 1890.

A Poetic Drama
> First appeared, under the titles *The Poetic Drama. Some Interesting Attempts to Revive it in London. Dr. Todhunter's Important Work in "The Poison Flower"*, in *The Providence Sunday Journal,* July 26, 1891.

174

THE WORDS UPON THE WINDOW | PANE: A PLAY IN ONE ACT, WITH | NOTES UPON THE PLAY AND ITS SUB- | JECT, BY WILLIAM BUTLER YEATS. | [woodcut, *Monoceros de Astris,* as in No. 111] | THE CUALA PRESS | DUBLIN, IRELAND | MCMXXXIV

$8\frac{3}{10} \times 5\frac{1}{2}$; pp. xvi, 64: comprising pp. [i–viii] blank; title, verso blank, pp. [ix–x]; dedication [in red], verso blank, pp. [xi–xii]; fly-title [in red], verso blank, pp. [xiii–xiv]; p. [xv] blank; Persons of the Play [in red], p. [xvi]; text, pp. [1]–58; colophon, in red, p. [59]; pp. [60–64] blank.

Issued in sugar-bag blue paper boards with buff linen spine, lettered in black on front cover, white paper label, printed in black, on spine; blue end-papers matching binding; all edges untrimmed.

350 copies printed on paper made in Ireland and published by Elizabeth Corbet Yeats at The Cuala Press 133 Lower Baggot Street, Dublin. Finished in the last week of January 1934. Published in April 1934.

Contents

Dedication to the memory of Lady Gregory
Introduction
> First appeared, under the title *The Words upon the Window Pane: a Commentary*, in *The Dublin Magazine*, October–December 1931 and January–March 1932.

The Words upon the Window Pane

175

WHEELS | AND | BUTTERFLIES | BY | W. B. YEATS | [design of masks] | MACMILLAN AND CO. LIMITED | ST. MARTIN'S STREET, LONDON | 1934

$7\frac{2}{8} \times 5$; pp. 2, x, 184: comprising one leaf not counted in pagination; half-title, Macmillan's monogram and addresses on verso, pp. [i–ii]; title, notice about performing rights, copyright notice and imprint on verso, pp. [iii–iv]; couplet, verso blank, pp. [v–vi]; Preface, verso blank, pp. vii–[viii]; list of contents, verso blank, pp. ix–[x]; fly-title, verso blank, pp. [1–2]; dedication, Persons in the Play on verso, pp. 3–4; text, pp. 5–155; p. [156] blank; couplet, verso blank, pp. [157–158]; fly-title, verso blank, pp. [159–160]; music, pp. 161–181; imprint, Printed in Great Britain by R. & R. Clark, Limited, Edinburgh, p. [182]; pp. [183–184] blank.

Issued in bright green cloth, lettered in gold on spine, design of masks in gold on front cover; white end-papers; top edges trimmed, others untrimmed. Published on November 13, 1934; the edition consisted of 3000 copies.

Contents

Couplet
Preface. Dated 4th August 1934.
Introduction to "The Words upon the Window-pane". Dated 1931.
The Words upon the Window-pane
> From the Cuala Press edition, 1934 (No. 174).

Introduction to "Fighting the Waves."
> First appeared in *The Dublin Magazine*, April–June 1932.

Fighting the Waves

Introduction to "The Resurrection"
The Resurrection
> From *Stories of Michael Robartes and his Friends*, Cuala Press,
> 1931. (No. 167.)

Introduction to "The Cat and the Moon"
The Cat and the Moon
> From *The Cat and the Moon*, Cuala Press, 1924. (No. 145.)

Couplet
Music to "Fighting the Waves". By George Antheil.

176

AMERICAN EDITION

WHEELS | AND | BUTTERFLIES | [design of masks] |
NEW YORK | THE MACMILLAN COMPANY | 1935

$8\frac{1}{5} \times 5\frac{1}{2}$; pp. x, 166: comprising half-title, Macmillan's monogram and
addresses on verso, pp. [i–ii]; title, notices concerning copyright and
performing rights, and imprint, Printed in the United States of
America by the Stratford Press, Inc., New York on verso, pp. [iii–
iv]; couplet, verso blank, pp. [v–vi]; Preface, verso blank, pp. [vii–
viii]; list of contents, verso blank, pp. [ix–x]; fly-title, verso blank,
pp. [1–2]; dedication, Persons in the Play on verso, pp. [3–4]; text,
pp. 5–138; p. [139] blank; couplet, p. [140]; fly-title, verso blank, pp.
[141–142]; music, pp. 143–163; p. [164–166] blank.

Issued in light green cloth, design of masks in gold on front cover,
lettering in gold on spine; white end-papers; all edges untrimmed.
Published on February 19, 1935.

The contents are the same as those of the English edition (No. 175).

177

THE | COLLECTED PLAYS | OF | W. B. YEATS | MAC-
MILLAN AND CO., LIMITED | ST. MARTIN'S STREET, LONDON |
1934

$7\frac{3}{5} \times 5\frac{1}{5}$; pp. vi, 618: comprising half-title, Macmillan's monogram and
addresses on verso, pp. [i–ii]; title, notice concerning performing
rights, copyright, and imprint, Printed in Great Britain by R. & R.
Clark, Limited, Edinburgh on verso, pp. [iii–iv]; Preface, p. v;
contents, p. vi; fly-title, dedication on verso, pp. [1–2]; text, pp.
3–617; imprint, Printed in Great Britain by R. & R. Clark, Limited,

Edinburgh, at foot of p. 617; p. [618] blank. Frontispiece portrait of
the author from a charcoal drawing by John S. Sargent, first used in the
Collected Works of 1908, Volume I. (No. 75.)

Issued in purple red cloth, design in gold and blind on spine, lettering
in gold on spine; white end-papers; top edges gilt, others trimmed.
Published on November 30, 1934; the edition consisted of 2000 copies.

Contents

The Countess Cathleen (1892)
The Land of Heart's Desire (1894)
Cathleen ni Houlihan (1902)
The Pot of Broth (1904)
The King's Threshold (1904)
The Shadowy Waters (1911). Acting version
Deirdre (1907)
At the Hawk's Well (1917)
The Green Helmet (1910)
On Baile's Strand (1904)
The Only Jealousy of Emer (1919)
The Hour-Glass (1914)
The Unicorn from the Stars (1908)
The Player-Queen (1922)
The Dreaming of the Bones (1919)
Calvary (1920)
The Cat and the Moon (1924)
Sophocles' "King Oedipus" (1928)
Sophocles' "Oedipus at Colonus" (1934)
The Resurrection (1931)
The Words upon the Window-pane (1934)

All commentaries, notes, and the music for the plays have been
omitted.

This volume contains the first printing of *Oedipus at Colonus*.

178

AMERICAN EDITION

THE | COLLECTED PLAYS | OF | W. B. YEATS | NEW
YORK | THE MACMILLAN COMPANY | 1935

$7\frac{4}{5} \times 5\frac{1}{2}$; pp. x, 618. On the verso of title is imprint, Printed in the

United States of America by the Polygraphic Company of America, N.Y. Frontispiece portrait by John S. Sargent, R.A.

Issued in dark blue cloth, design [by Charles Ricketts] stamped blind on front cover, lettering in gold between gold bands on spine; white end-papers; top and bottom edges trimmed, fore-edges untrimmed. Published on August 27, 1935.

The contents are the same as those of the English edition (No. 177).

179

THE KING OF THE GREAT CLOCK | TOWER, COMMENTARIES AND POEMS, | BY WILLIAM BUTLER YEATS. | [woodcut, *in red*, of bell and fish by Robert Gregory] | THE CUALA PRESS | DUBLIN, IRELAND | MCMXXXIV

$8\frac{3}{10} \times 5\frac{7}{10}$; pp. xvi, 56: comprising pp. [i–viii] blank; title, verso blank, pp. [ix–x]; Preface, pp. [xi–xiii]; contents, pp. [xiv]; fly-title and notice of first performance [*in red*], The Persons of the Play [*in red*] on verso, pp. [xv–xvi]; text, pp. [1]–[12]; fly-title [*in red*], verso blank, pp. [13–14]; text, pp. 15–[45]; p. [46] blank; colophon, *in red*, on p. [47]; pp. [48–56] blank.

Issued in sugar-bag blue paper boards with buff linen spine, lettered in black on front cover, white paper label printed in black THE GREAT CLOCK TOWER: W. B. YEATS on spine; blue end-papers matching binding; all edges untrimmed.

400 copies printed on paper made in Ireland and published by Elizabeth Corbet Yeats at The Cuala Press, 133 Lower Baggot Street, Dublin. Finished in the last week of October 1934. Published on December 14, 1934.

Contents

Preface, including poem *God guard me from those thoughts men think*.
> The poem first appeared, under the title *Old Age*, in *The Spectator*, November 2, 1934. Also printed in *Poetry* (Chicago), May 1935.

The King of the Great Clock Tower
> Also printed in *Life and Letters*, November 1934.

Commentary on "The Great Clock Tower," including poem *He had famished in a wilderness*.
> The poem first appeared, under the title *The Singing Head and the Lady*, in *The Spectator*, December 7, 1934.

A Parnellite at Parnell's Funeral.
> The third stanza first appeared in the introduction to *Fighting the Waves* in *The Dublin Magazine*, April–June 1932. The whole poem first appeared in *The Spectator*, October 19, 1934.

Commentary on "A Parnellite at Parnell's Funeral," including poem *The rest I pass, one sentence I unsay.* This is section II. of *Parnell's Funeral,* and first appeared, under the title *Forty Years Later,* in *The Spectator,* October 19, 1934.

Three Songs to the Same Tune
> First appeared in *The Spectator,* February 23, 1934. Printed in *Poetry,* December, 1934.

Commentary on the "Three Songs." Dated April, 1934.

Postscript, containing poem *Here is fresh matter, poet,* dated August 1934.
> The *Commentary* and *Postscript* appeared in *Poetry,* December 1934. The poem appeared separately, under the title *A Vain Hope,* in *The Spectator,* November 23, 1934.

Supernatural Songs
> 1. *Ribh at the Tomb of Baile and Aillinn*
> 2. *Ribh prefers an Older Theology*
> 3. *Ribh considers Christian Love insufficient*
> 4. *He and She*
> 5. *The Four Ages of Man*
> 6. *Conjunctions*
> 7. *A Needle's Eye*
> *Meru*
> These eight poems first appeared in *The London Mercury,* and in *Poetry,* December 1934.

Commentary on "Supernatural Songs"

179A

AMERICAN EDITION

THE KING OF THE GREAT CLOCK | TOWER, COMMENTARIES | AND POEMS | BY | WILLIAM BUTLER YEATS | NEW YORK | THE MACMILLAN COMPANY | 1935

$8 \times 5\frac{1}{4}$; pp. x, 46: comprising half-title, Macmillan's monogram and addresses on verso, pp. [i–ii]; title, copyright notice and place of printing on verso, pp. [iii–iv]; Preface, pp. v–vii; p. [viii] blank; contents, verso blank, pp. [ix–x]; half-title and notice of first performance, The Persons of the Play on verso, pp. [1–2]; text, pp. 3–46.

Issued in light yellow-green boards with black cloth spine, lettered in gold on spine; white end-papers; all edges untrimmed. Published in May 1935.

The contents are the same as those of the Cuala Edition (No. 179).

180

THE | SINGING | HEAD | AND | THE | LADY | [asterisk] | W. B. | YEATS | [asterisk] | XMAS | 1934

$6\frac{1}{2} \times 4\frac{1}{2}$; pp. 12, unnumbered: comprising pp. [1–4] blank; title-page, p. [5]; text, pp. [6–7]; colophon on p. [8]; pp. [9–12] blank.

The colophon reads:

Twenty copies of this poem were printed for the author: six on Oland, numbered 1–6; six on Dresden, numbered I–VI; six on rice paper, numbered a–f; and two on Imperial vellum, numbered A and B. This is number . . .

Issued in different patterned paper covers with white or gold labels printed in black on front cover; a duplicate label is tipped in at end; stitched with different coloured silk cords; all edges untrimmed.

The poem first appeared in *The Spectator*, December 7, 1934, and was printed, without title, in the *Commentary on "The Great Clock Tower,"* in *The King of the Great Clock Tower*, Cuala Press, 1934. (No. 179.)

This booklet was printed by Mr. Frederic Prokosch at his own press at Bryn Maur, Pennsylvania, in December 1934. Mr. Prokosch tells me that he sent all the copies but four to Yeats, who signed and inscribed two or three copies and sent these back.

181

REALE ACCADEMIA D'ITALIA | [long rule] | WILLIAM BUTLER YEATS | [short rule] | THE IRISH NATIONAL THEATRE | [short rule] | ESTRATTO DAGLI ATTI | DEL IV CONVEGNO DELLA "FONDAZIONE ALESSANDRO VOLTA" | TEMA: IL TEATRO DRAMMATICO | ROMA 8–14 OTTOBRE 1934 —XII | [short rule] | ROMA | REALE ACCADEMIA D'ITALIA | 1935—XIII

10×7; pp. 16: comprising pp. [1–2] blank; title, imprint, Roma, 1935—XIII—Tipografia del Senato dal dott. G. Bardi. beneath a long rule at foot of verso, pp. [3–4]; text, pp. [5]–15; p. [16] blank.

Issued in stiff white paper covers, lettered in black, as title-page, on front cover.

Contents

Relazione di William Butler Yeats
The Irish National Theatre

The text of the lecture runs from p. [5] to more than half way down

p. 11. This is followed by Riassunto and Résumé, printed in parallel
columns, the Italian on the left of the page, the French on the
right, and running from p. 11 to p. 15.

182

A FULL MOON | IN MARCH | BY | W. B. YEATS | LONDON
| MACMILLAN AND CO LTD | 1935

$7\frac{9}{10} \times 5\frac{1}{4}$; pp. viii, 72: comprising half-title, Macmillan's monogram
and addresses on verso, pp. [i–ii]; title, copyright notice and imprint,
Printed in Great Britain by R. & R. Clark, Limited, Edinburgh, on
verso, pp. [iii–iv]; Preface, pp. v–vi; contents, verso blank, pp. vii–
[viii]; fly-title, Characters on verso, pp. [1–2]; text, pp. 3–22;
fly-title, dedication and Characters on verso, pp. [23–24]; text, pp.
25–41; p. [42] blank; fly-title, verso blank, pp. [43–44]; text, pp.
45–[70]; imprint, Printed in Great Britain by R. & R. Clark, Ltd,
Edinburgh, on p. [71]; p. [72] blank.

Issued in dark green cloth, lettered in gold on spine; white end-papers;
top edges trimmed, others untrimmed. Published on November
22, 1935; the edition consisted of 2000 copies.

Contents

Preface. Dated May 30, 1935.

A Full Moon in March
> First appeared in *Poetry* (Chicago), March 1935.
> The poem *He had famished in a wilderness* (pp. 15–16) had
> appeared in the Commentary on *The Great Clock Tower* in the
> Cuala Press edition, 1934. (No. 179.)

The King of the Great Clock Tower
> A new version in verse.
> The final song first appeared, under the title *The Wicked Haw-
> thorn Tree*, in *A Broadside*, February 1935. (See No. 249.)

Parnell's Funeral and other Poems:
> *Parnell's Funeral*
>> I. First appeared, under the title *A Parnellite at Parnell's
>> Funeral*, in *The Spectator*, October 19, 1934.
>> II. First appeared, under the title *Forty Years Later*, in
>> *The Spectator*, October 19, 1934. Printed in the Cuala Press
>> edition (No. 179) without title.

Three Songs to the Same Tune
> From *The King of the Great Clock Tower*, 1934. (No. 179.)

*Alternative Song for the Severed Head in "The King of the Great Clock
Tower"*

This appeared in the prose version of the play, Cuala Press,
1934. (No. 179.)

Two Songs Rewritten for the Tune's Sake

A Prayer for Old Age

First appeared, under the title *Old Age*, in *The Spectator*,
November 2, 1934. Printed, without title, in the Preface to
The King of the Great Clock Tower, 1934 (No. 179), and, under
the title *God Guard me from those Thoughts Men Think*, in
Poetry, May 1935.

Church and State. Dated August 1934.

First appeared, under the title *A Vain Hope*, in *The Spectator*,
November 23, 1934. Appeared, without title, in the Postscript
to the *Commentary on the "Three Songs"* in *The King of the Great
Clock Tower*, 1934. (No. 179.)

Supernatural Songs

12 poems. Numbers 1, 2, 5, 6, 9, 10, 11 and 12 are taken from *The
King of the Great Clock Tower*, 1934 (No. 179). The others are:

3. *Ribh in Ecstasy*
4. *There*
7. *What Magic Drum?*
8. *Whence had they Come?*

The title of number 2 is changed from *Ribh Prefers an Older
Theology* to *Ribh Denounces Patrick*.

183

DRAMATIS PERSONÆ | BY | WILLIAM BUTLER YEATS. |
[woodcut as in No. 162] | THE CUALA PRESS | DUBLIN,
IRELAND | MCMXXXV

$8\frac{1}{8} \times 5\frac{1}{2}$; pp. viii, 96: comprising pp. [i–iv] blank; title, verso blank,
pp. [v–vi]; pp. [vii–viii] blank; text, pp. [1]–[89]; colophon, in red, on
p. [89]; pp. [90–96] blank. An Errata slip correcting "blackmail" to
"blackball" is inserted loose between pp. 58 and 59.

Issued in sugar-bag blue paper boards with buff linen spine, lettered in
black on front cover, white paper label, printed in black, on spine;
blue end-papers matching binding, all edges untrimmed.

400 copies printed and published by Elizabeth Corbet Yeats, at the
Cuala Press 133 Lower Baggot Street, Dublin. Finished in the second
week in October 1935. Published on December 9, 1935.

Contents

Dramatis Personæ

These memoirs first appeared in *The London Mercury*, November and December 1935 and January 1936; they were also printed in *The New Republic*, February 26, March 11 and 25, and April 8 and 22, 1936.

184

POEMS | BY | WILLIAM BUTLER YEATS | THE CUALA PRESS | DUBLIN, IRELAND | MCMXXXV

6½ × 4¾; pp. xvi, 24: comprising pp. [i–xii] blank; title, verso blank, pp. [xiii–xiv]; p. [xv] blank; coloured frontispiece on p. [xvi]; text, pp. 1–[10]; colophon, in red, on p. [11]; pp. [12–24] blank. Each poem has a hand-coloured initial and, where necessary, a hand-coloured ornament to fill out the line after the title of the poem.

Issued in light blue stiff paper covers without lettering; white end-papers; all edges untrimmed.

30 copies were privately printed for Eleanor Lady Yarrow, by The Cuala Press, 133 Lower Baggot Street, Dublin, in 1935.

Contents
The Lover Tells of the Rose in his Heart; Into the Twilight; He Wishes for the Cloths of Heaven; The Fiddler of Dooney; The Lake Isle of Innisfree; When You are Old; A Faery Song; The Song of Wandering Aengus; The Pity of Love.

185

LEDA | AND | THE | SWAN | [asterisk] | W. B. YEATS | CHRISTMAS: | PRIVATELY PRINTED

6⅖ × 4½; pp. 12, unnumbered: comprising pp. [1–4] blank; title, verso blank, pp. [5–6]; text, p. [7]; colophon on p. [8]; pp. [9–12] blank.

The colophon reads:

Of this poem twenty-two copies were printed for the author: five copies bound in Sicily paper, numbered 1–5; five bound in Sardinia, numbered I–V; five bound in Abruzzo, numbered a–e; five bound in Umbria, numbered A–E; and two bound in Marche, numbered X and XX. This is number . . .

Issued in various patterned paper covers, label printed in black on front cover; stitched with coloured silk cord; all edges trimmed. Printed at Florence, Christmas, 1935.

These booklets were printed by Mr. Frederic Prokosch. Mr. Prokosch tells me that at the moment the printing was finished he was
called to America on his father's death and went leaving all his books
and papers behind him. In 1948 he returned to Florence and discovered the copies of the booklet still intact.

186

w. b. yeats | [rule] | DRAMATIS PERSONAE | 1896–
1902 | [fleuron] | ESTRANGEMENT | [fleuron] | THE
DEATH OF SYNGE | [fleuron] | THE BOUNTY OF
SWEDEN | [rule] | NEW YORK | THE MACMILLAN COMPANY |
1936

$8\frac{3}{4} \times 5\frac{1}{2}$; pp. viii, 200: comprising half-title, Macmillan's monogram
and addresses on verso, pp. [i–ii]; title, copyright notice and imprint,
Set up by Brown Brothers Linotypers Printed in the United States of
America by the Ferris Printing Company on verso, pp. [iii–iv];
contents, verso blank, pp. [v–vi]; List of Illustrations, verso blank,
pp. [vii–viii]; fly-title, verso blank, pp. [1–2]; text, pp. 3–82; fly-title,
verso blank, pp. [83–84]; text, pp. 85–122; fly-title, verso blank, pp.
[123–124]; text, pp. 125–154; fly-title, verso blank, pp. [155–156];
text, pp. 157–200. Frontispiece of the author from the portrait by
Augustus John, R.A., in the Kelvingrove Art Gallery, Glasgow.
Illustrations facing pp. 12, 20, 28 and 76; that facing p. 28 is from a
pastel of Coole House by W. B. Yeats.

Issued in blue-green cloth, lettered in gold inside double rules on
front cover, lettered in gold on spine, the title between two double
rules; white end-papers; top edges trimmed, others untrimmed.
Published on May 12, 1936.

Contents

Dramatis Personae, 1896–1902
    From the Cuala Press volume of 1935. (No. 183.)
Estrangement
    From the Cuala Press volume of 1926. (No. 150.)
The Death of Synge
    From the Cuala Press volume of 1928. (No. 162.)
The Bounty of Sweden
    From the Cuala Press volume of 1925. (No. 146.)
    The six notes which followed the lecture on *The Irish Dramatic
    Movement* are here omitted.

187

ENGLISH EDITION

W. B. YEATS | [rule] | DRAMATIS PERSONAE | 1896–
1902 | [fleuron] | ESTRANGEMENT | [fleuron] | THE
DEATH OF SYNGE | [fleuron] | THE BOUNTY OF
SWEDEN | [rule] | MACMILLAN & CO. LTD. | 1936

$8\frac{4}{5} \times 5\frac{3}{4}$; pp. viii, 192. Printed in Great Britain by R. & R. Clark
Limited Edinburgh.

Issued in brown-and-yellow patterned paper boards with yellow linen
spine, lettered in gold on spine; off-white end-papers; top edges
stained yellow, others untrimmed. Published on May 15, 1936; the
edition consisted of 2000 copies.

The contents are the same as those of the American edition (No. 186).

188

MODERN POETRY | BY | W. B. YEATS | THE EIGHTEENTH
OF THE | BROADCAST NATIONAL LECTURES DELIVERED ON |
11 OCTOBER 1936 | [ornament] | THE BRITISH BROADCASTING
CORPORATION | BROADCASTING HOUSE LONDON, W.1 | 1936

$7\frac{1}{5} \times 4\frac{4}{5}$; pp. 28: comprising half-title, list of Previous National Lectures
on verso, pp. [1–2]; title, place of printing on verso, pp. [3–4]; text,
pp. 5–[28]; imprint, Cambridge: Printed by W. Lewis, M.A., at the
University Press B.B.C. No. 1113, at foot of p. [28].

Issued in bright green paper covers, lined with white end-papers, and
lettered in black on front cover; all edges trimmed. Published in
December 1936. The edition consisted of 1000 copies, but 200 of
these were destroyed by incendiary bombs in 1940–41.

Contents

Modern Poetry
    First appeared in *The Listener*, October 14, 1936. Also printed in
    The Living Age, December 1936.

189

THE | KING'S THRESHOLD | BY | W. B. YEATS | MAC-
MILLAN AND CO., LIMITED | ST. MARTIN'S STREET, LONDON |
1937

$7\frac{1}{5} \times 5$; pp. 52: comprising title, copyright notice and imprint, Printed
in Great Britain By R. & R. Clark, Limited, Edinburgh, on verso,
pp. [63–64]; Persons in the Play, verso blank, pp. 65–[66]; text, pp.
67–114.

Issued in light blue paper covers stitched on with blue thread, lettered
in black on front cover; all edges trimmed. Published on March 25,
1937; the edition consisted of 1000 copies.

Contents

The King's Threshold

This edition is reprinted from the type of *Plays in Prose and Verse*,
1922 (No. 136) with new title-page.

190

NINE ONE-ACT PLAYS | BY | W. B. YEATS | MACMILLAN
AND CO., LIMITED | ST. MARTIN'S STREET, LONDON | 1937

$6\frac{9}{10} \times 4\frac{1}{4}$; pp. vi, 218: comprising half-title, Macmillan's monogram
and addresses on verso, pp. [i–ii]; title, Note concerning music for the
plays, notice concerning performing rights, copyright notice and
imprint, Printed in Great Britain by R. & R. Clark, Limited, Edinburgh on verso, pp. [iii–iv]; contents, verso blank, pp. v–[vi]; fly-
title bearing quotation, dedication on verso, pp. [1–2]; text, pp. 3–127;
imprint, Printed in Great Britain by R. & R. Clark, Limited, Edinburgh. at foot of p. 217; p. [218] blank.

Issued in dark red cloth, design stamped blind on front cover,
lettering and design in gold on spine; white end-papers; all edges
trimmed. A volume of the *New Eversley Series*. Published on June 8,
1937; the edition consisted of 1500 copies.

Contents

The Land of Heart's Desire (1894)
Cathleen ni Houlihan (1902)

The Hour-Glass (1903). Prose version
The Pot of Broth (1904)
On Baile's Strand (1904)
Deirdre (1907)
The Green Helmet (1910)
The Shadowy Waters (1911). Acting version
The Words upon the Window-pane (1934)

191

A VISION | BY | W. B. YEATS | [three asterisks arranged in a triangle] | MACMILLAN & CO., LTD. | ST. MARTIN'S ST., LONDON | 1937

$7\frac{4}{5} \times 5\frac{1}{5}$; pp. viii, 308: comprising half-title, Macmillan's monogram and addresses on verso, pp. [i–ii]; title, copyright notice and imprint on verso, pp. [iii–iv]; contents, verso blank, pp. v–[vi]; list of Illustrations, verso blank, pp. vii–[viii]; fly-title, verso blank, pp. [1–2]; text, pp. 3–305; imprint, Printed in Great Britain by R. & R. Clark, Limited, Edinburgh, on p. [306]; list of Works by W. B. Yeats, pp. [307–308]. Frontispiece portrait of the author from an etching by Augustus John, R.A. Illustrations [by Edmund Dulac] on pp. 39, 64 and 66. Design of The Historical Cones on p. 266.

Issued in decorated black and brown paper boards with black cloth spine, lettered in gold on spine; white end-papers; all edges trimmed. Published on October 7, 1937; the edition consisted of 1500 copies.

Contents

A Packet for Ezra Pound
> From the Cuala Press edition of 1929 (No. 163).
> *Rapallo.* Dated March and October 1928.
>> Section VI of this essay is omitted, as also the two poems which followed it.
> *Introduction to "A Vision"*
>> This is revised and is now dated November 23rd 1928, and later.
> *To Ezra Pound*
Stories of Michael Robartes and his Friends: an Extract from a Record made by his Pupils
> From the Cuala Press edition of 1931 (No. 167).
> A long passage is added to section III.

The Phases of the Moon
    Book I: *The Great Wheel*
        Part I: *The Principal Symbol*
        Part II: *Examination of the Wheel*
        Part III: *The Twenty-eight Incarnations*
        Finished at Thoor Ballylee, 1922, in a time of Civil War.
    Book II: *The Completed Symbol*
    Book III: *The Soul in Judgment*
    Book IV: *The Great Year of the Ancients*
    Book V: *Dove or Swan*
        Written at Capri, February 1925.
The End of the Cycle. Dated 1934–1936.
All Souls' Night: an Epilogue. Dated Oxford, Autumn 1920.

So much which appeared in the first version of *A Vision*, 1925 (No. 149) has been omitted and so much new material added, that this is almost a new book.

192

AMERICAN EDITION

A VISION | BY | W. B. YEATS | [three asterisks in the form of an inverted triangle] | THE MACMILLAN COMPANY | NEW YORK. 1938

$8\frac{1}{2} \times 5\frac{3}{4}$; pp. 2, viii, 310. Frontispiece portrait of W. B. Yeats, 1907. From an etching by Augustus John, R.A.

Issued in black cloth with light green cloth spine, lettered blind on front cover, lettering in silver on spine; white end-papers; all edges trimmed. Published on February 23, 1938; the edition consisted of 1200 copies.

The contents are the same as those of the English edition of 1937 (No. 191).

193

A SPEECH AND | TWO POEMS BY | W. B. YEATS

$7\frac{1}{2} \times 5$; pp. 12: comprising title, verso blank, pp. [1–2]; text, pp. 3–5; p. [6] blank; Dedication, verso blank, pp. 7–[8]; text, pp. 9–11; colophon, Printed for W. B. Yeats at the Sign of the Three Candles, Ltd. Dublin, December, 1937 Edition limited to Seventy copies of which this is No. . . . . , at foot of p. [12].

70 copies issued in grey paper covers, lettered (in dark-green), as on title-page, on front cover; stitched; all edges untrimmed. Issued for presentation, not for sale.

Contents

From a Speech delivered at the Banquet of the Irish Academy of Letters, on 17th August, 1937
Dedication (Poem)
The Municipal Gallery Re-Visited (Poem)

194

ESSAYS | BY W. B. YEATS. | 1931 TO 1936 | [woodcut as in No. 179] | THE CUALA PRESS | DUBLIN, IRELAND | 1937
$8\frac{3}{10} \times 5\frac{1}{2}$; pp.xvi, 144: comprising pp. [i–xii] blank; title, verso blank, pp. [xiii–xiv]; Preface, on verso; contents, pp. [xv–xvi]; text, pp. [1]–[132]; colophon, in red, on p. [133]; pp. [134–144] blank.

Issued in sugar-bag blue paper boards with buff linen spine, lettered in black on front cover, white paper label, printed in black, on spine; blue end-papers matching binding; all edges untrimmed.

300 copies printed on paper made in Ireland and published by Elizabeth Corbet Yeats at The Cuala Press, 133 Lower Baggot Street, Dublin. Finished in the last week of October 1937. Published on December 14, 1937.

Contents

Preface
Parnell
Come Gather Round Me Parnellites. Dated August 1936.
    First appeared in *A Broadside*, New (3rd) Series, No. 1. January 1937. (See No. 254.)
Modern Poetry: a Broadcast. Dated 1936.
    Published separately in 1936 (No. 188).
Bishop Berkeley. Dated July 1931.
    First appeared as introduction to *Bishop Berkeley* by J. M. Hone and M. M. Rossi, 1931 (No. 280).
My Friend's Book
    First appeared in *The Spectator*, April 9, 1932. Printed in *Spectator's Gallery*, 1933 (No. 322).
N

Prometheus Unbound
    First appeared in *The Spectator*, March 17, 1933.
Louis Lambert
    First appeared in *The London Mercury*, July 1934.
Introduction to "An Indian Monk"
    First appeared in *An Indian Monk* by Shri Purohit Swami, 1932.
    (No. 281.)
Introduction to "The Holy Mountain"
    First appeared in *The Holy Mountain* by Bhagwan Shri Hamsa,
    1934. (No. 282.)
Introduction to "Mandukya Upanishad"
    First appeared, under the title *Introduction to a short Upanishad*,
    in *The Criterion*, July 1935.

195

THE | HERNE'S EGG | A STAGE PLAY | BY | W. B. YEATS |
LONDON | MACMILLAN AND CO LTD | 1938

$7\frac{9}{10} \times 5$; pp. vi, 74: comprising half-title, verso blank, pp. [i–ii]; title,
notice of copyright and imprint on verso, pp. [iii–iv]; Persons, verso
blank, pp. v–[vi]; text, pp. 1–[73]; imprint, Printed in Great Britain
by R. & R. Clark, Ltd, Edinburgh, on p. [74].

Issued in maroon cloth, lettering and design in gold on spine; white
end-papers; all edges trimmed. Published on January 21, 1938; the
edition consisted of 1600 copies.

Contents

The Herne's Egg

196

THE | HERNE'S EGG | AND OTHER PLAYS | BY | W. B.
YEATS | NEW YORK | THE MACMILLAN COMPANY | 1938

$7\frac{9}{10} \times 5\frac{1}{4}$; pp. viii, 136: comprising half-title, Macmillan's monogram
and addresses on verso, pp. [i–ii]; title, copyright notice and imprint,
Printed in the United States of America Norwood Press Linotype,
Inc. Norwood, Mass., U.S.A. on verso, pp. [iii–iv]; Preface, pp.
v–vi; contents, verso blank, pp. vii–[viii]; fly-title, Persons on verso,
pp. [1]–2; text, pp. 3–136.

Issued in black cloth, lettering and design in silver on front cover and on spine; off-white end-papers; all edges trimmed. Published on April 12, 1938.

Contents

Preface
The Herne's Egg
A Full Moon in March
The King of the Great Clock Tower (In verse)
Alternative Song for the Severed Head in "The King of the Great Clock Tower"

197

NEW POEMS: BY W. B. YEATS. | [woodcut, Monoceros de Astris, as in No. 111] | THE CUALA PRESS | DUBLIN, IRELAND | MCMXXXVIII

$8\frac{1}{8} \times 5\frac{3}{16}$; pp. xvi, 56: comprising pp. [i–xii] blank; title, verso blank, pp. [xiii–xiv]; contents, pp. [xv–xvi]; text, pp. [1]–[39]; p. [40] blank; Music, pp. [41–45]; p. [46] blank; colophon, in red, p. [47]; pp. [48–56] blank.

Issued in sugar-bag blue paper boards with buff linen spine, lettered in black on front cover, white paper label, printed in black, on spine; blue end-papers matching binding; all edges untrimmed.

450 copies printed and published by Elizabeth Corbet Yeats, at The Cuala Press, 133 Lower Baggot Street, Dublin. Finished on April 9, 1938. Published on May 18, 1938.

Contents

The Gyres
Lapis Lazuli
> First appeared in The London Mercury, March 1938; also printed in The New Republic, April 13, 1938.

Imitated from the Japanese
Sweet Dancer
> First appeared in The London Mercury, March 1938.

The Three Bushes
> First appeared in The London Mercury, January 1937, and printed in A Broadside, March 1937. (See No. 254.)

The Lady's First Song
The Lady's Second Song
The Lady's Third Song

The Lover's Song
The Chambermaid's First Song
The Chambermaid's Second Song
An Acre of Grass
    First appeared in *The London Mercury*, April 1938; also printed in *The Atlantic Monthly*, April 1938.
What Then?
    First appeared in *The Year's Poetry 1936* (No. 322A). Reprinted in *The Erasmian* (Dublin), April 1937.
Beautiful Lofty Things
A Crazed Girl
    First appeared, under the title *At Barcelona*, in *The Lemon Tree*, 1937. (No. 284.)
To a Friend
    First appeared in *The London Mercury*, March 1938; also printed in *The Nation* (New York), March 12, 1938.
The Curse of Cromwell
    First appeared in *A Broadside*, August 1937. (See No. 254.)
Roger Casement
    First appeared in *The Irish Press*, February 2, 1937. Reprinted, in a revised version and with an accompanying letter, in *The Irish Press*, February 13, 1937.
The Ghost of Roger Casement
The O'Rahilly
Come Gather Round Me Parnellites
    From *Essays, 1931 to 1936*, 1937 (No. 194).
The Wild Old Wicked Man
    First appeared in *The London Mercury*, April 1938; also printed in *The Atlantic Monthly*, April 1938.
The Great Day
    First appeared in *The London Mercury*, March 1938.
Parnell
    First appeared in *The London Mercury*, March 1938.
What was Lost
    First appeared in *The London Mercury*, March 1938.
The Spur
    First appeared in *The London Mercury*, March 1938.
A Drunken Man's Praise of Sobriety
The Pilgrim
    First appeared in *A Broadside*, October 1937. (See No. 254.)
Colonel Martin
    First appeared in *A Broadside*, December 1937. (See No. 254.)

A Model for the Laureate
The Old Stone Cross
> First appeared in *The London Mercury*, March 1938; also printed in *The Nation* (New York), March 12, 1938.

The Spirit Medium
Those Images
> First appeared in *The London Mercury*, March 1938; also printed in *The New Republic*, April 13, 1938.

The Municipal Gallery Re-Visited
> First appeared in *A Speech and Two Poems*, 1937 (No. 193).

Are You Content
> First appeared in *The London Mercury*, April 1938; also printed in *The Atlantic Monthly*, April 1938.

Music for "The Three Bushes". By Edmund Dulac.

Music for "The Curse of Cromwell"
Music for "Come Gather Round Me Parnellites"
Music for "The Pilgrim"
Music for "Colonel Martin"
> These four tunes are from traditional Irish airs.

198

THE | AUTOBIOGRAPHY | OF | WILLIAM BUTLER YEATS | [rule] | CONSISTING OF | REVERIES OVER CHILDHOOD AND YOUTH | THE TREMBLING OF THE VEIL | AND | DRAMATIS PERSONAE | [rule] | NEW YORK | THE MACMILLAN COMPANY | 1938

$8 \times 5\frac{1}{2}$; pp. viii, 480: comprising half-title, Macmillan's monogram and addresses on verso, pp. [i–ii]; title, copyright notice and imprint, Printed in the United States of America, on verso, pp. [iii–iv]; contents, verso blank, pp. [v–vi]; list of Illustrations, verso blank, pp. [vii–viii]; fly-title, verso blank, pp. [1–2]; fly-title, dedication on verso, pp. [3–4]; Preface, verso blank, pp. [5–6]; text, pp. 7–479; p. [480] blank. Frontispiece portrait of the author, aged 21, from a drawing by his Father. Illustrations facing pp. 30, 100, 308, 325, 336, 342, 348 and 384.

Issued in green cloth, lettered in gold inside gold panel on front cover, lettered in gold between two gold bars on spine; white end-papers; edges trimmed at head and foot, fore-edge untrimmed. Published on August 30, 1938.

Contents

Reveries over Childhood and Youth (1914)
The Trembling of the Veil (1922)
Dramatis Personae, 1896–1902
Estrangement
The Death of Synge
The Bounty of Sweden
    This omits the lecture on *The Irish Dramatic Movement*, and its
    notes.
Notes to "The Trembling of the Veil"
    I. *The Hermetic Students*
    II. *The Vision of an Archer*

†   †   †   †   †

199

SELECTED POEMS | OF | W. B. YEATS | AMSTERDAM |
A. A. BALKEMA | 1939

$7\frac{4}{8} \times 5$; pp. 60: comprising half-title, verso blank, pp. [1–2]; title,
verso blank, pp. [3–4]; text, pp. 5–56; contents, pp. [57–58]; colophon
on p. [59]; p. [60] blank.

Issued in light blue paper covers, with white paper lining, not pasted
down, lettered in blue on front cover SELECTED POEMS | OF | W. B.
YEATS, lettered in blue on spine W. B. YEATS—SELECTED POEMS; white
end-papers; all edges untrimmed.

The colophon reads:

These poems have been selected from the Collected Poems of W. B.
Yeats by A. Roland Holst and printed by J. F. Duwaer & Sons in
200 copies on Haesbeek Imperial.

According to D. de Jong's bibliography of works published without
permission of the Germans during the period of the Occupation the
date of publication was 1944.

Contents

Crossways (1889)
    *The Sad Shepherd; Down by the Salley Gardens; The Meditation
    of the Old Fisherman.*
The Rose (1893)
    *The Rose of the World; The Lake Isle of Innisfree; The Pity of
    Love; When You are Old; A Dream of Death.*

The Wind among the Reeds (1899)
> *The Lover tells of the Rose in his Heart; The Host of the Air; The Lover mourns for the Loss of Love ; He reproves the Curlew; A Poet to his Beloved; He hears the Cry of the Sedge; He wishes for the Cloths of Heaven; The Fiddler of Dooney.*

In the Seven Woods (1904)
> *Never give all the Heart; Red Hanrahan's Song about Ireland; The Old Men admiring Themselves in the Water; O do not love too Long.*

The Green Helmet and other Poems (1910)
> *No Second Troy; Reconciliation; The Fascination of What's Difficult; A Drinking Song; These are the Clouds.*

Responsibilities (1914)
> *September 1913 ; Fallen Majesty; That the Night come; A Coat.*

The Wild Swans at Coole (1919)
> *A Song; The Scholars; The Fisherman; A Deep-sworn Vow.*

Michael Robartes and the Dancer (1921)
> *Easter 1916; The Leaders of the Crowd; The Second Coming.*

The Tower (1928)
> *Sailing to Byzantium; Nineteen Hundred and Nineteen; Leda and the Swan; First Love; The Mermaid.*

The Winding Stair and other Poems (1933)
> *Death; The Nineteenth Century and After; Vacillation* (III): *Vacillation* (IV); *Vacillation* (VII).

200

LAST POEMS AND TWO PLAYS | BY WILLIAM BUTLER YEATS. | [woodcut as in No. 167] | THE CUALA PRESS | DUBLIN IRELAND | MCMXXXIX

$8\frac{3}{10} \times 5\frac{1}{2}$; pp. viii, 64: comprising pp. [i–iv] blank; title, verso blank, pp. [v–vi]; contents, verso blank, pp. [vii–viii]; text, pp. [1]–[59]; p. [60] blank; colophon, in red, on p. [61]; pp. [62–64] blank.

Issued in sugar-bag blue paper boards with buff linen spine, lettered in black on front cover, white paper label, printed in black, on spine; blue end-papers matching binding; all edges untrimmed.

500 copies printed and published by Elizabeth Corbet Yeats at The Cuala Press, 133 Lower Baggot Street, Dublin. Finished in the second week in June 1939. Published on July 10, 1939.

Contents

Under Ben Bulben. Dated September 4th 1938.
> First appeared in *The Irish Times* and in *The Irish Independent*, February 3, 1939. The last stanza of the poem also appeared in *The Irish Press*, February 3, 1949.

Three Songs to the one Burden
> First appeared in *The Spectator*, May 26, 1939.

The Black Tower. Dated January 21st. 1939.

Cuchulain Comforted. Dated January 13th. 1939.

Three Marching Songs

In Tara's Halls

The Statues. Dated April 9th. 1938.
> First appeared in *The London Mercury*, March 1939; also printed in *The Nation* (New York), April 15, 1939.

News for the Delphic Oracle
> First appeared in *The London Mercury*, March 1939; also printed in *The New Republic*, March 22, 1939.

Long-Legged Fly
> First appeared in *The London Mercury*, March 1939; also printed in *The Nation* (New York), April 15, 1939.

A Bronze Head
> First appeared in *The London Mercury*, March 1939; also printed in *The New Republic*, March 22, 1939.

A Stick of Incense

Hound Voice
> First appeared, under the title *Hound's Voice*, in *The London Mercury*, December 1938; also printed in *The Nation*, December 10, 1938.

John Kinsella's Lament for Mrs. Mary Moore
> First appeared in *The London Mercury*, December 1938; also printed in *The New Republic*, February 15, 1939.

High Talk
> First appeared in *The London Mercury*, December 1938; also printed in *The Nation*, December 10, 1938.

The Apparitions
> First appeared, under the title *Apparitions*, in *The London Mercury*, December 1938; also printed in *The New Republic*, February 15, 1939.

A Nativity
> First appeared, under the title *Nativity*, in *The London Mercury*, December 1938; also printed in *The New Republic*, February 15, 1939.

The Man and the Echo
> First appeared, under the title *Man and the Echo*, in *The London Mercury*, and in *The Atlantic Monthly*, January 1939.

The Circus Animal's Desertion
> First appeared in *The London Mercury*, and in *The Atlantic Monthly*, January 1939.

Politics
> First appeared in *The London Mercury*, and in *The Atlantic Monthly*, January 1939.

The Death of Cuchulain

Purgatory

201

ON THE BOILER | BY | W. B. YEATS | [rule] | THE CUALA PRESS | 133 LOWER BAGGOT STREET, | DUBLIN

$9\frac{3}{10} \times 7\frac{2}{5}$; pp. 48: comprising title, verso blank, pp. [1–2]; contents, verso blank, pp. [3–4]; Preface, verso blank, pp. [5–6]; text, pp. 7–45; advertisement of The Cuala Press, p. [46]; pp. [47–48] blank.

Issued in light blue-green covers, lettered and with reproduction of a drawing by Jack B. Yeats, R.H.A. in black on front cover, the lettering reading ON THE BOILER | BY. W. B. YEATS | [rule] | PRICE THREE SHILL-INGS AND SIXPENCE | [rule] | THE CUALA PRESS, DUBLIN the whole enclosed in double rules with corners indented, advertisement of The Cuala Press inside back cover; all edges trimmed.

Contents

Preface. Dated October, 1938.

The Name; including poem *Why should not old men be mad.*

Preliminaries

Tomorrow's Revolution

Private Thoughts

Ireland after the Revolution; including poem *I am tired of cursing the Bishop.*

Other Matters; including poem *I lived among great houses.*

Purgatory. Dated April, 1938.
> Already printed in *Last Poems and Two Plays*, 1939. (No. 200.)

Mrs. W. B. Yeats says that only about four copies of this edition had been issued when it was decided to reprint the book; the whole remainder of the edition was then destroyed and the new edition substituted.

202

ON THE BOILER | BY | W. B. YEATS | PUBLISHED BY |
THE CUALA PRESS | 133 LOWER BAGGOT STREET | DUBLIN |
PRINTED BY ALEX. THOM & CO., LTD. DUBLIN

$9\frac{3}{10} \times 7\frac{2}{5}$; pp. 48: comprising half-title, verso blank, pp. [1–2]; title,
copyright notice on verso, pp. [3–4]; contents, verso blank, pp.
[5–6]; Preface, verso blank, pp. [7–8]; text, pp. 9–46; advertisements,
verso blank, pp. [47–48].

Issued in blue paper covers, lettered and with a reproduction of a
drawing by Jack B. Yeats, R.H.A., on front cover, the lettering read-
ing ON THE BOILER | BY | W. B. YEATS | [drawing] | THE CUALA PRESS—
DUBLIN | PRICE: THREE SHILLINGS AND SIXPENCE; advertisement of
The Cuala Press inside back cover; no end-papers; all edges trimmed.
Published in the autumn of 1939.

The contents are the same as those of No. 201.

The copy in the British Museum Library is of the second printing.
This bears the date stamp September 4, 1939.

203

LAST POEMS | & | PLAYS | BY | W. B. YEATS | LONDON |
MACMILLAN & CO. LTD | 1940

$8\frac{1}{2} \times 5\frac{1}{2}$; pp. viii, 128: comprising half-title, verso blank, pp. [i–ii];
title, copyright notice and imprint on verso, pp. [iii–iv]; contents,
pp. v–vii; p. [viii] blank; fly-title, verso blank, pp. [1–2]; text, pp.
3–[126]; imprint, Printed in Great Britain by R. &. R. Clark, Limited,
Edinburgh, at foot of p. [126]; pp. [127–128] blank.

Issued in green cloth, design, signed Sturge Moore del, stamped
blind on front cover, design and lettering in gold on spine; white
end-papers; all edges trimmed. Published in January 1940; the edition
consisted of 2000 copies.

Contents

Last Poems 1936–1939:
> 35 poems from *New Poems*, 1938 (No. 197), the title of poem
> *To a Friend* changed to *To Dorothy Wellesley.*

19 poems from *Last Poems and Two Plays*, 1939 (No. 200), the order of the poems being changed.

3 poems from *On the Boiler*, 1939 (No. 201), here given titles *Why should not Old Men be Mad, Crazy Jane on the Mountain*, and *The Statesman's Holiday*.

Last Plays 1938–1939:
  Purgatory
  The Death of Cuchulain
  Both from *Last Poems and Two Plays*, 1939 (No. 200).

204

AMERICAN EDITION

LAST POEMS | & | PLAYS | BY | W. B. YEATS | NEW YORK | THE MACMILLAN COMPANY | 1940

$8\frac{1}{16} \times 5\frac{3}{16}$; pp. vi, 126: comprising half-title, Macmillan's monogram and addresses on verso, pp. [i–ii]; title, copyright notice and imprint, Printed in the United States of America American Book—Stratford Press, Inc., New York on verso, pp. [iii–iv]; contents, pp. [v–vi]; fly-title, verso blank, pp. [1–2]; text, pp. 3–[126].

Issued in green cloth, design, signed Sturge Moore del, stamped blind on front cover, design and lettering in gold on spine; white end-papers; all edges trimmed. Published on May 14, 1940.

The contents are the same as those of *Last Poems and Plays*, Macmillan & Co., London, 1940 (No. 203).

There was a further impression in December 1940.

205

IF I WERE FOUR-AND-TWENTY | BY | WILLIAM BUTLER YEATS | [woodcut as in No. 167] | THE CUALA PRESS | DUBLIN, IRELAND | MCMXL

$8\frac{3}{10} \times 5\frac{7}{10}$; pp. viii, 72: comprising pp. [i–iv] blank; title, verso blank, pp. [v–vi]; p. [vii] blank; contents [in red], p. [viii]; text, pp. [1]–[68]; colophon, in red, on p. [69]; pp. [70–72] blank.

Issued in sugar-bag blue paper boards with buff linen spine, lettered in black on front cover, white paper label, printed in black, on spine; blue end-papers matching binding; all edges untrimmed.

450 numbered copies printed on paper made in Ireland by Esther Ryan and Maire Gill, and published by the Cuala Press, 133 Lower

Baggot Street, Dublin. Finished in the first week of September 1940. Published on September 28, 1940.

Contents

If I were Four-and-Twenty (1919)
> First appeared in *The Irish Statesman*, August 23 and 30, 1919; also printed in *The Living Age*, October 4, 1920.

Swedenborg, Mediums and the Desolate Places (1914)
> First appeared in *Visions and Beliefs in the West of Ireland* by Lady Gregory: Second Series, 1920 (No. 312).

206

MOSADA | BY | W. B. YEATS | PRIVATELY PRINTED OCTOBER 1943. | CUALA PRESS DUBLIN

$8\frac{3}{10} \times 5\frac{7}{10}$; pp. vi, 22: comprising pp. [i–ii] blank; title, verso blank, pp. [iii–iv]; p. [v] blank; facsimile of MS., p. [vi]; text, pp. [1]–[17]; pp. [18–20] blank; colophon on p. [21]; p. [22] blank.

Issued in cream parchment covers lined with white paper, lettered in black on front; no end-papers; all edges untrimmed.

The colophon reads:
Fifty copies only of this edition of MOSADA have been privately printed from the text of 1889 published in THE WANDERINGS OF OISIN with the manuscript corrections made by the author on his own copy.
This is number

Contents

Frontispiece facsimile from manuscript dated June 7th, 1886.
Mosada

207

PAGES FROM A DIARY WRITTEN IN | NINETEEN HUN-DRED AND THIRTY | BY WILLIAM BUTLER YEATS | [woodcut of Giraldus as in No. 149] | THE CUALA PRESS | DUBLIN IRELAND | MCMXLIV

$8\frac{3}{10} \times 5\frac{3}{5}$; pp. viii, 64: comprising pp. [i–iv] blank; title, verso blank, pp. [v–vi]; p. [vii] blank; note on p. [viii]; text, pp. [1]–[58]; colophon, in red, on p. [59]; pp. [60–64] blank.

Issued in bright yellow paper boards with buff linen spine, lettered in black on front cover, white paper label, printed in black, PAGES FROM A DIARY BY W. B. YEATS on spine; bright yellow end-papers matching binding; all edges untrimmed.

280 numbered copies, of which 250 for sale, printed on paper made in Ireland by Esther Ryan and Maire Gill and published by The Cuala Press, 46 Palmerston Road, Dublin. Finished in the second week of September 1944. Published in November, 1944.

Contents

Note, signed George Yeats
Pages from a Diary
> The entries are dated and run from April 7 to November 18, 1930.

208

TRIBUTE | TO | THOMAS DAVIS | BY | W. B. YEATS | WITH AN ACCOUNT OF THE THOMAS DAVIS CENTENARY | MEETING HELD IN DUBLIN ON NOVEMBER 20TH, | 1914, INCLUDING DR. MAHAFFY'S PROHIBITION | OF THE "MAN CALLED PEARSE", AND AN | UNPUBLISHED PROTEST BY "A.E." | CORK UNIVERSITY PRESS | OXFORD: B. H. BLACKWELL, LTD. | 1947

$8\frac{3}{10} \times 5\frac{1}{2}$; pp. 24: comprising title, address of Dublin Agents on verso, pp. [1–2]; contents, verso blank, pp. [3–4]; text, pp. [5]–22; p. [23] blank; imprint, Printed by the Eagle Printing Works Ltd., South Mall, Cork. below rule at foot of p. [24].

Issued in stiff light blue paper covers, stitched, lettered in black on front cover as on title-page with the addition of the words ONE SHILLING AND SIXPENCE at foot; all edges trimmed. Published in August 1947.

Contents

Foreword. By Denis Gwynn
Thomas Davis. By W. B. Yeats
> First appeared in *New Ireland*, July 17, 1915.

An Unpublished Letter. By A.E.
> This letter is addressed to W. B. Yeats and is signed Geo. W. Russell.

209

THE DEFINITIVE EDITION

THE POEMS OF | W. B. YEATS | VOLUME ONE | [asterisk] | THE WANDERINGS OF OISIN · CROSSWAYS | THE ROSE · THE WIND AMONG THE REEDS | THE OLD AGE OF QUEEN MAEVE | BAILE AND AILLINN · IN THE SEVEN WOODS | THE SHADOWY WATERS | FROM 'THE GREEN HELMET AND OTHER POEMS' | RESPONSIBILITIES | MACMILLAN AND CO. LTD | ST. MARTIN'S STREET, LONDON | 1949

$9\frac{4}{5} \times 6\frac{1}{4}$; pp. 4, x, 276: comprising 3 pp. blank, on the fourth, limitation notice signed by the author; half-title, verso blank, pp. [i–ii]; title, copyright notice and notice of place of printing on verso, pp. [iii–iv]; contents, pp. v–ix; p. [x] blank; fly-title, quotation on verso, pp. [1–2]; dedication, verso blank, pp. [3–4]; text, pp. 5–[275]; imprint, Printed by R. & R. Clark, Ltd., Edinburgh p. [276]. Frontispiece portrait as in No. 75 by J. S. Sargent, R.A.

Issued in olive green buckram with bevelled boards, monogram of author's initials inside circle in gold on front cover, lettering inside frame in gold on spine; white end-papers; silk head-bands, top edges gilt, others untrimmed.

The edition was limited to 375 copies, printed on specially made Glastonbury Ivory Toned Antique Laid paper, and signed by the author, of which 350 were for sale. Published on November 25, 1949.

Contents

The Wanderings of Oisin
Crossways
The Rose
The Wind Among the Reeds
The Old Age of Queen Maeve
Baile and Aillinn
In the Seven Woods
The Shadowy Waters. A Dramatic Poem.
From 'The Green Helmet and other Poems'
Responsibilities
Notes

> The notes are the same as those printed in the *Collected Poems*, 1933 (No. 171); the first note is, however, now dated 1938.

210

THE POEMS OF | W. B. YEATS | VOLUME TWO | [asterisk] | THE WILD SWANS AT COOLE | MICHAEL ROBARTES AND THE DANCER | THE TOWER | THE WINDING STAIR AND OTHER POEMS | FROM 'A FULL MOON IN MARCH' | LAST POEMS | MACMILLAN AND CO. LTD. | ST. MARTIN'S STREET, LONDON | 1949

$9\frac{4}{5} \times 6\frac{1}{4}$; pp. xii, 308: comprising half-title, verso blank, pp. [i–ii]; title, copyright notice and notice of place of printing on verso, pp. [iii–iv]; contents, pp. v–xii; fly-title, verso blank, pp. [1–2]; text, pp. 3–282; fly-title, verso blank, pp. [283–284]; Index to Titles, pp. 285–295; p. [296] blank; Index to First Lines, pp. 297–[307]; imprint, Printed by R. & R. Clark, Ltd., Edinburgh, p. [308]. Frontispiece portrait from a Painting by Augustus John, O.M., R.A.

Issued in binding uniform with that of Volume One (No. 209).

Contents

The Wild Swans at Coole
Michael Robartes and the Dancer
The Tower
> The original poem *The Hero, the Girl and the Fool* is printed here, as in *The Tower*, 1928 (No. 158), instead of the final lyric only, *The Fool by the Roadside*, as in the *Collected Poems*, 1933 (No. 171).

The Winding Stair and other Poems
From 'A Full Moon in March'
Last Poems
Notes
> These are the same as those printed in *Collected Poems*, 1933, with one slight alteration and one short passage omitted. There is a new final note giving the original version of a stanza in *The Municipal Gallery Revisited*.

Index to Titles
Index to First Lines

The two volumes were issued together in a brown cardboard slip case.

From the Publishers' note in the prospectus for this edition:

For some time before his death, W. B. Yeats was engaged in revising the text of this edition of his poems, of which he had corrected the proofs, and for which he had signed the special page to appear at the beginning of Volume I.

211

THE | COLLECTED POEMS | OF | W. B. YEATS | MAC-
MILLAN AND CO., LIMITED | ST. MARTIN'S STREET, LONDON |
1950

$7\frac{7}{10} \times 5$; pp. xviii, 566: comprising half-title, verso blank, pp. [i–ii]; title, copyright notice, bibliographical note and place of printing on verso, pp. [iii–iv]; contents, pp. v–xviii; fly-title, verso blank, pp. [1–2]; fly-title, quotation on verso, pp. [3–4]; dedication, verso blank, pp. [5–6]; text, pp. 7–538; Index to Titles, pp. 539–551; p. [552] blank; Index to First Lines, pp. 553–[565]; imprint, Printed by R. & R. Clark, Ltd., Edinburgh at foot of p. [565]; p. [566] blank.

Issued in maroon cloth, lettering and design of unicorn and fountain in gold on spine; white end-papers; top edges stained maroon, others trimmed. Frontispiece portrait of W. B. Yeats, 1907, from the portrait by Augustus John, O.M., R.A. Published on July 4, 1950; the edition consisted of 10,000 copies.

Contents

Lyrical
> *Crossways* (1889)
> *The Rose* (1893)
> *The Wind Among the Reeds* (1899)
> *In the Seven Woods* (1904)
> From *The Green Helmet and other Poems* (1910)
> *Responsibilities* (1914)
> *The Wild Swans at Coole* (1919)
> *Michael Robartes and the Dancer* (1921)
> *The Tower* (1928)
> *The Winding Stair and other Poems* (1933), including *Words for Music Perhaps* and *A Woman Young and Old*
> From *A Full Moon in March* (1935)
> *Last Poems* (1936–1939)

Narrative and Dramatic
> *The Wanderings of Oisin* (1889)
> *The Old Age of Queen Maeve* (1903)
> *Baile and Aillinn* (1903)
> *The Shadowy Waters* (1906)

The Two Kings (1914)
The Gift of Harun Al-Rashid (1923)
Notes
Index to Titles
Index to First Lines

This book is described in the bibliographical note as Second Edition with later poems added. It follows the text of the First Edition, (No. 171), in printing *The Fool by the Roadside* in the section *The Tower* instead of the longer poem *Cuchulain, the Girl and the Fool* which appeared in the Definitive Edition of 1949 (Nos. 209 and 210).

In the Notes, that on the spelling of Gaelic names is now dated 1933 as in the First Edition, and the alteration and omission made in the Definitive Edition are not observed. The additional note on *The Municipal Gallery Revisited* is, however, printed.

There were further impressions in 1952, 1955, 1958, 1960, 1962, and 1965.

211A

THE | COLLECTED POEMS OF | W. B. YEATS | [monogram] WBY | THE MACMILLAN COMPANY | NEW YORK · 1951

$8\frac{3}{10} \times 5\frac{1}{2}$; pp. xvi, 480: comprising half-title, the Macmillan Company monogram and addresses on verso, pp. [i–ii]; title, copyright notices, bibliographical note and place of printing on verso, pp. [iii–iv]; contents, pp. v–[xvi]; fly-title, verso blank, pp. [1–2]; fly-title, quotation on verso, pp. [3–4]; dedication, verso blank, pp. [5–6]; text, pp. 7–458; Index to Titles, pp. 459–469; Index to First Lines, pp. 470–480.

Issued in dark blue cloth, monogram WBY in gold on front cover, lettering and design in gold on spine; white end-papers; all edges trimmed. Frontispiece portrait of W. B. Yeats. 1907, from the portrait by Augustus John, O.M., R.A. Published in March 1951; the edition consisted of 5000 copies.

This book is described in the bibliographical note as Second Edition, with later poems added, 1950. The contents are the same as those of the English edition of 1950 (No. 211).

There were further impressions in October 1951; December 1951; July 1952; August 1953; March 1954; and February 1955. The eighth impression, 7500 copies published April 3, 1956, is described in a bibliographical note as the "definitive edition with the author's final corrections." The "corrections" bring this impression into conformity with Nos. 209 and 210. There were further impressions of this

o

"definitive edition" in February 1957; January 1958; January 1959; November 1959; September 1960; July 1961; March 1962; March 1963; March 1964; July 1965; and February 1966.

211B

DIARMUID AND GRANIA | A PLAY IN THREE ACTS | BY | GEORGE MOORE | AND | W. B. YEATS | NOW FIRST PRINTED | WITH AN INTRODUCTORY NOTE | BY | WILLIAM BECKER | [short rule] | [REPRINTED FROM THE DUBLIN MAGAZINE, APRIL–JUNE, 1951]

$9\frac{1}{2} \times 7$; pp. 42: comprising title, p. [1]; text, pp. 2–41; p. [42] blank. The text is printed exactly as in the magazine except that the signature letter D on p. 41 has been taken out.

Issued in thick whitish-grey paper covers measuring $10 \times 7\frac{3}{8}$ and overlapping; lettered in black on front cover; all edges of the text trimmed.

This is an off-print from *The Dublin Magazine*; 25 copies were printed in April, 1951.

It may be noted that in this version the play does not contain the song in Act I., *There are seven that pull the thread* (No. 39).

211C

SELECTED POEMS | LYRICAL AND NARRATIVE | BY | W. B. YEATS | [design] | MACMILLAN AND CO., LIMITED | ST. MARTIN'S STREET, LONDON | 1951

6×4; pp. 2, x, 204: comprising one leaf not included in pagination; half-title, verso blank, pp. [i–ii]; title, copyright notice, bibliographical note and place of printing on verso, pp. [iii–iv]; Preface, verso blank, pp. v–[vi]; contents, pp. vii–x; fly-title, verso blank, pp. [1–2]; text, pp. 3–199; p. [200] blank; Index to first lines, pp. 201–[203]; imprint, Printed by R. & R. Clark, Ltd., Edinburgh at foot of p. [203]; p. [204] blank.

Issued in blue cloth, design in gold and rules round edges stamped blind on front cover, lettering in gold with gold line at head and foot on spine; white end-papers; all edges trimmed. A volume of the *Golden Treasury Series*. Published on May 11, 1951; the edition consisted of 3000 copies. There was a further impression in 1952.

The contents are the same as those of *Selected Poems*, 1929. (No. 165.)

211D

THE | COLLECTED PLAYS | OF | W. B. YEATS | MACMILLAN AND CO., LIMITED | ST. MARTIN'S STREET, LON-
DON | 1952

$7\frac{4}{5} \times 5\frac{1}{5}$; pp. vi, 706. On verso of title: First published 1934. Second
Edition, with additional plays, 1952.

Issued in maroon cloth, uniform with the Collected Poems published in
1950. (No. 211.) Frontispiece portrait from the charcoal drawing by
John S. Sargent, R.A. Published on September 26, 1952.

There were further impressions in 1953, 1960, and 1963.

Contents

The twenty-one plays included in the volume of 1934 (No. 177) to
which are added:

> *A Full Moon in March* (1935)
> *The King of the Great Clock Tower* (1935)
> *The Herne's Egg* (1938)
> *Purgatory* (1939)
> *The Death of Cuchulain* (1939)

211E

AMERICAN EDITION

THE | COLLECTED PLAYS | OF | W. B. YEATS |
NEW EDITION | WITH FIVE ADDITIONAL PLAYS | THE MAC-
MILLAN COMPANY | NEW YORK | 1953.

$8\frac{3}{10} \times 5\frac{1}{2}$; pp. viii, 448: comprising half-title, Macmillan's monogram
and addresses on verso, pp. [i–ii]; title, copyright notices, imprint,
Printed in the United States of America and notice concerning performing rights on verso, pp. [iii–iv]; preface, dated 1934, verso blank, pp.
[v–vi]; contents, verso blank, pp. [vii–viii]; fly-title, quotation, and
dedication, p. [1]; text, pp. 2–446; pp. [447–448], blank. Frontispiece
portrait of W. B. Yeats from a photograph by Martin Vos, New York.

Issued in similar style and binding to No. 211A. Published in 1953.

There were further impressions in July 1961; March 1962; November
1963; and July 1965.

Issued also in cerise-coloured cloth with gold lettering.

211F

SOME LETTERS FROM | W. B. YEATS | TO JOHN
O'LEARY AND HIS SISTER | FROM ORIGINALS IN
THE BERG COLLECTION | EDITED BY ALLAN WADE |
[ornament] | NEW YORK | THE NEW YORK PUBLIC LIBRARY |
1953

10 × 7; pp. 28: comprising title, copyright notice, and certificate of
printing on verso, pp. 1–2; introduction, pp. 3–5; text of letters, pp.
6–18; Notes, pp. 19–25; pp. 26–28 blank.

Issued in stiff cream paper covers, lettered in dark green on front cover;
all edges trimmed. Frontispiece reproduction in facsimile of first and
last pages of the first letter to John O'Leary, the paper on which this
is printed being carried through to the back of the book. Published
on March 28, 1953. The edition consisted of 300 copies.

211G

THE | AUTOBIOGRAPHY OF | WILLIAM BUTLER
YEATS | CONSISTING OF | REVERIES OVER
CHILDHOOD AND YOUTH | THE TREMBLING OF
THE VEIL | AND | DRAMATIS PERSONAE | [device] |
NEW YORK · THE MACMILLAN COMPANY · 1953. [*A re-issue of
No.* 198.]

$8\frac{3}{10} \times 5\frac{1}{2}$; pp. viii, 344: comprising half-title, Macmillan's monogram
and addresses on verso, pp. [i–ii]; title, copyright notices, and imprint,
Printed in the United States of America, on verso, pp. [iii–iv]; fly-
title and dedication, Preface dated 1914 on verso, pp. [1–2]; text, pp.
3–344. Frontispiece portrait of William Butler Yeats from British
Information Services.

Issued in red cloth, lettered in white on spine; white end-papers; all
edges trimmed. Published in 1953.

211H

W. B. YEATS | LETTERS TO | KATHARINE TYNAN | EDITED BY | ROGER MCHUGH | DUBLIN | CLONMORE AND REYNOLDS LTD | LONDON | BURNS OATES AND WASHBOURNE LTD.

$8\frac{1}{2} \times 5\frac{3}{8}$; pp. 192. Illustrations facing pp. 96, 97, 112, 113.

Issued in bright blue cloth, lettering in gold on spine; white end-papers; top edge blue, others trimmed. Published in 1953.

Contains 72 letters from Yeats to Katharine Tynan, transcribed from the originals in the Henry E. Huntington Library; and extracts from another eleven letters from Yeats to Katharine Tynan.

211I

AMERICAN EDITION

W. B. YEATS | LETTERS TO | KATHARINE TYNAN | EDITED BY | ROGER MCHUGH | MCMULLEN BOOKS, INC. | NEW YORK.

Issued in similar style and binding, and with the same contents and pagination, as No. 211H. Published in 1953.

Copies are known bound in black cloth.

211J

THE LETTERS | OF | W. B. YEATS | EDITED BY | ALLAN WADE | [Publisher's design] | RUPERT HART-DAVIS | 36 SOHO SQUARE LONDON W I | 1954

$9\frac{3}{8} \times 5\frac{1}{4}$; pp. 938. Frontispiece portrait of W. B. Yeats from a photograph by Howard Coster; illustrations facing pp. 52, 146(2), 288, 400, 412, 596, 600, 722, 830.

Issued in dark-blue cloth, lettered in gold on spine; white end-papers; top edges blue, others trimmed. Published on September 24, 1954. The edition consisted of 3000 copies.

211K

THE LETTERS | OF | W. B. YEATS | EDITED BY | ALLAN
WADE | THE MACMILLAN COMPANY | NEW YORK | 1955

$9\frac{3}{8} \times 5\frac{1}{4}$; pp. 940. 11 illustrations.

Issued in black cloth, lettered in silver on front cover and spine; white
end-papers; top edges green, others trimmed. Identical with the English edition, except that the Macmillan monogram and addresses appear
on the half-title verso, and there are two blank pages at the end, pp.
[939–940]. Published on February 21, 1955. The edition consisted of
2500 copies.

211L

W. B. YEATS | [swelled rule] | AUTOBIOGRAPHIES |
[ornament] | LONDON | MACMILLAN & CO LTD | 1955

$8\frac{4}{8} \times 5\frac{1}{2}$; pp. viii, 592. Frontispiece portrait; illustrations facing pp.
32, 48, 336, 353, 368, 400 and 512.

Issued in olive-green cloth, lettered in gold on spine; white end-
papers; all edges trimmed. Published on March 11, 1955.

Contents

Reveries over Childhood and Youth
The Trembling of the Veil
Dramatis Personae
Estrangement
The Death of Synge
The Bounty of Sweden
Notes

The Bounty of Sweden includes the lecture on *The Irish Dramatic
Movement* which had appeared in No. 146 and in Nos. 152 and 153,
but was omitted from No. 198. Two notes to *The Bounty of Sweden*
which had hitherto appeared only in No. 146 are now included. There
is a new footnote on p. 235.

2IIM

A VISION | BY | W. B. YEATS | [three asterisks in the form of an inverted triangle] | A REISSUE | WITH THE AUTHOR'S | FINAL REVISIONS | THE MACMILLAN COMPANY | NEW YORK | 1956

8⅛ × 5½; pp. viii, 310: comprising half-title, Macmillan's monogram and addresses on verso, pp. [i–ii]; title, copyright notice, bibliographical note and place of printing on verso, pp. [iii–iv]; contents, verso blank, pp. [v–vi]; list of illustrations, verso blank, pp. [vii–viii]; fly-title, verso blank, pp. [1–2]; text, pp. 3–305; pp. [306–310] blank.

Issued in dark-blue cloth, lettering in silver on spine; white end-papers; all edges trimmed. Frontispiece portrait of W. B. Yeats, 1907, from an etching by Augustus John, R.A. Published on April 17, 1956; the edition consisted of 1500 copies.

There was a second impression in 1961.

Issued also as a paperback in 1961, no. 75 of Macmillan Paperbacks. Published in Great Britain by Macmillan & Co. Ltd. in 1956. A slightly revised edition of this printing was published in 1958 and reprinted in 1962.

2IIN

THE VARIORUM EDITION | OF THE POEMS OF | W. B. YEATS | [rule] | EDITED BY | PETER ALLT | LATE OF TRINITY COLLEGE, DUBLIN | AND | RUSSELL K. ALSPACH | UNITED STATES MILITARY ACADEMY | THE MACMILLAN COMPANY . NEW YORK | [rule] | 1957

6⅛ × 9¼; pp. xxxvi, 884: comprising half-title, Macmillan's monogram and addresses on verso, pp. [i–ii]; title, copyright notice, Library of Congress catalogue card number and imprint, Printed in the United States of America, on verso, pp. [iii–iv]; dedication, verso blank, pp. [v–vi]; contents, verso blank, pp. [vii–viii]; preface, pp. ix–x; tribute to Peter Allt, pp. xi–xiv; introduction, pp. xv–xvi; list of poems, pp. xvii–xxviii; bibliography, pp. xxix–xxxiv; the collations, verso blank, pp. xxxv–[xxxvi]; text, pp. 1–884.

Issued in light blue linen with dark blue linen spine; title, editors' and publisher's names stamped in gold on spine; white end-papers; all edges trimmed. Published on October 29, 1957; the edition consisted of 3175 copies.

There was a second impression in May 1965.

A revised edition was published in September 1966.

Limited Edition

The pagination is the same, except that an additional leaf, unnumbered, is inserted after the half-title leaf, and reads This Special Printing of *The Variorum Edition of the Poems of W. B. Yeats* consists of eight hundred and twenty-five copies on paper specially made by Oxford Paper Company, each containing the Poet's autograph. This is Number . . ., verso blank.

Issued in wheat-coloured buckram with red buckram spine; title, editors' and publisher's names stamped in gold on spine; ivory end-papers; all edges trimmed. Each copy is inserted in a slip case. Published on October 29, 1957.

211O

THE | AUTOBIOGRAPHY OF | WILLIAM BUTLER YEATS | CONSISTING OF | REVERIES OVER CHILDHOOD AND YOUTH | THE TREMBLING OF THE VEIL | AND | DRAMATIS PERSONÆ | DOUBLE-DAY ANCHOR BOOKS | DOUBLEDAY & COMPANY, INC. | GARDEN CITY, NEW YORK | 1958.

$7\frac{1}{8} \times 4\frac{1}{8}$; pp. viii, 384, followed by 4 pp. of advertisements and 2 blank pages.

Issued in blue and white paper covers; lettered in white and black with design in gold of bird on bough on front cover; lettered in black on back cover; and lettered in black and white on spine; no end-papers, all edges trimmed. Published in 1958.

No. A142 of Doubleday Anchor Books.

211P

W. B. YEATS | [swelled rule] | MYTHOLOGIES | [ornament] | THE CELTIC TWILIGHT | THE SECRET ROSE | STORIES OF RED HANRAHAN | ROSA ALCHEMICA | THE TABLES OF THE LAW | THE ADORATION OF THE MAGI | PER AMICA SILENTIA LUNAE | LONDON | MACMILLAN & CO LTD. | 1959

$8\frac{4}{5} \times 5\frac{5}{8}$; pp. viii, 376: comprising half-title, verso blank, pp. [i–ii]; title, copyright notice, Macmillan's addresses and place of printing on verso, pp. [iii–iv]; contents, pp. v–vii; title of frontispiece, p. [viii]; note, verso blank, pp. 1–[2]; fly-title, verso blank, pp. [3–4]; text, pp. 5–140; poem Into the Twilight, verso blank, pp. 141–[142]; fly-title, epigraphs on verso, pp. [143–144]; poem To the Secret Rose, pp. 145–146; text, pp. 147–210; fly-title, verso blank, pp. [211–212]; text pp. 147–261; p. [262] blank; fly-title, epigraph on verso, pp. [263–264]; dedication, verso blank, pp. [265–266]; text, pp. 167–315; p. [316] blank; fly-title, verso blank, pp. [317–318]; prologue, verso blank, pp. 319–[320]; text, pp. 321–[369]; imprint, printed by R. & R. Clark, Ltd., Edinburgh, at foot of p. [369]; pp. [370–376] blank. Frontispiece portrait of W. B. Yeats from a charcoal drawing by John S. Sargent, R.A.

Issued in olive-green cloth, lettered in gold on spine; white end-papers; all edges trimmed. Published on March 12, 1959; the edition consisted of 3000 copies. There was a second impression in 1962

Contents

The Celtic Twilight (1893):
[The Note that precedes The Celtic Twilight is from the Notes to *Early Poems and Stories* (No. 147).] Reprinted from *Early Poems and Stories* (No. 147) with some changes in hyphenation and capitalisation. The poem 'Into the Twilight,' has been brought into conformity with the version in *The Variorum Edition* (No. 211n).

The Secret Rose (1897):
Reprinted from *Early Poems and Stories* (No. 147) with some changes in punctuation and hyphenation, and including 'Where There is Nothing There is God' from *The Secret Rose, Rosa Alchemica*, etc. (No. 81). The quotation from Leonardo da Vinci on verso of the fly-title is identified, and the poem 'To the Secret Rose' has been brought into conformity with the version in *The Variorum Edition* (No. 211n).

Stories of Red Hanrahan (1897):
Reprinted from *Early Poems and Stories* (No. 147) with some changes in punctuation, spelling, and hyphenation. The poem 'Red Hanrahan's Song About Ireland' in the story 'Hanrahan and Cathleen the Daughter of Houlihan' has been brought into conformity with the version in *The Variorum Edition* (No. 211n).

Rosa Alchemica, The Tables of the Law, and The Adoration of the Magi (1897):
Reprinted from *Early Poems and Stories* (No. 147).

Per Amica Silentia Lunae (1917):

> Reprinted from *Essays* (No. 141) with some changes in capitalisa-
> tion and punctuation. The poem 'Ego Dominus Tuus' has
> been brought into conformity with the version in *The Variorum
> Edition* (No. 211N).

211Q

AMERICAN EDITION

W. B. YEATS | [swelled rule] | MYTHOLOGIES |
[ornament] | THE CELTIC TWILIGHT | THE SECRET ROSE |
STORIES OF RED HANRAHAN | ROSA ALCHEMICA | THE TABLES
OF THE LAW | THE ADORATION OF THE MAGI | PER AMICA
SILENTIA LUNAE | NEW YORK | THE MACMILLAN COMPANY |
1959

$9\frac{1}{4} \times 6$; pp. viii, 374. The page breakdown is the same as the English
Edition (No. 211P).

Issued in light green cloth with black cloth spine; lettered in gold on
spine; white end-papers; all edges trimmed. Published on July 28
1959; the edition consisted of 4500 copies.

The contents are the same as the English edition (No. 211P).

211R

[publisher's device] | THE SENATE SPEECHES OF |
W. B. YEATS | EDITED BY | DONALD R. PEARCE | INDIANA
UNIVERSITY PRESS | BLOOMINGTON

$8 \times 5\frac{1}{4}$; pp. 184: comprising half-title, verso blank, pp. [1–2]; title,
acknowledgements, copyright notice, imprint, Manufactured in the
United States of America, and Library of Congress catalog card
number on verso, pp. [3–4]; preface, pp. 5–6; contents, pp. [7–9];
p. [10] blank; text, pp. 11–183; p. [184] blank. Illustrations facing
pp. 30 and 31.

Issued in blue-green cloth, lettered in silver on spine, with design in
silver stamped on front cover; sand-coloured end-papers; top edges
red, others untrimmed. Published in 1960.

211s

THE SENATE SPEECHES OF | W. B. YEATS | EDITED
BY | DONALD R. PEARCE | FABER AND FABER | 24 RUSSELL
SQUARE | LONDON.

Published in 1961. The contents are the same as the American edition
(No. 211R).

211T

W. B. YEATS | [swelled rule] | ESSAYS | AND |
INTRODUCTIONS | [ornament] | LONDON | MACMILLAN
& CO LTD | 1961

$8\frac{4}{5} \times 5\frac{1}{2}$; pp. xii, 532: comprising one leaf not included in pagination;
half-title, bibliographical note on verso, pp. [i–ii]; title, copyright
notice, Macmillan's addresses and place of printing on verso, pp.
[iii–iv]; contents, pp. v–vi; Introduction, pp. vii–xi; p. [xii], blank;
fly-title, verso blank, pp. [xiii–xiv]; fly-title, verso blank, pp. [1–2];
text, pp. 3–216; fly-title, verso blank, pp. [217–218]; Preface, verso
blank, pp. 219–[220]; text, pp. 221–383; p. [384] blank; fly-title, verso
blank, pp. [385–386]; text, pp. 387–530; imprint, Printed by R. & R.
Clark, Ltd., Edinburgh, verso blank, pp. [531–532]. Frontispiece
portrait of W. B. Yeats by John Butler Yeats the Elder, and a picture
of W. B. Yeats from the photograph by Howard Coster facing p.
[385].

Issued in olive-green cloth, lettered in gold on spine; white end-
papers; all edges trimmed. Published February 16, 1961; the edition
consisted of 2800 copies.

Contents

Introduction

Printed for the first time. A footnote on p. vii reads Written
for a complete edition of Yeats's works which was never produced.

Essays

I. *Ideas of Good and Evil:*
II. *The Cutting of an Agate:*

This section follows the edition of *Essays*, 1924 (No. 141), but
without the Dedication to Lennox Robinson.

Later Essays and Introductions

Gitanjali
       From *Gitanjali*, 1921 (No. 263)
Bishop Berkeley
My Friend's Book
Prometheus Unbound
An Indian Monk
Louis Lambert
The Holy Mountain
The Mandukya Upanishad
Parnell
Modern Poetry
       These nine selections from the Cuala Press edition of *Essays*,
       1931 to 1936 (No. 194).
A General Introduction for My Work
An Introduction for My Plays
       These two selections printed for the first time. Identical foot-
       notes on pp. 509 and 527 read Written for a complete edition of
       Yeats's works which was never produced.

211U

AMERICAN EDITION

W. B. YEATS | [swelled rule] | ESSAYS | AND |
INTRODUCTIONS | [ornament] | NEW YORK | THE
MACMILLAN COMPANY | 1961

$9\frac{1}{4} \times 6$; pp. xii, 532: comprising half-title, portrait of W. B. Yeats
by John Butler Yeats the Elder on verso, pp. [i–ii]; title, copyright
notice, imprint, Printed in the United States of America, and Library
of Congress catalog card number on verso, pp. [iii–iv]; contents, pp.
v–vi; Introduction, pp. vii–xi; p. [xii] blank; fly-title, verso blank,
pp. [1–2]; text, pp. 3–216; fly-title, verso blank, pp. [217–218];
Preface, verso blank, pp. 219–[220]; text, pp. 221–383; picture of W.
B. Yeats from the photograph by Howard Coster, p. [384]; fly-title,
verso blank, pp. [385–386]; text, pp. 387–530; pp. [531–532] blank.

Issued in beige-coloured cloth with black cloth spine; lettered in
gold on spine; cream-coloured end-papers; all edges trimmed.
Published on May 31, 1961; the edition consisted of 5000 copies.
The contents are the same as the English edition (No. 211T).

211v

THE | CELTIC TWILIGHT | AND A SELECTION
OF | EARLY POEMS | BY W. B. YEATS | INTRODUCTION BY
WALTER STARKIE | [publisher's device] | A SIGNET CLASSIC
| PUBLISHED BY THE NEW AMERICAN LIBRARY

7¼ × 4⅜: pp. 224, numbered i–xxvii, 28–[224]: comprising biographical
note and pen-and-ink sketch of Yeats, verso blank, pp. [i–ii]; title,
publisher's notices, copyright notices, date of printing and imprint,
Printed in the United States of America, on verso, pp. [iii–iv]; contents, pp. [v–vii]; p. [viii] blank; Introduction, pp. ix–xxv; p. [xxvi]
blank; half-title, poem Time drops in decay, on verso, pp. [xxvii]–28;
poem The Hosting of the Sidhe, verso blank, pp. 29–[30]; text, pp.
31–129; poem Into the Twilight, p. 130; fly-title, verso blank, pp.
[131–132]; text, pp. 133–[222]; advertisements, pp. [223–224].

Issued in paper covers coloured tan, brown, and white; lettered in
white with design of red rose, reproduction of sketch of Yeats, and
publisher's insignia on front cover; lettered in black and red on back
cover and in black on spine; no end-papers; all edges trimmed.
Published in March, 1962.

No. CP120 of the Signet Classics of The New American Library.

Contents

Introduction
The Celtic Twilight
    The text is from No. 35.
The Poems
    54 poems.
Notes on the Poems
Sources of the Poems
Selected Bibliography

211w

SELECTED | POEMS | OF | WILLIAM | BUTLER
YEATS | EDITED | AND WITH AN | INTRODUCTION BY | M. L.
ROSENTHAL | [swelled rule] | NEW YORK | THE MACMILLAN
COMPANY | 1962.

$8\frac{1}{4} \times 5\frac{3}{8}$; pp. xlii, 283: comprising half-title, verso blank, pp. [i–ii]; title, copyright notices, bibliographical note, imprint, Printed in the United States of America, and Library of Congress catalog card number, on verso, pp. [iii–iv]; Foreword, pp. [v–vi]; contents, pp. vii–xiii; p. [xiv] blank; Introduction, pp. xv–xxxix; p. [xl] blank; fly-title, verso blank, pp. [xli–xlii]; text, pp. 1–236; pp. [237–238] blank.

Issued in dark-grey paper covers, lettering in white, black, and red on front and back covers and spine, with design in red on front cover; no end-papers. Published on February 2, 1962; the edition consisted of 17,500 copies.

Contents

Foreword
Introduction: The Poetry of Yeats
From *Crossways* (1889) 5 poems.
From *The Rose* (1893) 14 poems.
From *The Wind Among the Reeds* (1899) 14 poems.
From *In the Seven Woods* (1904) 4 poems.
From *The Green Helmet and Other Poems* (1910) 13 poems.
From *Responsibilities* (1914) 20 poems.
From *The Wild Swans at Coole* (1919) 26 poems.
From *Michael Robartes and the Dancer* (1921) 10 poems.
From *The Tower* (1928) 12 poems.
From *The Winding Stair and Other Poems* (1933) 15 poems.
From *Words for Music Perhaps* 15 poems.
From *A Woman Young and Old* 3 poems.
From *A Full Moon in March* (1935) 9 poems.
From *Last Poems* (1936–1939) 35 poems.
Plays
Calvary (1921)
Purgatory (1939)
Notes
Glossary of Names and Places
Selective Bibliography
Index to Titles

211x

W. B. YEATS | SELECTED POETRY | EDITED | WITH AN INTRODUCTION AND NOTES | BY | A. NORMAN JEFFARES | PROFESSOR OF ENGLISH LITERATURE | UNIVERSITY OF LEEDS | LONDON | MACMILLAN & CO LTD | 1962

$6\frac{3}{4} \times 4\frac{1}{2}$; pp. xxii, 234: comprising half-title, list of publications of St. Martin's Library on verso, pp. [i–ii]; title, notice of copyright, Macmillan's addresses, and place of printing on verso, pp. [iii–iv]; contents pp. v–xii; Introduction, pp. xiii–xxi; p. [xxii] blank; text, pp. 1–232; imprint, Printed in Great Britain by Richard Clay and Company, Ltd., Bungay, Suffolk, below rule at foot of p. 232; pp. [233–234] blank.

Issued in paper covers coloured grey and green, with photograph of Yeats and publisher's insignia on front cover; lettered in white on front cover and spine with publisher's insignia repeated at foot of spine, lettered in black on back cover; no end-papers; all edges trimmed.

Contents

Introduction

From *Crossways* (1889) 6 poems.

From *The Rose* (1893) 11 poems.

From *The Wind Among the Reeds* (1899) 18 poems.

From *In the Seven Woods* (1904) 6 poems.

From *The Green Helmet and Other Poems* (1910) 8 poems.

From *Responsibilities* (1914) 14 poems.

From *The Wild Swans at Coole* (1919) 15 poems.

From *Michael Robartes and the Dancer* (1921) 10 poems.

From *The Tower* (1928) 13 poems.

From *The Winding Stair and Other Poems* (1933) 14 poems.

From *Words for Music Perhaps* 10 poems.

From *A Woman Young and Old* 9 poems.

From *A Full Moon in March* (1935) 8 poems.

From *Last Poems* (1936–1939) 23 poems.

Notes

Index to Titles

Index to First Lines

211Y

W. B. YEATS | [swelled rule] | EXPLORATIONS | [ornament] | SELECTED BY | MRS. W. B. YEATS | LONDON | MACMILLAN & CO LTD | 1962

$8\frac{4}{5} \times 5\frac{1}{2}$; pp. viii, 456: comprising half-title, bibliographical note on verso, pp. [i–ii]; title, copyright notice, Macmillan's addresses and place of printing on verso, pp. [iii–iv]; publisher's note, verso blank, pp. v–[vi]; contents, pp. vii–viii; fly-title, verso blank, pp. [1–2]; text, pp. 3–70; fly-title, note on verso, pp. [71–72]; text, pp. 73–259; p. [260] blank; fly-title, verso blank, pp. [261–262]; text, pp. 263–286; fly-title, verso blank, pp. [287–288]; text, pp. 289–340; fly-title, verso blank, pp. [341–342]; text, pp. 343–404; fly-title, verso blank, pp. [405–406]; text, pp. 407–[453]; imprint, Printed by R. & R. Clark, Ltd., Edinburgh at foot of p. [453]; pp. [454–456] blank. Frontispiece portrait of William Butler Yeats from a painting by Augustus John.

Issued in olive-green cloth, lettered in gold on spine; white endpapers; all edges trimmed. Published on July 23, 1962; the edition consisted of 3000 copies.

Contents

I

Explorations I

Cuchulain of Muirthemne (1902)
Gods and Fighting Men (1904)
> These two selections reprinted, slightly revised, from *Discoveries. Edmund Spenser. Poetry and Tradition; & Other Essays* (No. 82).

Swedenborg, Mediums and the Desolate Places (1914)
> From the Cuala Press edition of *If I Were Four-and-Twenty* (No. 205).

II

The Irish Dramatic Movement: 1901–1919
> From *Plays and Controversies* (No. 139) and including 'Samhain: 1908. First Principles,' that first appeared in *Samhain*, November 1908.

III

Explorations II

If I Were Four-and-Twenty (1919)
> From the Cuala Press edition of *If I Were Four-and-Twenty* (No. 205).

The Midnight Court (1926)
> First appeared as the Introduction to *The Midnight Court* (No. 276).

IV

Pages from a Diary Written in Nineteen Hundred and Thirty: 1944
> From the Cuala Press edition of *Pages from a Diary Written in Nineteen Hundred and Thirty* (No. 207).

V

From *Wheels and Butterflies:* 1934

Introduction to The Words upon the Window-pane
Fighting the Waves
Introduction to The Resurrection
Introduction to The Cat and the Moon

These four selections from *Wheels and Butterflies* (No. 175). Section IV of the *Introduction to The Cat and the Moon* is omitted.

From *On the Boiler:* 1939

The Name
Preliminaries
To-morrow's Revolution
Private Thoughts

Section V is omitted.

Ireland after the Revolution

Sections IV (the poem 'Crazy Jane on the Mountain') and V are omitted.

Other Matters

Section V is omitted; section VI has become section V; section VII has become section VI; section VIII has become section VII.

These six selections are from the Cuala Press edition of *On the Boiler* (Nos. 201–202).

211z

AMERICAN EDITION

W. B. YEATS | [swelled rule] | EXPLORATIONS | [ornament] | SELECTED BY | MRS. W. B. YEATS | THE MAC-MILLAN COMPANY | NEW YORK.

$9\frac{1}{4} \times 6\frac{1}{4}$; pp. viii, 456: comprising half-title, portrait of William Butler Yeats by Augustus John on verso, pp. [1–ii]; title, copyright notice, imprint, Printed in the United States of America, and Library of Congress catalog card number on verso, pp. [iii–iv]; publishers note, verso blank, pp. [v–vi]; contents, pp. vii–viii; fly-title, verso blank, pp. [1–2]; text, pp. 3–70; fly-title, note on verso, pp. [71–72]; text, pp. 73–[259]; p. [260] blank; fly-title, verso blank, pp. [261–262]; text, pp. 263–286; fly-title, verso blank, pp. [287–288]; text, pp. 289–340; fly-title, verso blank, pp. [341–342]; text, pp. 343–404; fly-title, verso blank, pp. [405–406]; text, pp. 407–[453]; pp. [454–456] blank.

P

Issued in light-green cloth with dark-green spine; lettered in purple and white on spine, monogram stamped in purple on front cover; blue end-papers; top and bottom edges trimmed. Published on April 1, 1963; the edition consisted of 3000 copies.

The contents are the same as the English edition (No. 211Y).

211AA

A CONCORDANCE TO THE POEMS OF | W. B. YEATS | edited by | Stephen Maxfield Parrish | programmed by | James Allan Painter | Cornell University Press | Ithaca, New York

$6\frac{1}{8} \times 9\frac{3}{16}$; pp. xl, 968: comprising half-title, information about The Cornell Concordances on verso, pp. [i–ii]; title, copyright notice, Library of Congress catalog card number and imprint, Printed in the United States of America on verso, pp. [iii–iv]; editor's preface, pp. v–xxvii; p. [xxviii] blank; programmer's preface, pp. xxix–xxxxvii; p. [xxxviii] blank; fly-title, verso blank, [pp. xxxix–xl]; text, pp. 1–967; p. [968] blank.

Issued in dark-red cloth; lettered in silver on spine and front cover; white end-papers; all edges trimmed. Published on September 10, 1963; the edition consisted of 1500 copies.

211BB

W. B. Yeats | SELECTED PLAYS | edited | with an introduction and notes | by | A. Norman Jeffares | Professor of English Literature | University of Leeds | London | Macmillan & Co Ltd | 1964

$6\frac{3}{4} \times 4\frac{1}{2}$; pp. viii, 280: comprising pp. [i–ii] blank; half-title, verso blank, pp. [iii–iv]; title, notice of copyright, Macmillan's addresses, and place of printing on verso, pp. [v–vi]; contents, pp. [vii–viii]; introduction, pp. 1–15; note on the text, p. [16]; text, pp. [17]–276; imprint, Printed in Great Britain by Richard Clay and Company, Ltd., Bungay, Suffolk, below rule at foot of p. 276; pp. [277–278] blank; list of St. Martin's library, verso blank, pp. [279–280].

Issued in white paper covers with design of mask in black, green, and gold on front cover; lettered in black on front cover and spine with publisher's insignia in green at foot of spine, lettered in black on back cover; no end-papers; all edges trimmed.

Contents

Introduction
Note on the Text
On Baile's Strand
Deirdre
The Player Queen
The Only Jealousy of Emer
The Resurrection
The Words upon the Window-pane
A Full Moon in March
The Herne's Egg
Purgatory
The Death of Cuchulain
Cathleen ni Hoolihan
Notes
Select Bibliography

211cc

W. B. Yeats | SELECTED PROSE | edited | with an introduction and notes | by | A. Norman Jeffares | Professor of English Literature | University of Leeds | London | Macmillan & Co Ltd | 1964

$6\frac{3}{4} \times 4\frac{1}{2}$; pp. 288: comprising half-title, list of publications of St. Martin's library on verso, pp. [1–2]; title, notice of copyright, Macmillan's addresses, and place of printing on verso, pp. [3–4]; contents, pp. [5–6]; acknowledgements, verso blank, pp. [7–8]; introduction, pp. 9–18; text, pp. 19–286; imprint, Printed in Great Britain by Richard Clay and Company Ltd., Bungay, Suffolk, verso blank, pp. [287–288].

Issued in similar style and binding to No. 211BB except that the design on front cover is of an inkpot rather than a mask.

Contents

Acknowledgements
Introduction
Autobiographical Writings
Letters
Essays, Stories, Introductions, Speeches and Other Prose
Notes

211DD

W. B. Yeats | SELECTED CRITICISM | edited | with an
introduction and notes | by | A. Norman Jeffares | Pro-
fessor of English Literature | University of Leeds | London |
Macmillan & Co Ltd | 1964

$6\frac{3}{4} \times 4\frac{1}{2}$; pp. 292: comprising half-title, list of publications of St.
Martin's library on verso, pp. [1–2]; title, notice of copyright, Mac-
millan's addresses, and place of printing on verso, pp. [3–4]; contents,
acknowledgements on verso, pp. [5–6]; introduction, pp. 7–16; text,
pp. 17–292; imprint, Printed in Great Britain by Richard Clay and
Company, Ltd., Bungay, Suffolk, at foot of page 292.

Issued in similar style and binding to No 211BB except that the design
on front cover is of a quill pen.

Contents

Acknowledgements
Introduction
Twenty-three critical essays
Notes

211EE

THE VARIORUM EDITION | OF THE PLAYS OF |
W. B. YEATS | edited by | Russell K. Alspach | United
States Military Academy | assisted by | Catharine C. Als-
pach | Macmillan | London · Melbourne · Toronto | 1966

$6 \times 9\frac{1}{4}$; pp. xxvi, 1338: comprising half-title, The Variorum Edition
of the Poems of W. B. Yeats, edited by Peter Allt and Russell K.
Alspach, and Irish Poetry from the English Invasion to 1798 by
Russell K. Alspach listed on verso, pp. [i–ii]; title, copyright notice,
Macmillan's addresses and imprint, Printed in Great Britain, on verso,
pp. [iii–iv]; dedication To the memory of Peter Allt, verso blank, pp.
[v–vi]; contents, verso blank, pp. vii–[viii]; preface, verso blank, pp.
ix–[x]; introduction, pp. xi–xvi; list of plays, pp. xvii–xviii; bibliography, pp. xix–xxiv; the collations, verso blank, pp. xxv–[xxvi]; text,
pp. 1–1319; index, pp. 1320–1336; pp. [1337–1338], blank.

Issued in dark-blue linen; title and editor's name stamped in gold
against a red leaf-design on spine, publisher's name in gold at foot of

spine; white end-papers; all edges trimmed. Published in January 1966; the edition consisted of 500 copies.

There was a second printing, with some slight revisions, in August 1966.

211FF

THE VARIORUM EDITION | OF THE PLAYS OF | W. B. YEATS | [rule] | edited by | Russell K. Alspach | United States Military Academy | assisted by | Catharine C. Alspach | The Macmillan Company · New York | [rule] | 1966

Identical with the English edition (No. 211EE) except that the verso of the title contains the words First Printing, the imprint reads Printed in Great Britain by R. & R. Clark Ltd. Edinburgh, and the Library of Congress catalog card number is at the foot of the page. The binding is identical with the English edition except that the title, the editor's name, and the publisher's name are stamped in gold on the spine.

Published in March 1966; the edition consisted of 1000 copies.

There was a second printing, with some slight revisions, in 1967.

BOOKS BY YEATS
ADDENDA

PART II

1. BOOKS AND PERIODICALS EDITED BY W. B. YEATS

2. BOOKS WITH A PREFACE OR INTRODUCTION
BY W. B. YEATS

3. BOOKS CONTAINING CONTRIBUTIONS BY W. B. YEATS
INCLUDING LETTERS FROM HIM

1. BOOKS AND PERIODICALS
EDITED BY W. B. YEATS

212

FAIRY AND FOLK TALES | OF THE IRISH PEASAN-
TRY: | EDITED AND SELECTED BY | W. B. YEATS. | LONDON |
WALTER SCOTT, 24 WARWICK LANE | NEW YORK: THOMAS
WHITTAKER | TORONTO: W. J. GAGE AND CO. | 1888

$6\frac{3}{5} \times 4\frac{1}{2}$; pp. xx, 326, followed by 6 pp. of advertisements. An Errata
slip was inserted, sometimes facing p. xviii and sometimes facing
p. 326.

No. 32 of The Camelot Series, issued simultaneously (1) in dark blue
cloth with paper label on spine, printed in black within a red line
border and headed Camelot Series; white end-papers; all edges untrimmed; and (2) in red cloth, lettering and design in black on front
cover, lettering and two rules in gold, lettering and design in black,
on spine; white end-papers; all edges trimmed. Some copies were also
issued in red leather with lettering in gold. There were also copies
issued in sage-green cloth, lettered in gold on front cover IRISH FAIRY |
AND FOLK TALES over decorated panel, with design of Irish bog land in
colours and gold, lettered in gold on spine FAIRY & FOLK | TALES OF
THE | IRISH PEASANTRY and design of Irish cabin in colours and gold;
yellow patterned end-papers; all edges gilt. This binding may have
been specially designed for this particular volume of the series. My
copy is dated on title 1888 and has evidently never had a half-title.

Yeats contributed:
Dedication: 'Inscribed to my mystical friend G.R.'* P. v.
Introduction. Signed. Pp. ix–xviii.
The Trooping Fairies. Pp. 1–3.
    Notes on pp. 16, 33, 37, 38.
Changelings. P. 47.
The Stolen Child. Signed. Pp. 59–60.
    Previously printed in *Poems and Ballads of Young Ireland,*
    1888. (No. 289.)

  * I am convinced that this refers to George Russell (A.E.), but I cannot
prove it.

The Merrow. P. [61.]

The Solitary Fairies. Pp. 80–81.

The Pooka. P. 94.

  Note: *The Banshee.* P. 108.

Ghosts. Pp. 128–129.

  Note. P. 131.

Witches, Fairy Doctors. Pp. 146–149.

  Notes on pp. 150, 155, 160, 161, 168, 191, 199.

  Note: *Tir-na-n-Og.* P. 200.

  Note. P. 207.

Saints, Priests. P. 214.

The Priest of Coloony. (A poem, with a note in prose.) Signed. Pp.
  220–221. The poem previously appeared in *Irish Minstrelsy*,
  1888. (No. 290.)

  Note. P. 232.

Giants. P. 260.

  Notes on pp. 268, 295, 299, 309, 319–326.

This series of books was first issued in 1886 under title of The
Camelot Classics, but the name appears to have been changed to
Camelot Series in 1887 or 1888. Some copies are found with Camelot
Classics on the paper label and Camelot Series on the half-title, which
may indicate a return to the earlier nomenclature. The copy described
above is in the British Museum and has neither name on the half-title;
it bears the date-stamp 27 September 1888. Later issues had title-pages
reading (*a*) Fairy and Folk Tales of the | Irish Peasantry. Edited and |
Selected by W. B. Yeats. | The Walter Scott Publishing Co., Ltd. |
London and Felling-on-Tyne. | New York: 3 East 14th Street. [n.d.];
or (*b*) Fairy and Folk Tales of the | [&c. as in (*a*)] || London: Walter
Scott, Ltd. | Paternoster Square. [n.d.]

Later the name of the series was changed to The Scott Library and
the volumes were issued in dark green cloth, lettering and design
in gold on front cover, lettering in gold on spine; top edges gilt,
others trimmed. The half-title was omitted and the imprint at foot of
title read LONDON: | WALTER SCOTT, 24 WARWICK LANE. | NEW YORK:
3 EAST 14TH STREET. The date of publication was omitted. The
volume is No. 37 in the series. A Scott Library copy has recently been
reported with a half-title and with the Paternoster Square title-page.

Later still the volumes were issued in smooth dark red cloth, publisher's device stamped blind on front cover, lettering and medallion
carrying the words SCOTT LIBRARY in gold on spine; all edges trimmed.

212A

AMERICAN EDITION

IRISH FAIRY | AND FOLK TALES | EDITED AND SELECTED | BY W. B. YEATS | [black-and-white drawing] | PROFUSELY ILLUSTRATED | A. L. BURT COMPANY, | PUBLISHERS, NEW YORK.

7½ × 5; pp. xvi, 416, followed by 2 pp. of advertisements.

Issued in green cloth with pictorial design in pink, black, and yellow on front cover and on spine; white end-papers; all edges trimmed. There are full-page black-and-white illustrations facing title-page, pp. 60, 88, 120, 196, 210, and 318, as well as numerous smaller ones. Except for the addition of *The Fate of the Children of Lir* at the beginning, and the deletion of the dedication, the contents are the same as No. 212. Published in 1902.

212B

IRISH FAIRY AND | FOLK TALES | EDITED BY | W. B. YEATS | [device] | NEW YORK | CARLTON HOUSE

7¾ × 5¼; pp. viii, 344.

Issued in red cloth with gold line design in a blue background on front cover, three similar designs on spine. Lettered on spine GREAT | SHORT | STORIES | | IRISH | FOLK | TALES | YEATS; top edges blue, other edges trimmed. A volume in a set of Great Short Stories. Except for the deletion of the dedication and introduction the contents are the same as No. 212. No date.

213

IRISH FAIRY AND FOLK TALES | [rule] | EDITED BY W. B. YEATS | [rule] | [device] | [rule] | BONI AND LIVERIGHT, INC. | [rule] | PUBLISHERS NEW YORK

6½ × 4¼; pp. xviii, 354.

No. 44 of The Modern Library. This series has been issued, from time to time, in a considerable variety of binding styles. The records of Messrs. Boni and Liveright do not exist to show what style was first used, although it probably was blue fabricoid and later brown fabricoid; all edges trimmed for both bindings. Roth gives the date of publication as 1918. In 1925 The Modern Library was acquired by Random House, Inc. The title-page of No. 44 is now IRISH | FAIRY | AND | FOLK | TALES | EDITED BY | W. B. YEATS | THE | MODERN LIBRARY | NEW YORK [all set in a double panel: device in lower r.h. corner]; the pagination is xviii, 2, 352, followed by 8 pp. of advertisements and 2 blank leaves; the binding is grey cloth with lettering in gold inside black panels on front cover and spine; all edges trimmed.

Yeats's contributions are the same as those to *Fairy and Folk Tales of the Irish Peasantry*, 1888. (NO. 212.)

213A

IRISH FOLK STORIES | AND | FAIRY TALES | edited by | William Butler Yeats | Grosset's Universal Library | Grosset & Dunlap · New York

8 × 5⅜; pp. xviii, 298.

Issued in paper covers coloured grey, green, and yellow; lettered in white, yellow, green, and black, with designs in green, on front cover; lettered in black on back cover; and lettered in white, black, and yellow on spine; no end-papers; all edges trimmed. Published in 1957.

No. UL-21 of Grosset's Universal Library.

214

STORIES FROM CARLETON: | WITH AN INTRODUCTION | BY W. B. YEATS. | LONDON: | WALTER SCOTT, 24 WARWICK LANE. | NEW YORK AND TORONTO: | W. J. GAGE & CO.

6⅗ × 4½; pp. xx, 302.

No. 48 in The Camelot Series, issued in two binding styles similar to those of No. 212. Published in August 1889.

Yeats contributed:

Dedication: "To my friend the Author of 'Shamrocks',* W.B.Y."
    P. v.

William Carleton. Pp. [ix]–xvii.

For description of the binding of later issues in The Camelot Classics and The Scott Library, see note to *Fairy and Folk Tales of the Irish Peasantry*, 1888. (No. 212.)

* Katharine Tynan.

In Quinn's copy Yeats wrote: "I thought no end of Carleton in those days & would still I dare say if I had not forgotten him. W. B. Yeats, 1904."

215

REPRESENTATIVE | IRISH TALES | COMPILED, WITH AN INTRODUCTION AND NOTES | BY | W. B. YEATS | [rule] | FIRST [SECOND] SERIES | [rule] | [medallion, *in red*, bearing the words KNICKERBOCKER NUGGETS] | NEW YORK AND LONDON | G. P. PUTNAM'S SONS | THE KNICKERBOCKER PRESS [*Entire title printed on a yellow ground and enclosed within a red line border.*]

$5\frac{2}{8} \times 3\frac{1}{2}$; Vol. I., pp. 4, vi, 340, followed by pp. vii of advertisements and 3 blank pages unnumbered. Vol. II., pp. 6, iv, 356, followed by pp. vii of advertisements and 3 blank pages unnumbered.

Issued in decorated paper boards, half bound in dark blue cloth decorated in gold and lettered in gold on spine IRISH TALES | [rule] | FIRST [SECOND] SERIES, and, at foot, KNICKERBOCKER NUGGETS arranged in a circle; white end-papers; top edges gilt, others untrimmed. Published in March 1891.

Copies are also found in pink cloth decorated in dark blue; lettered on spine IRISH TALES | [rule] | FIRST [SECOND] SERIES; top edges stained red, others untrimmed. The Second Series has two blank pages before the title. Half-titles and advertisements do not appear, and except for the panel on titles there is no reference to Knickerbocker Nuggets.

Yeats contributed:

VOLUME I.

Dedication. "There was a green branch hung with many a bell." Pp. iii–iv.

Introduction. Pp. 1–17.

Maria Edgeworth. Pp. 19–24.

John and Michael Banim. Pp. 141–150.

William Carleton. Pp. 191–196.

VOLUME II.

Samuel Lover. Pp. 1–3.

William Maginn. Pp. 91–92.

T. Crofton Croker. Pp. 129-130.

Gerald Griffin. Pp. 161–164.
Charles Lever. Pp. 205–209.
Charles Kickham. Pp. 243–245.
Miss Rosa Mulholland. P. 281.
Note. P. 331.

Quinn's copy was inscribed "This book was reviewed by the Saturday Review under the idea that it was written by a barbarous super-republican American. I read a lot, innumerable good and bad novels before I made this. W. B. Yeats. March, 1904."

There was a later issue, also undated:

REPRESENTATIVE | IRISH TALES | COMPILED WITH AN IN-TRODUCTION AND | NOTES BY | W. B. YEATS | FIRST [SECOND] SERIES [*between rules*] | [decorative rule] | NEW YORK AND LONDON | G. P. PUTNAM'S SONS | THE KNICKERBOCKER PRESS [*All in a decorative black-letter in a panel of two lines with design between them*]

The contents are similar to those of the earlier issue, but lack the advertisements and blank pages.

Issued in decorated boards with dark green leather spine and corners, lettered on spine in gold REPRE | SENTATIVE | IRISH TALES | [rule] | W. B. YEATS. in a decorative panel with VOL I [II] below the title panel; cream end-papers; top edges gilt, others untrimmed, with green marker.

215A

IRISH TALES | by | Maria Edgeworth [in red] | and | John and Michael Banim [in red] | Castlerackrent. The Stolen Sheep | The Mayor of Wind-Gap | with introduction by | W. B. Yeats [in red] | [publisher's device] | New York and London | G. P. Putnam's Sons [in red] | The Knicker-bocker Press

$5\frac{1}{2} \times 3\frac{3}{4}$; pp. iv, 192.

Issued in red limp leather boards lettered in gilt on spine and within a publisher's device on front cover. Except for the deletion of the dedication and the introduction to Carleton, Yeats's contributions are the same as in No. 215, volume I. No date.

216

IRISH | FAIRY TALES [*in red*] | EDITED | WITH AN INTRO-
DUCTION [*in red*] | BY | W. B. YEATS [*in red*] | AUTHOR OF 'THE
WANDERINGS OF OISIN,' ETC. | ILLUSTRATED BY JACK B.
YEATS | LONDON | T. FISHER UNWIN [*in red*] | 1892

6⅛ × 4; pp. viii, 236, followed by 8 pp. of advertisements, imprint, and
3 blank pages. Illustrations facing title, and p. 71.

A volume of The Children's Library, issued in pinafore cloth, lettered
in blue, inside panel, on front cover; lettered in blue on spine IRISH |
FAIRY | TALES | THE | CHILDREN'S | LIBRARY | T. FISHER UNWIN;
decorated end-papers matching binding; all edges trimmed and
decorated to match binding. Published in 1892.

Yeats contributed:

Where my books go. (Poem.) Dated January 1892. P. v.
Introduction: "An Irish Story-teller." Dated July 1891. Pp. 1–7.
Note. Pp. 8–9.
A Fairy Enchantment. Story-teller—Michael Hart. Recorder—
W. B. Yeats. Pp. 49–52.
Appendix. Classification of Irish Fairies. Dated June 1891. Pp. 223–
233.
Authorities on Irish Folklore. Pp. 234–236.

There was a second impression, undated, issued in buff paper boards
with pictorial design of children on front cover and on spine; white
end-papers; all edges trimmed. No advertisements at end.

217

AMERICAN EDITION

IRISH | FAIRY TALES [*in red*] | EDITED | WITH AN INTRO-
DUCTION [*in red*] | BY | W. B. YEATS [*in red*] | AUTHOR OF 'THE
WANDERINGS OF OISIN,' ETC. | ILLUSTRATED BY JACK B. YEATS
| NEW YORK | CASSELL PUBLISHING COMPANY [*in red*] | 104 &
106 FOURTH AVENUE | 1892

6⅛ × 4; pp. viii, 236 plus 4 blank.

Issued in blue and white pinafore cloth, lettered in blue on front cover
and on spine; blue and white end-papers, matching binding; edges
stamped with the same design in blue. Published in 1892.

English sheets with new title pasted in, and Cassell | Publishing Company at foot of spine.

218

THE WORKS | OF | WILLIAM BLAKE | POETIC, SYMBOLIC, AND CRITICAL | EDITED WITH LITHOGRAPHS OF THE ILLUSTRATED | "PROPHETIC BOOKS," AND A MEMOIR | AND INTERPRETATION | BY | EDWIN JOHN ELLIS | AUTHOR OF "FATE IN ARCADIA," &c. | AND | WILLIAM BUTLER YEATS | AUTHOR OF "THE WANDERINGS OF OISIN," "THE COUNTESS KATHLEEN," &c. | [rule] | "BRING ME TO THE TEST | AND I THE MATTER WILL RE-WORD, WHICH MADNESS | WOULD GAMBOL FROM" | HAMLET | [rule] | IN THREE VOLS. | VOL. I [II III] | LONDON | BERNARD QUARITCH, 15 PICCADILLY | 1893 | [ALL RIGHTS RESERVED]

$10 \times 6\frac{1}{4}$; Vol. I., pp. xiv, 420. (ERRATA slip facing p. xvi.) Vol. II., pp. viii, 436. Vol. III., pp. x, 100, 2, followed by 71 pp. of facsimile reproductions, followed by *Tiriel*, 16 pp. followed by 225 pp. of reproductions, followed by *Vala* and notes, 174 pp. At the end of Vol. III., advertisements of books by E. J. Ellis and W. B. Yeats, pp. [175]–176.

Issued in light green cloth, designs by Blake and lettering on gold on front cover and on spine; grey or dark-brown end-papers lined white; top edges gilt, others untrimmed. Published in February 1893. The edition consisted of 500 copies.

Contents

VOLUME I
Preface. Signed by both editors.
Memoir
Literary Period
The Symbolic System

VOLUME II
Interpretation and Paraphrased Commentary
Blake the Artist
Some References

VOLUME III
Text of Blake's Writings, Facsimilies and Reproductions
For Yeats's contributions see note below.

$11 \times 7\frac{3}{8}$. Issued in brown imitation leather with leather spine and corners, lettered in gold on spine; top edges gilt, others untrimmed.

The edition was limited to 150 copies.

In his own (vellum bound) copy Yeats wrote:

The writing of this book is mainly Ellis's, the thinking is as much mine as his. The biography is by him. He re-wrote and trebled in size a biography of mine. The greater part of the 'symbolic system' is my writing; the rest of the book was written by Ellis working over short accounts of the books by me, except in the case of the 'literary period' the account of the minor poems, & the account of Blake's art theories which are all his own except in so far as we discussed everything together.

W. B. Y. May 3. 1900

P.S. The book is full of misprints. There is a good deal here & there in the biography etc with which I am not in agreement. I think that some of my own constructive symbolism is put with too much confidence. It is mainly right but parts should be used rather as an interpretive hypothesis than as a certainty. The circulation of the Zoas, which seems to me unlike anything in traditional symbolism, is a chief cause of uncertainty, but most that I have written on the subject is at least part of Blake's plan. There is also uncertainty about the personages who are mentioned by him too seldom to make one know them perfectly; & here and there elsewhere.

W. B. Y.   May. 1900.

219

THE POEMS | OF | WILLIAM BLAKE [*in red*] | EDITED BY | W. B. YEATS. | [publisher's device] | LONDON: | LAWRENCE & BULLEN [*in red*] | 16, HENRIETTA STREET, W.C. | 1893 | NEW YORK: | CHARLES SCRIBNER'S SONS [*in red*] | 743 & 745 BROADWAY | 1893 | [*The two imprints are arranged side by side.*]

$6\frac{1}{5} \times 3\frac{7}{10}$; pp. liv, 252.

Issued in light blue cloth, design in gold including words THE · MUSES' · LIBRARY · on front cover, gold design and lettering on spine; white end-papers; top edges gilt, others untrimmed.

Q

Yeats contributed:

Introduction. Pp. [xv]–liii.

Note of acknowledgement. P. [liv].

Notes. Pp. [235]–251.

220

LARGE PAPER EDITION

THE POEMS | OF | WILLIAM BLAKE [*in red*] | EDITED
BY | W. B. YEATS. | [publisher's device] | LONDON: | LAWRENCE
& BULLEN [*in red*] | 16, HENRIETTA STREET, COVENT GARDEN,
W.C. | 1893

$7 \times 4\frac{1}{4}$; pp. 4, liv, 252. On p. [iv]:

Two hundred copies of this Edition have been printed on Large
Paper. No. . .

On verso of title is imprint London: Printed by Henderson &
Spalding, Ltd. Marylebone Lane, W.

Issued in light green cloth with vellum spine, lettered in gold on spine
BLAKE'S | POEMS | [rule] | W. B. YEATS; white end-papers; top edges
gilt, others untrimmed.

On Quinn's large paper copy Yeats wrote:

"I am well pleased with this little [book] but I am sorry that I made
Westminster Abbey a Cathedral. I thought a Church was a Cathedral
when big enough. W. B. Yeats. March, 1904."

221

POEMS | OF | WILLIAM BLAKE | EDITED BY | W. B.
YEATS | LONDON: GEORGE ROUTLEDGE & SONS, LIMITED |
NEW YORK: E. P. DUTTON CO.

$6 \times 3\frac{3}{4}$; pp. l, 278, followed by 6 pp. of advertisements.

Issued in dark blue cloth, design and lettering in gold BLAKE | THE
MUSES' | LIBRARY | ROUTLEDGE on spine; white end-papers; all edges
trimmed. Published in June 1905.

In 1904 The Muses' Library was transferred to Messrs. George
Routledge & Sons.

The volume was also issued in lambskin, gilt.

A second edition, undated, has a publisher's device on title, following line 5, and has no advertisements at end.

In 1910 the book appeared in a different series:

MR WILLIAM BUTLER | YEATS INTRODUCES THE | POETICAL WORKS OF WILLIAM | BLAKE, BORN IN 1757, DIED IN 1827, | AS THE SECOND VOLUME IN THE SERIES OF | 'BOOKS THAT MARKED EPOCHS,' PUBLISHED | IN THE YEAR 1910 BY GEORGE | ROUTLEDGE & SONS, LIMITED. [*all within a border of double rules*]

$6\frac{1}{4} \times 4$; pp. l, 280.

Issued in blue linen boards with parchment spine and corners, a gilt line at join and at corners; lettering in gilt on spine; grey end-papers; top edges gilt, others trimmed. Published in 1910.

The introduction has been revised.

222

AMERICAN EDITION

POEMS OF | WILLIAM BLAKE | [rule] | EDITED BY WILLIAM BUTLER YEATS | [rule] | [publisher's device] | [rule] | THE MODERN LIBRARY | [rule] | PUBLISHERS [Two rectangles of four dots] NEW YORK

$6\frac{1}{2} \times 4\frac{1}{4}$; pp. xlii, 278.

No. 91 of The Modern Library. Undated. This series has been issued, from time to time, in a considerable variety of binding styles. The records of Messrs. Boni and Liveright do not exist to show what style was first used, although it was probably green fabricoid. The book is not mentioned in Roth. In 1925 The Modern Library was acquired by Random House, Inc. but this volume does not at present figure in the series.

Yeats contributed:

Introduction. Pp. xi–xli.
Acknowledgements. P. [xlii].
Notes. Pp. 261–278.

223

ILLUSTRATED EDITION

IRISH | FAIRY AND FOLK TALES | SELECTED AND EDITED, | WITH INTRODUCTION, | BY W. B. YEATS. | TWELVE

ILLUSTRATIONS BY JAMES TORRANCE. | LONDON: WALTER
SCOTT, LTD. | 24 WARWICK LANE.

7⅕ × 4½; pp. xviii, 326, followed by 22 pp. of advertisements.

Issued in green, white and brown cloth with pictorial designs on front
and back covers and on spine, lettering in gold on front cover and on
spine, a golden sun on back cover; pictorial end-papers; all edges gilt.
There are illustrations facing title-page, pp. 6, 46, 92, 122, 132, 160,
192, 202, 226, 262, 284 and 312.

Except for the preliminaries, this book seems to have been printed
from the same types as the original edition (No. 212). The errors have
been corrected. Published in October 1893.

There was a later edition, undated, issued in light buff cloth, lettered
in gold on front cover and on spine; pictorial end-papers; top edges
gilt, others untrimmed. I have seen a copy with only 6 pp. of advertisements at the end; the Walter Scott publications, however, vary much
in this respect.

223A

IRISH [*in red*] | FAIRY TALES [*in red*] | [publisher's
device] | EDITED BY W. B. YEATS | WITH TWELVE FULL- |
PAGE ILLUSTRATIONS BY | JAMES TORRANCE. | [publisher's
DEVICE] | LONDON | WALTER SCOTT, LTD. | PATERNOSTER SQ.

7⅛ × 4¾; pp. xviii, 326, followed by 20 pp. of advertisements.

Issued in brown cloth with design stamped in black and gold on front
cover and spine, and in black on back cover; lettering in brown against
gold background on front cover and spine, and publisher's name
stamped in gold letters at foot of spine; pictorial end-papers; all edges
trimmed.

224

AMERICAN EDITION

IRISH | FAIRY AND FOLK | TALES | SELECTED AND
EDITED, | WITH INTRODUCTION BY W. B. YEATS. | TWELVE
ILLUSTRATIONS BY JAMES TORRANCE. | LONDON | WALTER
SCOTT, LTD, PATERNOSTER SQUARE | CHARLES SCRIBNER'S
SONS, | 154–157 FIFTH AVENUE, NEW YORK | 1895

7⅕ × 4½; pp. xviii, 2, 326, followed by 14 pp. of advertisements.

Issued in green, white and brown cloth. This is composed of the English sheets imported with new title as above, and SCRIBNERS at foot of spine. Published in 1895.

In Quinn's copy Yeats wrote: "A good book with my part pretty reckless and ill written. W. B. Yeats, 1904."

225

A BOOK OF | IRISH VERSE | SELECTED FROM MODERN WRITERS | WITH AN INTRODUCTION | AND NOTES | BY W. B. YEATS | METHUEN AND CO. | 36 ESSEX STREET, W.C. | LONDON | 1895

$7\frac{1}{2} \times 5$; pp. xxviii, 260, followed by 32 pp. of advertisements, numbered [1]–32.

Issued in green buckram, lettered in gold on spine; white end-papers; top edges trimmed, others untrimmed. Published in March 1895.

Yeats contributed:

Dedication: To the Members of the National Literary Society of Dublin and the Irish Literary Society of London. P. v.

Introduction. Dated August 5, 1894. Pp. xi–xxvii.

Note of acknowledgement. P. xxviii.

Notes. Pp. 250–257.

There was a revised edition published in January 1900. Pp. xxxii, 260.

Yeats contributed:

Dedication. P. v.

Preface. Dated August 15, 1899. Pp. xiii–xv.

Modern Irish Poetry. Pp. xvii–xxxi.

This is the former *Introduction,* much revised.

Note of acknowledgement. P. xxxii.

Notes. Pp. 250–257.

There were further editions in January 1912 and in 1920.

226

THREEPENCE—INCLUDING PROGRAMME. | BELTAINE | [rule] | AN OCCASIONAL PUBLICATION. NUMBER ONE. MAY 1899. | [rule] | THE ORGAN OF THE IRISH LITERARY THEATRE |

[rule] | LONDON: AT THE SIGN OF THE UNICORN. | [rule] |
DUBLIN: AT THE "DAILY EXPRESS" OFFICE. [*All except the
top line enclosed within rules.*]

$8\frac{1}{2} \times 6\frac{3}{8}$; pp. 24.

Issued in pale blue paper covers, lettered in dark blue on front cover;
fastened with one metal staple; all edges untrimmed.

Yeats contributed:

Plans and Methods. Signed Editor of 'Beltaine.' Pp. 6–9.
     Some of these notes first appeared as part of an essay *The Irish
     Literary Theatre* in *The Dublin Daily Express*, January 14, 1899.
Two lyrics reprinted from *The Countess Cathleen*. P. 13.
The Theatre. Pp. 20–23.
     First appeared in *The Dome*, April 1899.

This first number of *Beltaine* was originally issued without title-page,
the above description being taken from the front cover. W. B. Yeats
was not definitely named as editor in this number as first issued.

THE ORGAN OF THE IRISH LITERARY THEATRE | [rule] |
BELTAINE | [rule] | NUMBER TWO · FEBRUARY MDCCCC ·
EDITED BY W. B. YEATS | [rule] CONTENTS [12 lines giving
list of contributions and authors] | [rule] | LONDON: AT THE
SIGN OF THE UNICORN | [rule] | VII CECIL COURT, SAINT
MARTIN'S LANE, W.C. [*The whole enclosed within rules.*]

$8\frac{1}{2} \times 6\frac{3}{8}$; pp. 32.

Issued in light brown paper covers, lettered in blue on front cover;
fastened with two metal staples; all edges untrimmed.

Yeats contributed:

Plans and Methods. Signed Editor of 'Beltaine.' Pp. 3–6.
'*Maive,*' *and certain Irish Beliefs.* Pp. 14–17.
Footnote. Signed Editor of 'Beltaine.' P. 21.
The Irish Literary Theatre, 1900. Pp. 22–24.
     First appeared in *The Dome*, January 1900.

This number was issued at the price of sixpence net.

THE ORGAN OF THE IRISH LITERARY THEATRE | [rule] |
BELTAINE | [rule] | NUMBER THREE APRIL MDCCCC EDITED
BY W. B. YEATS | [rule] | CONTENTS | [3 lines naming con-

tents] | [rule] | LONDON: AT THE SIGN OF THE UNICORN | [rule] | VII CECIL COURT, SAINT MARTIN'S LANE, W.C. [*The whole enclosed within rules.*]

$8\frac{1}{2} \times 6\frac{3}{5}$; pp. 8 including covers.

Issued in white paper covers, lettered in black on front cover; fastened with one metal staple; all edges untrimmed.

This number contained only an essay by Yeats:

'*The Last Feast of the Fianna,*' '*Maive,*' *and* '*The Bending of the Bough,*' *in Dublin.* Pp. 4–6.

This number was issued at the price of one halfpenny net.

The three numbers of *Beltaine* were afterwards issued in one volume, with the addition of a general title and a title for Number One which also included a list of contents of the Number. The volume was issued in brown paper boards, labels printed in red brown on front cover and on spine; white end-papers; all edges untrimmed; all wrappers and advertisements bound in.

227

SAMHAIN EDITED | FOR THE IRISH LITERARY THEATRE | BY W. B. YEATS. | PUBLISHED IN OCTOBER 1901 BY | SEALY BRYERS & WALKER AND | BY T. FISHER UNWIN.

$8\frac{1}{2} \times 6\frac{7}{10}$; pp. 40.

Issued in brown paper covers, lettered in black on front cover, fastened with one metal staple; all edges untrimmed.

Yeats contributed:
Windlestraws. Pp. 3–10.
Footnote. Signed Editor of SAMHAIN. P. 12.

228

SAMHAIN: AN OCCASIONAL | REVIEW EDITED BY W. B. YEATS. | PUBLISHED IN OCTOBER 1902 BY | SEALY BRYERS & WALKER AND | BY T. FISHER UNWIN.

$8\frac{1}{2} \times 6\frac{7}{10}$; pp. 32.

Issued in brown paper covers, lettered in black on front cover, fastened with one metal staple; all edges untrimmed.

Yeats contributed:

Notes. Pp. 3–10.

Footnote. Signed W. B. Y. P. 12.

Cathleen ni Hoolihan. Pp. 24–31.

229

SAMHAIN: AN OCCASIONAL | REVIEW EDITED BY W. B.
YEATS. | PUBLISHED IN SEPTEMBER 1903 | BY SEALY BRYERS
& WALKER | AND BY T. FISHER UNWIN.

$8\frac{1}{2} \times 6\frac{7}{10}$; pp. 36. Frontispiece portrait of William Fay by J. B. Yeats.
Issued in brown paper covers, lettered in black on front cover,
fastened with one metal staple; all edges untrimmed.

Yeats contributed:

Notes. Pp. 3–8.

The Reform of the Theatre. Pp. 9–12.

   Part of this essay first appeared in *The United Irishman*, April
   4, 1903.

There was a second issue of this number which differed only in the
covers. Beneath the title on the front cover appeared the words "(An
Occasional Review)" and lower down the date of publication was
altered from September 1903 to October 1903. On the third page of
cover the words "Dublin: Hodges, Figgis & Co." are added to an
advertisement of Lady Gregory's *Poets and Dreamers*.

230

SAMHAIN: AN OCCASIONAL | REVIEW EDITED BY W. B.
YEATS. | PUBLISHED IN DECEMBER 1904 | BY SEALY BRYERS &
WALKER | AND BY T. FISHER UNWIN.

$8\frac{4}{5} \times 6\frac{9}{10}$; pp. 56. Frontispiece portrait of Frank Fay as Cuchullain,
portrait of J. M. Synge facing p. 34, both by J. B. Yeats.

Issued in brown paper covers, lettered in black on front cover, fastened
with two metal staples; all edges untrimmed.

Yeats contributed:

The Dramatic Movement. Pp. 3–12.

First Principles. Pp. 12–24.

The Play, the Player, and the Scene. Dated December 1904. Pp. 24–33.

Footnote to 'An Opinion.' P. 55.

231

TWENTY ONE POEMS WRITTEN BY | LIONEL JOHNSON:
SELECTED BY | WILLIAM BUTLER YEATS | THE DUN EMER
PRESS | DUNDRUM | MCMIV

$8\frac{3}{10} \times 5\frac{3}{4}$; pp. xvi, 40.

Issued in blue paper boards with buff linen spine, white label printed in
black on spine; blue end-papers matching binding; all edges untrimmed.

220 copies printed on paper made in Ireland and published by Elizabeth
Corbet Yeats at the Dun Emer Press, Dundrum. Finished on All
Hallows' Eve, 1904. Published on February 21, 1905.

There is no introduction by Yeats.

In 1908 an edition of this book was issued by T. B. Mosher of Portland,
Maine. There were 950 copies on Van Gelder paper.

232

SOME ESSAYS AND PASSAGES BY JOHN | EGLINTON;
SELECTED BY WILLIAM | BUTLER YEATS | THE DUN EMER
PRESS | DUNDRUM | MCMV

$8\frac{3}{10} \times 5\frac{3}{4}$; pp. xvi, 64.

Issued in blue paper boards with buff linen spine; white label printed in
red on spine; blue end-papers matching binding; all edges untrimmed.

200 copies printed on paper made in Ireland and published by Elizabeth
Corbet Yeats at the Dun Emer Press, Dundrum. Finished on April 16,
1905. Published on August 25, 1905.

There is no introduction by Yeats.

233

SAMHAIN: AN OCCASIONAL | REVIEW EDITED BY W. B.
YEATS. | PUBLISHED IN NOVEMBER 1905 | BY MAUNSEL &
CO., LTD., | AND BY A. H. BULLEN.

$8\frac{4}{5} \times 6\frac{7}{10}$; pp. 36. Frontispiece portrait of Padraic Colum by J. B. Yeats
Issued in brown paper covers, lettered in black on front cover, fastened
with two metal staples; all edges untrimmed.

Yeats contributed:

Notes and Opinions. Pp. 3–14.

234

SIXTEEN POEMS by william | allingham: selected
by | william butler yeats | the dun emer press | dun-
drum | mcmv

$8\frac{3}{10} \times 5\frac{3}{4}$; pp. xvi, 48.

Issued in blue paper boards with buff linen spine, white label printed
in red on spine; blue end-papers matching binding; all edges untrimmed.

200 copies printed on paper made in Ireland and published by Elizabeth
Corbet Yeats at the Dun Emer Press, Dundrum. Finished on September 15, 1905. Published on November 27, 1905.

There is no introduction by Yeats.

235

POEMS | OF | SPENSER | selected and with | an
introduction by | w. b. yeats. | t. c. & e. c. jack. |
edinburgh. [*The whole forms part of a design by A. S.
Hartrick.*]

$6\frac{4}{5} \times 4\frac{1}{2}$; pp. xlviii, 292.

A volume of The Golden Poets, issued in dark heliotrope cloth,
lettering and design in gold on front cover, lettered in gold between
gold rules poems | of | spenser | w. b. yeats | ill^{TD} by | jessie m |
king on spine; white end-papers; top edges gilt, others untrimmed.

Also issued in green leather, lettered as above in gold on front cover
and spine, but rules in blind, page trimmed to $6\frac{1}{2} \times 4\frac{1}{2}$, dark green
endpapers, green silk marker, all edges gilt.   Published in October
1906.

Yeats contributed:
Introduction. Pp. xiii–xlvii.

Sets of The Golden Poets were taken over by the Caxton Publishing
Company and reissued with new titles, the caxton publishing co. |
london substituted in the Hartrick design in place of t. c. & e. c.
jack | edinburgh.

The volumes were issued in at least two different bindings: (1) Brown
cloth, lettering in gold on front cover poems of | spenser | w·b |
yeats | illustrated by | jessie m. king within all-over design in
orange. Lettered on spine in gold poems | of | spenser | w·b | yeats |
illustrated | by jessie | m. king | caxton (at foot). Design in yellow.

(2) Dark-blue cloth, design and lettering in gold THE | GOLDEN | POETS on front cover, within double frame of yellow lines. Lettered in gold on spine POEMS | OF | SPENSER | · | W. B. | YEATS | · | design | CAXTON within single yellow line frame. Top edges gilt, others trimmed.

The Caxton Publishing Company have no record of the dates of these issues. The latest is 1960.

236

[Design of girl and wolf-hound by Elinor Monsell, as in No. 54] | THE ARROW | EDITED BY W. B. YEATS.

NUMBER 1

$9\frac{1}{2} \times 7\frac{1}{4}$; pp. 8, unnumbered.

Issued in dark grey paper covers, lettering and design, as above, on front cover; fastened with two metal staples; no title; all edges trimmed. Published on October 20, 1906.

Yeats contributed:

The Season's Work. Pp. [1–2].

A Note on The Mineral Workers. Pp. [2–3].

Notes on "The Doctor in spite of Himself", "The Eloquent Dempsy" and on other Plays. P. [4].

NUMBER 2

Pp. 8, unnumbered. Published on November 24, 1906.

Notes. P. [1].

A Note on "Deirdre". P. [2].

A Note on "The Shadowy Waters". Pp. [3–4].

NUMBER 3

Pp. 12, unnumbered. Published on February 23, 1907.

The Controversy over "The Playboy". Pp. [1–2].

Answers to some of these criticisms from the 'Samhain' of 1905. Pp. [4–6].

Mr. Yeats' opening Speech at the Debate of February 4th, at the Abbey Theatre. Pp. [6–9].

NUMBER 4.

$9\frac{4}{5} \times 7\frac{1}{4}$; pp. 8, unnumbered. Published on June 1, 1907.

W. B. Yeats contributes a note without heading, afterwards called *On Taking "The Playboy" to London.* Pp. [1–2].

NUMBER 5

$9\frac{1}{2} \times 7\frac{1}{4}$; pp. 8, unnumbered. Published on August 25th, 1909.

The Shewing-up of Blanco Posnet. Statement by the Directors. Signed W. B. Yeats, *Managing Director.* A. Gregory, *Director and Patentee.* Dated Abbey Theatre, *August 22nd, 1909.* Pp. [1–2].
The Religion of Blanco Posnet. P. [7].

[In the Summer of 1939 the Abbey Theatre issued:

THE | ARROW | W. B. YEATS COMMEMORATION NUMBER | [List of Contributors and of Illustrations] | [design of girl and wolf-hound, as in No. 54] | SUMMER, 1939 PRICE 1/-
$9\frac{3}{8} \times 7\frac{1}{4}$; pp. 24.

Issued in light grey paper covers, lettered in black as above on front covers; fastened with two metal staples; all edges trimmed.

The contents include memories of and tributes to W. B. Yeats by Gordon Bottomley, Austin Clarke, Edmund Dulac, Oliver St. J. Gogarty, Richard Hayes, F. R. Higgins, John Masefield, Lennox Robinson, Sir William Rothenstein and W. J. Turner; portraits of him by J. B. Yeats, Charles Shannon and Sean O'Sullivan; caricatures of him by Sir Max Beerbohm and Edmund Dulac; and a facsimile reproduction of a letter by Yeats facing p. 13.

This memorial number of *The Arrow* was edited by Lennox Robinson.]

237

SAMHAIN: AN OCCASIONAL | REVIEW EDITED BY W. B. YEATS. | PUBLISHED IN DECEMBER 1906 | BY MAUNSEL & CO., LTD., | DUBLIN.
$8\frac{4}{5} \times 6\frac{7}{10}$; pp. 40. Frontispiece portrait of Miss A. E. F. Horniman from the picture by J. B. Yeats, R.II.A.

Issued in brown paper covers, lettered in black on front cover, fastened by two metal staples; all edges untrimmed.

Yeats contributed:
Notes. P. 3.
Literature and the Living Voice. Pp. 4–14.
    First appeared in *The Contemporary Review*, October 1906.

238

TWENTY ONE POEMS BY KATHARINE | TYNAN: SELECTED BY W. B. YEATS. | [woodcut as in No. 84] | DUN EMER PRESS | DUNDRUM | MCMVII
$8\frac{3}{10} \times 5\frac{3}{4}$; pp. xvi, 48.

Issued in blue paper boards with buff linen spine, lettered in black on front cover, no label on spine; blue end-papers matching binding; all edges untrimmed.

200 copies printed on paper made in Ireland by Elizabeth C. Yeats, Esther Ryan and Beatrice Cassidy, and published by Elizabeth Corbet Yeats at the Dun Emer Press, Dundrum. Finished on March 20, 1907. Published on August 6, 1907.

There is no introduction by Yeats.

239

[Design of girl and wolf-hound by Elinor Monsell, as in No. 54] | BRITISH ASSOCIATION VISIT, | ABBEY THEATRE, | SPECIAL PROGRAMME.
$9\frac{4}{5} \times 7\frac{1}{4}$; pp. 8, unnumbered.

Issued in grey paper covers, lettering and design as above in black on front cover; fastened with two metal staples; all edges trimmed. Illustrated. Published on September 4, 1908.

Yeats contributed:
The Abbey Theatre. Dated August 1908. Pp. [1-2].

240

Second visit of the British Association:

The cover of the programme is exactly the same as that of the foregoing entry. The size and shape are also the same. This programme was published on September 8, 1908.

Yeats contributed:
W. B. Yeats' Speech at the Matinee of the British Association Friday, September 4th, 1908. Pp. [6-8].

241

SAMHAIN | AN OCCASIONAL REVIEW, EDITED | BY W. B. YEATS, CONTAINING | NOTES BY THE EDITOR. A NEW | VERSION OF SOME PASSAGES IN | DEIRDRE; PORTRAITS OF SARA | ALLGOOD AND ARTHUR SINCLAIR, | AND DERVORGILLA, A

PLAY IN ONE | ACT, BY LADY GREGORY. THE | SEVENTH
NUMBER. PUBLISHED IN | NOVEMBER, 1908, BY MAUNSEL |
& CO., LTD., DUBLIN, AND BY | T. FISHER UNWIN, LONDON;
| AND SOLD FOR SIXPENCE NET. [*This number has no title-page; the above description is taken from the front cover.*]

$8\frac{1}{2} \times 6\frac{1}{2}$; pp. 36. Frontispiece portrait of Sara Allgood from a drawing by Robert Gregory; portrait of Arthur Sinclair as James II. in "The White Cockade" from a painting by Robert Gregory facing p. 12.

Issued in light brown paper covers, lettered in black on front cover; stitched; all edges untrimmed.

Yeats contributed:
Events. Pp. 1–5.
First principles. Dated October, 1908. Pp. 6–12.
Alterations in "Deirdre." Pp. 28–33.
Footnote. P. [34].

Later issues of *Samhain* 1908 contained an Errata slip pasted to the back of frontispiece. This read:

Measure for Measure was not produced by the Elizabethan Stage Society, as stated in mistake on page 4, but by Miss Horniman's company, in the Elizabethan fashion, with Mr. Poel as producer.

Copies are also found with trimmed edges.

242

POETRY AND IRELAND: ESSAYS BY | W. B. YEATS AND
LIONEL JOHNSON. | [woodcut as in No. 84] | CUALA PRESS |
CHURCHTOWN | DUNDRUM | MCMVIII

$8\frac{3}{5} \times 5\frac{3}{4}$; pp. xvi, 64.

Issued in blue-grey paper boards with buff linen spine, lettered in black on front cover, no label on spine; blue end-papers matching binding; all edges untrimmed.

250 copies printed and published by Elizabeth C. Yeats at the Cuala Press, Churchtown, Dundrum. Finished on October 8, 1908. Published on December 1, 1908.

Yeats contributed:
Poetry and Patriotism. Dated August 1907. Pp. [1]–[18].
A note, unheaded, on Lionel Johnson. Printed in red. P. [19].

243

POEMS AND TRANSLATIONS | BY JOHN M. SYNGE |
[woodcut as in No. 84] | CUALA PRESS | CHURCHTOWN |
DUNDRUM | MCMIX

$8\frac{3}{10} \times 5\frac{1}{2}$; pp. viii, XVI, 56.

Issued in blue paper boards with buff linen spine, lettered in black on
front cover, white paper label, printed in black, on spine; blue end-
papers matching binding; all edges untrimmed.

250 copies printed and published by Elizabeth C. Yeats at the Cuala
Press, Churchtown, Dundrum. Finished on April 8, 1909. Published
on July 5, 1909.

Yeats contributed:

J. M. Synge. Dated April 4, 1909. Pp. VI–XIV.

244

POEMS AND TRANSLATIONS | BY JOHN M. SYNGE |
PRINTED FOR JOHN QUINN | NEW YORK | 1909

$8\frac{1}{2} \times 5\frac{3}{4}$; pp. xx, 44. On verso of half-title "Fifty copies of this book
have been printed, of which five are on vellum."

Issued in grey boards with linen spine; white end-papers; top edges
gilt, others untrimmed. Some copies have a printed label on front
cover, reading POEMS AND TRANSLATIONS | BY JOHN M. SYNGE, printed
in black on cream paper and framed within a black line.

Yeats contributed:

John M. Synge. Pp. viii–xvi.

244A

PARAGRAPHS FROM THE FORTH- | COMING
NUMBER OF "SAMHAIN." | AN OCCASIONAL REVIEW,
EDITED | BY W. B. YEATS.

$8\frac{3}{8} \times 6\frac{1}{4}$; pp. 8.

Issued in white paper covers, lettering as above in black on front cover.

Yeats contributed:

Private and Confidential. Pp. 3–5. Signed W. B. Yeats. Abbey
Theatre, Dublin, September, 1909.

The last formal issue of Samhain was No. 248, published in November
1908.

244B

[Design of girl and wolf-hound by Elinor Monsell, as in
No. 54] | PARAGRAPHS WRITTEN IN NOV., | 1909,
WITH SUPPLEMENT AND | FINANCIAL STATEMENT
$8\frac{1}{2} \times 6\frac{1}{2}$; pp. 8.

Issued in white paper covers, lettering as above in black on front
cover; printer's device on back cover.

Yeats and Lady Gregory contributed:
Private and Confidential Paragraphs written in No. 1909. Pp. 2–4
Signed W. B. Yeats./A. Gregory. Abbey Theatre, Dublin, November,
1909.

This pamphlet, that contains besides the Paragraphs a listing of plays
produced by the Abbey Theatre Co., was probably distributed to
subscribers sometime in March 1910 because the last play in the listing
is dated March 2, 1910.

245

DEIRDRE OF THE SORROWS: A PLAY | BY JOHN M.
SYNGE | [woodcut as in No. 84] | CUALA PRESS | CHURCH-
TOWN | MCMX
$8\frac{3}{10} \times 5\frac{3}{4}$; pp. xvi, 88.

Issued in blue paper boards with buff linen spine, lettered in black on
front cover, white paper label, printed in red, on spine; blue end-
papers matching binding; all edges untrimmed.

250 copies printed and published by Elizabeth Corbet Yeats at the
Cuala Press, Churchtown, Dundrum. Finished on May Eve, 1910.
Published on July 5, 1910.

Yeats contributed:
Preface. Dated April 1910. Pp. [xiii–xiv].

246

DEIRDRE OF THE SORROWS: | A PLAY BY JOHN M.
SYNGE | PRINTED FOR JOHN QUINN | NEW YORK | 1910
$8\frac{1}{2} \times 5\frac{3}{4}$; pp. viii, 92. On verso of half-title "Fifty copies of this book
have been printed, of which five are on vellum."

Issued in grey boards with linen spine, printed label with lettering running vertically on spine DEIRDRE OF THE SORROWS, BY JOHN M. SYNGE; white end-papers; top edges gilt, others untrimmed. [Some copies have a printed label on front cover, reading DEIRDRE OF THE SORROWS: | A PLAY BY JOHN M. SYNGE, printed in black on cream paper and framed within a black line.]

Yeats contributed:

Preface. Pp. v–vi.

I am indebted to Mr. P. S. O'Hegarty for the descriptions of the two Quinn copyright editions of POEMS AND TRANSLATIONS and DEIRDRE OF THE SORROWS from copies in his possession. He has also given me the following note on the Corrected Edition of DEIRDRE OF THE SORROWS, 1910:

Identical with previous item, save that at the end of the Text there are twelve unnumbered pages, nine of them containing corrections obtained by comparison with the original manuscript, and three blank, with, at the head of the first page, a note by Quinn that he had destroyed all copies of this edition save five on vellum and five on hand-made paper, and had printed a new edition of fifty, adding "The corrections indicated below should be made in this edition." It is clear however, from the Quinn Sale catalogue, item 9982a, that this new edition never got beyond the proof stage, and it is not known exactly how many copies of the original issue had the corrections inserted.

247

SELECTIONS FROM THE WRITINGS | OF LORD DUNSANY | [woodcut as in No. 84] | THE CUALA PRESS | CHURCHTOWN | DUNDRUM | MCMXII

$8\frac{3}{10} \times 5\frac{3}{4}$; pp. xxviii, 112.

Issued in grey paper boards with white linen spine; lettered in black on front cover, no label on spine; grey end-papers matching binding; all edges untrimmed.

250 copies printed and published by Elizabeth Corbet Yeats at the Cuala Press, Churchtown, Dundrum, Dublin. Finished on Lady Day, 1912. Published in October 1912.

Yeats contributed:

Introduction. Dated 1912. Pp. xix–xxvii.

The selection of Lord Dunsany's writings was made by Yeats.

R

248

Announcement of a Private Performance of *The Shewing-up of Blanco Posnet* by Bernard Shaw at the Court Theatre, London, on Monday, July 14th [1913] to provide funds for the Dublin Municipal Gallery of Modern Art.

$7\frac{2}{5} \times 4\frac{4}{5}$; pp. 4, unnumbered.

A note by Yeats begins at the foot of p. [1] and continues on p. [2]. Pp. [3–4] are perforated for tearing off.

249

BROADSIDES | A COLLECTION OF OLD AND NEW SONGS | 1935 | SONGS BY W. B. YEATS, JAMES STEPHENS, F. R. HIGGINS, | FRANK O'CONNOR, LYNN DOYLE, | BRYAN GUINESS, | PADRAIC COLUM. | ILLUSTRATIONS BY JACK B. YEATS, VICTOR BROWN, SEAN O'SULLIVAN, | E. C. PEET, HARRY KERNOFF, MAURICE MCGONIGAL. | MUSIC BY ARTHUR DUFF. | THE CUALA PRESS | DUBLIN, IRELAND. | MCMXXXV

$11\frac{1}{2} \times 8\frac{1}{2}$; pp. xii, followed by twelve broadsides of 4 pp. each, followed by 4 pp. blank at end of volume.

Issued in blue boards with buff linen spine, label printed in black on front cover, no label on spine; blue end-papers matching binding; all edges trimmed.

Yeats contributed:

Anglo-Irish Ballads. Signed by F. R. Higgins and W. B. Yeats.
　　Pp. [ix–xii].

The Wicked Hawthorn Tree
　　Broadside No. 2 (New Series), February 1935.

The Rose Tree
　　Broadside No. 5 (New Series), May 1935.
　　From *Michael Robartes and the Dancer*, 1920. (No. 127.)

The Soldier takes Pride
　　Broadside No. 12 (New Series), December 1935.
　　This is one of the *Three Songs to the Same Tune* from *The King of the Great Clock Tower*, 1934. (No. 179.)

The Broadsides were edited by W. B. Yeats and F. R. Higgins and were issued monthly during 1935.

The number of Broadsides printed was limited to 300.

The number of bound volumes was 100, issued in December 1935.

250

THE | OXFORD BOOK | OF MODERN VERSE | 1892–1935 | CHOSEN BY | W. B. YEATS | OXFORD | AT THE CLARENDON PRESS | 1936

$7\frac{3}{10} \times 4\frac{4}{5}$; pp. 2, xlviii, 452.

Issued in dark blue cloth, lettered in gold on front cover and on spine, with frame in gold on front cover and spine and stamped blind on back cover; medallion of Oxford arms stamped in gold on spine; white end-papers; top edges gilt, others trimmed. It was issued also in leather binding of which there were five different kinds, of varying colours.

Yeats contributed :

Introduction. Dated September 1936. Pp. v–xlii.
Acknowledgements. Signed W. B. Y. Pp. xliii–xlviii.

Yeats included fourteen of his own poems: *After Long Silence, Three Things, Lullaby, Symbols, Vacillation* (part viii), *Sailing to Byzantium, The Rose Tree, On a Political Prisoner, In Memory of Eva Gore-Booth and Con Markiewicz, To a Friend whose work has come to Nothing, An Irish Airman Foresees his Death, Coole Park 1929, Coole and Ballylee 1931,* and *From 'Oedipus at Colonus'.*

I am indebted to the courtesy of the Secretary of the Clarendon Press for the following information regarding the publication of this book:

Before the date of publication certain omissions were detected in the acknowledgements list of an advance copy. A slip containing these was inserted in review copies, still before publication. Then further omissions in the list were discovered and the original correction slip was withdrawn and replaced by a paste-in (pp. xlvii–xlviii). It was in this form that the book was published on 19 November 1936. There may be a very few copies with the slip in its earlier form in cases where review copies were not returned for correction. We should not consider these true copies of the first edition.

Apart from some minor corrections to the index and list of acknowledgements, correction of minor errors and misprints, and the correction of no. 368 to 368 and 368a, there have been no important alterations in the successive issues; and of these corrections the majority were made in the second issue.

The book was published on November 19, 1936, and eight impressions had appeared up to February 1949.

251

AMERICAN EDITION

THE | OXFORD BOOK | OF MODERN VERSE |
1892–1935 | CHOSEN BY | W. B. YEATS | NEW YORK | OXFORD
UNIVERSITY PRESS | 1936

$7\frac{1}{2} \times 5$; pp. xlvi, 458.

Issued in blue cloth, lettered in gold on front cover and on spine, with
gold border design on spine; white end-papers; all edges trimmed.
Published in November 1936.

The contents are the same as those of the English edition. (No. 250.)

There was a second printing in 1937, and a third in 1947.

252

THE TEN | PRINCIPAL UPANISHADS | [rule] |
PUT INTO ENGLISH BY | SHREE PUROHIT SWAMI | AND |
W. B. YEATS | FABER AND FABER LIMITED | 24 RUSSELL SQUARE
| LONDON

$8\frac{3}{5} \times 5\frac{1}{2}$; pp. 160.

Issued in bright blue cloth, lettered in gold on spine; off-white end-
papers; top edges trimmed, others untrimmed. Published in April
1937. There was a further printing in 1952.

Yeats contributed:

Preface. Pp. 7–12.

Yeats collaborated in making this English version of the Upanishads.

253

AMERICAN EDITION

THE TEN | PRINCIPAL UPANISHADS | [rule] | PUT
INTO ENGLISH BY | SHREE PUROHIT SWAMI | AND | W. B.
YEATS | NEW YORK | THE MACMILLAN COMPANY | 1937

$8\frac{5}{8} \times 5\frac{3}{4}$; pp. 160.

Issued in brown cloth, lettered in gold on spine. Printed in the United
States of America by the Polygraphic Company of America. Published
in 1937. There was a further printing in 1952.

Yeats contributed:

Preface. Pp. 7–12.

Yeats collaborated in making this English version of the Upanishads.

254

BROADSIDES | A COLLECTION OF NEW IRISH AND ENGLISH
SONGS | 1937 | SONGS BY W. B. YEATS, W. J. TURNER, OLIVER
GOGARTY, | HILAIRE BELLOC, DOROTHY WELLESLEY, JAMES |
STEPHENS, EDITH SITWELL, FRANK O'CONNOR, | GORDON
BOTTOMLEY, F. R. HIGGINS, PADRAIC | COLUM, WALTER DE LA
MARE. | ILLUSTRATIONS BY JACK B. YEATS, VICTOR BROWN,
HARRY KERNOFF, MAURICE MCGONIGAL. | MUSIC BY W. J.
TURNER, ARTHUR DUFF, EDMUND DULAC, | FRANK LIEBICH,
HILDA MATHESON, ART O'MURNAGHAN, | HILAIRE BELLOC. |
THE CUALA PRESS | DUBLIN IRELAND | MCMXXXVII

$11\frac{1}{2} \times 8\frac{3}{10}$; pp. xii, followed by 12 Broadsides of 4 pp. each, unnumbered,
followed by 4 pp. blank at end of volume. In Broadside No. 11 (New
Series), November, 1937 an Errata slip was inserted loose. This read:

The music to the first poem in the September number should have
been described as an old English Ballad called "The Brisk Young
Bachelor" arranged by Mrs. Gordon Woodhouse. Both poem and
music were incorrectly printed. An additional sheet with correct
versions will be added to the December Broadside. W. B. Y.

An Errata page, measuring $8\frac{1}{2} \times 7\frac{9}{10}$, printed on both sides, duly
appeared and was inserted loose at end of the bound volume.

Issued in blue boards with buff linen spine, label printed in black on
front cover, no label on spine; blue end-papers matching binding;
all edges trimmed.

Yeats contributed:

Music and Poetry. Signed by W. B. Yeats and Dorothy Wellesley.
　　Pp. [ix–x].
Come Gather Round me Parnellites
　　Broadside No. 1 (New Series), January 1937.
The Three Bushes
　　Broadside No. 3 (New Series), March 1937.
The Curse of Cromwell
　　Broadside No. 8 (New Series), August 1937.

The Pilgrim
>Broadside No. 10 (New Series), October 1937.

Colonel Martin
>Broadside No. 12 (New Series), December 1937.

The Broadsides were edited by Dorothy Wellesley and W. B. Yeats and were issued monthly during 1937.

The number of Broadsides printed was limited to 300.

The number of bound volumes issued was 150, issued in December 1937.

2. BOOKS WITH A PREFACE OR INTRODUCTION BY W. B. YEATS

255

A BOOK OF IMAGES | DRAWN BY W. T. | HORTON & INTRO- | DUCED BY W. B. YEATS | LONDON AT THE UNICORN | PRESS VII CECIL COURT ST. | MARTIN'S LANE MDCCCXCVIII $8\frac{1}{2} \times 6\frac{3}{4}$; pp. 64.

No. 2 of *The Unicorn Quartos*, issued in bright yellow cloth, design in black by W. T. Horton on front cover, lettering in black on spine; white end-papers; all edges untrimmed. A slip inserted loose refers to p. 14, line 4, saying: The Publishers are asked to state that "The Brotherhood of New Life" claims to be practical rather than visionary, and that the "waking dreams" referred to in the above passage are a purely personal matter. Published in March, 1898.

Yeats contributed:

Introduction. Pp. 7–16.
> The first two sections of this introduction are reprinted, under the title, *Symbolism in Painting*, in *Ideas of Good and Evil*, 1903 (No. 46); the third section has not been reprinted.

256

CUCHULAIN OF MUIRTHEMNE: | THE STORY OF THE MEN OF | THE RED BRANCH OF ULSTER | ARRANGED AND PUT INTO | ENGLISH BY LADY GREGORY. | WITH A PREFACE BY W. B. YEATS | LONDON | JOHN MURRAY, ALBEMARLE STREET | 1902 8×5; pp. xx, 364.

Issued in blue cloth, lettering and design in white on front cover, lettering in gold, design in yellow, on spine; off-white end-papers; top edges gilt, fore edges trimmed; a blue silk marker is attached to headband. Published in April 1902. There were further printings in 1903, 1907, 1911, 1915, 1919, 1926 and 1934.

Yeats contributed:
Preface. Dated March 1902. Pp. vii–xvii.
Note on the Conversation of Cuchulain and Emer. Pp. 351–353.

COLONIAL EDITION

A few copies of this book were included in Murray's Imperial Library. These were made up of sheets of the original first edition with title-page unaltered, and were issued in grey green cloth with the title in gold on spine, as in the London edition, but without the ornamentation. The front cover bore the words MURRAY'S IMPERIAL LIBRARY in gold at the head, beneath which was a panel of a map of the world in red and gold on the grey cloth background. This panel, reduced in size, was repeated on the spine immediately above the publisher's name at the foot.

Inset at the end of the volume were four pages advertising Murray's Imperial Library.

257

CUCHULAIN OF MUIRTHEMNE: | THE STORY OF THE MEN OF | THE RED BRANCH OF ULSTER | ARRANGED AND PUT INTO | ENGLISH BY LADY GREGORY. | WITH A PREFACE BY W. B. YEATS | NEW YORK | CHARLES SCRIBNER'S SONS | 153– 157 FIFTH AVENUE | 1903
8 × 5; pp. xx, 360.

Issued in blue cloth, similar in decoration to that of the English edition, copies of this American edition having been imported from England already bound. Published in 1903.

Yeats's contributions are the same as those to the English edition.

258

GODS AND FIGHTING MEN: | THE STORY OF THE TUATHA DE | DANAAN AND OF THE FIANNA | OF IRELAND,

ARRANGED AND | PUT INTO ENGLISH BY LADY | GREGORY.
WITH A PREFACE | BY W. B. YEATS | LONDON | JOHN MURRAY,
ALBEMARLE STREET, W. | 1904

$7\frac{4}{5} \times 5$; pp. xxviii, 480.

Issued in dark blue cloth, lettering and design in yellow on front cover, design in yellow and lettering in gold on spine; white end-papers; top edges gilt, others untrimmed. A blue silk marker attached to headband. Published in February 1904. There were further printings in 1905, 1910, 1913, 1919 and 1926.

Yeats contributed:
Preface. Pp. ix–xxiv.

COLONIAL EDITION

A few copies of this book were included in Murray's Imperial Library. These were issued in similar style to that of *Cuchulain of Muirthemne* in the same series. For description of this see No. 256.

259

GODS AND FIGHTING MEN: | THE STORY OF THE
TUATHA DE | DANAAN AND OF THE FIANNA | OF IRELAND,
ARRANGED AND | PUT INTO ENGLISH BY LADY | GREGORY.
WITH A PREFACE | BY W. B. YEATS | NEW YORK | CHARLES
SCRIBNER'S SONS | 153–157 FIFTH AVENUE | 1904

$7\frac{4}{5} \times 5$; pp. xxviii, 480.

Issued in blue cloth, similar in decoration to that of the English edition, copies of this American edition having been imported from England already bound. Published in 1904.

Yeats's Preface is the same as that in the English edition.

260

THE LOVE SONGS OF CONNACHT BE- | ING THE
FOURTH CHAPTER OF THE | SONGS OF CONNACHT, COLLECTED |
AND TRANSLATED BY DOUGLAS HYDE | LL.D., 'AN CRAOBHIN
AOIBHINN' PRE- | SIDENT OF THE GAELIC LEAGUE

$8\frac{2}{5} \times 5\frac{3}{4}$; pp. xvi, 136.

Issued in grey blue paper boards with fawn linen spine; label printed in black on front cover, no label on spine; grey blue end-papers matching binding; all edges untrimmed. Copies are known that have a label on the spine.

300 copies printed at the Dun Emer Press in Dundrum, County Dublin. Published on July 4, 1904.

Yeats contributed:

Preface. P. [xi].

261

IRISH | LITERATURE | JUSTIN MCCARTHY M.P. | EDITOR IN CHIEF | MAURICE F. EGAN, LL.D. DOUGLAS HYDE, LL.D. | LADY GREGORY JAMES JEFFREY ROCHE. LL.D. | ASSOCIATE EDITORS | CHARLES WELSH, | MANAGING EDITOR | VOL. [design] III. | JOHN D. MORRIS & COMPANY | PHILADELPHIA [*The title-page is surrounded by a green and gold ornamental border.*]

$9\frac{1}{16} \times 5\frac{3}{4}$; pp. xxxii, 811–1240.

Issued in green buckram, lettering in gold on brown label at head of spine; white end-papers. Published in 1904.

Yeats contributed:

Modern Irish Poetry. Pp. vii–xv.

> This is the revised version of the Introduction to *A Book of Irish Verse*, 1900. (No. 225.)

This anthology comprised ten volumes. Yeats is listed as one of the authors of "Biographies and Literary Appreciations" but these are mostly unsigned. There was a reissue, undated, the ten volumes bound as five. The title was identical except that BIGELOW, SMITH & COMPANY | NEW YORK replacesJ OHN D. MORRIS & COMPANY | PHILADELPHIA.

262

THE WELL OF THE SAINTS. | BY J. M. SYNGE. WITH AN INTRO- | DUCTION BY W. B. YEATS. BE- | ING VOLUME FOUR OF PLAYS | FOR AN IRISH THEATRE | LONDON: A. H. BULLEN, 47, GREAT | RUSSELL STREET, W.C. 1905.

$7\frac{1}{2} \times 5$; pp. xviii, 92.

Issued in grey paper boards with green cloth spine; white label printed in green within green panel on spine; white end-papers; all edges untrimmed.

Yeats contributed:

Mr. Synge and his Plays. Dated Abbey Theatre, January 27th, 1905.

The *English Catalogue* gives the date of publication as December 1905. I find, however, a note which I made on receipt of the book from the publisher saying that the book was not published until the end of January 1906. Copies of the play, using Bullen's sheets but without Yeats's introduction, had been issued in Dublin by Maunsel and Co. as Volume I. of their *Abbey Theatre Series* in February 1905. (See note by P. S. O'Hegarty in *The Dublin Magazine*, April–June 1947.) As Yeats's introductory essay is dated 27th January, 1905, it is not easy to account for the delay in issuing the English edition.

263

GITANJALI [*in red*]] (SONG OFFERINGS) | BY | RABINDRA NATH TAGORE | A COLLECTION OF PROSE TRANSLATIONS MADE | BY THE AUTHOR FROM THE | ORIGINAL BENGALI | WITH AN INTRODUCTION BY | W. B. YEATS | [fleuron, *in red*] | LONDON | PRINTED AT THE CHISWICK PRESS FOR | THE INDIA SOCIETY | 1912

$9 \times 5\frac{3}{4}$; pp. xvi, 64.

Issued in white linen, lettered in gold on front cover and on spine; white end-papers; all edges untrimmed.

750 copies printed for the India Society of which 250 only were for sale.

Yeats contributed:

Introduction. Signed W. B. Yeats, September 1912. Pp. vii–xvi.

264

GITANJALI | (SONG-OFFERINGS) | BY | RABINDRANATH TAGORE | A COLLECTION OF PROSE TRANSLATIONS | MADE BY THE AUTHOR FROM | THE ORIGINAL BENGALI | WITH AN INTRODUCTION BY | W. B. YEATS | MACMILLAN AND CO., LIMITED | ST. MARTIN'S STREET, LONDON | 1913

$7\frac{1}{2} \times 5$; pp. 2, xxii, 104.

Issued in blue cloth, gilt rules round edge of front cover, lettered in gold on front cover and on spine; white end-papers; all edges untrimmed. Published in March 1913.

Yeats contributed:

Introduction. Dated September 1912. Pp. [vii]–xxii.

> This is the same introduction as that to the edition of 1912. (No. 263.)

There were further impressions in April, May, June, July (2), September, October (3), November (2) and December (2), 1913; January (2), February, April (2), June, 1914; January, March, 1915.

265

AMERICAN EDITION

GITANJALI | (SONG OFFERINGS) | BY | RABINDRANATH TAGORE | A COLLECTION OF PROSE TRANSLATIONS | MADE BY THE AUTHOR FROM | THE ORIGINAL BENGALI | WITH AN INTRODUCTION BY | W. B. YEATS | NEW YORK | THE MACMILLAN COMPANY | 1914 | ALL RIGHTS RESERVED

$7\frac{3}{8} \times 4\frac{7}{8}$; pp. xxii, 101, followed by 5 pp., unnumbered, of advertisements.

Issued in blue cloth, lettered in gold on spine, monogram, R T, on front cover; white end-papers. Published in 1914.

Yeats contributed:

Introduction. Dated September 1912. Pp. vii–xxii.

> This is the same introduction as that to the edition of 1912. (No. 263.)

There was a new edition in 1928.

Published as a paperback by The Colonial Press, Inc., Clinton, Mass. 1960? A volume in the International Pocket Library Series.

266

GITANJALI | (SONG OFFERINGS) | BY | RABINDRANATH TAGORE | A COLLECTION OF PROSE TRANSLATIONS | MADE BY THE AUTHOR FROM | THE ORIGINAL BENGALI | WITH AN INTRODUCTION BY | W. B. YEATS | INDIAN EDITION | MACMILLAN AND CO., LIMITED | CALCUTTA · BOMBAY · MADRAS · LONDON. | 1919

$7 \times 4\frac{7}{10}$; pp. xxii, 102, followed by 2 pp. of advertisements.

Issued in dull green cloth, lettered in black on front cover, no lettering on spine; white end-papers; all edges trimmed. Published in 1919.

Yeats contributed:

Introduction. Dated September 1912. Pp. vii–xxii.

This is the same introduction as that to the edition of 1912. (No. 263.)

267

THE POST OFFICE: A PLAY BY RAB- | INDRANATH TAGORE TRANSLAT- | ED BY DEVABRATA MUKERJEA | [woodcut as in No. 84] | THE CUALA PRESS | CHURCHTOWN | DUNDRUM | MCMXIV

$8\frac{2}{5} \times 5\frac{3}{4}$; pp. xii, 44.

Issued in blue paper boards with white linen spine; lettered in black on front cover; no label on spine; blue end-papers matching binding; all edges untrimmed.

400 numbered copies printed and published by Elizabeth C. Yeats at the Cuala Press, Churchtown, Dundrum, County Dublin. Finished on Saint John's Eve, 1914. Published on July 27, 1914.

Yeats contributed:

Preface. Printed in red. P. [xii].

268

THE POST OFFICE | BY | RABINDRANATH TAGORE | TRANSLATED BY | DEVABRATA MUKERJEA | MACMILLAN AND CO., LIMITED | ST. MARTIN'S STREET, LONDON | 1914

$7\frac{3}{5} \times 5$; pp. viii, 88, followed by 2 pp. of advertisements for books by Tagore.

Issued in dark blue cloth, lettered in gold inside gold rules on front cover, lettered in gold on spine between two gold bands; white end-papers; all edges untrimmed. Published in October 1914.

Yeats contributed:

Preface. Pp. v–vi.

This is the same as that in the Cuala Press Edition. (No. 267.)

Issued in New York by The Macmillan Company in 1914.

269

CERTAIN NOBLE PLAYS OF JAPAN: | FROM THE MANUSCRIPTS OF ERNEST | FENOLLOSA, CHOSEN AND

FINISHED | BY EZRA POUND, WITH AN INTRODUC- | TION BY
WILLIAM BUTLER YEATS. | [woodcut as in No. 179] | THE
CUALA PRESS | CHURCHTOWN | DUNDRUM | MCMXVI

$8\frac{3}{10} \times 5\frac{1}{2}$; pp. xi, XXI, 56.

Issued in grey paper boards with buff linen spine, lettered in black on
front cover, no label on spine; grey end-papers matching binding;
all edges untrimmed.

350 numbered copies printed and published by Elizabeth Corbet
Yeats at The Cuala Press, Churchtown, Dundrum. Finished on July
20, 1916. Published on September 16, 1916.

Yeats contributed:
Introduction. Pp. i–[xix].

270

GITANJALI AND | FRUIT-GATHERING | BY | SIR
RABINDRANATH TAGORE | WITH ILLUSTRATIONS BY | NAN-
DALAL BOSE, SURENDRANATH KAR | ABINDRANATH TAGORE,
AND | NOBINDRANATH TAGORE | MACMILLAN AND CO.,
LIMITED | ST. MARTIN'S STREET, LONDON | 1919

$7\frac{3}{5} \times 5\frac{1}{4}$; pp. 2, xxii, 224.

Issued in dark blue cloth, with lettering and ornamental design in
gold on front cover and on spine; white end-papers; all edges untrimmed. Published in 1919.

Yeats contributed:
Introduction. Dated September 1912. Pp. vii–xxii.
    This is the same introduction as that to *Gitanjali*, 1912. (No. 263.)

271

THE COMPLETE WORKS OF | OSCAR WILDE |
[double rule] | THE HAPPY PRINCE [*in red*] | AND OTHER
FAIRY TALES [*in red*] | WITH AN INTRODUCTION | BY | W. B.
YEATS | [ornament, impressed] | VOLUME | III | GARDEN
CITY NEW YORK | DOUBLEDAY, PAGE & COMPANY [*in red*] |
1923

$8 \times 5\frac{1}{2}$; pp. xviii, 264.

A volume of the Patrons' Edition de Luxe of the *Complete Works of Oscar Wilde*, issued in green paper boards with elephant grey parchment spine, a gold line at the joining of the half binding on front and back covers; label printed in black on spine; white end-papers; top edges gilt, others untrimmed. Published in 1923.

Yeats contributed:
Introduction. Pp. ix–xvi.

272

EARLY MEMORIES; SOME CHAPTERS | OF AUTOBIOGRAPHY | BY JOHN BUTLER YEATS. | [woodcut as in No. 84] | THE CUALA PRESS | CHURCHTOWN | DUNDRUM | MCMXXIII
$8\frac{3}{10} \times 5\frac{4}{5}$; pp. xii, 104.

Issued in blue paper boards with buff linen spine, lettered in black on front cover, white paper label, printed in black, on spine; blue end-papers matching binding; all edges untrimmed.

500 copies printed and published by Elizabeth C. Yeats at the Cuala Press, Churchtown, Dundrum. Finished in the last week of July 1923. Published in September 1923.

Yeats contributed:
Preface. Dated June, 1923. Pp. [vii–ix].

273

AN OFFERING OF SWANS: BY | OLIVER GOGARTY. | [woodcut as in No. 84] | THE CUALA PRESS | MERRION SQUARE | DUBLIN IRELAND | MCMXXIII
$8\frac{3}{10} \times 5\frac{7}{10}$; pp. xvi, 32.

Issued in light blue paper boards with buff linen spine, lettered in black on front cover, white paper label, printed in black, on spine; light blue end-papers matching binding; all edges untrimmed.

300 copies printed and published by Elizabeth Yeats's Cuala Press, Merrion Square, Dublin. Finished on October 20, 1923. Published in January 1924.

Yeats contributed:
Preface. Dated August 30th. 1923. Pp. [xi–xii].

274

AN OFFERING OF | SWANS | AND | OTHER POEMS | BY |
OLIVER ST. JOHN GOGARTY | [ornament] | LONDON: | EYRE
& SPOTTISWOODE, LTD. | 2 GOLDSMITH STREET, FLEET
STREET, E.C.

$8\frac{9}{10} \times 6$; pp. 60. Portrait frontispiece of the Author by Augustus John.

Issued in dark blue cloth, lettered in gold on front cover and on spine;
off-white end-papers; top edges trimmed, others untrimmed.
Published in August 1924.

Yeats contributed:

Preface. Pp. 3–4.
  This is the same as that to the Cuala Press edition, 1923. (No.
  273.)

275

AXEL | [rule] | BY | JEAN MARIE MATTHIAS | PHILIPPE
AUGUSTE | COUNT DE VILLIERS DE L'ISLE-ADAM | TRANSLATED
| INTO ENGLISH BY H. P. R. FINBERG | WITH A PREFACE BY |
WILLIAM BUTLER YEATS | [rule] | [heraldic design] | [rule] |
JARROLDS PUBLISHERS · LONDON · LTD | [rule] | MCMXXV
[*The whole is enclosed in a line border with an additional line
on the right.*]

$9 \times 5\frac{3}{4}$; pp. iv (blank), 296.

Issued in white buckram with lettering and designs by T. Sturge
Moore in gold on front cover and on spine; white end-papers; top
edges gilt, others untrimmed. Decorated throughout by T. Sturge
Moore.

500 copies, numbered, and signed by the translator, for sale in Great
Britain and America. Published in May 1925.

Yeats contributed:

Preface. Dated September 20th, 1924. Pp. 7–11.
  Some passages of this preface first appeared in an essay *A
  Symbolical Drama in Paris* in *The Bookman*, April 1894.

276

THE MIDNIGHT COURT | AND | THE ADVENTURES OF
A LUCKLESS FELLOW | TRANSLATED FROM THE GAELIC |
BY | PERCY ARLAND USSHER | [publisher's device] | WITH
A PREFACE BY | W. B. YEATS | & | WOODCUTS BY | FRANK W.
PEERS | LONDON | JONATHAN CAPE 30 BEDFORD SQUARE
$8\frac{1}{10} \times 5\frac{4}{5}$; pp. 80.

Issued in orange cloth with white label, printed in blue, on spine;
white end-papers; top edges trimmed, others untrimmed. Published in
1926.

Yeats contributed:
Introduction. Pp. 5–12.

277

AMERICAN EDITION

THE MIDNIGHT COURT | AND | THE ADVENTURES OF
A LUCKLESS FELLOW | TRANSLATED FROM THE GAELIC | BY |
PERCY ARLAND USSHER | WITH A PREFACE BY | W. B. YEATS |
& | WOODCUTS BY | FRANK W. PEERS | [device] | BONI AND
LIVERIGHT | PUBLISHERS NEW YORK
$8 \times 5\frac{4}{5}$; pp. 80.

Sheets of the English edition issued in green-specked silver boards,
with geometric designs in green and silver, green cloth spine with
silver label lettered in green; white end-papers. Published in 1926.

Yeats's Preface is the same as that to the English edition. (No. 276.)

278

SONGS OF INNOCENCE | WILLIAM BLAKE | ILLUSTRATED
BY | JACYNTH PARSONS | [decoration] | WITH A PREFATORY
LETTER BY W. B. YEATS | LONDON AND BOSTON | THE MEDICI
SOCIETY. [*The whole enclosed within a decorative border.*]
$9\frac{3}{4} \times 7\frac{2}{5}$; pp. xii, 44.

S

Issued in blue cloth, design and lettering in gold on front cover, lettering in gold on spine; white end-papers; all edges trimmed. Published in November 1927.

Yeats contributed:
Prefatory Letter. To the Medici Society. Pp. vii–viii.

279

WILD APPLES: BY OLIVER GOGARTY, | WITH PREFACE BY | WILLIAM BUTLER YEATS. | [woodcut as in No. 72, in red] | THE CUALA PRESS | DUBLIN, IRELAND | MCMXXX

$8\frac{3}{10} \times 5\frac{3}{4}$; pp. xvi, 40.

Issued in blue paper boards with buff linen spine, lettered in black on front cover, white label printed in black on spine; blue end-papers matching binding; all edges untrimmed.

250 copies printed on paper made in Ireland and published by Elizabeth Corbet Yeats at the Cuala Press, 133 Lower Baggot Street, Dublin. Finished in the last week of February 1930. Published in April 1930.

Yeats contributed:
Preface. Pp. [xi–xiv].

280

BISHOP BERKELEY | HIS LIFE, WRITINGS, AND | PHILOSOPHY | BY | J. M. HONE & M. M. ROSSI | WITH AN INTRODUCTION | BY | W. B. YEATS | LONDON | FABER & FABER LIMITED | 24 RUSSELL SQUARE

$8\frac{3}{8} \times 5\frac{1}{2}$; pp. xxx, 290.

Issued in brown linen, lettered in gold on spine; white end-papers; top edges stained blue, bottom edges trimmed, others untrimmed. Published in October 1931.

Yeats contributed:
Introduction. Dated July, 1931, followed by a postscript. Pp. xv–xxix.

Issued in New York by The Macmillan Company in 1931.

281

AN INDIAN MONK │ HIS LIFE AND ADVENTURES │ BY │
SHRI PUROHIT SWAMI │ WITH INTRODUCTION │ BY │ W. B.
YEATS │ MACMILLAN AND CO., LIMITED │ ST. MARTIN'S STREET,
LONDON │ 1932

$7\frac{2}{5} \times 5$; pp. 2, xxvi, 208.

Issued in blue cloth, lettered in gold on spine; white end-papers; top
edges trimmed, others untrimmed. Published in November 1932.

Yeats contributed:

Introduction. Dated 5th September 1932. Pp. xv–xxvi.

282

THE │ HOLY MOUNTAIN │ BEING THE STORY OF A │
PILGRIMAGE TO LAKE MĀNAS │ AND OF INITIATION │ ON
MOUNT KAILĀS IN TIBET │ BY │ BHAGWĀN SHRI HAMSA │
TRANSLATED │ FROM THE MARĀTHI BY │ SHRI PUROHIT
SWĀMI │ WITH AN INTRODUCTION BY │ W. B. YEATS │ LONDON │
FABER AND FABER LIMITED │ 24 RUSSELL SQUARE

$8\frac{1}{10} \times 5\frac{1}{8}$; pp. 204.

Issued in light blue cloth, lettered in gold on spine; white end-
papers; top edges stained yellow, other edges trimmed. Published in
September 1934.

Yeats contributed:

Introduction. Pp. 11–41.

> First appeared, under the title *Initiation on a Mountain,* in *The
> Criterion,* July 1934.

A Biographical Note. P. 43.

283

SELECTIONS │ FROM │ THE POEMS │ OF │ DOROTHY
WELLESLEY │ [asterisk] │ WITH AN INTRODUCTION BY │
W. B. YEATS │ AND A DRAWING BY │ SIR WILLIAM ROTHEN-
STEIN │ LONDON │ MACMILLAN AND CO. LTD. │ 1936

$7\frac{1}{2} \times 5$; pp. xviii, 126.

Issued in pale yellow linen, lettered in gold on spine; white end-papers; top edges trimmed, others untrimmed. Published in June 1936.

Yeats contributed:
Introduction. Dated 1935. Pp. vii–xv.

Most of this edition was destroyed by fire during the air raids on London.

283A

THE POETS | AND | OTHER POEMS | BY | [autograph of Dorothy Wellesley] | [ornament] | PENNS IN THE ROCKS SERIES. | 1943 | COPYRIGHT. |

$9\frac{5}{8} \times 5\frac{3}{4}$; pp. 27.

Issued in tan paper covers, lettered in red and black on cream-coloured paper label pasted on front cover; no end-papers; all edges trimmed.

300 copies printed and published by H. W. Baldwin, Grosvenor Road, Tunbridge Wells, Kent.

Yeats contributed an introduction, pp. 3–6, that follows a foreword by Dorothy Wellesley.

This is the same introduction as that to *Selections from the Poems of Dorothy Wellesley*, 1936 (No. 283; and see No. 288).

284

THE LEMON TREE | MARGOT | RUDDOCK | WITH AN INTRODUCTION BY | W. B. YEATS | LONDON: J. M. DENT & SONS LTD.

$7\frac{1}{5} \times 5\frac{1}{4}$; pp. 4, xiv, 30.

Issued in grey-green paper boards, lettered in blue on spine; white end-papers; top edges stained blue, others trimmed. Published in May 1937.

Yeats contributed:
At Barcelona. (Poem.) Pp. vii.
Introduction. I. Dated June 1936.   Pp. ix–xiii.
        First appeared, under the title *Prefatory Note on the Author*, in *The London Mercury*, July 1936.
                II. Dated December 1936. Pp. xiii–xiv.
Footnotes. Pp. 1, 3 and 7.

285

OTHERS TO ADORN | BY | OLIVER ST. JOHN GOGARTY |
PREFACE BY W. B. YEATS | FOREWORDS BY | A. E. [GEORGE
RUSSELL] | AND HORACE REYNOLDS | LONDON | RICH &
COWAN | 37 BEDFORD SQUARE, W.C.1 | 1938

$7\frac{2}{5} \times 5$; pp. xxxviii, 186.

Issued in dark blue linen, lettered in gold on spine; white end-papers;
top edges trimmed, others untrimmed. Published in April 1938.

Yeats contributed:
Preface (from the introduction to the *Oxford Book of Modern Verse,
1892–1935*, Section V, p. xv). P. ix.

Issued in Canada by the Ryerson Press, Toronto, in 1938.

286

[Symbol, *in red*] | APHORISMS OF YOGA | BY | BHAGWAN
SHREE PATANJALI | DONE INTO ENGLISH | FROM THE ORIGINAL
IN SANSKRIT | WITH A COMMENTARY | BY | SHREE PUROHIT
SWAMI | AND AN INTRODUCTION | BY | W. B. YEATS | FABER
AND FABER LIMITED | 24 RUSSELL SQUARE | LONDON

$8\frac{7}{10} \times 5\frac{1}{2}$; pp. 96.

Issued in yellow cloth, lettered in gold on spine; off-white end-papers;
top edges trimmed, others untrimmed. Published in June 1938.

Yeats contributed:
Introduction. Dated Dublin 1937. Pp. 11–21.

Issued in Canada by the Ryerson Press, Toronto, in 1938.

287

LIGHTNING | FLASH | BY | MARGARET O'LEARY |
[publisher's device] | JONATHAN CAPE | THIRTY BEDFORD
SQUARE | LONDON

$7\frac{1}{2} \times 5$; pp. 384.

Issued in light brown cloth, lettered in green on front cover and on spine; white end-papers; top and side edges trimmed. Published in November 1939.

At the beginning is printed a letter :

W. B. Yeats to Lennox Robinson. Dated April 16th, 1929. Pp. 7–9.
This letter criticises the play by the same author on which the novel is founded.

Issued in Canada by Thomas Nelson & Sons, Toronto, in 1939.

288

SELECTED | POEMS | [ornament] | DOROTHY WELLESLEY | (DUCHESS OF WELLINGTON) | LONDON | WILLIAMS & NORGATE LTD. | 36 GREAT RUSSELL STREET, W.C.1

$7\frac{1}{5} \times 4\frac{7}{10}$; pp. xii, 13–160.

Issued in green cloth, lettered in gold within impressed panel on front cover, lettered in gold on spine; white end-papers; all edges trimmed. Published in April 1949.

Yeats contributed:
Introduction. Pp. vii–xi.
This is the same introduction as that to *Selections from the Poems of Dorothy Wellesley*, 1936. (No. 283.)

288A

SCHARMEL IRIS | [device] | BREAD OUT | OF STONE | PREFACE BY | WILLIAM BUTLER YEATS | EPILOGUE BY | OLIVER ST. JOHN GOGARTY | [device] | HENRY REGNERY COMPANY | PUBLISHERS CHICAGO

$6\frac{1}{8} \times 9\frac{1}{4}$; pp. 62.

Reproduction of portrait-drawing of Scharnel Iris by Diego Rivera on verso of the unnumbered half-title. Gogarty's Epilogue is at pp. 60–62.

Issued in blue cloth, lettered in gold on spine; all edges trimmed. Published on September 16, 1953.

Yeats contributed:
Preface. Pp. 5–6. Dated "Riverdale | Willbrook | Rathfarnham, | Dublin. | 1934".

3. BOOKS CONTAINING CONTRIBUTIONS BY W. B. YEATS, INCLUDING LETTERS FROM HIM

289

POEMS AND BALLADS | OF | YOUNG IRELAND | 1888 | "WE'RE ONE AT HEART IF YOU BE IRELAND'S FRIEND, | THOUGH LEAGUES ASUNDER OUR OPINIONS TEND; | THERE ARE BUT TWO GREAT PARTIES IN THE END." | ALLINGHAM. | DUBLIN | M. H. GILL AND SON | O'CONNELL STREET | 1888
$6\frac{3}{4} \times 4$; pp. viii, 80.

Issued in white cloth, lettered in gold and with design of harp on front cover; thick black end-papers, lined white; top edges untrimmed, others trimmed. Published in 1888.

I take this description from a copy of the book, now in the possession of Mr. P. S. O'Hegarty, who tells me that it is a presentation copy from Count Plunkett, one of the contributors, to his wife, and that it bears the date 1st May, 1888. He believes, therefore, that it is the first issue.

Copies are also found with yellow end-papers, lined white; all edges untrimmed; and with an Errata slip facing p. iv. The copy in the British Museum is of this issue; it bears the date stamp 25 February, 1889.

Yeats contributed:
The Stolen Child. Pp. 12–14.
King Goll (Third Century). Pp. 43–46.
    First appeared in *The Leisure Hour*, September 1887.
The Meditation of the Old Fisherman. P. 59.
    First appeared in *The Irish Monthly*, October 1886.
Love Song. From the Gaelic. P. 80.

In 1890 there was a reissue, described on the title-page as a New Edition but actually made up of the original sheets, the running headlines on the recto pages of text reading OF YOUNG IRELAND, 1888. and the Errata slip of the first edition still remaining. Only pp. i–iv, on slightly thicker paper, appear new.

Issued in brown paper covers, lettered in gold on front cover POEMS & BALLADS | OF | YOUNG IRELAND | PRICE SIXPENCE | NEW EDITION.

The British Museum copy is dated May 17, 1890.

In 1903 there was a further reissue in grey paper covers with lettering in gold on front cover. This is described on the cover as New Edition and on the title-page as Re-Issue. That the latter description is correct may be deduced from the facts that the sheets have running headlines 'Poems and Ballads of Young Ireland, 1888.' and that the Errata slip again appears.

It has been stated that this book was edited by W. B. Yeats. Messrs. M. H. Gill and Son, the publishers, kindly inform me that though they have no record of any editor's name, they do not believe that Yeats was the editor. In letters to John O'Leary, Yeats refers to certain poems as suitable for "our ballad book," and it seems probable that the actual editing was informal, under the general direction of O'Leary. In an article, dated April 11, 1891, on Rose Kavanagh in *The Boston Pilot* (reprinted in *Letters to the New Island*, 1934), Yeats refers to the book and says "It was planned out by a number of us, including Miss Rose Kavanagh, Miss Katharine Tynan, Miss Ellen O'Leary, Dr. Todhunter, and Dr. Douglas Hyde, the eminent Gaelic scholar."

290

IRISH MINSTRELSY: [*in red*] | BEING A SELECTION OF | IRISH SONGS, LYRICS, AND BALLADS. | EDITED, | WITH NOTES AND INTRODUCTION, | BY | H. HALLIDAY SPARLING. [*in red*] | [rule] | LONDON | WALTER SCOTT | 24 WARWICK LANE, PATER- NOSTER ROW | [short rule] | 1888

$7\frac{1}{2} \times 5$; pp. xxviii, 516.

Issued in dark blue cloth, design and lettering in gold on front cover and on spine; decorated blue end-papers; top edges gilt, others untrimmed.

Yeats contributed:
The Priest of Coloony. Pp. 378–379.
Copies of this book are also found in red cloth with purple end-papers;

all edges gilt. These appear to be a later issue. The British Museum copy is in this binding, and bears the date stamp 8 January '91.

The first edition of *Irish Minstrelsy* appeared in 1887 when it formed part of the series of Canterbury Poets, issued by Walter Scott, but Yeats's poem does not appear in this edition.

291

THE BOOK | OF THE | RHYMERS' CLUB | [publisher's device] | LONDON | ELKIN MATHEWS | AT THE SIGN OF THE BODLEY HEAD [*in red*] | IN VIGO STREET | 1892 | ALL RIGHTS RESERVED

$6\frac{2}{5} \times 5$; pp. xvi, 94.

Issued in dark yellow cloth with white label, printed in black, on spine; white end-papers; all edges untrimmed. Published in February 1892.

On p. iv, facing half-title:

"Four hundred and fifty copies of this edition printed, of which three hundred and fifty are for sale."

Yeats contributed:

A Man who dreamed of Fairyland. Pp. 7–9.
  First appeared in *The National Observer*, February 7, 1891.
Father Gilligan. Pp. 38–40.
  First appeared in *The Scots Observer*, July 5, 1890.
Dedication of 'Irish Tales.' Pp. 54–55.
  First appeared in *Representative Irish Tales*, 1890. (No. 215.)
A Fairy Song. P. 71.
  First appeared in *The National Observer*, September 12, 1891.
The Lake Isle of Innisfree. P. 84.
  First appeared in *The National Observer*, December 13, 1890.
An Epitaph. P. 88.
  First appeared in *The National Observer*, December 12, 1891.

LARGE PAPER EDITION

THE BOOK | OF THE | RHYMERS' CLUB [*in red*] | [publisher's device] | LONDON | ELKIN MATHEWS | AT THE SIGN OF THE BODLEY HEAD [*in red*] | IN VIGO STREET | 1892 | ALL RIGHTS RESERVED

$7\frac{3}{10} \times 5\frac{1}{2}$; pp. xvi, 96.

Issued in blue paper boards with parchment spine; white end-papers; all edges untrimmed; a yellow silk marker is attached to headband.

On verso of p. iv facing half-title:

"Only fifty copies of this Large Paper Edition Printed, of which this is No. . . ."

Quinn's Large Paper copy was inscribed "I got the Rhymers to publish this book because I wanted copies of Dowson's verse. W. B. Yeats, March, 1904."

292

THE | POETS [*in red*] | AND THE | POETRY [*in red*] | OF THE | CENTURY [*in red*] | CHARLES KINGSLEY | TO | JAMES THOMSON | EDITED BY [*in red*] | ALFRED H. MILES [*in red*] | HUTCHINSON & CO. | 25, PATERNOSTER SQUARE, LONDON
$6\frac{7}{10} \times 4\frac{1}{4}$; pp. xx, 652. [Vol. V.]

Issued in three styles: (1) On art paper, bound in parchment lettered in gold on front cover and on spine; white end-papers; top edges gilt, others untrimmed.   Limited to 110 copies, numbered, 100 only being for sale; sold in sets only. (2) On fine paper, bound in buckram; top edges gilt, others untrimmed. Limited to 300 copies. (3) On antique paper, bound in cloth; top edges gilt, others untrimmed. Published in 1892.

Yeats contributed:
William Allingham. Pp. 209–212.

293

THE | POETS [*in red*] | AND THE | POETRY [*in red*] | OF THE | CENTURY [*in red*] | JOANNA BAILLIE | TO | MATHILDE BLIND | EDITED BY [*in red*] | ALFRED H. MILES [*in red*] | HUTCHINSON & CO. | 25, PATERNOSTER SQUARE, LONDON
$6\frac{7}{10} \times 4\frac{1}{4}$; pp. xvi, 640. [Vol. VII.]

Issued in three styles, as No. 292. Published in 1892.

Yeats contributed:
Ellen O'Leary. Pp. 449–452.

294

THE SECOND BOOK | OF | THE RHYMERS' CLUB |
LONDON: ELKIN MATHEWS & JOHN LANE | NEW YORK: DODD,
MEAD & COMPANY | 1894 | ALL RIGHTS RESERVED

$6\frac{3}{10} \times 5$; pp. xvi, 136. At end is a List of Books in Belles Lettres, dated 1894, pp. 16.

Issued in brown buckram, lettered in gold on spine; white end-papers, all edges untrimmed. Published in June 1894.

On p. iv, facing half-title: ".·. Of this Edition Five Hundred Copies have been printed for England (of which Four Hundred only are for Sale). One Hundred and Fifty Copies also have been printed for America."

Yeats contributed:

The Rose in my Heart. P. 11.
　　First appeared in *The National Observer*, November 12, 1892.
The Folk of the Air. Pp. 37–39.
　　First appeared, under the title *The Stolen Bride*, in *The Bookman*, November 1893.
The Fiddler of Dooney. Pp. 68–69.
　　First appeared in *The Bookman*, December 1892.
A Mystical Prayer to the Masters of the Elements—Finvarra, Feacra, and Caolte. Pp. 91–92.
　　First appeared, under the title *A Mystical Prayer to the Masters of the Elements, Michael, Gabriel, and Raphael*, in *The Bookman*, October 1892.
The Cap and Bells. Pp. 108–109.
　　First appeared, under the title *Cap and Bell*, in *The National Observer*, March 17, 1894.
The Song of the Old Mother. P. 126.
　　First appeared in *The Bookman*, April 1894.

LARGE PAPER EDITION

THE SECOND BOOK | OF | THE RHYMERS' CLUB [*in red*] |
LONDON: ELKIN MATHEWS & JOHN LANE | NEW YORK:
DODD, MEAD & COMPANY | 1894] | ALL RIGHTS RESERVED

$7\frac{3}{10} \times 5\frac{1}{2}$; pp. xvi, 136.

Issued in blue paper boards with parchment spine, label, printed in black, on spine; white end-papers; all edges trimmed; an orange silk marker is attached to headband.

On p. [iv], facing half-title:

Of this Edition Fifty Copies have been printed for England, and Twenty Copies for America.

295

MDCCCXCVI. | THE | PAGEANT [*the title forms part of a design by Selwyn Image*] | EDITED BY C. HAZELWOOD | SHANNON AND J. W. GLEE- | SON WHITE. PUBLISHED BY | HENRY & CO. FROM THEIR | OFFICES AT 93 SAINT | MARTIN'S LANE | LONDON.

$10 \times 7\frac{1}{2}$; pp. xvi, 244, followed by pp. x of advertisements.

Issued in brown cloth, lettering and designs in gold by Charles Ricketts on front cover and on spine; white end-papers with design in brown by Lucien Pissarro; all edges untrimmed. Published in December 1896.

Yeats contributed:

Costello the Proud, Oona Macdermott, and the Bitter Tongue. Pp. 2–13.

There were also 150 copies printed on large paper. These measured $11\frac{9}{10} \times 8\frac{4}{5}$. They were issued in brown cloth with the same design by Charles Ricketts as that of the ordinary edition.

295A

ROMA | RECUEIL ARTISTIQUE INTERNATIONAL | PUBLIÉ PAR LA COMITÉ | = CARITÀ E LAVORO =

$16 \times 11\frac{1}{4}$; pp. ii, 46.

Issued in heavy paper boards, with elaborate design in buff, yellow and blue, on white. Design on front cover signed G. Cellini, that on back cover V. Moraldi. Lettering on front cover reads RECUEIL ARTISTIQUE INTERNATIONAL | ROMA | CARITÀ E LAVORO | MDCCCXCVII | INCISIONI DELLO STABILIMENTO DANESI. TIPI DELLA STAMPERIA FORZANI E C. On back cover COMITATO | CARITÀ E LAVORO | ROMA | CHARITAS | 1897 EDITION INTERNATIONALE | PRIX 7 FR. 50 CENT.

Yeats contributed:

The Glove and The Cloak. P. 27.

The poem was reprinted, with a note by Professor Marion Witt, in *Modern Language Notes*, January, 1955, and in *The Variorum Edition of the Poems of W. B. Yeats* (No. 211N).

296

'98 CENTENNIAL ASSOCIATION | OF GREAT
BRITAIN AND FRANCE. | [double rule] | REPORT OF
SPEECHES | DELIVERED AT THE | INAUGURAL BANQUET | HELD
AT | THE HOLBORN RESTAURANT, LONDON, | ON | WEDNESDAY,
13TH APRIL, 1898. | [double rule] | PRINTED FOR THE |
'98 CENTENNIAL ASSOCIATION OF GREAT BRITAIN AND
FRANCE | BY BERNARD DOYLE, PRINTER AND PUBLISHER, | 9
UPPER ORMOND QUAY, DUBLIN. | [rule] | 1898. | IRISH-MADE
PAPER. [*The whole enclosed in frame of one thick and one thin
rule.*]

$8\frac{3}{8} \times 5\frac{5}{12}$; pp. 16 of which the first page serves as front cover.

On white paper, fastened with one metal staple; all edges trimmed.
Published in 1898.

Yeats, who was Chairman of the Banquet, contributed:

The Union of the Gael. (A speech.) Pp. 8–10.

297

LITERARY | IDEALS IN | IRELAND. | BY JOHN
EGLINTON; | W. B. YEATS | A.E.; | W. LARMINIE. | PUBLISHED
BY T. FISHER UNWIN, LONDON. | AND AT THE DAILY EXPRESS
OFFICE, DUBLIN.

$8\frac{2}{5} \times 4\frac{3}{5}$; pp. ii, 88, followed by 7 pp. of advertisements and one blank
page.

Issued in sage green paper covers, lettered in black on front cover;
the lettering repeats that of the title-page but restores the semi-colon
dropped after Yeats's name, and adds at foot PRICE ONE SHILLING.
MDCCCIC.; the title-page is not part of the first gathering, but is tipped
in; no end-papers; all edges trimmed. Published in May 1899.

The description given is that of my own copy which I bought in England shortly after publication; it agrees with that of the copy in the
British Museum which bears the date stamp 19 June '99. I have, however, seen two variants, both in Dublin, one of which has the date
MDCCCIC on the title, on the left-hand side of the page at the foot, and
does not restore the semi-colon after Yeats on the cover, the other has
both date on title and semi-colon after Yeats on cover.

Two other binding variants are known: one, pp. 16, 88, 8, comprising 16 blank pp. preceding the text and 8 blank pp. following the text, the half-title leaf missing, bound in brown paper boards with grey canvas back, white label lettered in red LITERARY IDEALS IN IRELAND BY EGLINGTON [*sic*], YEATS, & OTHERS on spine, brown end-papers matching binding, all edges gilt; the other, pp. 2, ii, 88, 2, comprising 2 blank pp. preceding the half-title leaf and 2 blank pp. following the text, title-page adds at foot MDCCCIC, bound in white cloth, lettering in gold on front cover repeating accurately lettering on title-page but without place or date of publication, white end-papers, top edges gilt, others trimmed.

Yeats contributed:

A Note on National Drama. Pp. 17–20.

> First appeared, as part of an essay under the title *The Poems and Stories of Miss Nora Hopper*, in *The Dublin Daily Express*, September 24, 1898.

John Eglinton and Spiritual Art. Pp. 31–37.

> First appeared in *The Dublin Daily Express*, October 29, 1898.

The Autumn of the Flesh. Pp. 69–75.

> First appeared in *The Dublin Daily Express*, December 3, 1898.

Quinn's copy was inscribed: "This was a stirring row while it lasted and we were all very angry. W. B. Yeats. New York, 1904."

298

A TREASURY | OF | IRISH POETRY | IN THE | ENGLISH TONGUE | EDITED BY | STOPFORD A. BROOKE | AND | T. W. ROLLESTON | LONDON | SMITH, ELDER, & CO., 15 WATERLOO PLACE | 1900 | ALL RIGHTS RESERVED

$7\frac{3}{10} \times 5\frac{1}{2}$; pp. xlvi, 586.

Issued in blue cloth, lettered in gold on spine; white end-papers; all edges untrimmed. Published in December 1900.

Yeats contributed:

Lionel Johnson. Pp. 465–467.

> First appeared, under the title *Mr. Lionel Johnson and certain Irish Poets*, in *The Dublin Daily Express*, August 27, 1898.

Nora Hopper. Pp. 471–473.

> First appeared, as part of an essay *The Poems and Stories of Miss Nora Hopper*, in *The Dublin Daily Express*, September 24, 1898.

Althea Gyles. P. 475.

A.E. Pp. 485–487.

> First appeared, under the title *The Poetry of A.E.*, in *The Dublin Daily Express*, September 3, 1898.

In addition to these original contributions the compilers selected the following poems by Yeats for inclusion in their Anthology:

The Hosting of the Sidhe; Michael Robartes remembers Forgotten Beauty; The Rose of the World; The Lake Isle of Innisfree; When you are Old; A Dream of a Blessed Spirit; The Lamentation of the Old Pensioner; The Two Trees; The Island of Sleep (a passage from *The Wanderings of Oisin*).

Copies are known bound in green ribbed cloth with black or white end-papers, lettering or design in gold on the front cover, and lettering in gold on spine.

299

AMERICAN EDITION

A TREASURY | OF | IRISH POETRY | IN THE ENGLISH TONGUE | EDITED BY | STOPFORD A. BROOKE | AND | T. W. ROLLESTON | NEW YORK | THE MACMILLAN COMPANY. | LONDON: MACMILLAN & CO., LTD. | 1900 | ALL RIGHTS RESERVED.

$7\frac{3}{10} \times 5\frac{1}{2}$; pp. xlvi, 578 plus 2 pp. of advertisements.

Issued in blue cloth, lettered in gold on spine; white end-papers; all edges trimmed. Published in December 1900.

Yeats's contributions are the same as those in the English edition. (No. 298.)

The volume was reprinted in March and May 1905, in March 1910, and in July 1915. There was a new edition, pp. xlvi and 610, published in February 1932.

300

IDEALS IN | IRELAND | EDITED BY LADY GREGORY | WRITTEN BY "A.E.," D.P. | MORAN, GEORGE MOORE, | DOUGLAS HYDE, STANDISH | O'GRADY, AND W. B. YEATS | LONDON: AT THE UNICORN | VII CECIL COURT MDCCCCI

$7\frac{1}{2} \times 5$; pp. 112.

Issued in dark blue cloth, design in light green on front cover, lettered IDEALS | IN | IRELAND | UNICORN | PRESS in light green on spine; white end-papers; all edges untrimmed. Published in January 1901.

Yeats contributed:

The Literary Movement in Ireland. Pp. 87–102.

First appeared in *The North American Review*, December 1899.

A Postscript. Pp. 105–107.

> First appeared, under the title *A Postscript to a Forthcoming Book of Essays by Irish Writers*, in *The All Ireland Review*, December 1, 1900.

Some copies, including Lady Gregory's, have a small slip pasted on to p. 45, printed in red and reading as follows:

IDEALS IN IRELAND

Page 45, last three lines:

> MR GEORGE MOORE wishes to add that at the time he wrote this passage he did not know of the extraordinary revival of the Irish language in Dublin.

301

AMERICAN EDITION

An edition of *Ideals in Ireland* was also published in America. This was made up of the English sheets and was issued in similar style of binding, the only differences being that the words NEW YORK: M. F. MANSFIELD. 1901 were substituted for VII CECIL COURT MDCCCCI in the last line of title-page and MANSFIELD for UNICORN | PRESS at foot of spine.

302

WAYFARER'S LOVE | CONTRIBUTIONS FROM LIVING POETS | EDITED BY | THE DUCHESS OF SUTHERLAND. | COVER DESIGN BY MR. WALTER CRANE. | "LET ME TAKE YOUR HAND FOR LOVE AND SING YOU A SONG. | SAID THE OTHER TRAVELLER—THE JOURNEY IS A HARD JOURNEY, BUT | IF WE HOLD TOGETHER IN THE MORNING AND IN THE EVENING, | WHAT MATTER IF IN THE HOURS BETWEEN THERE IS SORROW." | OLD TALE. | WESTMINSTER | ARCHIBALD CONSTABLE & CO., LTD. | 1904

$8\frac{1}{2} \times 6\frac{3}{4}$; pp. 80.

Issued in green cloth, design and lettering in gold on front cover, lettering in gold on spine; white paper lining pasted to boards; all edges untrimmed. Published in October 1904.

Yeats contributed:

Old Memory. P. 37.

There was also an edition of 100 copies on large paper, measuring $10\frac{1}{4} \times 7\frac{3}{4}$, issued in vellum binding.

303

A BIBLIOGRAPHY OF THE WRITINGS | OF WIL-
LIAM BUTLER YEATS | BY ALLAN WADE | THE SHAKES-
PEARE HEAD PRESS | STRATFORD-ON-AVON | MCMVIII
$8\frac{4}{5} \times 5\frac{1}{2}$; pp. 96.

Part IV. *American Editions* (pp. [88]–95) was compiled from notes by
John Quinn.

Issued in grey paper boards with green cloth spine, white label, printed
in black inside frame of green lines, on spine; white end-papers; all
edges untrimmed.

Sixty copies printed, numbered in ink. Published in November 1908.
Yeats contributed:

Four-line poem *Accursed who brings to light of day*. P. [7].

A Prologue (to *The King's Threshold*). Pp. 32–34, with footnote
    dated W.B.Y. 1904.
    (This prologue was included at Yeats's request as it had been
    omitted from all editions except Nos. 55, 56 and 57.)

304

SEVEN SHORT PLAYS | BY LADY GREGORY | DUBLIN:
MAUNSEL & CO., LTD. | 96 MIDDLE ABBEY STREET | 1909
$7\frac{3}{10} \times 5$; pp. viii, 212.

Issued in blue paper boards with buff linen spine, label, printed in
black, on spine; white end-papers; top edges trimmed, others untrimmed. Published in June 1909.

In her note on *The Travelling Man* Lady Gregory writes:

"I owe the Rider's Song, and some of the rest, to W. B. Yeats."

Issued in Boston by John W. Luce & Co., in 1911; and in New York
by G. P. Putnam's Sons, in 1915.

305

WILLIAM SHARP [*in red*] | (FIONA MACLEOD) | A MEMOIR
| COMPILED BY HIS WIFE | ELIZABETH A. SHARP | [pub-
lisher's device] | LONDON | WILLIAM HEINEMANN [*in red*] |
1910
9×6; pp. 2, viii, 434.
    T

Issued in black cloth, facsimile signatures of William Sharp and of Fiona Macleod in gold on front cover, lettering in gold on spine, publisher's device stamped blind on back cover; yellowish white end-papers; top edges gilt, others untrimmed. Published in October 1910.

Letters from Yeats appear on pp. 269–270, 276–277, 280–282, 334–336, and quotations from a letter and from a lecture on p. 424.

Issued in New York by Duffield & Co. in 1910.

306

TWENTY-FIVE YEARS: | REMINISCENCES | BY | KATHA-RINE TYNAN | (MRS. H. A. HINKSON) | WITH A PORTRAIT | LONDON | SMITH, ELDER & CO., 15 WATERLOO PLACE | 1913 | [ALL RIGHTS RESERVED]

$8\frac{4}{5} \times 5\frac{1}{2}$; pp. viii, 360.

Issued in red cloth, lettered in gold on front cover and on spine; white end-papers; top edges trimmed, others untrimmed. Published in October 1913.

In 1916 John Murray took over Smith, Elder, and sometime thereafter copies, still dated 1913, were issued with the Murray imprint on the title-page. They were lettered in blind on front cover and in gold on spine; all edges trimmed. Pp. [357–360] still contained advertisements for Smith, Elder books.

Letters from Yeats are quoted on pp. 259–263 and 264–272.

Issued in New York by The Devin-Adair Co. in 1914.

307

OUR IRISH THEATRE | A CHAPTER OF AUTOBIOGRAPHY | BY | LADY GREGORY | ILLUSTRATED | G. P. PUTNAM'S SONS | NEW YORK AND LONDON | THE KNICKERBOCKER PRESS | 1913

$7\frac{3}{5} \times 5$; pp. vi, 328.

Issued in blue paper boards with buff linen spine, label printed in black within black rules on spine; white end-papers; all edges trimmed. Published in January 1914.

This contains the text of Yeats's

Advice to Playwrights who are sending Plays to the Abbey, Dublin. Pp. 100–102, and quotes short passages from many letters written by him. It also reprints the greater part of the first dedication to Lady Gregory of *Where There is Nothing*, New York, 1902. (No. 42.)

Issued in New York by G. P. Putnam's Sons in 1913.

308

ROYAL SOCIETY OF LITERATURE | THE ACADEMIC COMMITTEE | ADDRESSES OF RE-CEPTION | TO | JOHN MASEFIELD | BY SIR WALTER RALEIGH | TO | MRS. MARGARET LOUISA WOODS | BY MAURICE HEWLETT | TO | THE DEAN OF ST. PAUL'S | BY A. C. BENSON | TO | MAX BEERBOHM | BY LAURENCE BINYON | AWARD OF THE EDMOND DE POLIGNAC PRIZE | TO | JAMES STEPHENS | BY W. B. YEATS | FRIDAY, NOVEMBER 28TH, 1913 | LONDON | HUMPHREY MILFORD | OXFORD UNIVERSITY PRESS, AMEN CORNER, E.C. | 1914

$8\frac{7}{16} \times 5\frac{1}{2}$; pp. 42.

Issued stitched in grey paper covers, lettered in black on front cover, the lettering as that on title with the addition of the words Price One Shilling at foot; no end-papers; all edges trimmed. Imprint, Adlard and Son, Impr., London and Dorking at foot of p. 42.

Yeats contributed:
The Polignac Prize. Pp. 37–42.

309

CATHOLIC | ANTHOLOGY | 1914–1915 | [publisher's device] | LONDON | ELKIN MATHEWS, CORK STREET | 1915

$7\frac{1}{2} \times 5$; pp. viii, 100.

Issued in pale mauve paper boards with design in black on front and back covers signed D.S.; lettered in black on spine. Published in November 1915.

Yeats's contribution, *The Scholars* appears on p. 1 and is the only contribution printed in italics.

310

THE | BOOK OF THE HOMELESS | (LE LIVRE DES SANS-FOYER) | EDITED BY EDITH WHARTON | ORIGINAL ARTICLES IN VERSE AND PROSE | ILLUSTRATIONS REPRODUCED FROM ORIGINAL PAINTINGS & DRAWINGS | [ornament] | THE BOOK IS SOLD | FOR THE BENEFIT OF THE AMERICAN HOSTELS FOR REFUGEES | (WITH THE FOYER FRANCO-BELGE) | AND OF THE CHILDREN OF FLANDERS RESCUE COMMITTEE | LONDON | MACMILLAN & CO., LIMITED | MDCCCCXVI

$10\frac{9}{10} \times 8\frac{1}{4}$; pp. 2, xxvi, 160. Decorative half-title not included in pagination. There are 22 illustrations with fly-titles before each; these fly-titles are unnumbered and are not reckoned in the pagination.

Issued in dark brown paper boards with dark red linen spine, lettering in black and decoration in green on front cover, lettering and ornament in gold on spine; white end-papers; all edges trimmed. Published in March 1916.

On p. 157: Of this book, in addition to the regular edition, there have been printed and numbered one hundred and seventy-five copies de luxe, of larger format.

Numbers 1–50 on French hand-made paper, containing four facsimiles of manuscripts and a second set of illustrations in portfolio.

Numbers 51–175 on Van Gelder paper.

Yeats contributed:
A Reason for Keeping Silent (Poem). P. 45.

Issued in New York by Charles Scribner's Sons in 1915.

311

THE MIDDLE YEARS | BY | KATHARINE TYNAN | AUTHOR OF | "TWENTY-FIVE YEARS: REMINISCENCES" | LONDON | CONSTABLE & COMPANY LTD | 1916

$8\frac{3}{5} \times 5\frac{1}{2}$; pp. viii, 416.

Issued in green ribbed cloth, lettering and design in gold on front cover, lettering in gold on spine; white end-papers; top edges gilt, others untrimmed. Published in November 1916.

Letters from Yeats are quoted on pp. 31–48; pp. 49–71; and pp. 356–357.

Yeats adds footnotes on pp. 35, 36, 38, 39 and 46 concerning the right order of the letters.

Issued in Boston by Houghton, Mifflin Co. in 1917.

312

VISIONS AND BELIEFS IN | THE WEST OF IRE-LAND | COLLECTED AND ARRANGED BY | LADY GREGORY: WITH TWO ES- | SAYS AND NOTES BY W. B. YEATS | [four-line quotation] | FIRST [SECOND] SERIES | G. P. PUTNAM'S SONS | NEW YORK AND LONDON | THE KNICKERBOCKER PRESS | 1920.

$7\frac{2}{5} \times 5$; Vol. I., pp. 2, viii, 294. Vol. II., pp. 4, iv, 344.

Issued in blue cloth, label printed in black on spine; white end-papers; all edges trimmed. Published in September 1920.

Yeats contributed:

Vol. I. *Witches and Wizards and Irish Folk-Lore.* Dated 1914. Pp. 247–262.
    Notes. Pp. 265–293.

Vol. II. *Swedenborg, Mediums and the Desolate Places.* Dated 14th October, 1914. Pp. 295–339.
    This essay was reprinted in *If I were Four-and-Twenty*, 1940. (No. 205.)
    Notes. P. 343.

313

HUGH LANE'S LIFE AND | ACHIEVEMENT, WITH | SOME ACCOUNT OF THE | DUBLIN GALLERIES. BY | LADY GREGORY | WITH ILLUSTRATIONS | LONDON | JOHN MURRAY, ALBEMARLE STREET, W. I | 1921

$8\frac{1}{2} \times 5\frac{1}{2}$; pp. xvi, 290, followed by 6 pp. of advertisements.

Issued in olive green cloth, with white label printed in black on spine; white end-papers; top edges trimmed, others untrimmed. Published in February 1921.

Quotations from letters by Yeats appear on pp. 42, 45 n., 59–60, 61, 64, 79, 80, 87, 93–94, 103, 107, 111, 113, 117–118, 124, 127–128, 129, 158, 202, 203 and 219–220.

Memoranda, dictated or spoken, by Yeats appear on pp. 21–24, 32–33, 43–44, 59, 68–69 and 72–73.

Portions of the article *Sir Hugh Lane's Pictures. Mr. W. B. Yeats's Reply*, reprinted from *The Observer*, January 21, 1917, appear on pp. 221–225 and 228–229.

313A

THE JOHN KEATS | MEMORIAL VOLUME | ISSUED BY | THE KEATS HOUSE COMMITTEE, HAMPSTEAD | ILLUSTRATED WITH 5 FACSIMILES | VARIOUS PORTRAITS, 2 SKETCHES, ETC. | LONDON: JOHN LANE, THE BODLEY HEAD, VIGO STREET, W. | NEW YORK: JOHN LANE COMPANY. | FEBRUARY 23, 1921

$9\frac{3}{8} \times 7$; pp. xxii, 276.

Issued in pale olive-green cloth; on front cover in red is a circular monogram containing a large K, a sheaf of corn (gilt) and Grecian Urn; lettering and tooling in gilt on top and bottom of spine; no end-papers, the book opening directly upon the title; top edges coloured red, others untrimmed. There are four pages of advertisements at the end of the book.

Yeats contributed:

A Letter about the Book. Dated Dec. 22. P. 216.

314

MY LIFE AND SOME | LETTERS.   BY MRS. PATRICK CAMPBELL (BEATRICE STELLA CORNWALLIS-WEST) | [double rule] | WITH A PHOTOGRAVURE FRONTISPIECE AND | 40 OTHER ILLUSTRATIONS ON ART PAPER | LONDON: HUTCHIN-SON & CO. | PATERNOSTER ROW

$8\frac{7}{8} \times 5\frac{1}{2}$; pp. xii, 360.

Issued in dark blue cloth, lettered in gold on spine; white end-papers; all edges trimmed. Published in October 1922.

Letters from Yeats appear on pp. 162–163.

Issued in New York by Dodd, Mead & Co. in 1922.

314A

THE VOICE OF IRELAND | (Glór na h-Éireann) | A
survey of the race and nation | from all angles, | by | the
foremost leaders at home and abroad. | edited by | William
G. Fitz-Gerald. | [shamrock] | "Ba món epert in cach ré
airle Dé fri hErind uill"— | ("God's counsel concerning
glorious Erin is at all times | greater than the power of man
can tell.") | From *An Leabhar Laighneach* (The Book | of
Leinster, of the Twelfth Century). | [dotted rule] | Pub-
lished by: | John Heywood Ltd., | Dublin, Manchester,
London and Blackburn. | [All Rights Reserved.]

$10\frac{3}{4} \times 8\frac{3}{8}$; pp. xx, 612.

Issued in green cloth, lettered in gold on front cover and spine;
mottled-green end-papers; all edges trimmed. Published probably in
April 1924; a first edition, that I have not seen, was published by Virtue
and Company in 1923.

Yeats contributed:

*The Irish Dramatic Movement. A Letter to the Students of a Cali-
fornia School.* Pp. 460–465.

This essay has not been published elsewhere.

315

SEANAD EIREANN | DÍOSBÓIREACHTAÍ PÁIR-
LIMINTE | (PARLIAMENTARY DEBATES) | TUAIRISG OIFI-
GIÚIL | (OFFICIAL REPORT) | [double rule] | IMLEABHAR I. |
(VOLUME I.) | [double rule] | I GCÓIR NA TRÉIMHSE ÓN
11ADH MÍ NA NODLAG, 1922, GO 9ADH LUGHNASA, 1923, |
SA TSIOSÓN DAR TOSACH 11ADH MÍ NA NODLAG, 1922, AGUS
DAR CRIOCHNÚ | 9ADH LUGHNASA, 1923. | (COMPRISING THE
PERIOD FROM 11TH DECEMBER, 1922, TO 9th AUGUST, 1923,
IN THE SESSION | BEGINNING THE 11TH DECEMBER, 1922,
AND ENDING THE 9TH AUGUST, 1923.) | BAILE ATHA CLIÁTH |
(DUBLIN) | ALEX. THOM & CO., LTD., CLÓDÓIRÍ. | A CLÓ-
BHUAILEANN AGUS OIFIG AN TSOLATHÁIR A FHOILLSIGHEANN.
| PRINTED BY ALEX. THOM & CO., LTD., AND PUBLISHED BY
THE STATIONERY OFFICE | PRICE 20/-

$9\frac{1}{2} \times 6$. Issued in red cloth, lettered in gold on spine; white end-papers; all edges trimmed.

The above is taken from the first volume. The succeeding volumes have similar title-pages, with the necessary alterations of date, and are printed by Cahill & Co. Ltd.

The volumes are printed with two columns to each page; the figures given in the following list of subjects on which W. B. Yeats spoke refer to columns, not to pages.

Volume I. Session 1922–1923.

 Election of Chairman. 11–12.
 Standing Committees. 114, 115.
 Report of Committee on Standing Orders. 156, 531–533, 542.
 Indemnity (British Military) Bill. 167–168.
 Enforcement of Law (Occasional Powers) Bill. 277–278, 284–285.
 College of Science, Occupation of. 298.
 Griffith Settlement Bill. 470–471.
 League of Nations. 599, 972, 978, 979, 980, 981, 983.
 Electoral Bill. 619.
 Oireachtas Staff. 671.
 Damage to Property Bill. 724, 877.
 Cathaoirleach, powers and functions of. 742–743, 745.
 Compensation for Personal Injuries. 922–923.
 Irish Manuscripts. 992–995.
 Motion re The Lane Pictures. 1037–1041.
 Oireachtas (Payment of Members) Bill. 1121.
 Censorship of Films Bill. 1147–1148.
 Health Insurance Bill. 1274, 1307–1308.
 The Dowling Case. 1364.
 Oireachtas Accommodation. 1390–1391.
 Public Safety Bill. 1440–1441, 1579, 1638–1639.
 Valuation Bill. 1987.
 Defence Forces Bill. 1991.
 Civic Guard Bill. 2003.
 Land Bill. 2129–2130.

Volume II. Session 1923–1924.

 Resignation of a Senator. 65.
 Report of Committee on Standing Orders. 85, 89–90.
 Civil Service Regulation Bill. 369, 378, 379, 383.
 Saorstat Representation at British Empire Exhibition. 398.
 Public Safety Bill. 489–490.
 Courts of Justice Bill. 519, 714–715, 770, 792.

Volume IX. June–August 1927.

    Public Safety Bill. 318.

Volume X. October 1927–November 1928.

    Constitution Amendment Bill. 1097.

316

LES PRIX NOBEL | EN 1923 | STOCKHOLM | IMPRIMERIE ROYALE. P. A. NORDSTEDT & SÖNER | 1924.

$9\frac{3}{4} \times 6\frac{1}{2}$; pp. 100 followed by the five Conferences Nobel, each paged separately: pp. 1–13, p. [14] blank; pp. 1–7, p. [8] blank; pp. 1–15 p. [16] blank; pp. 1–12; pp. 1–11, p. [12] blank.

Issued in stiff white paper covers, lettered in red LES PRIX NOBEL | EN 1923 on front cover, lettered in red on spine; on back cover in red PRIS 10 KRONOR and at foot, beneath rule, imprint STOCKHOLM 1924. KUNGL. BOKTRYCKERIET. P. A. NORDSTEDT & SÖNER. 241553; no end-papers; all edges untrimmed.

Yeats's lecture *The Irish Dramatic Movement* is the last in the volume, and is paged separately, pp. 1–11.

On p. 97 is a short biographical note, and, facing this, is a reproduced photograph by A. B. Lagrelius & Westphal, Stockholm, with the poet's signature, W. B. Yeats, in facsimile beneath it.

Yeats delivered his lecture in Stockholm to the Swedish Royal Academy on December 13, 1923. In his preface to *The Bounty of Sweden,* dated June 15, 1924, he wrote that "a couple of months ago" he had dictated as many of his words as he could remember and added thereto "certain explanatory notes."

316A

[Reproduction of the Thomas William Lyster Memorial in the National Library of Ireland] | MEMORIAL TO THE LATE T. W. LYSTER | [small rule]

$10\frac{5}{8} \times 8\frac{1}{4}$; pp. 4: comprising text, pp. [1]–2; list of subscribers, p. 3; p. [4] blank.

Issued in white paper with lettering in black. 150 copies printed and distributed to the subscribers to the Lyster Memorial. Published in June 1926.

Contains the speech made by Yeats when, on behalf the Committee and the subscribers, he handed over the memorial to Sir Philip Hanson, C.B., Chief Commissioner of the Board of Works, on March 27, 1926.

317

COINAGE OF SAORSTÁT ÉIREANN | 1928 | DUBLIN: | PUBLISHED BY THE STATIONERY OFFICE. | TO BE PURCHASED THROUGH MESSRS. EASON AND SON, LTD., 40 AND 41 | LOWER O'CONNELL STREET, DUBLIN .| [PRICE THREE SHILLINGS AND SIXPENCE NETT.]

$9\frac{7}{10} \times 7\frac{3}{10}$; pp. viii, 68.

Issued in light brown buckram, lettered in gold on front cover; white end-papers; all edges trimmed. Published in 1928.

Yeats contributed:
What we did or tried to do. Pp. 1–7.

317A

SATIRE & FICTION | BY | WYNDHAM LEWIS | PRECEDED BY | THE HISTORY OF A | REJECTED REVIEW | BY ROY CAMPBELL | THE ARTHUR PRESS | 53. OSSINGTON STREET | LONDON. W.2.

$11 \times 8\frac{2}{5}$; pp. 64.

Issued in paper covers; all edges trimmed. Published in 1930.

Part of a letter from Yeats to Wyndham Lewis appears on p. 29.

Reprinted in *The Letters of W. B. Yeats*, 1954.

318

THE GOLDEN BOOK OF TAGORE | A HOMAGE TO RABINDRANATH TAGORE | [square] FROM INDIA AND THE WORLD [square] | IN CELEBRATION OF HIS SEVENTIETH BIRTHDAY | [ornament in red] | EDITED BY RAMANANDA CHATTERJEE | PUBLISHED BY THE GOLDEN BOOK COMMITTEE | CALCUTTA 1931

$11\frac{3}{10} \times 8\frac{1}{5}$; pp. xxii, 376. Illustrated.

Issued in yellow linen with decorative medallion in red and gold pasted on front cover, red label printed in gold on spine; yellow end-papers; all edges untrimmed.

Limited to 1500 copies. Published in 1931.

Yeats contributed:
A letter to Tagore. P. 269.

319

COOLE | BY LADY GREGORY | [woodcut as in No. 84] | THE CUALA PRESS | DUBLIN, IRELAND | MCMXXXI
$8\frac{3}{10} \times 5\frac{3}{4}$; pp. viii, 56.

Issued in blue paper boards with buff linen spine, lettered in black on front cover, white label, printed in black, on spine; blue end-papers matching binding; all edges untrimmed.

250 copies printed on paper made in Ireland and published at the Cuala Press, 133 Lower Baggot Street, Dublin, by Elizabeth Corbet Yeats. Finished on May Eve, 1931. Published in July 1931.

Yeats contributed:
Coole Park. (A poem.) Dated September 7th. 1929. Pp. [vii–viii].

319A

WRITERS AT WORK | by | Louise Morgan | [publisher's device] | London | Chatto & Windus | 1931
$7\frac{1}{4} \times 4\frac{7}{8}$; pp. viii, 76.

Issued in light-yellow cloth, lettered in red on front cover and spine, with design in red of dolphin, sea, and marginal decoration on front cover; white and-papers; all edges trimmed. One of the Dolphin Books series.

A conversation with Yeats is on pp. 1–9.

320

THE NEW KEEPSAKE | CONTRIBUTIONS BY | MAURICE BARING H. J. MASSINGHAM | MAX BEERBOHM RAYMOND MORTIMER | CLIVE BELL HAROLD NICOLSON | HILAIRE BELLOC NAOMI ROYDE SMITH | STELLA BENSON V. SACKVILLE-WEST |

LORD BERNERS SIEGFRIED SASSOON | EDMUND BLUNDEN
J. C. SQUIRE | IVOR BROWN H. M. TOMLINSON | LORD DAVID
CECIL HUGH WALPOLE | CYRIL CONNOLLY DOROTHY
WELLESLEY | ALDOUS HUXLEY R. H. WILENSKI | ROSE
MACAULAY W. B. YEATS | DECORATED BY | REX WHISTLER |
COBDEN-SANDERSON | 1 MONTAGUE STREET | LONDON
$8\frac{2}{5} \times 5\frac{3}{5}$; pp. x, 150.

Issued in white cloth, lettering and designs by Rex Whistler in pink
and black on front cover and on spine; white end-papers; top edges
trimmed and stained pink, other edges trimmed. Published in November 1931.

Yeats contributed:
Lullaby. Pp. 21–22.

321

MEN AND MEMORIES | RECOLLECTIONS | OF | WILLIAM
ROTHENSTEIN | 1900–1922 | [two asterisks] | 'BUT IT MAKES
NO MATTER, IT SHALL SERVE THE | TURNE, MEN ARE NOT WISE
AT ALL TIMES.' | THOMAS WENTWORTH, | EARL OF STRAFFORD
| [publisher's device] | LONDON | FABER & FABER
LIMITED | 24 RUSSELL SQUARE
$8\frac{3}{4} \times 5\frac{3}{4}$; pp. xii, 396.

Issued in black cloth, lettered in gold on spine; white end-papers;
top edges gilt, others untrimmed. Published in April 1932.

Letters from Yeats appear on pp. 20, 144–145 and 266–267, and a
passage from a letter is quoted on p. 263.

This is the second volume of *Men and Memories*.

Issued in New York by Coward-McCann Inc. in 1937.

322

SPECTATOR'S GALLERY | ESSAYS, SKETCHES, SHORT |
STORIES & POEMS | FROM | THE SPECTATOR | 1932 | [publisher's
device] | EDITED BY | PETER FLEMING | AND DEREK
VERSCHOYLE | JONATHAN CAPE | THIRTY BEDFORD SQUARE |
LONDON
$7\frac{1}{2} \times 5$; pp. 416.

Issued in light buff cloth, lettering in red on spine, publisher's device in red on back cover; white end-papers; all edges trimmed. Published in June, 1933.

Yeats contributed:

Three Poems: For Anne Gregory; Swift's Epitaph; Symbols. Pp. 20–21.
> *Swift's Epitaph* first appeared in *The Dublin Magazine*, October 1931. The other two poems first appeared in *Words for Music Perhaps*, 1932, and were printed in *The Spectator*, December 2, 1932.

Ireland, 1921–1931. Pp. 117–122.
> First appeared in *The Spectator*, January 30, 1932.

Remorse for Intemperate Speech. P. 123.
> First appeared in *Words for Music Perhaps*, 1932, and printed in *The Spectator*, November 18, 1932.

My Friend's Book. Pp. 335–341.
> (A review of *Song and its Fountains* by A.E.)
> First appeared in *The Spectator*, April 9, 1932. Reprinted in *Essays 1931 to 1936.* (No. 194.)

322A

THE YEAR'S POETRY | 1936 | A REPRESENTATIVE SELECTION | COMPILED BY | DENYS KILHAM ROBERTS | JOHN LEHMANN | JOHN LANE THE BODLEY HEAD | BURY STREET LONDON WC

$7\frac{1}{4} \times 4\frac{3}{4}$; pp. 136.

Issued in light yellow cloth, lettered in blue on spine; off-white end-papers; top edges stained purple, others trimmed. Published in 1936.

Yeats contributed three poems: *What Then?* reprinted in *The Erasmian* (Dublin), April 1937, in *New Poems*, 1938, and in *Last Poems and Plays*, 1940; *Parnell's Funeral.* First appeared as *A Parnellite at Parnell's Funeral* in *The Spectator*, October 19, 1934; and *Ribh at the Tomb of Baile and Aillinn.* First appeared in *The London Mercury* and *Poetry* (Chicago), December 1934.

323

ERNEST RHYS | [double rule with fleuron at each end] | LETTERS FROM LIMBO | WITH 63 REPRODUCTIONS | OF LETTERS | LONDON | J. M. DENT AND SONS LTD.

$8\frac{1}{6} \times 5\frac{1}{4}$; pp. 2, xviii, 292.

Issued in red cloth, lettered in gold on spine, the title being enclosed in gold double rules; white end-papers; top edges stained red, others trimmed. Published in October 1936.

Letters from Yeats appear on pp. 155–159.

A part of the letter on p. 155 is reproduced in facsimile on p. [156].

323A

A | POET'S LIFE | SEVENTY YEARS | IN A CHANGING WORLD | BY | HARRIET MONROE | [*ornament*] | NEW YORK | THE MAC-MILLAN COMPANY | 1938

$9\frac{1}{4} \times 6$; pp. xii, 488.

Issued in green cloth, lettered in black on front cover and spine; white end-papers; all edges trimmed. Published in March 1938.

Contains the following contributions by Yeats:

Letters. Pp. 330–331.
Speech at Banquet. Pp. 336–338.
Extract from speech at presentation to Wilfrid Blunt. P. 331.

324

SELF-PORTRAIT | TAKEN FROM THE | LETTERS & JOURNALS | OF | CHARLES RICKETTS, R.A. | COLLECTED AND COMPILED BY | T. STURGE MOORE | EDITED BY | CECIL LEWIS | LONDON: PETER DAVIES

$8\frac{1}{2} \times 5\frac{1}{2}$; pp. xx, 444.

Issued in dark blue cloth, lettered in gold on spine; white end-papers; all edges trimmed. Published in December, 1939.

Letters from Yeats appear on pp. 110 and 196–7.

Issued in Canada by S. J. Reginald Saunders & Co., Ltd., Toronto, in 1939.

325

LETTERS ON POETRY | FROM | W. B. YEATS | TO |
DOROTHY WELLESLEY | OXFORD UNIVERSITY PRESS | LONDON
NEW YORK TORONTO | 1940

$8\frac{3}{5} \times 5\frac{2}{5}$; pp. viii, 216. Frontispiece photograph of Yeats reading.

Issued in blue cloth, with lettering in gold on spine; white end-papers, top edges stained blue, fore-edges trimmed, bottom edges untrimmed. Published in June 1940.

This volume contains 172 letters written by Yeats; a draft of his Introduction to the *Selections from the Poems of Dorothy Wellesley*, 1936, (No. 283); the text of his letter on George II. which appeared in *The Irish Times*, May 14, 1937; and earlier versions of a number of poems which are printed in *Last Poems and Plays*, 1940 (No. 203). A facsimile of a letter from Yeats faces p. 112.

Published as a paperback by the Oxford Press in 1964 with an introduction by Kathleen Raine. No. 82 of Oxford Paperbacks.

325A

AMERICAN EDITION

LETTERS ON POETRY | FROM | W. B. YEATS | TO |
DOROTHY WELLESLEY | OXFORD UNIVERSITY PRESS | LONDON
NEW YORK TORONTO | 1940

$8\frac{2}{5} \times 5\frac{2}{5}$; pp. viii, 216. The facsimile of a letter from Yeats is on p. [ii]. There is no frontispiece photograph. Notice of copyright and Printed in the United States of America, p. [iv].

Issued in yellow cloth, with lettering in dark brown on spine, facsimile signature of W. B. Yeats in dark brown on lower right-hand corner of front cover.

326

FRIENDS OF A | LIFETIME | LETTERS TO | SYDNEY
CARLYLE COCKERELL | EDITED BY | VIOLA MEYNELL |
[publisher's device] | JONATHAN CAPE | THIRTY BEDFORD
SQUARE | LONDON

$8\frac{4}{5} \times 5\frac{3}{4}$; pp. 384.

Issued in blue cloth, lettered in gold on spine; white end-papers; top edges stained blue, fore-edges trimmed, bottom edges untrimmed. Published in October 1940.

Letters from Yeats appear on pp. 268–273.

Issued in Canada by Thomas Nelson & Sons, Toronto, in 1940.

327

FLORENCE FARR, BERNARD SHAW | AND W. B. YEATS. | EDITED BY CLIFFORD BAX | [woodcut as in No. 131] | THE CUALA PRESS | DUBLIN IRELAND | MCMXLI
$8\frac{3}{10} \times 5\frac{3}{5}$; pp. xvi, 96.

Issued in dark blue paper boards with white linen spine, lettered in black on front cover, white paper label, printed in black, on spine; dark blue end-papers matching binding; all edges untrimmed.

500 numbered copies printed on paper made in Ireland by Esther Ryan and Maire Gill and published by the Cuala Press, 133 Lower Baggot Street, Dublin. Finished in the second week of October 1941. Published on November 1, 1941.

Yeats's letters to Florence Farr occupy pp. 45–85.

328

AMERICAN EDITION

FLORENCE FARR | BERNARD | SHAW | W. B. YEATS | LETTERS | EDITED BY CLIFFORD BAX | NEW YORK | DODD, MEAD & COMPANY | 1942
$8 \times 5\frac{1}{2}$; pp. xiv, 98.

Issued in old rose paper boards with dark blue cloth spine, lettered in gold on spine; white end-papers; top edges trimmed, others untrimmed. Published in 1942.

Yeats's letters occupy pp. 51–96.

329

ENGLISH EDITION

FLORENCE FARR | BERNARD SHAW | W. B. YEATS | LETTERS | EDITED BY CLIFFORD BAX | LONDON | HOME & VAN THAL LTD. | 1946

U

$7\frac{3}{10} \times 4\frac{4}{5}$; pp. x, 68.

Issued in sage green cloth, lettered in gold on front cover, no lettering on spine; white end-papers; all edges trimmed. Published in 1946.

Yeats's letters occupy pp. 37–67.

330

THE | LATER LIFE AND LETTERS | OF | SIR HENRY NEWBOLT | EDITED BY HIS WIFE | MARGARET NEWBOLT | FABER AND FABER | 24 RUSSELL SQUARE | LONDON

$8\frac{4}{5} \times 5\frac{1}{2}$; pp. xii, 428.

Issued in light brown cloth, lettered in gold on spine; off-white end-papers; top edges trimmed. Published in November, 1942.

Letters from Yeats appear on pp. 4 and 5.

Issued in Canada by The Ryerson Press, Toronto, in 1932.

331

W. B. YEATS | 1865–1939 | BY | JOSEPH HONE | LONDON | MACMILLAN & CO. LTD | 1942 [*The whole enclosed within a decorative border inside rules.*]

$8\frac{7}{10} \times 5\frac{3}{4}$; pp. 2, x, 504.

Issued in red cloth, black label lettered in gold between gold rules on spine, publishers' name in gold at foot of spine; off-white end-papers; all edges trimmed. Published in February 1943.

Letters from Yeats are quoted on pp. 39, 83, 90, 94, 111, 124, 143–144, 149, 151, 152–153, 153–154, 158, 160, 171, 185, 189, 195–198, 206, 212, 222–223, 240, 247, 249–250, 252, 266, 269, 270, 273, 278–279, 280, 288, 291, 295, 296, 298, 300, 303, 306, 307–308, 310, 311–312, 313–314, 315–316, 319, 320–321, 322, 323, 325, 335–336, 340, 345–346, 348, 350–351, 353–354, 358, 361–362, 372, 373, 377–378, 380–381, 383, 385, 387, 392, 394, 395–396, 396–397, 397–398, 401, 402, 403, 404–405, 408, 409, 410–411, 420–421, 423, 424–425, 426, 428, 429, 430, 432, 435–436, 437–438, 440, 441, 446, 447, 448, 454, 455, 458, 461, 464–465, 465–466, 469, 470, 471, 473, 475–476, 476.

A note for a lecture is quoted on p. 190.

Yeats's Journals are quoted on pp. 228–229, 237–238, 282, 379–380, 389, 412, 417–418.

A revised edition was published in February 1962, similar to the first edition except that the binding is blue cloth, there is a Publisher's Note to the Second Edition dated February 1962 on p. vi, and there are some slight textual changes. Published by Macmillan & Co. Ltd. London and Toronto.

331A

AMERICAN EDITION

W. B. YEATS | 1865–1939 | by | Joseph Hone | New York | The Macmillan Company | 1943 [The whole enclosed within a decorative border inside rules]

$8\frac{1}{2} \times 5\frac{1}{2}$; pp. xii, 536.

Issued in green cloth, lettered in gold on spine, publisher's name in gold at foot of spine; off-white end-papers; all edges trimmed. Frontispiece portrait from the charcoal drawing by John S. Sargent, R.A.

The contents are the same as those of No. 331.

There was a second printing in 1943.

332

J. B. YEATS | LETTERS TO HIS SON W. B. YEATS | AND OTHERS | 1869–1922 | EDITED WITH A MEMOIR BY | JOSEPH HONE | AND A PREFACE BY | OLIVER ELTON | LONDON | FABER AND FABER LIMITED | 24 RUSSELL SQUARE

$8\frac{4}{5} \times 5\frac{3}{4}$; pp. 296. Printed on yellowish paper. Illustrated.

Issued in old rose linen, lettering in gold on spine; off-white end-papers; top edges trimmed, others untrimmed. Published in January 1944.

Letters from W. B. Yeats are printed on pp. 122–123, 137–138, 152–154, 164–165, 203–204, 222–223, 237–238, 248–249, 249–250, 251, 261, 288–289.

333

AMERICAN EDITION

J. B. YEATS | LETTERS TO HIS SON W. B. YEATS | AND OTHERS | 1869–1922 | EDITED WITH A MEMOIR BY | JOSEPH HONE | AND A PREFACE BY | OLIVER ELTON | E. P. DUTTON & COMPANY, INC. | NEW YORK, 1946.

$8\frac{1}{2} \times 5\frac{3}{4}$; pp. 304.

Issued in pale yellow rough cloth, publisher's monogram in brown and yellow on front cover, lettered in brown on spine; white end-papers; all edges trimmed. Published in 1946.

W. B. Yeats's letters occur on the same pages as in the English edition. (No. 332.)

(This edition has an appendix, not included in the English edition, containing Elizabeth Yeats's Diary, 1888–9.)

333A

LADY GREGORY'S | JOURNALS | 1916–1930 | EDITED BY | LENNOX ROBINSON | PUTNAM & COMPANY LTD. | 42 GREAT RUSSELL STREET

$8 \times 5\frac{1}{2}$; pp. 344.

Issued in dark blue linen, lettered in gold on spine; white end-papers; all edges trimmed. Published in September 1946.

Letters from Yeats are quoted on pp. 89–90, 121–122. An early version of one stanza of ' Another Troy must rise and set ', *Two Songs from a Play*, is given on p. 263. Two versions of his translation of *Swift's Epitaph* appear on p. 266.

An American edition was published by The Macmillan Co., New York, in 1947.

334

YEATS | THE MAN AND THE MASKS | [ornament] | BY RICHARD ELLMANN | THE MACMILLAN COMPANY | NEW YORK: 1948

$8\frac{1}{8} \times 5\frac{2}{8}$; pp. x, 332.

Issued in black cloth, initials W B Y in gold on front cover, lettering and design in gold on spine; white end-papers; all edges trimmed. Published in 1948.

Unpublished manuscripts and notes by Yeats are quoted on pp. 5, 6, 96, 104, 122, 126, 136, 168, 173, 183, 188–189, 199, 208 n., 210–211 216, 234–235, 248, 262 n., 278.

Unpublished letters from Yeats are quoted on pp. 13–14, 33, 95, 100, 101, 103, 121, 122, 125, 130, 148, 151, 153, 154–155, 165, 179, 181, 186, 196–197, 200, 200–201, 211, 229 n., 238, 239, 241, 243, 244, 246, 251, 257, 258–259, 260, 261, 262, 263, 266, 268, 272, 274, 278, 279, 282, 284, 285, 289, 291, 294.

An unpublished novel by Yeats is quoted on p. 24.

The first draft of *Autobiographies* is quoted on pp. 28, 62, 63, 75–76, 102, 103, 104, 106, 107, 108, 110, 111, 119, 123, 129–130, 147.

Unpublished poems and early drafts of poems are quoted on pp. 29, 30, 33, 33–34–35, 102, 142–143, 155, 157–158, 172, 255.

Unpublished speeches by Yeats are quoted on pp. 41–42, 113–114, 244–245.

Yeats's unpublished journals are quoted on pp. 65–67, 125, 138, 174–175, 177, 187, 189, 190–191.

The poem *Mourn—and then Onward* is reprinted from *United Ireland* on p. 100.

The manifesto *To All Artists and Writers* is reprinted from *To-Morrow* on pp. 246–247.

Published as a paperback by E. P. Dutton Inc. in 1958. A Dutton Everyman Paperback. D 24.

335

ENGLISH EDITION

YEATS | THE MAN | AND THE MASKS | BY | RICHARD ELLMANN | LONDON | MACMILLAN & CO. LTD | 1949

$8\frac{1}{2} \times 5\frac{1}{2}$; pp. x, 342.

Issued in green cloth, lettered in gold on spine; white end-papers; all edges trimmed. Published in 1949.

Unpublished manuscripts and notes by Yeats are quoted on pp. 5–6, 99, 107, 125, 129, 139, 171–172, 176–177, 186, 191–192, 202–203, 204, 219, 238, 252, 282.

Unpublished letters from Yeats are quoted on pp. 14, 34, 103, 104, 106, 125, 128, 133, 151, 154, 156, 157–158, 168, 182, 184–185, 189, 203, 213, 214, 219, 232 n., 242, 245, 247, 248, 250, 255–256, 261, 263, 264, 265, 266, 267, 270, 272, 276, 278, 282, 283, 286, 287, 288, 289, 292, 294, 297.

An unpublished novel by Yeats is quoted on p. 25.

The first draft of *Autobiographies* is quoted on pp. 28, 65, 78–79, 106 107, 109, 110, 111, 112, 113, 114, 122, 126, 132–133, 145, 150, 162.

Unpublished poems and early drafts of poems are quoted on pp. 30–31–32, 34, 35–36, 105, 145–146, 158, 161, 175, 259, 274 n.

Unpublished speeches by Yeats are quoted on pp. 43, 116–117, 248–249.

Yeats's unpublished journals are quoted on pp. 67–68, 69, 128, 141, 177–179, 181, 190, 192, 193–194, 214.

The poem *Mourn—and then Onward* is reprinted from *United Ireland* on p. 103.

The manifesto *To All Artists and Writers* is reprinted from *To-Morrow*, August 1924, on pp. 250–251.

336

W. B. YEATS | MAN AND POET | BY | A. NORMAN JEFFARES | M.A., PH.D. (DUBLIN), M.A., D.PHIL. (OXON.) | LECTURER IN ENGLISH, GRONINGEN UNIVERSITY | LONDON | ROUTLEDGE & KEGAN PAUL LTD.

$8\frac{1}{2} \times 5\frac{1}{2}$; pp. viii, 368. 10 illustrations.

Issued in green cloth, lettered in gold on spine; white end-papers; all edges trimmed. Published in May 1949.

Yeats's unpublished autobiography is quoted on pp. 49, 51, 52, 55, 57, 58, 59–60, 67, 68, 86–87, 99, 100–101, 105–107, 108–109, 109–110, 118, 306, 319.

Unpublished letters from Yeats are quoted on pp. 97, 134, 166, 167, 171–172, 173, 186, 188, 214, 231, 236, 237, 238, 239, 241, 243–244, 245, 246, 246–247, 250, 251, 252, 253, 254, 254–255, 256, 257, 268–269, 272, 277, 277–278, 279, 280–282, 283, 284–285, 286, 297, 321, 330, 331, 334.

Yeats's Diaries are quoted on pp. 141, 144, 145, 147–148, 150, 151, 156, 157, 159, 161, 162–163, 179–180, 182, 325, 335.

Unpublished fragments, in prose and verse, by Yeats are quoted on pp. 118, 120, 173–174, 241–242, 260, 294.

Speeches by Yeats are quoted on pp. 240 and 328.

Published in New Haven by The Yale University Press in 1949.

There was a revised edition in 1962.

336A

BEYOND THE GRAVE. | LETTERS ON POETRY, | TO W. B. YEATS, | FROM | DOROTHY WELLESLEY | THIS BOOK MAY BE PURCHASED FROM THE PRINTER | C. BALDWIN, GROSVENOR ROAD, TUNBRIDGE WELLS. |

$8\frac{1}{2} \times 5\frac{1}{2}$; pp. iv, 67. There is a frontispiece photograph of Yeats and his two children and six other photographs of rooms in Yeats's tower and of Dorothy Wellesley.

Issued in green cloth with darker green spine; lettering in black on front cover; white end-papers; all edges trimmed. An erratum slip is pasted on the front end-paper. [n.d. The last letter is dated 1949.]

A remark of Yeats is quoted on p. 5.

337

SINCE FIFTY | MEN AND MEMORIES, 1922–1938 | RECOLLECTIONS | OF | WILLIAM ROTHENSTEIN | [three asterisks] | LIFTING THE EYES WOULD BE SO EASY, YET IT | IS SELDOM DONE, AND WHEN A RAPT POET | COMPELS US TO DO SO, WE ARE ARRESTED, | WE ARE REBUKED, WE ARE DELIVERED. | GEORGE SANTAYANA | FABER AND FABER LIMITED | 24 RUSSELL SQUARE | LONDON

$9\frac{1}{2} \times 6$; pp. xvi, 352.

Issued in black cloth, lettered in gold on spine; off-white end-papers; top edges gilt, others untrimmed. Published in November, 1939.

Letters from Yeats appear on pp. 111–112, 178–179 and on pp. 305–306.

This is the third volume of *Men and Memories*.

Issued in Canada by The Ryerson Press, Toronto, in 1939; and in New York by The Macmillan Company in 1940.

337A

LETTERS | ADDRESSED | [ornament *in red*] TO [ornament *in red*] | A. P. WATT | [ornament *in red*] | LONDON [ornament *in red*] | A. P. WATT | & SON: HASTINGS HOUSE | NORFOLK ST: STRAND 1905

$7\frac{13}{16} \times 4\frac{1}{4}$; pp. xxiv, 172. There is a blank leaf before the title not included in pagination, and between this leaf and the wrapper a leaf has been inserted, printed in green, giving a list of authors letters from whom are first printed in this volume.

Issued in stiff wrappers, design in black and lettering in red on front cover, lettering in black on spine; all edges untrimmed. Issued in 1905. A letter from Yeats appears on p. 171.

337B

LETTERS | ADDRESSED | TO | A. P. WATT | AND | HIS SONS | 1883–1924 | LONDON | A. P. WATT & SON | 1924

$6\frac{3}{4} \times 4$; pp. xxiv, 220.

Issued in stiff blue paper covers, lettered in dark blue on front cover; blue end-papers; all edges trimmed. Issued in 1924.

Two letters from Yeats appear on pp. 217 and 218.

338

IRELAND'S | ABBEY THEATRE | A HISTORY | 1899–1951 | [star] | COMPILED BY | LENNOX ROBINSON | SIDGWICK AND JACKSON LIMITED | LONDON

$8\frac{1}{2} \times 5\frac{1}{2}$; pp. xvi, 224.

Issued in brown cloth, lettered in gold on spine; white end-papers; top edges green, others untrimmed. Published in 1951.

Letters from Yeats are on pp. 6–7; a letter of Lady Gregory and Yeats is on p. 87; a lecture of Yeats is quoted from on p. 32.

There was no American edition; Macmillan is the American distributor.

Copies were remaindered to Fred Hanna Ltd. and were bound in green cloth with Fred | Hanna | Dublin at foot of spine.

339

ROBERT ROSS | FRIEND OF FRIENDS | LETTERS TO ROBERT ROSS, ART CRITIC | AND WRITER, TOGETHER WITH EXTRACTS | FROM HIS PUBLISHED ARTICLES | EDITED BY | MARGERY ROSS | [publisher's device] | JONATHAN CAPE | THIRTY BEDFORD SQUARE | LONDON

$8\frac{3}{4} \times 5\frac{1}{2}$; pp. 368.

Issued in dark turquoise-blue cloth, lettered in gold on spine; white end-papers; all edges trimmed. Published in June 1952.

Yeats contributed:
A letter, dated Feb. 13 [1916]. Pp. 278–279.

340

W. B. YEATS | AND T. STURGE MOORE | THEIR
CORRESPONDENCE | 1901–1937 | EDITED BY | URSULA
BRIDGE | [design] | ROUTLEDGE & KEGAN PAUL LTD | BROAD-
WAY HOUSE, 68–74 CARTER LANE | LONDON
$8\frac{3}{8} \times 5\frac{1}{4}$; pp. xx, 216.

Issued in black cloth, lettered in gold on spine, partly within red label,
partly outside it; white end-papers; top edges coloured red, others
trimmed. 1996 copies printed, 780 of which formed the American
edition. Published on September 25, 1953.

341

AMERICAN EDITION

W. B. YEATS | AND T. STURGE MOORE | THEIR
CORRESPONDENCE | 1901–1937 | EDITED BY | URSULA
BRIDGE | [design] | NEW YORK | OXFORD UNIVERSITY PRESS |
1953

Identical with No. 340, except for title-page, verso of title-page, and
foot of spine, which reads OXFORD instead of ROUTLEDGE & | KEGAN
PAUL.

342

DIVIDED IMAGE | [waved rule] | A STUDY OF |
WILLIAM BLAKE AND W. B. YEATS | BY | MARGARET
RUDD | [publisher's device] | ROUTLEDGE & KEGAN PAUL
LTD | BROADWAY HOUSE, 68–74 CARTER LANE | LONDON
$8\frac{1}{2} \times 5\frac{1}{2}$; pp. xvi, 240.

Issued in green cloth, lettered in gold on spine; white end-papers; all
edges trimmed. Published in 1953.

Unpublished notes from journals by Yeats appear on pp. 26, 86, 107–
108, 229, 231.

Unpublished marginalia by Yeats appear on pp. 1, 66, 67, 230.

343

THE IDENTITY | OF | YEATS | BY RICHARD ELLMANN |
LONDON | MACMILLAN & CO LTD | 1954

$8\frac{5}{8} \times 5\frac{1}{2}$; pp. ix, 343.

Issued in maroon cloth, lettering and design in gold on spine; white
end-papers; all edges trimmed. Published in 1954.

Unpublished letters from Yeats are quoted on pp. 43, 53, 55, 56, 61,
79, 80, 119, 126, 128, 147, 170, 179, 188, 189, 213, 222, 242, 295, 297.

Unpublished manuscripts and notes by Yeats are quoted on pp. 7, 24,
26, 39, 40, 52, 55, 56, 60, 66, 72, 83, 105–106, 109, 157, 163, 164, 165,
166, 178, 217, 221, 225, 232, 235, 237, 239–240, 242, 243, 295, 296, 300,
313–314, 316, 321–323.

The first draft of *Autobiographies* is quoted on pp. 58 and 299.

Unpublished poems and early drafts of poems are quoted on pp. 36,
37, 101–102, 109, 123, 124, 131, 132, 147, 166, 176–179, 194–200, 209–
211, 221, 223, 225, 232, 234–235, 236–237, 243, 254, 261–262, 268,
270–273, 275–276, 278, 280, 310–311, 317.

The American edition of this book, published by the Oxford University Press in 1954, is identical in pagination.

344

THE UNICORN | WILLIAM BUTLER YEATS' | SEARCH
FOR REALITY | VIRGINIA MOORE | THE MACMILLAN COMPANY
—NEW YORK | 1954

$8\frac{1}{4} \times 5\frac{3}{8}$; pp. xxii, 522.

Issued in black cloth, blue-green device of unicorn and lettering on
front cover, blue-green lettering on spine; white end-papers; all
edges trimmed.

Unpublished material by Yeats appears on pp. 36, 38, 59, 168, 170,
197, 199, 200, 201, 202, 203, 205, 206, 207, 217, 219, 225, 226, 228,
229, 230, 231, 235, 241, 242, 243, 325, 337, 346, 370, 378, 379, 409,
433, 463.

Issued simultaneously by the Macmillan Co. in London.

345

BLAKE AND YEATS: | THE CONTRARY VISION
[*the whole enclosed within a decorative border*] | HAZARD ADAMS
| CORNELL UNIVERSITY PRESS | ITHACA, NEW YORK

9 × 6; pp. xvi, 328.

Issued in red cloth, lettered in silver on front cover and spine; white end-papers; all edges trimmed.   Published in 1955.

Unpublished manuscripts and notes by Yeats are quoted on pp. 46–48, 123, 125, 173–176, 189–190, 201, 256, 281, 287–288; and "Michael Robartes Foretells"—unpublished typescript written for *A Vision* and rejected—is quoted in Appendix B, pp. 301–305.

346

W. B. YEATS | MANUSCRIPTS AND PRINTED BOOKS |
EXHIBITED IN THE LIBRARY | OF TRINITY COLLEGE, DUBLIN |
1956 | CATALOGUE | COMPILED BY R. O. DOUGAN, DEPUTY
LIBRARIAN, AND | PRINTED FOR THE FRIENDS OF THE LIBRARY
OF | TRINITY COLLEGE, DUBLIN BY COLM O LOCHLAINN | AT
THE SIGN OF THE THREE CANDLES, FLEET STREET | DUBLIN

8½ × 5½; pp. 52.

Issued in white paper covers, lettered in black on front cover that also has on it a black and white photograph of Head in Bronze of Yeats by Albert Power.

References to unpublished manuscripts by Yeats are on pp. 6, 10, 13, 20–31, 34–38, 42.

347

WILLIAM BUTLER YEATS | a catalogue of an exhibi-
tion from | the P. S. O'Hegarty collection in | the University
of Kansas Library | by Hester M. Black | Lawrence 1958.

9 × 6; pp. 42.

Issued in white paper covers, lettered in black on the front cover that also has stamped on it the woodcut of a lone tree made by Elizabeth

C. Yeats for the Cuala Press. The verso of the front cover is a photo-graphic reproduction of the cover of Poems Written in Discourage-ment [No. 107] with an inscription by Yeats to Lady Ottilene Morrell dated December 20, 1921.

Unpublished letters from Yeats are quoted from on pp. 12, 29; and other unpublished letters are mentioned on pp. 35, 38.

An unpublished fragment in prose by Yeats is mentioned on p. 41.

Republished in 1966 in tan paper covers, lettered in green on front cover.

348

W. B. YEATS AND TRADITION | BY | F. A. C. WILSON | LONDON | VICTOR GOLLANCZ LTD | 1958

$8\frac{1}{2} \times 5\frac{1}{2}$; pp. 288.

Issued in dark blue cloth, lettered in gold on spine; white end-papers; all edges trimmed.

Unpublished manuscripts by Yeats are quoted on pp. 232, 246. Published in New York By The Macmillan Company in 1958.

348A

AGNES TOBIN | Letters · Translations · Poems | with some account of her life | Printed at the Grabhorn Press for John Howell | San Francisco 1958

$10\frac{5}{8} \times 8\frac{1}{4}$; pp. xxii, 102 with four pages not included in the pagination. There is a coloured frontispiece of Agnes Tobin as a child and facing p. [2] a side-face sketch of her as a young woman.

Issued in light-blue paper boards with grey linen spine, label printed in black on spine; white end-papers; top and bottom edges trimmed. Published in 1958.

Unpublished letters from Yeats appear on pp. 74, 75, and 76. A full-page facsimile of a letter from Yeats is inserted between pp. 76 and 77. A quotation from one of these letters appears on p. x.

349

THE MASTERPIECE | AND THE MAN | YEATS AS I KNEW HIM | MONK GIBBON | [publisher's device] | RUPERT HART-DAVIS | SOHO SQUARE LONDON | 1959

$8\frac{5}{8} \times 5\frac{1}{2}$; pp. 228. 8 illustrations.

Issued in dark-blue cloth, lettered in gold on spine; white end-papers; all edges trimmed. Published in 1959.

Unpublished letters from Yeats are quoted on pp. 131, 133–134, 137–138, 143–144.

Unpublished fragments, in prose, by Yeats are quoted on pp. 48, 49, 53–54, 75–76, 80, 82, 88, 97, 103–104, 109, 148, 153, 157–158, 165–167, 179, 186–187, 198–199, 201.

Published in New York by The Macmillan Company in 1959.

350

YEATS'S ICONOGRAPHY | BY | F. A. C. WILSON | NEW YORK | THE MACMILLAN COMPANY | 1960

$8\frac{1}{2} \times 5\frac{1}{2}$; pp. 350.

Issued in dark blue cloth, lettered in gold on spine; white end-papers; all edges trimmed.

Unpublished manuscripts by Yeats quoted on pp. 117, 200, 202, 323.

References to unpublished manuscripts by Yeats are on pp. 191, 241–244 (a précis of an unpublished play *The Bridegroom*), 327, 330.

Published in Great Britain by Victor Gollancz in 1960.

351

YEATS'S VISION | AND THE LATER PLAYS | HELEN HENNESSY VENDLER | HARVARD UNIVERSITY PRESS | CAMBRIDGE, MASSACHUSETTS | 1963.

$8\frac{1}{4} \times 5\frac{1}{2}$; pp. xiv, 286.

Issued in paper boards coloured light and dark grey, and tan, lettered in black on spine; white end-papers; all edges trimmed. References to unpublished MSS. of Yeats are on pp. 14, 69, 124, 133, 177, 237. Quotations from unpublished MSS. are on pp. 178, 220, 231–232.

Published in Great Britain by Oxford University Press in 1963.

352

JON STALLWORTHY | [MODIFIED RULE] | BETWEEN THE LINES | YEATS'S POETRY | IN THE MAKING | OXFORD | AT THE CLARENDON PRESS | 1963

$8\frac{3}{8} \times 5\frac{1}{2}$; pp. vii, 264.

Issued in dark-blue cloth, lettered in gold on spine; white end-papers; all edges trimmed. Frontispiece facsimile of page 2 of a manuscript of Byzantium, and facsimiles of the manuscript of The Black Tower are on pp. 224–225.

Unpublished poems and early drafts of poems are quoted on pp. 2–4, 17–23, 29–42, 47–49, 66–79, 82–84, 89–110, 116–136, 140–163, 168–176, 180–200, 205–221, 223, 226, 230–235, 237–242, 245–248.

Unpublished manuscripts and notes by Yeats are referred to and/or quoted from on pp. 9–13, 24–25, 29, 43–44, 80–81, 83–84, 88, 96–97, 100, 115, 139, 167–168, 205, 228–229, 236, 244–248, 251–253. The following poems by Yeats are reprinted: The Second Coming, p. 16; A Prayer for my Daughter, pp. 26–28; The Sorrow of Love, p. 46; The Gift of Harun Al-Rashid, pp. 54–59; Sailing to Byzantium, pp. 87–88; Byzantium, pp. 113–114; Chosen, p. 137; Parting, p. 138; In Memory of Eva Gore-Booth and Con Markiewicz; Coole Park, 1929, pp. 177–178; Memory, Consolation, After Long Silence, The Nineteenth Century and After, The Results of Thought, An Acre of Grass, A Bronze Head, pp. 201–204; The Black Tower, pp. 222–223.

353

WILLIAM BUTLER YEATS: A MEMOIR | by Oliver St. John Gogarty | with a preface by Myles Dillon | Dublin MCMLXIII | At the Dolmen Press

$4\frac{1}{4} \times 7\frac{1}{4}$; pp. 32.

Issued in dark-green mottled cloth, lettered in gold on spine; white end-papers; all edges trimmed. Frontispiece of Yeats medal struck in 1922; facsimile of a manuscript poem by Sir William Watson on p. 27. Unpublished prose fragments by Yeats are quoted on pp. 12–13, 15–17, 19–20, 22–23.

354

THE TIMES I'VE SEEN: | Oliver St. John Gogarty | [reproduction of painting of Gogarty by Sir William Orpen] | A Biography | by Ulick O'Connor

6×9; pp. xiv, 370.

Issued in green cloth, lettered in black on spine; white end-papers; all edges trimmed. Published in 1963 by Ivan Oblensky, Inc. New York. Remarks of Yeats's are referred to on pp. 107–108; remarks of Yeats's are quoted on pp. 154, 254, 306; a speech of Yeats's is quoted on p. 242; photographs that include Yeats are reproduced on pp. 181, 248, 250.

355

Thomas Parkinson | W. B. Yeats [in red] | THE LATER POETRY | Berkeley and Los Angeles | University of California Press—1964

$8\frac{3}{8} \times 5\frac{3}{8}$; pp. xiv, 264.

Issued in yellow cloth, lettered in black on spine; white end-papers; all edges trimmed. Facsimiles of manuscripts of After Long Silence and Among School Children are on pp. 83–86.

Early drafts of poems by Yeats are quoted on pp. 65, 83–91, 95–103, 105–107, 109–110, 131, 137, 140–141, 143–146, 166–168, 174, 198–199, 205–209, 212–214, 217–219, 222–225.

Unpublished manuscripts and notes by Yeats are referred to and/or quoted from on pp. 16, 20, 52, 64–65, 80, 93, 184–186.

The following poems are reprinted: After Long Silence, p. 90; The Wild Swans at Coole, pp. 127–128; Leda and the Swan, p. 141; Lines Written in Dejection, p. 151; An Acre of Grass, pp. 171–172; Her Anxiety, pp. 187–188; Mohini Chatterjee, pp. 210–211. Parts of other poems are reprinted *passim*.

356

A Symposium and Catalogue | edited by Robin Skelton | and Ann Saddlemyer | THE WORLD OF W. B. YEATS | Essays in Perspective | on the occasion of the W. B. Yeats | Centenary Festival held at the | University of Victoria | February 14 to March 16, 1965 | distributed in the United States of America | by the University of Washington Press, Seattle

9×6; pp. xviii, 278.

Issued in black cloth, lettered in gold on spine, white end-papers; all edges trimmed. Published in February 1965.

Unpublished material by Yeats appears on pp. 91–92, 96, 123.

(Contains contributions from David R. Clark, Joan Coldwell, Gwladys V. Downes, Liam Miller, Ann Saddlemyer, Robin Skelton.)

Published in Canada for the University of Victoria by the Adelphi Bookshop Limited, Victoria, B.C. in February 1965.

357

IRISH RENAISSANCE [in red] | A Gathering of | Essays, Memoirs, and Letters | from The Massachusetts Review | edited by | Robin Skelton & David R. Clark | MR [red ligature] | The Dolmen Press

$9\frac{3}{16} \times 6$; pp. 168.

Issued in tan cloth, black label printed in gold on spine, with publisher's device in gold at foot of spine; light-brown end-papers; all edges trimmed.

Published in 1965.

Material by Yeats appears on pp. 13–25, 29–30, 34–55, 99–105. This material appeared first in *The Massachusetts Review*, Winter 1964. [See contributions to Periodicals, 1964.]

[Contains contributions from Curtis Bradford (2), David R. Clark, Austin Clarke, Robin Skelton, John Unterecker.]

Distributed in Ireland, Canada, and America by Oxford University Press.

358

YEATS | AND THE HEROIC IDEAL | by Alex Zwerdling | [printer's device] | New York University Press 1965

$8\frac{1}{4} \times 5\frac{1}{2}$; pp. x, 198.

Issued in blue cloth, lettered in gold on spine; green end-papers; all edges trimmed.

Unpublished material by Yeats appears on pp. 22, 62.

359

W. B. YEATS AND JAPAN | by | Shotaro Oshima, D.Litt. | Professor of English Literature at Waseda University | 1965 | The Hokuseido Press

$10\frac{3}{8} \times 7\frac{1}{4}$; pp. xiv, 198: comprising half-title, verso blank, pp. [i–ii]; title, copyright notice and notice of limitation, number of copy marked by stamping machine, publisher's device and imprint, Printed in Japan at foot of page, pp. [iii–iv]; dedication, verso blank, pp. [v–vi]; preface, pp. vii–ix; acknowledgements, p. x; contents, pp. xi–xiv; text, pp. [1]–198.

Issued in dark-green cloth, lettered in gold on spine, off-white endpapers; all edges trimmed. Published in June 1965.

There are 43 plates: nos. 1–4 between pp. [ii] and [iii], no. 1 is a photograph of Yeats inscribed To S. Oshima from W. B. Yeats Jan 1934, nos. 2–3 are coloured photographs of a Japanese mask and costume, no. 4 is a photograph of a Tanto-sword; nos. 5–18 between pp. 2 and 3 are facsimiles of letters from Yeats (6) and others; nos. 19–21 between pp. 4 and 5 are photographs of the Yeats family and Thoor Ballylee; nos. 22–25 between pp. 30 and 31 are facsimiles of the autograph poems; nos. 26–37 between pp. 36 and 37 are photographs of scenes from several Yeats plays; nos. 38–41 between pp. 108 and 109, and nos. 42–43 between pp. 120 and 121 are miscellaneous photographs; no. 44 between pp. 170 and 171 is of Kōsaku Yamada's music for At the Hawk's Well.

Contents

Preface

Part I: Letters of W. B. Yeats

Part II: Four autograph poems by W. B. Yeats (Youth and Age, The Nineteenth Century and After, The Wheel, Symbols)

Part III: Some Essays on the Eastern Aspects of Yeats's Work

Part IV: Interviews with Yeats and Others

Part V: Books and Periodicals on Yeats in Japan
    Bibliography of W. B. Yeats in Japan
    Index
    List of Plates
    x

360

W. B. YEATS AND OCCULTISM | A study of his works in relation to Indian Lore, the | Cabbala, Swedenborg, Boehme and Theosophy | by | Harbans Rai Bachchan | Motilal Banarsidass | Delhi : : Varanasi : : Patna

$8\frac{7}{16} \times 5\frac{1}{8}$; pp. xxii, 296.

Issued in reddish-brown cloth, lettered in gold on spine; white end-papers; all edges trimmed. Published in 1965.

Unpublished material by Yeats is quoted on pp. 56, 223, 256, 264.

361

1865 | W. B. YEATS | 1965 | Centenary Essays | on the Art of W. B. Yeats | edited by | D. E. S. Maxwell and S. B. Bushrui | Ibadan University Press | 1965

$8\frac{1}{2} \times 5\frac{1}{2}$; pp. xvi, 252. 10 illustrations.

Issued in red cloth, lettered in gold on spine; white end-papers; all edges trimmed.

Unpublished material by Yeats appears on pp. 69, 72, 75.

(Contains contributions from S. B. Bushrui, MacD. Emslie, E. Engelberg, F. F. Farag, I. Fletcher, A. N. Jeffares, R. Fréchet, D. Gerstenberger, R. M. Kain, B. A. King, J. Kleinstück, L. D. Lerner, D. E. S. Maxwell, J. R. Moore, C. Okigbo, G. B. Saul, M. J. Sidnell, J. Simmons, W. H. Stevenson.)

362

W. B. YEATS | & | GEORGIAN | IRELAND | [rule] | Donald T. Torchiana [the whole enclosed within a decorative border] | Northwestern University Press | Evanston 1966

$9\frac{1}{4} \times 6\frac{1}{8}$; pp. xvi, 384.

Issued in black cloth, title lettered in silver within decorative border against red background on spine, author's and publisher's names in silver against black background on spine; grey end-papers; top and bottom edges trimmed. Published in 1966.

Unpublished material by Yeats is quoted and/or referred to on pp. 4–5, 9, 32, 63–65, 71, 74–76, 78, 80, 82–83, 91, 114, 133, 136–137, 139–141, 154–155, 162, 185–186, 188, 193, 195–196, 204, 207–209, 213–214, 218–219, 232, 242, 244, 246–247, 249, 255, 271–272, 276, 287–288, 296, 313, 318, 334, 341.

363

YEATS AND THE NOH: Types of | Japanese Beauty and their | Reflection in Yeats's Plays [all in red] | by Hiro Ishibashi. Edited by | Anthony Kerrigan Being No. | VI of the Dolmen Press Yeats | Centenary Papers MCMLXV

$8\frac{9}{16} \times 6$; pp. iv, 66. Illustrated.

Issued in brown paper covers, lettered in red and black on front cover and in black on spine; brown end-papers; all edges trimmed. Published in 1966.

Contains an unpublished letter from Yeats to Daisetz Suzuki on p. 196. [The numbering of these Papers is continuous]

364

YEATS'S 'LAST POEMS' AGAIN [in red] by | Curtis bradford Being No. VIII | of the Dolmen Press Yeats | Centenary Papers MCMLXV

$8\frac{9}{16} \times 6$; pp. ii, 28.

[for description see No. 363] Published in 1966.

Contains references to the order of the poems from Yeats's mss.

365

MEMORIES | 1898–1939 | [rule] | C. M. Bowra | Weidenfeld and Nicolson | 1 Winsley Street London W1

$8\frac{3}{8} \times 5\frac{3}{8}$; pp. ii, 369.

Issued in black cloth, silver lettering on orange label on spine; white end-papers; all edges trimmed. Published in November, 1966.

Unpublished letters from Yeats appear on pp. 236, 240–241, and an unpublished poem on p. 242.

There was a second impression in December 1966.

366

YEATS AND PATRICK MCCARTEN | A FENIAN FRIENDSHIP: | all in red] Letters | with a commentary by John | Unterecker & an address on | Yeats the Fenian by Patrick | McCarten. Being No. X of the | Dolmen Press Yeats Centen– | ary Papers MCMLXV

$8\frac{9}{16} \times 6$; pp. ii, 108. Frontispiece photograph of Yeats, and illustrations between pp. 364–365 and pp. 380–381.

[for description see No. 363] Published in 1967.

Unpublished letters from Yeats are on pp. 349, 350–351, 354–364, 367–369, 371–375, 382, 384–385, 392–393, 399–402, 404–405, 412, 414–416.

CONTRIBUTIONS TO PERIODICALS

CONTRIBUTIONS TO PERIODICALS

1885

SONG OF THE FAERIES

The Dublin University Review, March.
Reprinted in *The Island of Statues*, Act II, scene iii, in *The Dublin University Review*, July, and in *The Wanderings of Oisin*, 1889.

VOICES

The Dublin University Review, March.
Reprinted in *The Island of Statues*, Act II, scene iii, in *The Dublin University Review*, July, and in *The Wanderings of Oisin*, 1889. A rewritten version, *The Cloak, the Boat and the Shoes*, is printed in *Poems*, 1895.

THE ISLAND OF STATUES. AN ARCADIAN FAERY TALE—IN TWO ACTS

The Dublin University Review, April–July.
The third scene of Act II is reprinted, under the title *Island of Statues*, in *The Wanderings of Oisin*, 1889.
Lyrics from *The Island of Statues*, comprising *The Shepherds' Contest of Song* (from Act I, scene i), *The Fairy's Call* (from Act I, scene ii) and *The Fairy Voices* (from Act I, scene iii), were reprinted in *A Celtic Christmas* (*The Irish Homestead* Christmas number), December 1899.

LOVE AND DEATH

The Dublin University Review, May.

THE SEEKER. A DRAMATIC POEM—IN TWO SCENES

The Dublin University Review, September.
Reprinted, under the title *The Seeker*, in *The Wanderings of Oisin*, 1889.

AN EPILOGUE. TO 'THE ISLAND OF STATUES' AND 'THE SEEKER'

The Dublin University Review, October.

Reprinted, under the title *Song of the Last Arcadian*, in *The Wanderings of Oisin*, 1889. Also, under the title *The Song of the Happy Shepherd*, in *Poems*, 1895.

1886

IN A DRAWING-ROOM

(Unsigned)

The Dublin University Review, January.

Reprinted, as the sixth and second of *Quatrains and Aphorisms* in *The Wanderings of Oisin*, 1889.

LIFE

The Dublin University Review, February.

Five quatrains of which the first and fifth are reprinted as the first and fifth of *Quatrains and Aphorisms* in *The Wanderings of Oisin*, 1889.

THE TWO TITANS. A POLITICAL POEM

The Dublin University Review, March.

ON MR. NETTLESHIP'S PICTURE AT THE ROYAL HIBERNIAN ACADEMY

The Dublin University Review, April.

Reprinted in *The Wanderings of Oisin*, 1889.

MOSADA

The Dublin University Review, June.

Reprinted separately, 1886. Also in *The Wanderings of Oisin*, 1889.

REMEMBRANCE

The Irish Monthly, July.

MISERRIMUS

The Dublin University Review, October.

Reprinted in *The Wanderings of Oisin*, 1889. Also, under the title *The Sad Shepherd*, in *Poems*, 1895.

FROM THE BOOK OF KAURI THE INDIAN—SECTION V. ON THE
NATURE OF GOD

(Unsigned)

The Dublin University Review, October.

Reprinted, under the title *Kanva, the Indian, on God*, in *The Wanderings of Oisin*, 1889. Also, under the title *The Indian upon God*, in *Poems*, 1895.

THE MEDITATION OF THE OLD FISHERMAN

The Irish Monthly, October.

Reprinted in *Poems and Ballads of Young Ireland*, 1888. Also in *The Wanderings of Oisin*, 1889, and in *Poems*, 1895.

THE POETRY OF SIR SAMUEL FERGUSON

The Irish Fireside, October 9.

THE POETRY OF SIR SAMUEL FERGUSON

The Dublin University Review, November.

THE POETRY OF R. D. JOYCE

The Irish Fireside, November 27 and December 4.

THE STOLEN CHILD

The Irish Monthly, December.

Reprinted in *Poems and Ballads of Young Ireland*, 1888. Also in *Fairy and Folk Tales of the Irish Peasantry*, 1888, in *The Wanderings of Oisin*, 1889, and in *Poems*, 1895.

AN INDIAN SONG

The Dublin University Review, December.

Reprinted in *The Wanderings of Oisin*, 1889. Also, under the title *The Indian to his Love*, in *Poems*, 1895.

1887

A DAWN-SONG

The Irish Fireside, February 5.

THE FAIRY PEDANT

The Irish Monthly, March.

Reprinted in *The Wanderings of Oisin*, 1889. Also reprinted, under the title *The Solitary Fairy*, in *A Celtic Christmas* (*The Irish Homestead* Christmas number), December 1901.

CLARENCE MANGAN

The Irish Fireside, March 12.

MISS TYNAN'S NEW BOOK

The Irish Fireside, July 9.

HOW FERENCZ RENYI KEPT SILENT. HUNGARY—1848

The Boston Pilot, August 6.
Reprinted in *The Wanderings of Oisin*, 1889. Also reprinted in *A Celtic Christmas* (*The Irish Homestead* Christmas number), December 1900.

KING GOLL. AN IRISH LEGEND

The Leisure Hour, September.
Reprinted in *Poems and Ballads of Young Ireland*, 1888. Also in *The Wanderings of Oisin*, 1889, and in *Poems*, 1895.
An illustration by J. B. Yeats, representing King Goll, gives him a resemblance to the youthful bearded W. B. Yeats. The poem and illustration were reprinted in *A Celtic Christmas* (*The Irish Homestead* Christmas number), December 1898.

SHE WHO DWELT AMONG THE SYCAMORES

The Irish Monthly, September.
Reprinted in *The Wanderings of Oisin*, 1889. Also, under the title *She Dwelt Among the Sycamores*, in *A Celtic Christmas* (*The Irish Homestead* Christmas number), December 1902.

THE FAIRY DOCTOR

The Irish Fireside, September 10.
Reprinted in *The Wanderings of Oisin*, 1889.

[A LETTER]

The Gael (Dublin), November 26.
Reprinted in *The Irish Monthly*, July 1891; and in *The Letters of W. B. Yeats*, 1954.

1888

THE PROSE AND POETRY OF WILFRID BLUNT

United Ireland, January 28.

A LEGEND OF THE PHANTOM SHIP

> *The Providence Sunday Journal*, May 27.
> Reprinted, under the title *The Phantom Ship*, in *The Wanderings of Oisin*, 1889.

THE POET OF BALLYSHANNON

> (Review of William Allingham's *Irish Songs and Poems*)
> *The Providence Sunday Journal*, September 2.
> Reprinted in *Letters to the New Island*, 1934.

A LEGEND

> *The Vegetarian*, December 22.
> Reprinted in *The Wanderings of Oisin*, 1889.

1889

IRISH FAIRIES, GHOSTS, WITCHES, ETC.

> *Lucifer*, January 15.
> This essay ends "To be continued," but it never was.

DR. TODHUNTER'S LATEST VOLUME OF POEMS

> (Review of John Todhunter's *The Banshee and Other Poems*)
> *The Providence Sunday Journal*, February 10.
> Reprinted, under the title *The Children of Lir*, in *Letters to the New Island*, 1934.

SCOTS AND IRISH FAIRIES

> *The Scots Observer*, March 2.
> Reprinted, under the title *A Remonstrance with Scotsmen for having Soured the disposition of their Ghosts and Faeries*, in *The Celtic Twilight*, 1893 and 1902.

JOHN TODHUNTER

> (A biographical note, signed W. B. Y.)
> *The Magazine of Poetry* (Buffalo, New York), April.
> Reprinted in *W. B. Yeats Letters to Katharine Tynan*, 1953.

VILLAGE GHOSTS

> *The Scots Observer*, May 11.
> Reprinted in *The Celtic Twilight*, 1893 and 1902.

IN CHURCH

> (A poem with an illustration)
> *The Girl's Own Paper*, June 8.

KIDNAPPERS

> *The Scots Observer*, June 15.
> Reprinted in *The Celtic Twilight*, 1893 and 1902.

A SUMMER EVENING

> (A poem with an illustration)
> *The Girl's Own Paper*, July 6.

IRISH WONDERS

> (Review of D. R. McAnally's *Irish Wonders*)
> *The Providence Sunday Journal*, July 7.
> Reprinted in *Letters to the New Island*, 1934.

"THE WANDERINGS OF OISIN"

> (A letter)
> *The Spectator*, August 3.
> Reprinted in *The Letters of W. B. Yeats*, 1954.

THE CELT IN LONDON. IRISH WRITERS WHO ARE WINNING FAME

> (Dated London, July 10.) *The Boston Pilot*, August 3.
> Reprinted, under the title *Mr. William Wills*, in *Letters to the New Island*, 1934.

THE CELT IN LONDON. SOME FORTHCOMING IRISH BOOKS

> (Dated London, Sept. 7.) *The Boston Pilot*, September 28.
> Reprinted, under the title *Lady Wilde*, in *Letters to the New Island*, 1934.

COLUMKILLE AND ROSSES

> *The Scots Observer*, October 5.
> Reprinted, under the title *Drumcliffe and Rosses*, in *The Celtic Twilight*, 1893 and 1902.

WILLIAM CARLETON

> (Unsigned review of *Stories from Carleton* and *The Red-Haired Man's Wife* by William Carleton)
> *The Scots Observer*, October 19.
> Yeats wrote to Katharine Tynan on April 23, 1889: "The Scots Observer people have asked me to write an article on [Carleton] apropos of The Red Haired Man's Wife." The few words commending his own collection, *Stories from Carleton*,

which appear at the beginning of the article may well have been interpolated by the editor, W. E. Henley.

THE BALLAD OF THE OLD FOXHUNTER

East and West, November.
Reprinted in *United Ireland*, May 28, 1892, in *The Countess Kathleen*, 1892, and in *Poems*, 1895.

POPULAR BALLAD POETRY OF IRELAND

The Leisure Hour, November.

THE CELT IN LONDON. WHAT THE WRITERS AND THINKERS ARE DOING

(Dated London, Oct. 31. Signed W.B.Y.)
The Boston Pilot, November 23.
Reprinted, under the title *The Three O'Byrnes*, in *Letters to the New Island*, 1934.

THE CELT IN LONDON. CHEVALIER BURKE—"SHULE AROON" —CARLETON AND BANIM'S NOVELS—AN AUTOGRAPH SALE [AT] SOTHEBY'S—WILLIAM ALLINGHAM—MISS ELLEN O'LEARY

(Dated London, Dec. 3. Signed W.B.Y.)
The Boston Pilot, December 28.
Reprinted, under the title *Chevalier Burke and Shule Aroon*, in *Letters to the New Island*, 1934.

1890

BARDIC IRELAND

The Scots Observer, January 4.

CARLETON AS AN IRISH HISTORIAN

(A letter, dated January 3, 1890)
The Nation (Dublin), January 11.

THE CELT IN LONDON. BROWNING—A NEW SCHOOL— EDWARD CARPENTER—MR. CURTIN'S "IRISH MYTHS AND FOLK LORE"—LADY WILDE'S "ANCIENT CURES" —ALLINGHAM.

(Dated London, Eng. Jan. 23. Signed W.B.Y.)
The Boston Pilot, February 22.

Reprinted, under the title *Browning*, in *Letters to the New Island*, 1934.

TALES FROM THE TWILIGHT

(Review of Lady Wilde's *Ancient Cures, Charms and Usages of Ireland.*)
The Scots Observer, March 1.

IRISH WONDERS

(Unsigned review of *The Ghosts, Giants, Pookas, Demons, Leprechauns, Banshees, Fairies, Witches, Old Maids and other Marvels of the Emerald Isle* by D. R. M'Anally, Jr.)
The Scots Observer, March 30.
Reprinted, with Yeats's signature attached and a note by Horace Reynolds, in *The Tuftonian* (The Magazine of Tufts College, Medford, Mass., U.S.A.) January 1942.

STREET DANCERS

The Leisure Hour, April.
This poem appeared in *The Wanderings of Oisin*, 1889.

A CRADLE SONG

The Scots Observer, April 19.
Reprinted in *The Countess Kathleen*, 1892, and in *Poems*, 1895.

DR. TODHUNTER'S NEW PLAY

(A Sicilian Idyll)
The Nation (Dublin), May 17; and in *The Providence Sunday Journal*, June 8.

THE CELT IN LONDON. IRISH WRITERS OUGHT TO TAKE IRISH SUBJECTS. A SICILIAN IDYLL

(Dated London, April 21. Signed W.B.Y.)
The Boston Pilot, May 17.
Reprinted, under the title *Ireland's Heroic Age*, in *Letters to the New Island*, 1934.

THE CELT IN LONDON. DR. TODHUNTER'S SICILIAN IDYLL

(Dated London, May 12)
The Boston Pilot, June 14.
Reprinted, under the title *A Sicilian Idyll*, in *Letters to the New Island*, 1934.

A SCHOLAR POET

(Review of William Watson's *Wordsworth's Grave and Other Poems*)
The Providence Sunday Journal, June 15.
Reprinted in *Letters to the New Island*, 1934.

FATHER GILLIGAN (A LEGEND TOLD BY THE PEOPLE OF CASTLEISLAND, KERRY)

The Scots Observer, July 5.
Reprinted in *The Book of the Rhymers' Club*, 1892, in *The Countess Kathleen*, 1892, and in *Poems*, 1895.

IRISH FAIRIES

The Leisure Hour, October.
Reprinted in part, under the titles *Belief and Unbelief* and *The Three O'Byrnes and the Evil Faeries*, in *The Celtic Twilight*, 1893 and 1902.

POETRY AND SCIENCE IN FOLK-LORE

(A letter)
The Academy, October 11.

THE ARTS AND CRAFTS. AN EXHIBITION AT WILLIAM MORRIS'S

The Providence Sunday Journal, October 26.

THE OLD PENSIONER

The Scots Observer, November 15.
Reprinted in *The Countess Kathleen*, 1892, and in *Poems*, 1895.

THE LAKE ISLE OF INNISFREE

The National Observer, December 13.
Reprinted in *The Book of the Rhymers' Club*, 1892, in *The Countess Kathleen*, 1892, and in *Poems*, 1895.

1891

A MAN WHO DREAMED OF FAIRYLAND

The National Observer, February 7.
Reprinted in *The Book of the Rhymers' Club*, 1892, in *The Countess Kathleen*, 1892, and in *Poems*, 1895.

IRISH FOLK TALES

(Review of *Beside the Fire* by Douglas Hyde)
The National Observer, February 28.
Reprinted, under the title *The Four Winds of Desire*, in *The Celtic Twilight*, 1893.

IN THE FIRELIGHT

> (A poem)
> *The Leisure Hour*, March.

ROSE KAVANAGH. DEATH OF A PROMISING YOUNG IRISH POET.

> (Dated London, March 27)
> *The Boston Pilot*, April 11.
> Reprinted, under the title *Rose Kavanagh*, in *Letters to the New Island*, 1934.

THE CELT IN LONDON. SOME RECENT BOOKS BY IRISH WRITERS

> *The Boston Pilot*, April 18.
> Reprinted, under the title *The Poems of Ellen O'Leary*, in *Letters to the New Island*, 1934.

THE POETIC DRAMA. SOME INTERESTING ATTEMPTS TO REVIVE IT IN LONDON. DR. TODHUNTER'S IMPORTANT WORK IN "THE POISON FLOWER"

> (Dated London, July 10)
> *The Providence Sunday Journal*, July 26.
> Reprinted, under the title *A Poetic Drama*, in *Letters to the New Island*, 1934.

DR. TODHUNTER'S NEW PLAY

> (Dated London, June 27)
> *The Boston Pilot*, August 1.
> Reprinted, under the title *The Poison Flower*, in *Letters to the New Island*, 1934.

PLAYS BY AN IRISH POET

> (The work of Dr. John Todhunter)
> *United Ireland*, July 11.

CLARENCE MANGAN'S LOVE AFFAIR

> *United Ireland*, August 22.

A FAIRY SONG

> *The National Observer*, September 12.
> Reprinted in *The Book of the Rhymers' Club*, 1892, in *The Countess Kathleen*, 1892, and in *Poems*, 1895.

A RECKLESS CENTURY. IRISH RAKES AND DUELLISTS

> *United Ireland*, September 12.

THE CELT IN IRELAND

The Boston Pilot, September 12.
Reprinted, under the title *A Ballad Singer*, in *Letters to the New Island*, 1934.

OSCAR WILDE'S LAST BOOK

(Review of *Lord Arthur Saville's Crime and other Stories*)
United Ireland, September 26.

AN IRISH VISIONARY

The National Observer, October 3.
Reprinted, under the title *A Visionary*, in *The Celtic Twilight*, 1893 and 1902.

THE YOUNG IRELAND LEAGUE

United Ireland, October 3.

MOURN—AND THEN ONWARD

(A poem)
United Ireland, October 10.
Reprinted in *The Irish Weekly Independent*, May 20, 1893, and in *Yeats The Man and the Masks* by Richard Ellmann, New York, 1948 and London, 1949.

KATHLEEN

The National Observer, October 31.
Reprinted in Scene v. of *The Countess Kathleen*, 1892; also, under the title *A Dream of a Blessed Spirit*, in *Poems*, 1895.

AN EPITAPH

The National Observer, December 12.
Reprinted in *The Book of the Rhymers' Club*, 1892, in *The Countess Kathleen*, 1892, and, under the title *A Dream of Death*, in *Poems*, 1895.

IRISH LITERATURE. A POET WE HAVE NEGLECTED

(William Allingham)
United Ireland, December 12.

1892

POEMS BY MISS TYNAN

(Review of *Ballads and Lyrics*)
The Evening Herald, January 2.
Reprinted in part in *W. B. Yeats Letters to Katharine Tynan*, 1953.
Y

ROSA MUNDI

> *The National Observer*, January 2.
> Reprinted, under the title *The Rose of the World*, in *The Countess Kathleen*, 1892, and in *Poems*, 1895.

THE NEW "SPERANZA"

> (Maud Gonne)
> *United Ireland*, January 16.

DR. TODHUNTER'S IRISH POEMS

> (Review of *The Banshee*)
> *United Ireland*, January 23.

CLOVIS HUGES ON IRELAND

> *United Ireland*, January 30.

THE PEACE OF THE ROSE

> *The National Observer*, February 13.
> Reprinted in *The Countess Kathleen*, 1892; also, under the title *The Rose of Peace*, in *Poems*, 1895.

'FATHER GILLIGAN'

> (A letter)
> *The Academy*, March 19.
> Reprinted in *The Letters of W. B. Yeats*, 1954.

THE CELT IN LONDON. THE RHYMERS' CLUB

> *The Boston Pilot*, April 23.
> Reprinted, under the title *The Rhymers' Club* in *Letters to the New Island*, 1934.

THE WHITE BIRDS

> *The National Observer*, May 7.
> Reprinted in *The Countess Kathleen*, 1892, and in *Poems*, 1895.

THE IRISH INTELLECTUAL CAPITAL : WHERE IS IT? THE PUBLICATION OF IRISH BOOKS

> (A letter)
> *United Ireland*, May 14.

FERGUS AND THE DRUID

> *The National Observer*, May 21.
> Reprinted in *The Countess Kathleen*, 1892, and in *Poems*, 1895.

THE DEATH OF CUCHULLIN

United Ireland, June 11.
Reprinted in *The Countess Kathleen*, 1892, and in *Poems*, 1895.

[MICHAEL FIELD'S] SIGHT AND SONG

(A review)
The Bookman, July.

SOME NEW IRISH BOOKS

(Unsigned reviews of The Works of George Armstrong, *Fand*
by W. Larminie, and *Songs of Arcady* by W. O'Reilly. Other
reviews included in the article are, I believe, not written by Yeats.)
United Ireland, July 23.

THE NEW "SPERANZA"

(Dated London, July 9)
The Boston Pilot, July 30.
Reprinted, under the title *Maude Gonne*, in *Letters to the New
Island*, 1934.

THE IRISH LITERARY SOCIETY, LONDON

(A letter)
United Ireland, July 30.

DUBLIN SCHOLASTICISM AND TRINITY COLLEGE

United Ireland, July 30.

A NEW POET

(Review of *Fate in Arcadia* by Edwin Ellis)
The Bookman, September.

'NOETRY' AND POETRY

(Review of Savage Armstrong's collected verse)
The Bookman, September.

THE NATIONAL PUBLISHING COMPANY. SHOULD THE BOOKS
BE EDITED?

The Freeman's Journal, September 6.

THE NATIONAL PUBLISHING COMPANY

(Two letters)
The Freeman's Journal, September 8 and 10.

[DAVIS, MANGAN, FERGUSON]

(A letter)
United Ireland, September 10.
Reprinted in *The Letters of W. B. Yeats*, 1954.

THE NATIONAL LITERARY SOCIETY—LIBRARIES SCHEME

(A letter)
United Ireland, September 24.

A MYSTICAL PRAYER TO THE MASTERS OF THE ELEMENTS, MICHAEL, GABRIEL AND RAPHAEL

The Bookman, October.
Reprinted, under the title *A Mystical Prayer to the Masters of the Elements—Finvarra, Feacra, and Caolte*, in *The Second Book of the Rhymers' Club*, 1894, and, under the title *Aodh pleads with the Elemental Powers*, in *The Dome*, December 1898.

INVOKING THE IRISH FAIRIES

(Signed D.E.D.I.)
The Irish Theosophist, October.

HOPES AND FEARS FOR IRISH LITERATURE

United Ireland, October 15.

THE QUESTION OF THE LAUREATESHIP, II

(A letter, unsigned, in response to an enquiry)
The Bookman, November.
Reprinted in *The Letters of W. B. Yeats*, 1954.

THE ROSE IN MY HEART

The National Observer, November 12.
Reprinted in *The Second Book of the Rhymers' Club*, 1894; also, under the title *Aedh tells of the Rose in his Heart*, in *The Wind Among the Reeds*, 1899.

THE CELT IN IRELAND. THE NEW NATIONAL LIBRARY—THE NATIONAL LITERARY SOCIETY—MR. O'GRADY'S STORIES —DR. HYDE'S FORTHCOMING BOOK—THEMES FOR IRISH LITERATEURS

(Dated Dublin, Nov. 6)
The Boston Pilot, November 19.
Reprinted, under the title *The Irish National Literary Society*, in *Letters to the New Island*, 1934.

THE DEVIL'S BOOK

> *The National Observer*, November 26.
> Reprinted, under the title *The Book of the Great Dhoul and Hanrahan the Red*, in *The Secret Rose*, 1897.

[TENNYSON'S] THE DEATH OF ŒNONE

> (A review)
> *The Bookman*, December.

THE FIDDLER OF DOONEY

> (Dated November, 1892)
> *The Bookman*, December.
> Reprinted in *The Second Book of the Rhymers' Club*, 1894, and in *The Wind Among the Reeds*, 1899.

THE DE-ANGLICISING OF IRELAND

> (A letter)
> *United Ireland*, December 17.

THE TWISTING OF THE ROPE

> *The National Observer*, December 24.
> Reprinted, under the title *The Twisting of the Rope and Hanrahan the Red*, in *The Secret Rose*, 1897.

1893

[KUNO MEYER'S] THE VISION OF MACCONGLINNE

> (A review)
> *The Bookman*, February.

[ROBERT BUCHANAN'S] THE WANDERING JEW

> (A review)
> *The Bookman*, April.

THE BALLAD OF EARL PAUL

> (Dated Sligo, April 4th)
> *The Irish Weekly Independent*, April 8.
> An essay *An Old Yeats Ballad* by R. H., noting the existence of this poem and quoting several verses, appeared in *The Dublin Magazine*, April–June, 1927.

THE HEART OF THE SPRING

> *The National Observer*, April 15.
> Reprinted in *The Secret Rose*, 1897.

THE DANAAN QUICKEN TREE

(A poem, with a note in prose)
The Bookman, May.

THE LAST GLEEMAN

The National Observer, May 6.
Reprinted in *The Celtic Twilight*, 1893 and 1902.

NATIONALITY AND LITERATURE

(A lecture to the National Literary Society)
United Ireland, May 27.

OUT OF THE ROSE

The National Observer, May 27.
Reprinted in *The Secret Rose*, 1897.

A BUNDLE OF POETS

(Unsigned review of *The Poems* of A. H. Hallam, *Anne Boleyn*, *Musa Consolatrix* by Charles Sayle, and *An Enchanted Castle* by Sarah Piatt)
The Speaker, July 22.

THE CELTIC TWILIGHT

The National Observer, July 29.
Reprinted, under the title *Into the Twilight*, in *The Celtic Twilight*, 1893 and 1902, and in *The Wind Among the Reeds*, 1899.

THE WRITINGS OF WILLIAM BLAKE

(Review of a volume of *The Parchment Library*)
The Bookman, August.

THE MOODS

The Bookman, August.
Reprinted, without title, in *United Ireland*, November 11, 1893, and, also without title, in *The Celtic Twilight*, 1893 and 1902; and in *The Wind Among the Reeds*, 1899.

THE CURSE OF THE FIRES AND OF THE SHADOWS

The National Observer, August 5.
Reprinted in *The Secret Rose*, 1897.

THE MESSAGE OF THE FOLK-LORIST

The Speaker, August 19.

TWO MINOR LYRISTS

(Unsigned review of *Verses by the Way* by J. D. Hosken, and *The Question at the Well* by Fenil Haig [Ford Madox Hueffer]) *The Speaker*, August 26.

OLD GAELIC LOVE SONGS

(Review of *The Love Songs of Connacht* by Douglas Hyde) *The Bookman*, October.

THE FAERY HOST

The National Observer, October 7.
Reprinted, under the title *The Host*, in *The Celtic Twilight*, 1893; and, under the title *The Hosting of the Sidhe*, in *The Wind Among the Reeds*, 1899 and in *The Celtic Twilight*, 1902.

THE AINU

(Unsigned review of *Life with Trans-Siberian Savages* by B. Douglas Howard) *The Speaker*, October 7.

AN IMPRESSION

The Speaker, October 21.
Reprinted, under the title *A Knight of the Sheep*, in *The Celtic Twilight*, 1893 and 1902.

THE STOLEN BRIDE

(A poem with a note in prose) *The Bookman*, November.
Reprinted, under the title *The Folk of the Air*, in *The Second Book of the Rhymers' Club*, 1894, and, under the title *The Host of the Air*, in *The Wind Among the Reeds*, 1899.

The note, not reprinted, read: "I heard the story on which this ballad is founded from an old woman at Balesodare [*sic*], Sligo. She repeated me a Gaelic poem on the subject, and then translated it to me. I have always regretted not having taken down her words, and as some amends for not having done so, have made this ballad. Any one who tastes fairy food or drink is glamoured and stolen by the fairies. This is why Bridget sets O'Driscoll to play cards. "The folk of the air" is a Gaelic name for the fairies."

'REFLECTIONS AND REFRACTIONS' BY CHARLES WEEKES

(A review) *The Academy*, November 4.

OUR LADY OF THE HILLS

The Speaker, November 11.
Reprinted in *The Celtic Twilight*, 1893 and 1902.

PREFACE TO THE CELTIC TWILIGHT

United Ireland, November 11.
Reprinted, under the title *This Book*, in *The Celtic Twilight*, 1893 and 1902.

WISDOM AND DREAMS

(A poem)
The Bookman, December.

MICHAEL CLANCY, THE GREAT DHOUL, AND DEATH

The Old Country, a Christmas Annual.
Reprinted, with a long preliminary letter by the author, in *The Kilkenny Moderator*, Christmas number, 1898. The letter was reprinted in *The Letters of W. B. Yeats*, 1954.

'THE SILENCED SISTER'

(Two letters)
United Ireland, December 23 and 30.

1894

IRISH FOLK-LORE

Extracts from a paper read by Yeats at a meeting of the Belfast Naturalists Field Club, November 20, 1893.
Annual Report and Proceedings: Belfast Naturalists Field Club 1894.

[E. J. ELLIS'S] SEEN IN THREE DAYS

(A review)
The Bookman, February.

CAP AND BELL

The National Observer, March 17.
Reprinted, under the title *The Cap and Bells*, in *The Second Book of the Rhymers' Club*, 1894, and in *The Wind Among the Reeds*, 1899.

A CRUCIFIXION

The National Observer, March 24.
Reprinted, under the title *The Crucifixion of the Outcast*, in *The Secret Rose*, 1897.

THE SONG OF THE OLD MOTHER

(With a short note in prose)
The Bookman, April.
Reprinted in *The Second Book of the Rhymers' Club*, 1894, and in
The Wind Among the Reeds, 1899.

The note, not reprinted, read: "The 'seed of the fire' is the
Irish phrase for the little fragment of burning turf and hot ashes
which remains in the hearth from the day before."

A SYMBOLICAL DRAMA IN PARIS

(Note on a performance of *Axel*)
The Bookman, April.
Some passages from this essay were included in Yeats's Preface
to an English translation of Villiers de l'Isle Adam's *Axel*, made
by H. P. R. Finberg. London: 1925. (No. 275.)

REGINA, REGINA PIGMEORUM, VENI

The Irish Home Reading Magazine, May.
This essay had already appeared in *The Celtic Twilight*, 1893;
the text in the magazine differs from that in the book and may
have been earlier.

THE EVANGEL OF FOLKLORE

(Review of William Larminie's *West Irish Folk Tales*)
The Bookman, June.

THOSE WHO LIVE IN THE STORM

The Speaker, July 21.
Reprinted, under the title *The Rose of Shadow*, in *The Secret
Rose*, 1897. This story was omitted from the *Collected Works* of
1908 and from later editions.

A NEW POET

(Review of *Homeward* by A.E.)
The Bookman, August.

SOME IRISH NATIONAL BOOKS

(Review of *The New Spirit of the Nation* and other works)
The Bookman, August.

KATHLEEN-NY-HOOLIHAN

The National Observer, August 4.
Reprinted, under the title *Kathleen the Daughter of Hoolihan
and Hanrahan the Red*, in *The Secret Rose*, 1897.

[THE NEW IRISH LIBRARY]
>   (A letter)
>   *United Ireland*, September 1.

THE CURSE OF O'SULLIVAN THE RED UPON OLD AGE
>   *The National Observer*, September 29.
>   Reprinted, under the title *The Curse of Hanrahan the Red*, in *The Secret Rose*, 1897.

THE STONE AND THE ELIXIR
>   (Review of Ibsen's *Brand*)
>   *The Bookman*, October.

[CRITICISM OF IRISH BOOKS]
>   (Two letters signed "A Student of Irish Literature.")
>   *United Ireland*, November 24 and December 1.
>   Reprinted in *The Letters of W. B. Yeats*, 1954.

THE LOVER TO HIS HEART | (*Specially written for* THE SOCIAL REGISTER)
>   *The Social Register*, December 7.
>   These 6 lines beginning "Impetuous heart, be still, be still" were reprinted in *The Countess Cathleen*, originally in scene I, later in scene IV.

1895

BATTLES LONG AGO
>   (Review of Standish O'Grady's *The Coming of Cuchullain*)
>   *The Bookman*, February.

PROFESSOR DOWDEN AND IRISH LITERATURE
>   (Two letters)
>   *The Dublin Daily Express*, January 26 and February 7.

THE BEST THIRTY IRISH BOOKS
>   (A letter)
>   *The Dublin Daily Express*, February 27.
>   Reprinted in *The Letters of W. B. Yeats*, 1954.

AN EXCELLENT TALKER
>   (Review of Oscar Wilde's *A Woman of No Importance*)
>   *The Bookman*, March.

IRISH LITERATURE
>   (A letter)
>   *The Dublin Daily Express*, March 8.

THE THIRTY BEST IRISH BOOKS
(A letter)
United Ireland, March 16.

TO SOME I HAVE TALKED WITH BY THE FIRE
The Bookman, May.
Reprinted in *Poems*, 1895.

DUBLIN MYSTICS
(Review of *Homeward* by A.E. and of *Two Essays on the Remnant* by John Eglinton)
The Bookman, May.

[DOUGLAS HYDE'S] THE STORY OF EARLY GAELIC LITERATURE
(A review)
The Bookman, June.

IRISH NATIONAL LITERATURE
[I.] *From Callanan to Carleton*
The Bookman, July.

[DOUGLAS HYDE'S] THE THREE SORROWS OF STORY TELLING
(An unsigned review)
The Bookman, July.

IRISH NATIONAL LITERATURE
[II.] *Contemporary Prose Writers. Mr. O'Grady, Miss Lawless, Miss Barlow, Miss Hopper and the Folk-Lorists*
The Bookman, August.
The first paragraph of this essay is reprinted, under the title *The Moods*, in *Ideas of Good and Evil*, 1903.

THAT SUBTLE SHADE
(Review of *London Nights* by Arthur Symons)
The Bookman, August.

IRISH NATIONAL LITERATURE
III. *Contemporary Irish Poets. Dr. Hyde, Mr. Rolleston, Mrs. Hinkson, Miss Nora Hopper, A.E., Mr. Aubrey de Vere, Dr. Todhunter and Mr. Lionel Johnson*
The Bookman, September.
The first paragraph of this essay is reprinted, under the title *The Body of the Father Christian Rosencrux*, in *Ideas of Good and Evil*, 1903.

WISDOM

> *The New Review*, September.
> Reprinted, under the title *The Wisdom of the King*, in *The Secret Rose*, 1897.

A SONG OF THE ROSY CROSS

> *The Bookman*, October.

IRISH NATIONAL LITERATURE

> IV. *A List of the best Irish Books*
> *The Bookman*, October.

[DR. TODHUNTER'S] THE LIFE OF PATRICK SARSFIELD

> (A review)
> *The Bookman*, November.

THE CHAIN OF GOLD BY STANDISH O'GRADY

> (Unsigned review)
> *The Bookman*, November.

THE TWILIGHT OF FORGIVENESS

> *The Saturday Review*, November 2.
> Reprinted, under the title *Michael Robartes asks Forgiveness because of his many Moods*, in *The Wind Among the Reeds*, 1899.

ST. PATRICK AND THE PEDANTS

> *The Weekly Sun Literary Supplement*, December 1. Also printed in *The Chap Book* (Chicago), June 1, 1896.
> Reprinted, under the title *The Old Men of the Twilight*, in *The Secret Rose*, 1897.

1896

THE SHADOWY HORSES

> *The Savoy*, January.
> Reprinted, under the title *Michael Robartes bids his Beloved be at Peace*, in *The Wind Among the Reeds*, 1899.

THE TRAVAIL OF PASSION

> *The Savoy*, January.
> Reprinted in *The Wind Among the Reeds*, 1899.

THE BINDING OF THE HAIR

> *The Savoy*, January.
> Reprinted in *The Secret Rose*, 1897; omitted from the *Collected Works*, 1908 and from later editions.

EVERLASTING VOICES

> *The New Review*, January.
> Reprinted, under the title *The Everlasting Voices*, in *The Wind Among the Reeds*, 1899.

WILLIAM CARLETON

> (Review of *The Life of William Carleton* by D. J. O'Donahue)
> *The Bookman*, March.

O'SULLIVAN THE RED TO MARY LAVELL

> *The Senate*, March.
> These two poems were reprinted in *United Ireland*, April 4, 1896; in the following issue, April 11, the paper stated that Yeats had written to say that his *Senate* proof-sheets had miscarried and that the poems, as printed, "got a good deal on his nerves." Then followed the corrected text, under the title *Two Poems by O'Sullivan the Red concerning Mary Lavell*. The poems were reprinted, under the titles *Aedh tells of the perfect Beauty* and *A Poet to his Beloved*, in *The Wind Among the Reeds*, 1899.

ROSA ALCHEMICA

> *The Savoy*, April.
> Reprinted in *The Secret Rose*, 1897.

TWO POEMS CONCERNING PEASANT VISIONARIES

> I. *A Cradle Song*. II. *The Valley of the Black Pig*. The latter poem is accompanied by a note in prose.
> *The Savoy*, April.
> Reprinted in *The Wind Among the Reeds*, 1899. The substance of the note is included in the notes to that volume.

VERLAINE IN 1894

> *The Savoy*, April.
> The greater part of this essay is reprinted in *The Trembling of the Veil*, 1922, and in *Autobiographies*, 1926.

THE VISION OF O'SULLIVAN THE RED

> *The New Review*, April.
> Reprinted, under the title *The Vision of Hanrahan the Red*, in *The Secret Rose*, 1897.

WILLIAM BLAKE

> (Review of Dr. Richard Garnett's *William Blake* in *The Portfolio* series of monographs)
> *The Bookman*, April.

AN IRISH PATRIOT

(Review of Lady Ferguson's *Sir Samuel Ferguson in the Ireland of his Day*)
The Bookman, May.

THE NEW IRISH LIBRARY

(Review of *Swift in Ireland, Owen Roe O'Neill*, and *A Short Life of Thomas Davis*)
The Bookman, June.

O'SULLIVAN RUA TO MARY LAVELL

The Savoy, July.
Reprinted, under the title *Michael Robartes remembers forgotten Beauty*, in *The Wind Among the Reeds*, 1899.

WILLIAM BLAKE AND HIS ILLUSTRATIONS TO THE DIVINE COMEDY

I. *His Opinions upon Art*
   The Savoy, July.
II. *His Opinions upon Dante*
    The Savoy, August.
III. *The Illustrations of Dante*
     The Savoy, September.
     Reprinted in *Ideas of Good and Evil*, 1903.

O'SULLIVAN RUA TO THE SECRET ROSE

The Savoy, September.
Reprinted, under the title *To the Secret Rose*, in *The Secret Rose*, 1897, and, under the title *The Secret Rose*, in *The Wind Among the Reeds*, 1899.

GREEK FOLK POETRY

(Review of *Greek Folk Poesy* by Lucy M. Garnett)
The Bookman, October.

WHERE THERE IS NOTHING THERE IS GOD

The Sketch, October 21.
Reprinted in *The Secret Rose*, 1897 and in subsequent collections, but excluded from *Early Poems and Stories*, 1925.

WINDLESTRAWS

> I. *O'Sullivan Rua to the Curlew*
> II. *Out of the Old Days*
>> *The Savoy*, November.
>> Reprinted, under the titles *Hanrahan reproves the Curlew*
>> and *To my Heart, bidding it have no Fear*, in *The Wind
>> Among the Reeds*, 1899.

THE TABLES OF THE LAW

> *The Savoy*, November.
> Privately printed in book form in 1897, and published in book
> form in 1904 and 1914. Included in *Early Poems and Stories*, 1925.

THE CRADLES OF GOLD

> (A story)
> *The Senate*, November.

[WILLIAM MORRIS'S] THE WELL AT THE WORLD'S END

> (A review)
> *The Bookman*, November.

MISS FIONA MACLEOD AS A POET

> (Review of *From the Hills of Dream*)
> *The Bookman*, December.

THE DEATH OF O'SULLIVAN THE RED

> *The New Review*, December.
> Reprinted, under the title *The Death of Hanrahan the Red*, in
> *The Secret Rose*, 1897.

1897

[SIR CHARLES GAVAN DUFFY'S] YOUNG IRELAND

> (A review)
> *The Bookman*, January.

THE VALLEY OF LOVERS

> *The Saturday Review*, January 9.
> Reprinted, under the title *Aedh tells of a Valley full of Lovers*,
> in *The Wind Among the Reeds*, 1899.

JOHN O'LEARY

> (Review of John O'Leary's *Recollections of Fenians and Fenianism*)
> *The Bookman*, February.

THE '98 CENTENARY

>   (A letter)
>   *United Ireland*, March 20.

MR. ARTHUR SYMONS'S NEW BOOK

>   (Review of *Amoris Victima*)
>   *The Bookman*, April.

THE BLESSED

>   *The Yellow Book*, April.
>   Reprinted in *The Wind Among the Reeds*, 1899.

MISS FIONA MACLEOD

>   (Review of *Spiritual Tales*, *Tragic Romances*, and *Barbaric Tales*)
>   *The Sketch*, April 28.

["THE CRUCIFIXION OF THE OUTCAST"]

>   (A letter dated Sligo, May 18th.)
>   *The Speaker*, May 22.
>   Reprinted in *The Letters of W. B. Yeats*, 1954.

MR. ROBERT BRIDGES

>   *The Bookman*, June.
>   Reprinted, under the title "*The Return of Ulysses*," in *Ideas of Good and Evil*, 1903.

THE DESIRE OF MAN AND OF WOMAN

>   (With a note in prose)
>   Dated Sligo, June 1897.
>   *The Dome*, June.
>   Reprinted, under the title *Mongan Laments the Change that has come upon him and his Beloved*, in *The Wind Among the Reeds*, 1899. The substance of the note is included in the notes to that volume.

WILLIAM BLAKE

>   *The Academy*, June 19.
>   Reprinted, under the title *William Blake and the Imagination*, in *Ideas of Good and Evil*, 1903.

[MAURICE MAETERLINCK'S] THE TREASURE OF THE HUMBLE
(A review)
The Bookman, July.

SONG

The Saturday Review, July 24.
Reprinted, under the title *The Poet pleads with his Friend for old Friends*, in *The Wind Among the Reeds*, 1899.

MR. STANDISH O'GRADY'S "FLIGHT OF THE EAGLE"
(A review)
The Bookman, August.

O'SULLIVAN THE RED UPON HIS WANDERINGS
(A poem with a note in prose)
The New Review, August.
Reprinted, under the title *Hanrahan Laments because of his Wanderings*, in *The Wind Among the Reeds*, 1899. The note explains allusions which were omitted from the revised text of the poem. In the *Collected Works*, 1908, and thereafter, the poem is rewritten in shorter form and renamed *Maid Quiet*.

A MAD SONG

The Sketch, August 4.
Reprinted, under the title *The Song of Wandering Aengus*, in *The Wind Among the Reeds*, 1899.

[MAURICE MAETERLINCK'S] AGLAVAINE AND SELYSETTE
(A review)
The Bookman, September.
Parts of this review and of the review of *Amoris Victima* (see above, April), have been incorporated in the essay *The Autumn of the Body*, in *Ideas of Good and Evil*, 1903.

THE TRIBES OF DANU

The New Review, November.
Reprinted in part, under the title *The Friends of the People of Faery*, in *The Celtic Twilight*, 1902.

THREE IRISH POETS

(A.E., Nora Hopper and Lionel Johnson)
A Celtic Christmas (Christmas number of *The Irish Homestead*), December.
z

1898

THE PRISONERS OF THE GODS

> *The Nineteenth Century*, January.

MR. LIONEL JOHNSON'S POEMS

> (Review of *Ireland; and other poems*)
> *The Bookman*, February.

AODH TO DECTORA

> *The Sketch*, February 9.
> Reprinted, under the title *Aedh wishes his Beloved were dead*, in *The Wind Among the Reeds*, 1899.

MR. RHYS' WELSH BALLADS
> (A review)
> *The Bookman*, April.

THE BROKEN GATES OF DEATH

> *The Fortnightly Review*, April.

LE MOUVEMENT CELTIQUE

> I. *Fiona Macleod*
> (A note, including a review of *The Laughter of Peterkin*)
> *L'Irlande Libre* (Paris), April 1.
> The essay is printed in French; no translator's name is given.

"A.E.'S" POEMS

> (Review of *The Earth Breath*)
> *The Sketch*, April 6.

IRISH FAIRY LAND

> (A letter)
> *The Outlook*, April 23.
> Reprinted in *The Letters of W. B. Yeats*, 1954.

AODH TO DECTORA. THREE SONGS

> *The Dome*, May.
> Reprinted, under the titles *Aedh hears the Cry of the Sedge*, *Aedh Laments the Loss of Love*, and *Aedh thinks of those who have spoken Evil of his Beloved*, in *The Wind Among the Reeds*, 1899. The third song, set to music by Thomas F. Dunhill, under the original title *Aodh to Dectora*, was reprinted in *The Dome*, January 1900, and afterwards issued separately with the music.

THE CELTIC ELEMENT IN LITERATURE

Cosmopolis, June.
Reprinted in *Ideas of Good and Evil*, 1903.

LE MOUVEMENT CELTIQUE

II. *M. John O'Leary*
L'Irlande Libre (Paris), June 1.
The essay is printed in French; no translator's name is given.

MR. LIONEL JOHNSON AND CERTAIN IRISH POETS

The Dublin Daily Express, August 27.
Reprinted, under the title *Lionel Johnson*, in *A Treasury of Irish Poetry*, 1900.

CELTIC BELIEFS ABOUT THE SOUL

(Review of *The Voyage of Bran* by Kuno Meyer and Alfred Nutt)
The Bookman, September.

THE POETRY OF A.E.

The Dublin Daily Express, September 3.
Reprinted, under the title *A.E.*, in *A Treasury of Irish Poetry*, 1900.

THE POEMS AND STORIES OF MISS NORA HOPPER

The Dublin Daily Express, September 24.
Reprinted in part, under the title *A Note on National Drama*, in *Literary Ideals in Ireland*, 1899; and in part, under the title *Nora Hopper*, in *A Treasury of Irish Poetry*, 1900.

SONG OF MONGAN

(With a note in prose)
The Dome, October.
Reprinted, under the title *Mongan thinks of his past Greatness*, in *The Wind Among the Reeds*, 1899. The substance of the note is included in the notes to that volume.

JOHN EGLINTON AND SPIRITUAL ART

The Dublin Daily Express, October 29.
Reprinted in *Literary Ideals in Ireland*, 1899.

A SYMBOLIC ARTIST AND THE COMING OF SYMBOLIC ART

The Dome, December.

AODH PLEADS WITH THE ELEMENTAL POWERS

(A poem with a note in prose)
The Dome, December.
Reprinted, under the title *Aedh pleads with the Elemental Powers*, in *The Wind Among the Reeds*, 1899. The substance of the note is included in the notes to that volume.

BRESSEL THE FISHERMAN

The Cornish Magazine, December.
Reprinted, under the title *Breasal the Fisherman*, in *The Wind Among the Reeds*, 1899. In the *Poetical Works*, I, 1906, the title is changed to *The Fisherman*, and in the *Collected Poems*, 1933, to *The Fish*.

THE AUTUMN OF THE FLESH

The Dublin Daily Express, December 3.
Reprinted in *Literary Ideals in Ireland*, 1899; and, under the title *The Autumn of the Body*, in *Ideas of Good and Evil*, 1903.

1899

THE IRISH LITERARY THEATRE

(A letter)
The Dublin Daily Express, January 12.

THE IRISH LITERARY THEATRE

The Dublin Daily Express, January 14.
Reprinted in part, under the title *Plans and Methods*, in *Beltaine*, May 1899.

HIGH CROSSES OF IRELAND

(Signed Rosicrux)
The Dublin Daily Express, January 28.

MR. MOORE, MR. ARCHER AND THE LITERARY THEATRE

(A letter, dated January 27, 1899)
The Daily Chronicle, January 30.
Reprinted in *The Letters of W. B. Yeats*, 1954.

THE ACADEMIC CLASS AND THE AGRARIAN REVOLUTION

The Dublin Daily Express, March 11.
Reprinted in *Gaelic League Pamphlets* No. 20. November [1901?]

THE THEATRE

> *The Dome*, April.
> Reprinted in *Beltaine*, May 1899; and in *Ideas of Good and Evil*,
> 1903.

PLANS AND METHODS

> *Beltaine*, May.

THE IRISH LITERARY THEATRE

> *Literature*, May 6.

THE COUNTESS CATHLEEN AND CARDINAL LOGUE

> (A letter)
> *The Morning Leader*, May 13.
> Reprinted in *The Letters of W. B. Yeats*, 1954.

[FIONA MACLEOD'S] THE DOMINION OF DREAMS

> (A review)
> *The Bookman*, July.

IRELAND BEWITCHED

> *The Contemporary Review*, September.

'DUST HATH CLOSED HELEN'S EYE'

> *The Dome*, October.
> Reprinted in *The Celtic Twilight*, 1902.

THE LITERARY MOVEMENT IN IRELAND

> *The North American Review*, December.
> Reprinted in *Ideals in Ireland*, 1901.

[A LETTER]

> *The Gael* (New York), December.

1900

THE IRISH LITERARY THEATRE, 1900

> *The Dome*, January.
> Reprinted in *Beltaine*, February 1900; a paragraph is also reprinted
> as part of the essay *The Theatre*, in *Ideas of Good and Evil*, 1903.

THE IRISH LITERARY THEATRE

> (A letter)
> *The Irish Literary Society Gazette*, January.

THE STATUE OF MR. PARNELL

(A letter)
The United Irishman, January 20.
Reprinted in *The Letters of W. B. Yeats*, 1954.

PLANS AND METHODS

Beltaine, February.

'MAIVE' AND CERTAIN IRISH BELIEFS

Beltaine, February.

THE QUEEN'S VISIT

(A letter)
The Freeman's Journal, March 20.
Reprinted in *The Letters of W. B. Yeats*, 1954.

A CORRECTION

(A letter)
The Dublin Daily Express, March 30.

THE SYMBOLISM OF POETRY

The Dome, April.
Reprinted in *Ideas of Good and Evil*, 1903.

'THE LAST FEAST OF THE FIANNA,' 'MAIVE,' AND 'THE BENDING OF THE BOUGH' IN DUBLIN

Beltaine, April.

THE QUEEN'S VISIT

(A letter)
The Dublin Daily Express, April 5.
Reprinted in *The Letters of W. B. Yeats*, 1954.

THE WAY OF WISDOM

The Speaker, April 14.
Reprinted, under the title *The Pathway*, in the Collected Works, Vol. VIII, 1908.

NOBLE AND IGNOBLE LOYALTIES

The United Irishman, April 21.

THE SHADOWY WATERS

The North American Review, May.
Reprinted in book form, 1900. A new version of the play is
printed in *Poems, 1899–1905*, 1906; and an acting version in
book form in 1907.

THE PHILOSOPHY OF SHELLEY'S POETRY

The Dome, July.
Reprinted in *Ideas of Good and Evil*, 1903.

THE FREEDOM OF THE PRESS IN IRELAND

(A letter)
The Speaker, July 7.

IRISH FAIRY BELIEFS

(Review of Daniel Deeny's *Peasant Lore from Gaelic Ireland*)
The Speaker, July 14.

ECHTGE OF STREAMS

The Speaker, August 25.
Reprinted, under the title *The Withering of the Boughs*, in *In
the Seven Woods*, 1903.

IRISH WITCH DOCTORS

The Fortnightly Review, September.

IRISH LANGUAGE AND IRISH LITERATURE

(A letter)
The Leader (Dublin), September 1.

MR. YEATS'S JUG

(A letter)
The Leader (Dublin), November 10.

INTRODUCTION TO A DRAMATIC POEM

The Speaker, December 1.
Reprinted, without title, in *The Shadowy Waters*, 1900.

POSTSCRIPT TO A FORTHCOMING BOOK OF ESSAYS BY IRISH WRITERS

The All Ireland Review, December.
Reprinted, under the title *A Postscript*, in *Ideals in Ireland*, 1901.

1901

CANTILATION

(A letter)
The Saturday Review, March 16.
Reprinted in *The Letters of W. B. Yeats*, 1954.

[ON A LETTER TO THE "DAILY MAIL"]

(A letter)
The Academy, May 4.

AT STRATFORD-ON-AVON

The Speaker, May 11 and 18.
Reprinted, with the omission of Chapter III, which deals with the actors and their performances, in *Ideas of Good and Evil*, 1903.

THE FOOL OF FAERY

The Kensington, June.
Reprinted, under the title *The Queen and the Fool*, in *The Celtic Twilight*, 1902.

UNDER THE MOON

The Speaker, June 15.
Reprinted in *In the Seven Woods*, 1903.

BY THE ROADSIDE

An Claideamh Soluis, July 13.
Reprinted in *The Celtic Twilight*, 1902.

IRELAND AND THE ARTS

The United Irishman, August 31.
Reprinted in *Ideas of Good and Evil*, 1903.

MAGIC

The Monthly Review, September.
Reprinted in *Ideas of Good and Evil*, 1903.

EXTRACTS FROM SPEECHES TO THE PAN-CELTIC CONGRESS

Dublin, August 1901. *Celtia*, September.

[ABOUT AN "INTERVIEW"]

(A letter)
The Free Lance, September 21.

WINDLESTRAWS

Samhain, October.
Reprinted in *The Irish Dramatic Movement* in the *Collected Works*, Vol. IV, 1908; and in *Plays and Controversies*, 1923.

JOHN EGLINTON
The United Irishman, November 9.

THE PROPOSED CENSORSHIP
(A letter)
The Freeman's Journal, November 15.
Reprinted in *The Letters of W. B. Yeats*, 1954.

LITERATURE AND THE CONSCIENCE
The United Irishman, December 7.

FAVOURITE BOOKS OF 1901
(Contribution to a symposium)
The Academy, December 7.

1902

THE BLOOD BOND
(From *Grania* by George Moore and W. B. Yeats)
A Broad Sheet, January.
Reprinted in *The Dublin Magazine*, April–June 1951, in the play
Diarmuid and Grania.

SPINNING SONG
A Broad Sheet, January.
Reprinted, under the title *There are Seven that pull the thread*,
with a musical setting by Edward Elgar, 1902.

THE FOLLY OF BEING COMFORTED
The Speaker, January 11.
Reprinted in *In the Seven Woods*, 1903.

NEW CHAPTERS IN THE CELTIC TWILIGHT
I. *Enchanted Woods*
The Speaker, January 18.
Reprinted in *The Celtic Twilight*, 1902.

EGYPTIAN PLAYS
(A note on the performance of *The Beloved of Hathor* and *The
Shrine of the Golden Hawk* by Florence Farr and O. Shakespear)
The Star, January 23.

NEW CHAPTERS IN THE CELTIC TWILIGHT
II. *Happy and Unhappy Theologians*
The Speaker, February 15.
Reprinted in *The Celtic Twilight*, 1902.

WHAT IS 'POPULAR POETRY'?

> *The Cornhill Magazine*, March.
> Reprinted in *Ideas of Good and Evil*, 1903.

THE PURCELL SOCIETY

> (A letter)
> *The Saturday Review*, March 8.
> Reprinted in *The Letters of W. B. Yeats*, 1954.

NEW CHAPTERS IN THE CELTIC TWILIGHT

> III. *The Old Town.* IV. *War.* V. *Earth, Fire and Water.*
> *The Speaker*, March 15.
> Reprinted in *The Celtic Twilight*, 1902.

AWAY

> *The Fortnightly Review*, April.
> In the preface to *The Celtic Twilight*, 1902 edition, Yeats wrote
> "I shall publish in a little while a big book about the common-
> wealth of faery." It is reasonable to suppose that the six essays
> *The Tribes of Danu*, 1897, *The Prisoners of the Gods*, *The Broken
> Gates of Death*, 1898, *Ireland Bewitched*, 1899, *Irish Witch
> Doctors*, 1900, and *Away*, 1902, would have furnished some of the
> material for this book; but he had abandoned the idea by 1907.
> Lady Gregory, who had helped him to gather the stories, made
> use of many in her *Visions and Beliefs in the West of Ireland*,
> 1920.

MR. YEATS' NEW PLAY

> (An interview with Yeats, describing the action of *Kathleen Ni
> Houlihan* and giving the lyrics which occur in the play)
> *The United Irishman*, April 5.

THE ACTING AT ST. TERESA'S HALL

> (Notes on the performance of *Deirdre* by A.E. and of *Cathleen
> ni Hoolihan*)
> *The United Irishman*, April 12 and 26.

NEW CHAPTERS IN THE CELTIC TWILIGHT

> V. *A Voice.* VI. *The Swine of the Gods.* VII. *The Devil.* VIII,
> *'And Fair, Fierce Women.'* IX. *Mortal Help.*
> *The Speaker*, April 19.
> Reprinted in *The Celtic Twilight*, 1902.
> A footnote, not reprinted, to these chapters read: "A few lines
> of this bundle of stories appeared in *Ideals in Ireland*, but I have
> put them into quite a new setting, that throws a new light upon
> them."

NEW CHAPTERS IN THE CELTIC TWILIGHT

> X. *Aristotle of the Books*. XI. *Miraculous Creatures*. XII. *An Enduring Heart*.
> *The Speaker*, April 26.
> Reprinted in *The Celtic Twilight*, 1902.

SPEAKING TO THE PSALTERY

> *The Monthly Review*, May.
> Reprinted in *Ideas of Good and Evil*, 1903.

MR. CHURTON COLLINS ON BLAKE

> (A letter)
> *The Times Literary Supplement*, May 30.

SPEAKING TO MUSICAL NOTES

> (A letter)
> *The Academy*, June 7.
> Reprinted in *The Letters of W. B. Yeats*, 1954.

MAETERLINCK AND THE CENSOR

> (A letter signed by thirteen writers including W. B. Yeats)
> *The Times*, June 20.
> This letter also appeared elsewhere in the London Press.

THE HILL OF TARA

> (A letter signed by Douglas Hyde, LL.D., George Moore and W. B. Yeats)
> *The Times*, June 27.

BAILE AND AILLINN

> (With a note in prose)
> *The Monthly Review*, July.
> Reprinted in *In the Seven Woods*, 1903.

> The note, not reprinted, reads: "It is better, I think, to explain at once some of the allusions to mythological people and things, instead of breaking up the reader's attention with a series of footnotes. What the 'long wars for the White Horn and the Brown Bull' were, and who 'Deirdre the harper's daughter' was, and why Cuchullain was called 'the hound of Ulad,' I shall not explain. The reader will find all that he need know about them, and about the story of Baile and Aillinn itself, in Lady Gregory's *Cuchulain of Muirthemne*, the most important book that has come out of Ireland in my time. 'The Great Plain' is the Land of the Dead

and of the Happy; it is called also 'The Land of the Living Heart,' and many beautiful names besides. And Findrias and Falias and Gorias and Murias were the four mysterious cities whence the Tuatha De Danaan, the divine race, came to Ireland, cities of learning out of sight of the world, where they found their four talismans, the spear, the stone, the cauldron, and the sword. The birds that flutter over the head of Aengus are four birds that he made out of his kisses; and when Baile and Aillinn take the shape of swans linked with a golden chain, they take the shape that other enchanted lovers took before them in the old stories. Midhir was a king of the Sidhe, or people of faery, and Etain his wife, when driven away by a jealous woman, took refuge once upon a time with Aengus in a house of glass, and there I have imagined her weaving harp-strings out of Aengus' hair. I have brought the harp-strings into *The Shadowy Waters*, where I interpret the myth in my own way. W.B.Y."

NOTES

Samhain, October.
Reprinted in *The Irish Dramatic Movement* in the *Collected Works*, Vol. IV, 1908; and in *Plays and Controversies*, 1925.

CATHLEEN-NI-HOOLIHAN

Samhain, October.
Reprinted separately in book form, 1902; and in *Plays for an Irish Theatre*, Vol. II, 1904.

THE FREEDOM OF THE THEATRE

The United Irishman, November 1.

ADAM'S CURSE

The Monthly Review, December.
Reprinted in *The Gael* (New York), February 1903; and in *In the Seven Woods*, 1903.

FAVOURITE BOOKS OF 1902

(Contribution to a symposium)
The Academy, December 6.
Reprinted in *The Letters of W. B. Yeats*, 1954.

1903

THE OLD MEN ADMIRING THEMSELVES IN THE WATER

The Pall Mall Magazine, January.
Reprinted in *The Gael* (New York), September 1903; and in *In the Seven Woods*, 1903.

THE HAPPIEST OF THE POETS

The Fortnightly Review, March.
Reprinted in *Ideas of Good and Evil*, 1903.

POETS AND DREAMERS

The New Liberal Review, March.
Reprinted, under the title *The Galway Plains*, in *Ideas of Good and Evil*, 1903.

THE OLD AGE OF QUEEN MAEVE

The Fortnightly Review, April.
Reprinted in *The Gael* (New York), June 1903; and in *In the Seven Woods*, 1903.

[CATHLEEN, THE DAUGHTER OF HOOLIHAN]

A Broad Sheet, April.
Reprinted, under the title *The Song of Red Hanrahan*, in *In the Seven Woods*, 1903.

THE REFORM OF THE THEATRE

The United Irishman, April 4.
Reprinted, with additions, in *Samhain*, September 1903; in *The Irish Dramatic Movement*, in the *Collected Works*, Vol. IV, 1908; and in *Plays and Controversies*, 1925.

EMOTION OF MULTITUDE

The All Ireland Review, April 11.
Reprinted in *Ideas of Good and Evil*, 1903.

A CANONICAL BOOK

(Review of *Poets and Dreamers* by Lady Gregory)
The Bookman, May.

IRISH PLAYS AND PLAYERS

(A letter)
The Academy, May 16.

THE LAND OF HEART'S DESIRE

(Revised version)
The Bibelot (Portland, Maine), June.
Reprinted in volume form by T. B. Mosher, July 1903 and in many later editions.

THE HAPPY TOWNLAND

The Weekly Critical Review (Paris), June 4.
Reprinted, under the title *The Rider from the North*, in *In the Seven Woods*, 1903; and, under its original title, in *Poems, 1899–1905*, 1906 and subsequent editions.

THE KING'S VISIT

(A letter)
The Freeman's Journal, July 13.
Yeats wrote another letter, about this time, on the same subject and to the same paper, the date of which I have not been able to trace.

[THE KING'S RECEPTION AT MAYNOOTH]

(A letter)
The United Irishman, August 1.
Reprinted in *The Letters of W. B. Yeats*, 1954.

THE HOUR-GLASS. A MORALITY

The North American Review, September.
Printed in pamphlet form for copyright purposes, 1903; reprinted in *Plays for an Irish Theatre*, Vol. II., 1904.

NOTES

Samhain, September.
Reprinted in *The Irish Dramatic Movement*, in the *Collected Works*, Vol. IV., 1908; and in *Plays and Controversies*, 1925.

A POT OF BROTH

The Gael (New York), September.
Reprinted in *Plays for an Irish Theatre*, Vol. II., 1904.

A PROLOGUE

The United Irishman, September 9.
Reprinted in *Plays for an Irish Theatre*, Vol. III., 1904; also in the *Collected Works*, Vol. VIII., 1908.

ANNOUNCEMENT

(Of forthcoming plays by the National Theatre Society)
The United Irishman, September 16.

FLAUBERT AND THE NATIONAL LIBRARY

(A letter)
The Irish Times, October 8.

AN IRISH NATIONAL THEATRE

The United Irishman, October 10.
Reprinted in *The Irish Dramatic Movement,* in the *Collected Works,* Vol. IV., 1908; and in *Plays and Controversies,* 1925.

THE THEATRE, THE PULPIT AND THE NEWSPAPERS

The United Irishman, October 17.
Reprinted in *The Irish Dramatic Movement,* in the *Collected Works,* Vol. IV., 1908; and in *Plays and Controversies,* 1925.

THE IRISH NATIONAL THEATRE AND THREE SORTS OF IGNOR-ANCE

The United Irishman, October 24.

DREAM OF THE WORLD'S END

The Green Sheaf, No. II.

THE LAKE AT COOLE

(Reproduction of a pastel)
The Green Sheaf, No. IV.

RED HANRAHAN

The Independent Review, December.
Reprinted in *Stories of Red Hanrahan,* 1904.

1904

WE ARE UNLIKE THE ENGLISH IN ALL EXCEPT LANGUAGE

The New York Daily News, March 4.
In spite of the title, evidently supplied by an American editor, this is a signed article by Yeats, giving his impressions of the United States at the end of his first visit.

EMMET THE APOSTLE OF IRISH LIBERTY

(A speech delivered at the New York Academy of Music to the Clan-Na-Gael on Sunday, February 28, 1904)
The Gaelic American, March 5.

THE BEST BOOK FROM IRELAND

(A letter)
The Daily News, May 11.

THE IRISH NATIONAL THEATRE

(A letter)
The Gael (New York), June.

[NOTE ON THE PERFORMING RIGHTS OF HIS PLAYS]

The United Irishman, June 4.

THE DRAMATIC MOVEMENT

First Principles. The Play, the Player and the Scene.
Samhain, December.
Reprinted in *The Irish Dramatic Movement* in the *Collected Works*, Vol. IV., 1908; and in *Plays and Controversies*, 1925.

MR. GEORGE MOORE AND THE ROYAL HIBERNIAN ACADEMY

(A letter)
The Dublin Daily Express, December 7.

1905

J. M. SYNGE'S THE SHADOW OF THE GLEN

(Three letters)
The United Irishman, January 28, February 4 and 11.

RED HANRAHAN'S VISION

McClure's Magazine, March.
Reprinted in *Stories of Red Hanrahan*, 1904 (1905).

AMERICA AND THE ARTS

The Metropolitan Magazine, April.

QUEEN EDAINE

McClure's Magazine, September.
Reprinted with an additional verse, under the title *The Praise of Deirdre*, in *The Shanachie*, No. I. Spring, 1906; in *Poems, 1899–1905*, under the title *The Entrance of Deirdre*; under the title *Chorus for a Play*, in the *Poetical Works*, I, 1906; and in *Deirdre*, 1907.

DO NOT LOVE TOO LONG

The Acorn, October.
Reprinted, under the title *O Do not Love Too Long*, in the section *In the Seven Woods*, in the *Collected Works*, Vol. I., 1908.

NOTES AND OPINIONS

Samhain, November.
Reprinted in *The Irish Dramatic Movement* in the *Collected Works*, Vol. IV., 1908; and in *Plays and Controversies*, 1925.

NEVER GIVE ALL THE HEART
> *McClure's Magazine*, December.
> Reprinted, in the section *In the Seven Woods*, in *Poems, 1899–1905*; and in the *Collected Works*, Vol. I., 1908.

1906

AGAINST WITCHCRAFT
> *The Shanachie*, Spring.
> Reprinted, in *On Baile's Strand*, in *Poems, 1899–1905*, 1906, and in the *Poetical Works*, II., 1907.

THE PRAISE OF DEIRDRE
> *The Shanachie*, Spring.
> See *Queen Edaine*, above (1905).

MY THOUGHTS AND MY SECOND THOUGHTS
> I.–X. (Unsigned.)
> *The Gentleman's Magazine*, September and October.
> Reprinted in *Discoveries*, 1907.

LITERATURE AND THE LIVING VOICE
> *The Contemporary Review*, October.
> Reprinted in *Samhain*, 1906; and, in *The Irish Dramatic Movement*, in the *Collected Works*, Vol. IV., 1908; and in *Plays and Controversies*, 1925. Sections III, IV, and V. of the essay appear, under the title *The Work of the National Theatre Society at the Abbey Theatre, Dublin*, in *Poetical Works*, Vol. II., Appendix IV., New York, 1907.

THE SEASON'S WORK
> *The Arrow*, October 20.
> Reprinted, in part, in *The Irish Dramatic Movement*, in the Collected Works, Vol. IV., 1908; and in *Plays and Controversies*, 1925.

A NOTE ON THE MINERAL WORKERS, AND OTHER NOTES
> *The Arrow*, October 20.

MY THOUGHTS AND MY SECOND THOUGHTS
> XI.–XVII. (Unsigned.)
> *The Gentleman's Magazine*, November.
> Reprinted in *Discoveries*, 1907.

NOTES ON DEIRDRE AND THE SHADOWY WATERS
> *The Arrow*, November 24.

A A

NOTES

Samhain, December.

1907

THE CONTROVERSY OVER THE PLAYBOY

MR. YEATS'S OPENING SPEECH AT THE DEBATE ON FEBRUARY 4TH, AT THE ABBEY THEATRE

The Arrow, February 23.
Both reprinted, in part, in *The Irish Dramatic Movement* in the *Collected Works*, Vol. IV., 1908; and in *Plays and Controversies*, 1925.

NOTES

The Arrow, June 1.
Reprinted in part, under the title *On Taking 'The Playboy' to London*, in *The Irish Dramatic Movement*, in the *Collected Works*, Vol. IV., 1908; and in *Plays and Controversies*, 1925.

DISCOVERIES

The Shanachie, October.
Reprinted in *Discoveries*, 1907.

[A CORINTHIAN CLUB DINNER]

(A letter)
The Leader (Dublin), November 30.

1908

W. FAY'S RESIGNATION

(A letter)
The Dublin Evening Mail, January 14.

THE ABBEY THEATRE

(Two letters)
The Dublin Evening Mail, January 16 and 18.

A CORRECTION

(A letter)
The Dublin Evening Mail, January 17.

MR. W. FAY AND THE ABBEY THEATRE

(A letter)
The Dublin Evening Mail, May 21.

A DREAM

(A poem, with a note in prose.) Dated July 3rd.
The Nation (London), July 11.
Reprinted, under the title *His Dream*, in *The Green Helmet and other poems*, 1910.
The note, which was not reprinted, read: 'A few days ago I dreamed that I was steering a very gay and elaborate ship upon some narrow water with many people upon its banks, and that there was a figure upon a bed in the middle of the ship. The people were pointing to the figure and questioning, and in my dream I sang verses which faded as I awoke, all but this fragmentary thought, "We call it, it has such dignity of limb, by the sweet name of Death." I have made my poem out of my dream and the sentiment of my dream, and can almost say, as Blake did, "The Authors are in Eternity." '

EVENTS

Samhain, November.

FIRST PRINCIPLES

Samhain, November.

1909

THREE POEMS

I. *On a Recent Government Appointment in Ireland.* II. *Galway Races.* III. *Distraction.*
The English Review, February.
II. and III. were reprinted, under the titles *At Galway Races* and *All Things can Tempt Me*, in *The Green Helmet and other poems*, 1910; I. was reprinted, under the title *An Appointment*, in *Responsibilities*, 1914.

THE ART OF J. M. SYNGE

(A letter, dated Abbey Theatre, Dublin, Apr. 6, 1909)
The Nation (London), April 10.
Reprinted in *The Letters of W. B. Yeats*, 1954.

MR. SHAW'S PLAY [*The Showing-Up of Blanco Posnet*]

(Two letters signed by W. B. Yeats and Lady Gregory)
The Irish Times, August 23.
Reprinted in *Modern Drama*, May 1966.

THE RELIGION OF BLANCO POSNET

The Arrow, August 25.

THE SHOWING-UP OF BLANCO POSNET

> (A letter signed by W. B. Yeats and Lady Gregory)
> *The Irish Times*, August 27.
> Reprinted in *Modern Drama*, May 1966.

1910

THE IRISH NATIONAL THEATRE

> (A letter, signed by Lady Gregory and W. B. Yeats)
> *The Times*, June 16.
> This letter also appeared elsewhere in the London Press and under the title The Future of the Abbey Theatre in *The Irish Independent*, June 16.
> Reprinted in *Modern Drama*, May 1966.

THE ART OF THE THEATRE

> (Contribution to a symposium)
> *The New Age*, June 16.

THE TRAGIC THEATRE

> *The Mask* (Florence), October.
> Reprinted, in part, as Preface to *Plays for an Irish Theatre*, 1911; and in *The Cutting of an Agate*, 1919.

YOUTH AND AGE

> *McClure's Magazine*, December.
> Reprinted, under the title *The Coming of Wisdom with Time*, in *The Green Helmet and other poems*, 1910.

TO A CERTAIN COUNTRY HOUSE IN TIME OF CHANGE

> *McClure's Magazine*, December.
> Reprinted, under the title *Upon a Threatened House*, in *The Green Helmet and other poems*, 1910.

CONTEMPORARY POETRY

> (Extensive extracts from a lecture delivered in Memorial Hall, Manchester, October 31, 1910)
> *The Path*, December.

1911

THE FOLLY OF ARGUMENT

> (Four extracts from a Diary, with a short introduction)
> *The Manchester Playgoer*, June.
> Three of the extracts were reprinted in *Estrangement*, 1926.

JOHN SHAWE-TAYLOR

> *The Observer*, July 2.
> Reprinted in *The Cutting of an Agate*, 1912.

J. M. SYNGE AND THE IRELAND OF HIS TIME

> *The Forum*, August.
> Printed as a separate volume by the Cuala Press, 1911.

THE GREEN HELMET, AN HEROIC FARCE

> *The Forum*, September.
> Already printed in *The Green Helmet and other poems*, 1910.

THE THEATRE OF BEAUTY

> (An address delivered before the Dramatic Club of Harvard
> University)
> *Harper's Weekly*, November 11.

ON THOSE WHO DISLIKE THE PLAYBOY

> *The Irish Review*, December.
> Reprinted, under the title *The Attack on the "Play Boy"*, in *The
> Green Helmet and other poems* (New York), 1912.

1912

THE STORY OF THE IRISH PLAYERS. WHAT WE TRY TO DO

> *The Sunday Record-Herald* (Chicago), February 4.

THE HAPPIEST OF THE POETS

> (Reprinted from *Ideas of Good and Evil*)
> *The Bibelot*, Vol. 18, pp. 112–128, April.

STAGE SCENERY

> (A letter dated Sept. 11)
> *The Times*, September 13.

AT THE ABBEY THEATRE. IMITATED FROM RONSARD

> *The Irish Review*, December.
> Already printed in *The Green Helmet and other poems* (New York),
> 1912.

THE REALISTS

> *Poetry* (Chicago), December.
> Reprinted in *Responsibilities*, 1914.

THE MOUNTAIN TOMB

Poetry (Chicago), December.
Reprinted in *A Selection from the Poetry of W. B. Yeats*, Tauchnitz edition, 1913; in *The Quest*, April 1913; and in *Responsibilities*, 1914.

TO A CHILD DANCING UPON THE SHORE

Poetry (Chicago), December.
Reprinted, under the title *To a Child dancing in the Wind*, in *A Selection from the Poetry of W. B. Yeats*, Tauchnitz edition. 1913; and in *Responsibilities*, 1914.

LOVE AND THE BIRD

Poetry (Chicago), December.
Reprinted, under the title *A Memory of Youth*, in *Responsibilities*, 1914.

FALLEN MAJESTY

Poetry (Chicago), December.
Reprinted in *A Selection from the Poetry of W. B. Yeats*, Tauchnitz edition, 1913; and in *Responsibilities*, 1914.

1913

THE GIFT

The Irish Times, January 8.
Reprinted, under the title *To a Wealthy Man who promised a second subscription if it were proved the people wanted pictures*, in *Poems Written in Discouragement*, 1913, and, under the title *To a Wealthy Man who promised a second subscription to the Dublin Municipal Gallery if it were proved the people wanted pictures*, in *Responsibilities*, 1914.

SYNGE. BY LADY GREGORY

Includes a passage from Yeats's diary and some excerpts from his letters.
The English Review, March.
The passage from the diary is reprinted, under the title "Detractions," in *The Death of Synge*, 1928, and in *Dramatis Personae*, 1936.

THE MUNICIPAL ART GALLERY

(A letter)
The Irish Times, March 18.
Reprinted in *The Letters of W. B. Yeats*, 1954.

THE GREY ROCK

> *The British Review*, April, and *Poetry* (Chicago), April.
> Reprinted in *Responsibilities*, 1914.

THE HOUR GLASS

> *With a Preface to the New Version*
> *The Mask* (Florence) April.
> Privately printed, without the Preface, in 1914; included in
> *Responsibilities*, 1914; and in *Plays in Prose and Verse*, 1922.

THE THREE HERMITS

> *The Smart Set*, September.
> Privately printed in *Nine Poems* (1914); included in *Responsibilities*, 1914.

ROMANCE IN IRELAND

> *The Irish Times*, September 8.
> Reprinted, under the title *September, 1913*, in *Poems Written in Discouragement*, 1913; under the title *Romantic Ireland (September, 1913)* in *Nine Poems*, 1914; and under the title *September, 1913* in *Responsibilities*, 1914.

THE TWO KINGS

> *The British Review*, October, and *Poetry* (Chicago), October.
> Reprinted in *Responsibilities*, 1914.

DUBLIN FANATICISM

> *The Irish Worker*, November 1.

MR. W. B. YEATS AND GHOSTS

> (A letter)
> *The Irish Times*, November 3.

THE THREE BEGGARS

> *Harper's Weekly*, November 15.
> Reprinted in *Responsibilities*, 1914.

"THE PLAYBOY" AT LIVERPOOL

> (Two letters)
> *The Times*, December 1 and 4.

1914

A WORD FROM MR. YEATS

(Excerpts from two letters)
Poetry (Chicago), January.
Reprinted in *A Poet's Life* by Harriet Monroe, 1938; and in *The Letters of W. B. Yeats*, 1954.

NOTORIETY

The New Statesman, February, 7.
Reprinted, without title, in *Responsibilities*, 1914.

POETRY'S BANQUET

(Yeats's speech to the Poetry Society of Chicago quoted at length)
Poetry (Chicago), April.
Reprinted in *A Poet's Life* by Harriet Monroe, 1938.

POEMS: TO A FRIEND WHOSE WORK HAS COME TO NOTHING; PAUDEEN; TO A SHADE; WHEN HELEN LIVED; BEGGAR TO BEGGAR CRIED; THE WITCH; THE PEACOCK; RUNNING TO PARADISE; THE PLAYER QUEEN (SONG FROM AN UNFINISHED PLAY); TO A CHILD DANCING IN THE WIND; THE MAGI; A COAT

Poetry (Chicago), May.

The first three already printed in *Poems Written in Discouragement*, 1913; all reprinted in *Responsibilities*, 1914.

PAUDEEN; TO A SHADE

The New Statesman, May 9.
Already printed in *Poems Written in Discouragement*, 1913; reprinted in *Responsibilities*, 1914.

THE MAGI

The New Statesman, May 9.
Reprinted in *Responsibilities*, 1914.

ART AND IDEAS

The New Weekly, June 20 and 27.
Reprinted in the section *The Cutting of an Agate*, in *Essays*, 1924.

1915

THOMAS DAVIS
New Ireland, July 17.
Reprinted as a pamphlet, 1947.

1916

POEMS: THE DAWN; ON WOMAN; THE FISHERMAN; THE HAWK;
MEMORY; THE THORN TREE; THE PHOENIX; THERE IS
A QUEEN IN CHINA
Poetry (Chicago), February.
Reprinted in *Form*, April 1916, and issued separately as a
pamphlet, 1916; included in *The Wild Swans at Coole*, 1917, *The
Thorn Tree* under the title *Her Praise*; *The Phoenix* under the
title *The People*; and *There is a Queen in China* under the title *His
Phoenix*.

THE SCHOLARS
Poetry (Chicago), February.
Already printed in *Catholic Anthology*, 1915; included in *The
Wild Swans at Coole*, 1917.

CERTAIN NOBLE PLAYS OF JAPAN
Drama, November.
This had already appeared as introduction to the Cuala Press
volume of the same title, September 16, 1916; included in *The
Cutting of an Agate*, 1919.

A CHANCE FOR THE NATIONAL GALLERY. IRELAND AND SIR
HUGH LANE
(Signed Y.)
The Observer, December 10.
I believe this to be written by Yeats.

SIR HUGH LANE'S PICTURES
(A letter, dated December 18.)
The Morning Post, December 19.

SIR HUGH LANE'S PICTURES
(A letter)
The Spectator, December 23.

THE HUGH LANE PICTURES
(A letter)
The Observer, December 24.

SIR HUGH LANE'S PICTURES

(A letter)
The Times, December 28.

1917

SIR HUGH LANE'S PICTURES. MR. W. B. YEATS'S REPLY

The Observer, January 21.
Passages from this article are reprinted in *Hugh Lane's Life and Achievement* by Lady Gregory, 1921; the complete text is reprinted in *The Letters of W. B. Yeats*, 1954.

AT THE HAWK'S WELL OR WATERS OF IMMORTALITY

With a Preface
Harper's Bazaar, March.
The play alone was printed in *To-Day* (London), June 1917.
Reprinted, under the title *At the Hawk's Well*, in *The Wild Swans at Coole*, 1917; in *Four Plays for Dancers*, 1921; and in *Plays and Controversies*, 1923.

INSTEAD OF A THEATRE

To-Day (London), May.
This essay had previously appeared as a Preface to *At the Hawk's Well* in *Harper's Bazar*, March 1917. Reprinted, under the title *A Note on 'At the Hawk's Well'*, in *The Wild Swans at Coole*, 1917; in *Four Plays for Dancers*, 1921; and in *Plays and Controversies*, 1923. The essay was also reprinted in *Theatre Arts Magazine* (Detroit), January 1919; and about half of it was reprinted in *Theatre Arts Monthly* (New York), April 1939.

POEMS: THE WILD SWANS AT COOLE; PRESENCES; MEN IMPROVE WITH THE YEARS; A DEEP SWORN VOW; THE COLLAR-BONE OF A HARE; BROKEN DREAMS; IN MEMORY

The Little Review, June.
Reprinted in *The Wild Swans at Coole*, 1917.

UPON A DYING LADY

(Seven Poems)
The Little Review, August; *The New Statesman*, August 11.
Reprinted in *The Wild Swans at Coole*, 1917.

THE BALLOON OF THE MIND; TO A SQUIRREL AT KYLE-NA-GNO

The New Statesman, September 29.
Reprinted in *The Wild Swans at Coole*, 1917.

EGO DOMINUS TUUS

Poetry (Chicago), October; *The New Statesman*, November 17.
Reprinted in *The Wild Swans at Coole*, 1917.

1918

DUBLIN AND THE HUGH LANE PICTURES

(A letter)
The Observer, February 3.

MAJOR ROBERT GREGORY. A NOTE OF APPRECIATION

The Observer, February 17.
Reprinted in *The Little Review*, November 1918.

WILLIAM BLAKE AND HIS SCHOOL

The Irish Times, April 15, 1918.
Report of a lecture given by Yeats at the Abbey Theatre on
Sunday, April 14, 1918.

IRISH WRITERS PROTEST [*against conscription*]

(A letter signed by W. B. Yeats, Lady Gregory, James Stephens,
Douglas Hyde)
The Evening Telegraph (Dublin), May 22.

IN MEMORY OF ROBERT GREGORY

The English Review, August; *The Little Review*, September.
Reprinted, under the title *In Memory of Major Robert Gregory*,
in *The Wild Swans at Coole*, 1919.

SEVEN POEMS: TO A YOUNG GIRL; A SONG; SOLOMON TO
SHEBA; THE LIVING BEAUTY; UNDER THE ROUND TOWER;
TOM O'ROUGHLEY; A PRAYER ON GOING INTO MY HOUSE

The Little Review, October.
Privately printed in *Nine Poems*, 1918; included in *The Wild
Swans at Coole*, 1919.

1919

THE DREAMING OF THE BONES

The Little Review, January.
Reprinted in *Two Plays for Dancers*, 1919; in *Four Plays for
Dancers*, 1921; and in *Plays and Controversies*, 1923.

THE ONLY JEALOUSY OF EMER

Poetry (Chicago), January.
Reprinted in *Two Plays for Dancers*, 1919; in *Four Plays for
Dancers*, 1921; and in *Plays and Controversies*, 1923.

IF I WERE FOUR-AND-TWENTY

> *The Irish Statesman*, August 23 and 30.
> Reprinted in *The Living Age*, October 4, 1920; and in *If I were Four-and-Twenty*, 1940.

A PRAYER FOR MY DAUGHTER

> *The Irish Statesman*, November 8; *Poetry* (Chicago), November.
> Reprinted in *Michael Robartes and the Dancer*, 1920.

A PEOPLE'S THEATRE. A LETTER TO LADY GREGORY

> *The Irish Statesman*, November 29 and December 6.
> Reprinted in *The Dial*, April 1920; included in the section *The Irish Dramatic Movement*, in *Plays and Controversies*, 1923.

1920

EASTER, 1916

> *The New Statesman*, October 23; *The Dial*, November.
> This poem had been previously printed privately, 1916; it is included in *Michael Robartes and the Dancer*, 1920.

MICHAEL ROBARTES AND THE DANCER; UNDER SATURN; SIXTEEN DEAD MEN; DEMON AND BEAST

> *The Dial*, November.
> Reprinted in *Michael Robartes and the Dancer*, 1920.

THE ROSE TREE

> *The Dial*, November; *The Nation* (London), November 6.
> Reprinted in *Michael Robartes and the Dancer*, 1920.

THE SECOND COMING; AN IMAGE FROM A PAST LIFE

> *The Nation* (London), November 6; *The Dial*, November.
> Reprinted in *Michael Robartes and the Dancer*, 1920.

A MEDI[T]ATION IN TIME OF WAR; TOWARDS BREAK OF DAY; ON A POLITICAL PRISONER

> *The Dial*, November; *The Nation* (London), November 13.
> Reprinted in *Michael Robartes and the Dancer*, 1920.

1921

ALL SOULS' NIGHT

> *The London Mercury*, March; *The New Republic*, March 9.
> Reprinted in *Seven Poems and a Fragment*, 1922; and in *The Tower*, 1928.

SIR HUGH LANE AND THE NATIONAL GALLERY
> (A letter)
> *The Times Literary Supplement*, March 31.

FOUR YEARS
> *The London Mercury* and in *The Dial*, June, July and August.
> Reprinted in *Four Years*, 1921; in *The Trembling of the Veil*,
> 1922; and in *Autobiographies*, 1926.

THOUGHTS UPON THE PRESENT STATE OF THE WORLD
> *The Dial*, September.
> Reprinted in *Seven Poems and a Fragment*, 1922; and, under the
> title *Nineteen Hundred and Nineteen*, in *The Tower*, 1928.

1922

MORE MEMORIES
> *The London Mercury*, May to August; *The Dial*, May to October.
> Reprinted in *The Trembling of the Veil*, 1922; and in *Auto-
> biographies*, 1926.

THE PLAYER QUEEN
> *The Dial*, November.
> Reprinted in *Plays in Prose and Verse*, 1922; and as a separate
> volume, 1922.

MY INTERVIEW WITH MR. YEATS. BY JUNZŌ SATŌ.
> *The Osaka Mainichi* [newspaper], Osaka, Japan, December 4.

1923

MEDITATIONS IN TIME OF CIVIL WAR
> (Seven poems)
> *The London Mercury* and in *The Dial*, January.
> Reprinted in *The Cat and the Moon and Certain Poems*, 1924; and
> in *The Tower*, 1928.

MISS SARA ALLGOOD
> (A letter)
> *The Irish Times*, January 19.
> Reprinted in *Threshold*. Autumn 1965; and in *Modern Drama*,
> May 1966.

A BIOGRAPHICAL FRAGMENT, WITH SOME NOTES
> *The Criterion* and in *The Dial*, July.
> Reprinted in *Autobiographies*, 1926.

1924

THE GIFT OF HAROUN EL RASHID

English Life and The Illustrated Review, January; *The Dial*, June.
Reprinted in *The Cat and the Moon and Certain Poems*, 1924; and in *The Tower*, 1928.

LEDA AND THE SWAN

The Dial, June; *To-Morrow* (Dublin), August.
Reprinted in *The Cat and the Moon and Certain Poems*, 1924; and in *The Tower*, 1928.

THE LOVER SPEAKS. THE HEART REPLIES

The Dial, June.
Reprinted in *The Cat and the Moon and Certain Poems*, 1924; and, the two poems under the single title *Owen Ahern and his Dancers*, in *The Tower*, 1928.

THE CAT AND THE MOON

The Criterion and in *The Dial*, July.
Reprinted in *The Cat and the Moon and Certain Poems*, 1924; in *Wheels and Butterflies*, 1934; and in *Collected Plays*, 1934.

A MEMORY OF SYNGE

The Irish Statesman, July 5.

TO ALL ARTISTS AND WRITERS

A manifesto, signed H. Stuart, Cecil Salkeld.
To-Morrow (Dublin), August.
Reprinted in *Yeats The Man and the Masks* by Richard Ellmann, New York, 1948, London, 1949. A note definitely ascribes this to Yeats, on the authority of Mrs. Stuart.

COMPULSORY GAELIC: A DIALOGUE

The Irish Statesman, August 2.
Reprinted in *The Living Age*, September 13, 1924.

THE BOUNTY OF SWEDEN

The London Mercury, and in *The Dial*, September.
Reprinted in *The Bounty of Sweden*, 1925; and in *Dramatis Personae*, 1936.

AN OLD POEM RE-WRITTEN

(New version, with a prefatory note, of *The Dedication to a Book of Stories Selected from the Irish Novelists*)
The Irish Statesman, November 8.
Reprinted in *Early Poems and Stories*, 1925.

1925

AN UNDELIVERED SPEECH

(On Divorce)
The Irish Statesman, March 14.
A synopsis of this speech was printed in Marion Witt's article
' "Great Art Beaten Down": Yeats on Censorship' in *College
English*, February 1952; it was printed in full in *The Senate
Speeches of W. B. Yeats*, 1960. (No. 211r)

THE BOUNTY OF SWEDEN

(A letter)
The Sunday Times, August 9.

THE CHILD AND THE STATE

(A speech)
The Irish Statesman, December 5 and 12.

1926

THE NEED FOR AUDACITY OF THOUGHT

The Dial, February.
Reprinted, under the title *Our Need for Religious Sincerity*, in
The Criterion, April 1926.

MORE SONGS FROM AN OLD COUNTRYMAN

(Four poems)
The London Mercury, April.
Reprinted, under the title *The Old Countryman*, in *October
Blast*, 1927; and, under the title *A Man Young and Old*, in *The
Tower*, 1928.

A DEFENCE OF THE ABBEY THEATRE

(A speech reconstituted from memory)
The Dublin Magazine, April–June.

THE HUGH LANE PICTURES. DUBLIN'S CHANCE

(A letter, dated July 26, signed W. B. Yeats, A. Gregory)
The Times, July 29.

ESTRANGEMENT: THOUGHTS FROM A DIARY KEPT IN 1909

The London Mercury, October and November. Also, under the
title *Estrangement: Being some Fifty Thoughts from a Diary*, in
The Dial, November.

Reprinted in *Estrangement*, 1926; and in *Dramatis Personae*, 1936.

1927

FOUR SONGS FROM THE YOUNG COUNTRYMAN

The London Mercury, May.
Reprinted, under the title *The Young Countryman*, in *October Blast*, 1927; and, under the title *A Man Young and Old*, in *The Tower*, 1928.

TWO SONGS FROM THE OLD COUNTRYMAN

The London Mercury, May.
Reprinted, under the title *The Old Countryman*, in *October Blast*; and, under the title *A Man Young and Old*, in *The Tower*, 1928.

A LETTER AND PHOTOGRAPHS TO SHŌTARŌ OSHIMA

Eigo kenkyu (The Study of English), Tokyo, May.

THE RESURRECTION

The Adelphi, June.
Two songs from this play were reprinted in *October Blast*, 1927; and in *The Tower*, 1928. The play, in a rewritten version, appeared in *Stories of Michael Robartes*, 1931; in *Wheels and Butterflies*, 1934; and in *Collected Plays*, 1934.

THE TOWER

The Criterion, June; *The New Republic*, June 29.
Reprinted in *October Blast*, 1927; and in *The Tower*, 1928.

AMONG SCHOOL CHILDREN

The London Mercury, and in *The Dial*, August.
Reprinted in *October Blast*, 1927; and in *The Tower*, 1928.

1928

SAILING TO BYZANTIUM

The Exile, Spring.
Already printed in *October Blast*, 1927; included in *Stories of Red Hanrahan*, 1927, and in *The Tower*, 1928.

BLOOD AND THE MOON

The Exile, Spring.
Reprinted in *The Winding Stair*, 1929.

THE DEATH OF SYNGE AND OTHER PASSAGES FROM AN OLD DIARY

The London Mercury, and in *The Dial*, April.
Reprinted in volume form, 1928; included in *Dramatis Personae*, 1936.

MR. YEATS'S LETTER TO SEAN O'CASEY ABOUT "THE SILVER TASSIE"

(Dated April 20, 1928)
The Observer, June 3.
Reprinted in *The Literary Digest*, August 4, 1928; and in *The Letters of W. B. Yeats*, 1954.

THE ABBEY DIRECTORS AND MR. SEAN O'CASEY

(Five letters signed by Yeats: (1) June 4 to the Editor; (2) April 20 and (3) April 25 to Lady Gregory; (4) April 20 and (5) May 4 to Sean O'Casey) *The Irish Statesman*, June 9.
Reprinted in *Modern Drama*, May 1966. The letter of April 20 is the only one included in *The Letters of W. B. Yeats*, 1954.
[See the item immediately above].

THE CENSORSHIP AND ST. THOMAS AQUINAS

The Irish Statesman, September 22.

IRISH CENSORSHIP

The Spectator, September 29.

WAGNER AND THE CHAPEL OF THE GRAIL

(A letter)
The Irish Statesman, October 13.

1929

A RECENT LETTER FROM MR. W. B. YEATS. BY SHŌTARŌ OSHIMA

Ei-bungaku kenkyu (Studies in English Literature), Tokyo, March.

THREE THINGS

The New Republic, October 2.
Reprinted separately, 1929; in *Words for Music Perhaps*, 1932; and in *The Winding Stair*, 1933.
B B

1930

SEVEN POEMS: GIRL'S SONG; YOUNG MAN'S SONG; HER
DREAM; HIS BARGAIN; HER ANXIETY; HIS CONFIDENCE;
LOVE'S LONELINESS

The New Republic, October 22.
Reprinted, arranged in different order, in *Words for Music Perhaps*, 1932; and in *The Winding Stair*, 1933.

EIGHT POEMS: A SONG FOR MUSIC; LOVE'S LONELINESS; HER
DREAM; HIS BARGAIN; MEDITATIONS UPON DEATH;
CRAZY JANE AND THE DANCERS; CRAZY JANE AND
THE BISHOP; CRAZY JANE REPROVED

The London Mercury, November.
Meditations upon Death had already appeared in *A Packet for
Ezra Pound*, 1929. Reprinted in *Words for Music Perhaps*, 1932,
the first poem under the title *Those Dancing Days are Gone*, the
fifth under the titles *A Meditation written during Sickness at
Algeciras* and *Mohini Chatterji;* the sixth under the title *Crazy
Jane grown old looks at the Dancers*. Reprinted also, with two
titles slightly altered, in *The Winding Stair*, 1933.

FOUR POEMS: A SONG FOR MUSIC; CRACKED MARY AND
THE BISHOP; CRACKED MARY AND THE DANCERS;
CRACKED MARY REPROVED

The New Republic, November 12.
Reprinted in *Words for Music Perhaps*, 1932; and in *The Winding
Stair*, 1933. In the titles "Cracked Mary" becomes "Crazy Jane";
for other changed titles see above.

1931

MEDITATIONS UPON DEATH

The New Republic, January 14.
See note above under *Eight Poems* in *The London Mercury*,
November 1930.

THE WORDS UPON THE WINDOW PANE: A COMMENTARY

The Dublin Magazine, October–December 1931 and January–
March 1932.
Reprinted in *The Words upon the Window Pane*, 1934; and in
Wheels and Butterflies, 1934. The verse, from the October–

December issue, is reprinted, under the title *Swift's Epitaph* in *Words for Music Perhaps*, 1932, and "Fragments. I." in *Collected Poems*, 1933.

1932

IRELAND, 1921–1931

The Spectator, January 30.
Reprinted in *Spectator's Gallery*, 1933.

MY FRIEND'S BOOK

The Spectator, April 9.
Reprinted in *Spectator's Gallery*, 1933, and in *Essays 1931 to 1936*, 1937.

INTRODUCTION TO FIGHTING THE WAVES

The Dublin Magazine, April–June.
Reprinted in *Wheels and Butterflies*, 1934.

REMORSE FOR INTEMPERATE SPEECH

The Spectator, November 18.
Reprinted in *Words for Music Perhaps*, 1932; in *Spectator's Gallery*, 1933; and in *The Winding Stair*, 1933.

FOR ANNE GREGORY; SYMBOLS; SWIFT'S EPITAPH

The Spectator, December 2.
Reprinted, the first poem under the title *Anne Gregory*, in *Words for Music Perhaps*, 1932; in *Spectator's Gallery*, 1933; and in *The Winding Stair*, 1933.

1933

PLAIN MAN'S "OEDIPUS"

The New York Times, January 15.

[AWARD OF PRIZES FOR POETRY]

(A letter to W. T. H. Howe)
The Gypsy (Cincinnati), March.

PROMETHEUS UNBOUND

The Spectator, March 17.
Reprinted in *Essays 1931 to 1936*, 1937.

CENSORSHIP

(A letter)
Time and Tide, May 27.
Reprinted in *The Irish Times*, May 20, 1963; in *Threshold*,
August 1965; and in *Modern Drama*, May 1966.

THE GREAT BLASKET

(Review of *Twenty Years a-Growing* by Maurice O'Sullivan)
The Spectator, June 2.

1934

THREE SONGS TO THE SAME TUNE

The Spectator, February 23; and in *Poetry* (Chicago), December.
Reprinted in *The King of the Great Clock Tower*, 1934; and in
A Full Moon in March, 1935.

THE GROWTH OF A POET

(A broadcast lecture)
The Listener, April 4. [see item 4, p. 469]

LOUIS LAMBERT

The London Mercury, July.
Reprinted in *Essays 1931 to 1936*, 1937.

INITIATION ON A MOUNTAIN

The Criterion, July.
With slight rearrangement of the numbered sections this was
later used as the introduction to *The Holy Mountain* (No. 282).

THE ABBEY THEATRE AND THE FREE STATE. A MISUNDER-
STANDING CORRECTED

(A letter)
The Sunday Times, October 7.

A PARNELLITE AT PARNELL'S FUNERAL. FORTY YEARS LATER.

The Spectator, October 19.
The first part reprinted, under the same title, in *The King of the
Great Clock Tower*, 1934, the third stanza having already
appeared in the Introduction to *Fighting the Waves*, in *The
Dublin Magazine*, April–June 1932; and, under the title *Parnell's
Funeral*, in *A Full Moon in March*, 1935. The second part
included without title in the Commentary on *A Parnellite at
Parnell's Funeral*, in *The King of the Great Clock Tower*, 1934;
and as *Parnell's Funeral*. II. in *A Full Moon in March* 1935.

THE KING OF THE GREAT CLOCK TOWER

Life and Letters, November.
Reprinted in volume form, 1934.

OLD AGE

The Spectator, November 2.
Reprinted without title in *The King of the Great Clock Tower,*
1934; and, under the title *A Prayer for Old Age,* in *A Full Moon
in March,* 1935.

A VAIN HOPE

The Spectator, November 23.
Reprinted without title in the Postscript to *Commentary on the
Three Songs,* in *The King of the Great Clock Tower,* 1934; and,
under the title *Church and State,* in *A Full Moon in March,* 1935.

COMMENTARY ON THE THREE SONGS

(Including poem *Church and State,* untitled)
Poetry (Chicago), December.
Reprinted in *The King of the Great Clock Tower,* 1934.

SUPERNATURAL SONGS: RIBH AT THE TOMB OF BAILE AND
AILLINN; RIBH PREFERS AN OLDER THEOLOGY; RIBH
CONSIDERS CHRISTIAN LOVE INSUFFICIENT; HE AND SHE;
THE FOUR AGES OF MAN; CONJUNCTIONS; A NEEDLE'S
EYE; MERU.

The London Mercury, and in *Poetry* (Chicago), December.
Reprinted in *The King of the Great Clock Tower,* 1934; and in
A Full Moon in March, 1935.

THE SINGING HEAD AND THE LADY

The Spectator, December 7.
Privately printed, 1934; reprinted without title in the Commentary, in *The King of the Great Clock Tower,* 1934; and without
title in *A Full Moon in March,* 1935.

1935

A FULL MOON IN MARCH

Poetry (Chicago), March.
Reprinted in book form, 1935.

MĀNDOOKYA UPANISHAD WITH AN INTRODUCTION BY WILLIAM BUTLER YEATS

The Criterion, July.
The introduction reprinted, under the title *Introduction to "Mandukya Upanishad,"* in *Essays 1931 to 1936,* 1937.

STATEMENT BY ABBEY DIRECTORS

(A letter signed by W. B. Yeats, Walter Starkie, Lennox Robinson, Richard Hayes, F. R. Higgins, Ernest Blythe)
The Irish Times, September 3.
Reprinted in *Threshold,* August 1965; and in *Modern Drama,* May 1966.

1936

DRAMATIS PERSONÆ

The London Mercury, November and December 1935 and January 1936; and in *The New Republic,* February 26, March 11 and 25, and April 8 and 22.
Reprinted in book form, 1935; and, with three other books, in *Dramatis Personae, 1896–1902,* 1936.

PREFATORY NOTES ON THE AUTHOR

(Margot Ruddock)
The London Mercury, July.
Reprinted, as the first section of the Introduction, in *The Lemon Tree,* 1937.

MODERN POETRY

(A broadcast lecture)
The Listener, October 14.
Reprinted in *The Living Age,* December 1936; as a separate pamphlet, 1936; and in *Essays 1931 to 1936,* 1937.

1937

COME GATHER ROUND ME PARNELLITES

A Broadside, January.
Reprinted in *Essays 1931 to 1936,* 1937; in *New Poems,* 1938; and in *Last Poems and Plays,* 1940.

THE THREE BUSHES

The London Mercury, January.
Reprinted in *A Broadside,* March 1937; in *New Poems,* 1938; and in *Last Poems and Plays,* 1940.

ROGER CASEMENT

The Irish Press, February 2.
Reprinted, in a revised version, and accompanied by a letter
[Mr. Noyes' "Noble Letter"] from W. B. Yeats, in *The Irish Press*,
February 13. Reprinted in *New Poems*, 1938; and in *Last Poems
and Plays*, 1940.

WHAT THEN?

The Erasmian (Dublin), April.
Reprinted in *New Poems*, 1938; and in *Last Poems and Plays*,
1940.

GEORGE II

(A letter)
The Irish Times, May 14.
Reprinted in *Letters on Poetry to Lady Dorothy Wellesley*, 1940;
and in *The Letters of W. B. Yeats*, 1954.

THE CURSE OF CROMWELL

A Broadside, August.
Reprinted in *New Poems*, 1938; and in *Last Poems and Plays*,
1940.

THE PILGRIM

A Broadside, October.
Reprinted in *New Poems*, 1938; and in *Last Poems and Plays*,
1940.

COLONEL MARTIN

A Broadside, December.
Reprinted in *New Poems*, 1938; and in *Last Poems and Plays*,
1940.

1938

FRAGMENTS: THE GREAT DAY; PARNELL; WHAT WAS LOST;
    THE SPUR

The London Mercury, March.
Reprinted in *New Poems*, 1938; and in *Last Poems and Plays*,
1940.

TO A FRIEND

The London Mercury, March; *The Nation* (New York), March 12.
Reprinted in *New Poems*, 1938; and, under the title *To Dorothy
Wellesley*, in *Last Poems and Plays*, 1940.

THE OLD STONE CROSS

The London Mercury, March; *The Nation* (New York), March 12.
Reprinted in *New Poems*, 1938; and in *Last Poems and Plays*, 1940.

THOSE IMAGES; LAPIS LAZULI

The London Mercury, March; *The New Republic*, April 13.
Reprinted in *New Poems*, 1938; and in *Last Poems and Plays*, 1940.

THE WILD OLD WICKED MAN; AN ACRE OF GRASS; ARE YOU CONTENT?; SWEET DANCER

The London Mercury, April; *The Atlantic Monthly*, April.
Reprinted in *New Poems*, 1938; and in *Last Poems and Plays*, 1940.

"I BECAME AN AUTHOR"

The Listener, August 4.

HOUND VOICE; HIGH TALK

The London Mercury, December; *The Nation* (New York), December 10.
Reprinted in *Last Poems and Two Plays*, 1939; and in *Last Poems and Plays*, 1940.

JOHN KINSELLA'S LAMENT FOR MRS. MARY MOORE; THE APPARITIONS; A NATIVITY

The London Mercury, December; *The New Republic*, February 15, 1939.
Reprinted in *Last Poems and Two Plays*, 1939; and in *Last Poems and Plays*, 1940.

1939

MAN AND THE ECHO; THE CIRCUS ANIMAL'S DESERTION; POLITICS

The London Mercury, and in *The Atlantic Monthly*, January.
Reprinted, the first poem under the title *The Man and the Echo*, in *Last Poems and Two Plays*, 1939; and in *Last Poems and Plays*, 1940 where the second poem has ANIMALS' for ANIMAL'S.

UNDER BEN BULBEN

The Irish Times, February 3.
In this issue of the paper there is also given a brief extract from
"W. B. Yeats's Last Letter" (to Dr. Kiernan).
The poem also appeared in *The Irish Independent,* February 3,
and Section VI. of the poem in *The Irish Press,* February 3.
Reprinted in *Last Poems and Two Plays,* 1939; and in *Last
Poems and Plays,* 1940.

NEWS FOR THE DELPHIC ORACLE; A BRONZE HEAD

The London Mercury, March; *The New Republic,* March 22.
Reprinted in *Last Poems and Two Plays,* 1939; and in *Last Poems
and Plays,* 1940.

THE STATUES; LONG LEGGED FLY

The London Mercury, March; *The Nation* (New York), April
15.
Reprinted in *Last Poems and Two Plays,* 1939; and in *Last
Poems and Plays,* 1940.

THREE SONGS TO THE ONE BURDEN

The Spectator, May 26.
Reprinted in *Last Poems and Two Plays,* 1939; and in *Last Poems
and Plays,* 1940.

SOME PASSAGES FROM THE LETTERS OF W. B. YEATS TO A.E.
The Dublin Magazine, July–September.
Reprinted in *The Letters of W. B. Yeats,* 1954.

1940

WILLIE YEATS AND JOHN O'LEARY. BY JOHN S. CRONE

(Four letters from W. B. Yeats)
The Irish Book Lover, November.
Reprinted, with the omission of one postscript, in *The Letters of
W. B. Yeats,* 1954.

LETTERS FROM W. B. YEATS. BY PAMELA HINKSON

The Yale Review, Winter.
The letters included in this article are reprinted in *The Letters of
W. B. Yeats,* 1954.

1941

THE SPECKLED BIRD

(Part of a chapter from an unfinished novel, with notes by
J. M. Hone)
The Bell (Dublin), March.

1946

THE BYZANTINE POEMS OF W. B. YEATS. BY A. NORMAN
JEFFARES.

The Review of English Studies, January.
Contains drafts of 'Sailing to Byzantium' and 'Byzantium.'

YEATS AND THE REVISION OF HIS EARLY VERSE. BY G. D. P.
ALLT

Hermathena, November.
Contains a manuscript version of 'The Sorrow of Love,' and
observations of the style of early poems in manuscript.

1947

TWO UNPUBLISHED LETTERS OF WILLIAM BUTLER YEATS

(To Mario M. Rossi) and further quotations from letters.
Cronos (Ohio State University), Fall.
Two letters and fragments of two others are reprinted from this
article in *The Letters of W. B. Yeats,* 1954.

1948

THE FAYS AT THE ABBEY THEATRE. BY WINIFRED LETTS

The Fortnightly, June.
Contains quotations from several unpublished letters.

"REPRISALS"

(A poem on Robert Gregory)
Rann. An Ulster Quarterly of Poetry. Autumn.
Reprinted in *The Variorum Edition of the Poems of W. B. Yeats,*
1957. (No. 211N)

1950

JOYCE AND YEATS. BY RICHARD ELLMANN

The Kenyon Review, Autumn.
This essay contains a hitherto unpublished Preface by Yeats;
it seems possible that it was intended for *Ideas of Good and Evil,*
1903.

1951

AN INTERVIEW WITH YEATS IN HIS LAST YEARS. BY SHŌTARŌ OSHIMA

Ei-bungaku kenkyu (Studies in English Literature), Tokyo, February.

DIARMUID AND GRANIA

A Play in Three Acts by George Moore and W. B. Yeats. Now first printed with an introductory note by William Becker. The note includes a previously unpublished quatrain titled *On George Moore.*

The Dublin Magazine, April–June.

1952

"GREAT ART BEATEN DOWN": YEATS ON CENSORSHIP. BY MARION WITT

College English, February.

Contains a synopsis of Yeat's "Divorce: An Undelivered Speech," that was printed in full in *The Irish Statesman,* March 14, 1925, and was reprinted in *The Senate Speeches of W. B. Yeats,* 1960.

PHILOSOPHY AND PHANTASY: NOTES ON THE GROWTH OF YEATS'S 'SYSTEM.' BY DONALD PEARCE

University of Kansas City Review, Spring.

Contains references to Yeats's unpublished notebooks.

WILLIAM BUTLER YEATS AT WELLESLEY

The Friends of the Wellesley College Library, July.

Contains several unpublished prose fragments.

1953

SOME LETTERS FROM W. B. YEATS TO JOHN O'LEARY AND HIS SISTER

Edited with notes by Allan Wade.

Bulletin of The New York Public Library, January and February.

Reprinted as a pamphlet, 1953; and in *The Letters of W. B. Yeats,* 1954.

YEATS'S "THE SONG OF THE HAPPY SHEPHERD." BY MARION WITT

Philological Quarterly, January.

Contains a comparison of an early holograph with the published versions.

W. B. YEATS: LETTERS TO MATTHEW RUSSELL, S.J.

Edited with notes by Roger McHugh.
The Irish Monthly, February, March and April.
Reprinted in *The Letters of W. B. Yeats*, 1954.

FIFTY YEARS OF THE CUALA PRESS. BY ERNEST C. MARRINER

Colby Library Quarterly, August.
Contains an unpublished autograph comment by Yeats on the
poems of Lionel Johnson; and an early version of 'Politics'
differing slightly from the version in *The Letters of W. B. Yeats*,
p. 909, and differing markedly from the versions in *The Variorum
Edition of the Poems of W. B. Yeats*. (NO. 211N)

FOURTEEN LETTERS BY W. B. YEATS

Edited by Allan Wade.
Encounter, November.
Reprinted in *The Letters of W. B. Yeats*, 1954.

1955

THE SPECKLED BIRD

(A further section from an unfinished novel, with a note by
Curtis Bradford)
Irish Writing, No. 31. Summer.

1957

YEATS'S THE COUNTRY OF THE YOUNG. BY HAZARD ADAMS

Publications of The Modern Language Association of America,
June.
Contains extracts from the unpublished play 'The Country of
the Young.'

1958

W. B. YEATS: AN UNPUBLISHED LETTER. BY C. G. MARTIN
Notes and Queries, June.

1959

W. B. YEATS & W. J. TURNER, 1935–1937 (WITH UNPUBLISHED
LETTERS). BY H. W. HAUSERMANN
English Studies, August.

1960

YEATS'S BYZANTIUM POEMS: A STUDY OF THEIR DEVELOP-
MENT. BY CURTIS BRADFORD
Publications of The Modern Language Association of America,
March.
Contains early drafts of 'Sailing to Byzantium' and 'Byzantium.'

W. B. YEATS & W. J. TURNER, 1935–1937 (WITH UNPUBLISHED
LETTERS). BY H. W. HAUSERMANN. [continued]
English Studies, August.

AN UNRECORDED YEATS ITEM
The Irish Book, Autumn.
Contains a reprinting of the Lyster Memorial Address (see No.
316A) and an unpublished letter from Yeats to Richard Irvine
Best dated June 21 (1926?).

1961

THE ORDER OF YEATS'S LAST POEMS. BY CURTIS BRADFORD
Modern Language Notes, June.
Contains a listing from Yeats's manuscripts.

VESTIGES OF CREATION. BY THOMAS PARKINSON
The Sewanee Review, Winter.
Contains a comparison of manuscript drafts of 'After Long
Silence' and 'Among School Children' with the published ver-
sions.

A LETTER FROM W. B. YEATS ON RILKE. BY WILLIAM ROSE
German Life and Letters, October.
The letter is dated August 17, 1938.

1962

MANUSCRIPT VERSIONS OF YEATS'S THE COUNTESS CATHLEEN.
BY M. J. SIDNELL
Papers of the Bibliographical Society of America, First Quarter.
Contains early drafts of 'The Countess Cathleen.'

A LITERARY FOUNDLING. ANON
Douglas Library Notes (Queen's University at Kingston, On-
tario), Summer.
Contains an early draft of 'The Sorrow of Love' entitled 'The
Sorrow of the World.'

YEATS AND MAUD GONNE. BY CURTIS BRADFORD

Texas Studies in Literature and Language, Winter.
Contains extracts from the first draft of *Autobiographies*, from 'The Speckled Bird,' and from unpublished manuscripts and journals.

1963

SOME NEW LETTERS FROM W. B. YEATS TO LADY GREGORY.
BY DONALD T. TORCHIANA AND GLENN O'MALLEY

A Review of English Literature, July.
Contains 23 letters; an account of an interview with a reporter for the *Daily News and Leader*; and partial reports of speeches printed in *The Irish Times* for January 25, 1914, in *The Manchester Guardian* for July 15, 1913, and in *The Chicago Tribune* for February 24, 1914.

TWO OF YEATS'S LAST POEMS. BY JON STALLWORTHY

A Review of English Literature, July.
A study of the drafts of 'Long-legged Fly' and 'The Statues.'

TWO LETTERS TO JOHN O'LEARY. EDITED BY LIAM MILLER

The Irish Book, Autumn.
Dated January 24, 1889, and December 26, 1889. Part of the second letter is included in *The Letters of W. B. Yeats*, 1951.

ADDITIONS TO ALLAN WADE'S BIBLIOGRAPHY OF W. B. YEATS.
BY RUSSELL K. ALSPACH

The Irish Book, Autumn.
Lists 82 items by and concerning Yeats that do not appear in Wade.

THE FIRST PRINTING OF W. B. YEATS'S 'WHAT THEN?'. BY ROBIN SKELTON

The Irish Book, Autumn.
Lists the differences between an hitherto unnoticed first printing of 'What Then?' in *The Year's Poetry*, *1936* (see No. 322A) and the final text.

BIBLIOGRAPHICAL NOTES. BY ANN SADDLEMYER AND MICHEÁL Ó HAODHA

The Irish Book, Autumn.
Contains details of Yeats's contributions to *Samhain*, 1909 (see Nos. 244A and 244B) and references to two contributions of Yeats

to periodicals in 1894 and 1901 (*Annual Report of the Belfast Naturalists Field Club* and *Celtia*).

A CORRECTED TYPESCRIPT OF YEATS'S 'EASTER 1916.' BY GEORGE MAYHEW
The Huntington Library Quarterly, November.
A study of a 'first typed copy' of the poem.

WILLIAM BUTLER YEATS AT COLBY COLLEGE. BY RICHARD CARY
Colby Library Quarterly, December.
Contains several unpublished prose fragments.

1964

AS YEATS WAS GOING DOWN GRAFTON STREET. BY DIARMUID BRENNAN
The Listener, February 6.
Contains several unpublished prose fragments.

ENGLISH LITERARY AUTOGRAPHS XLIX: WILLIAM BUTLER YEATS, 1865–1939. BY T. J. BROWN
Book Collector, Spring.
Contains a manuscript version of 'The Rose Tree.'

PROFILES OF A POET. BY GABRIEL FALLON
Modern Drama, December.
Contains records of conversations with Yeats.

AUBREY BEARDSLEY'S DRAWING OF THE "SHADOWS" IN W. B. YEATS'S *THE SHADOWY WATERS*. BY DAVID R. CLARK
Modern Drama, December.
Contains a quotation from an unpublished manuscript of 'The Shadowy Waters.'

MODERN IRELAND. EDITED BY CURTIS BRADFORD
The Massachusetts Review, Winter.
Contains an unpublished address by Yeats to American audiences, 1932–33. Some of the address appeared in 'Commentary on "A Parnellite at Parnell's Funeral," ' in *The King of the Great Clock Tower*, 1934. Reprinted in *Irish Renaissance* (No. 358).

DISCOVERIES: SECOND SERIES. EDITED BY CURTIS BRADFORD
The Massachusetts Review, Winter.
Contains unpublished manuscript material.
Reprinted in *Irish Renaissance* (No. 358).

A FAIR CHANCE OF A DISTURBED IRELAND: W. B. YEATS TO
MRS. J. DUNCAN. EDITED BY JOHN UNTERECKER

The Massachusetts Review, Winter.
Contains unpublished letters.
Reprinted in *Irish Renaissance* (No. 358).

1965

W. B. YEATS 1865–1965 A CENTENARY TRIBUTE

The Irish Times, June 10.
(Contains contributions from W. H. Auden, Eavan Boland, Ruth
Brandt, Sean Brooks, Rachel Burrows, V. C. Clinton-Bradley,
Elizabeth Coxhead, May Craig, Richard Ellman, Padraic Fallon,
T. R. Henn, John Horgan, Norman Jeffares, Patrick Kavanagh,
Brendan Kennelly, A. J. Leventhal, Norah McGuinness, Conor
Cruse O'Brien, Stephen Spender, Terence de Vere White. There
is a selection of letters from 'The Silver Tassie' controversy and
numerous illustrations.)
Remarks of Yeats are quoted on pp. ii, iii, iv; references to con-
versations are on p. iv; and a substitute first-line for 'Sailing to
Byzantium' is on p. iv.

W. B. YEATS—A GENERATION LATER. BY THOMAS MAC-
GREEVY

University Review, Vol. III, No. 8 [October?].
Contains quotations from conversations with Yeats.

LETTERS AND LECTURES OF W. B. YEATS. BY ROBERT
O'DRISCOLL

University Review, Vol. III, No. 8. [October?].
Contains unpublished letters to William Blackwood, Lord
Haldane, and Herbert Grierson. One of the lectures—Yeats's
speech in defence of Synge's *Playboy*—had been published in
The Arrow, February 23, 1907.

'THEATRE BUSINESS, MANAGEMENT OF MEN.' BY RONALD
AYLING

Threshold, Autumn.
Contains six letters: one to Christina Walshe and two to Mrs.
Cherrie Hobart Houghton never before published; one about
Sara Allgood previously printed in *The Irish Times*, January
19, 1924, and reprinted in *Modern Drama*, May 1966; one on
censorship previously printed in *Time and Tide*, May 27, 1933,

reprinted in *The Irish Times*, May 20, 1963, and in *Modern Drama*, May 1966; and one on the Abbey–O'Casey feud printed in *The Irish Statesman*, June 9, 1933, and reprinted in *Modern Drama*, May 1966.

SOME MEMORIES OF W. B. YEATS. BY BRIGIT PATMORE

Texas Quarterly, Winter.
Contains two facsimile pages of Yeats's handprints, and records of conversations with Yeats.

THE GENESIS OF A LYRIC. YEATS'S "THE LAKE ISLE OF INNISFREE." BY TOM MULVANY

Texas Quarterly, Winter.
Contains a facsimile reproduction of that part of Yeats's letter to Katharine Tynan which includes the first version of the poem.

1966

YEATS AND THE LOVE LYRIC. BY THOMAS PARKINSON

James Joyce Quarterly, Winter.
Contains an unpublished letter to Mabel Dickinson.

W. B. YEATS'S 'UNDER BEN BULBEN.' BY JON STALLWORTHY

The Review of English Studies, February.
Contains early drafts of 'Under Ben Bulben.'

W. B. YEATS ON PLAYS AND PLAYERS. BY RONALD AYLING

Modern Drama, May.
Contains ten letters and references to others: two to *The Irish Times*, August 23 and 27, 1909, signed by Yeats and Lady Gregory; one to *The London Times*, June 16, 1910, printed also in *The Irish Independent*, June 16, 1910, signed by Yeats and Lady Gregory; one to *The Irish Times*, January 19, 1924, signed by Yeats; four to *The Irish Statesman*, June 9, 1928, signed by Yeats; one to *Time and Tide*, May 27, 1933, reprinted in *The Irish Times*, May 20, 1963, and in *Threshold*, August 1965, signed by Yeats; one to *The Irish Times*, September 3, 1935, reprinted in *Threshold*, August 1965, signed by Yeats and five other Abbey directors.

PART IV

TRANSLATIONS INTO OTHER LANGUAGES

1. SEPARATE TRANSLATIONS

MÄRCHEN | AUS | IRLANDS GAUEN. | GESAMMELT | VON | W. B. YEATS. | AUS DEM ENGLISCHEN ÜBERSETZT | VON | EUGENIE JACOBI. | [design and rule] | NEUWIED & LEIPZIG. | AUGUST SCHUPP. | 1894

$7\frac{1}{2} \times 5$; pp. iv, 124.

Issued in light blue paper covers, design and lettering in blue on front cover; all edges untrimmed. Published in 1894.

A translation of *Irish Fairy Tales*, 1892. (No. 216.)

The introductory poem and note of acknowledgement are omitted; some of the notes are compressed and others omitted. The note "Authorities on Irish Folklore" is also omitted.

CAITLÍN NÍ UALLACÁIN | DRÁMA NÁISIÚNTA. | AN T-AŦAIR TOMÁS Ó CEALLAIŻ | D'AISTRIŻ Ó'N MBÉARLA. | [rule] | A PLAY | TRANSLATED FROM THE ENGLISH OF W. B. YEATS | BY | REV. THOS. O'KELLY, B.D.. | SUMMERHILL COLLEGE, SLIGO. | [rule] | DUBLIN: M. H. GILL & SON, LIMITED. | [rule] | 1905.

$7\frac{3}{10} \times 4\frac{3}{4}$; pp. 32: comprising title, advertisements on verso, pp. [1–2]; Preface, list of characters on verso, pp. [3–4]; text, pp. [5]–22; Glossary, pp. [23]–30; advertisements, p. [31]; imprint, O'Brien and Ards, Printers, Dublin. Irish Paper. on p. [32].

Issued in green paper covers, lettered in green on front cover; one metal fastener; all edges trimmed.

This translation first appeared in *The United Irishman*, February 11, 18 and 25, March 4 and 11, 1905.

DAS LAND DER SEHNSUCHT. EIN DRAMATISCHES
MÄRCHEN. AUS DEM IRISCHEN VON FRIEDA WEEKLEY UND
ERNST LEOPOLD STAHL. SCHROBSDORFF, DÜSSELDORF 1911.
(Englisches Theater in deutscher Übertragung, Heft 1)
Paper covers. Published price 50 Pfennig.

This is a translation of *The Land of Heart's Desire*, 1894.
I have not seen a copy of this book.

JETHRO BITHELL | TRAD. FRANZ HELLENS | W. B. YEATS
| [ornament *in orange*] | ÉDITIONS DU MASQUE | PARIS |
LIBRAIRIE GÉNÉRALE | DES | SCIENCES, ARTS ET LETTRES | RUE
DANTE, 5 | BRUXELLES | H. LAMERTIN | RUE COUDENBERG, 58.
[1912]

$7\frac{1}{2} \times 5$; pp. 56, comprising 2 pp. blank, title, verso blank; pp. [1-2]
blank; p. [3] W. B. YEATS; p. [4] blank; p. [5] title and design in black;
p. [6] blank; pp. [7-8] Dédicace; text, pp. [9]-49; p [50] blank; p. [51]
Imprimerie; [52] blank.

The only copy of this volume examined had been rebound; the original
binding is not recorded.

Translations

A l'Irlande des temps futurs (incomplete), pp. 12-13
La plainte du vieil invalide, p. 17
A quelques amis, avec qui j'ai parlé près du feu, pp. 22-23
La méditation du vieux pêcheur, pp. 31-32
Violoneux de Dooney, pp. 32-33
Le cœur de la femme, p. 37
Le bonnet et les sonnettes, pp. 38-40
Aedh tells of the Rose in his Heart (title in English), p. 41
Aedh écoute le cri du jonc, p. 42
Hanrahan fait des reproches au courlis, p. 42
He Wishes for the Cloths of Heaven (no title), pp. 43-44
L'Homme qui rêva du pays des Fées, pp. 44-47
L'Ile du lac d'Innisfree, pp. 48-49

ARCYDZIEŁA EUROPEJSKIEJ | POEZYI DRAMA-
TYCZNEJ | W PRZEKŁADZIE JANA KASPROWICZA | TOM II. |
PERCY B. SHELLEY: RODZINA CENCICH—ROBERT BROWNING- |
PIPPA PRZECHODZI, NA BALKONIE—WILLIAM BUTLER YEATS: |
KSIĘŻNICZKA KASIA—ALGERNON CHARLES SWINEBURNE:

ATALANTA W KALYDONIE | [ornament] | LWÓW—MCMXII |
NAKŁADEM TOW. WYDAWNICZEGO | WARSZAWA—E. WENDE
I SPÓŁKA

$9\frac{1}{10} \times 7$; pp. ii, 486.

On p. [49]

WILLIAM BUTLER YEATS [Four fleurons] | KSIĘŻNICZKA KASIA | (THE
COUNTESS CATHLEEN) [Six fleurons]

p. [50] blank; list of characters, verso blank, pp, [51–52]; text of
translation, pp. 53–117; p. [118] blank; notes, pp. 119–121; p. [122]
blank.

Issued in light brown paper covers, lettered in red on front cover.
The copy in the British Museum bears the date stamp November 7,
1912.

ZEN-AKU NO KANNEN (IDEAS OF GOOD AND EVIL).
TRANSLATED INTO JAPANESE BY MAKOTO SANGU. TOUNDO,
TOKYO, MARCH, 1914.

$8 \times 5\frac{1}{2}$; pp. xxxiv, 418: comprising half-title, verso blank, pp. [i-ii];
Portrait of W. B Yeats in collotype, title-page, verso blank, pp.
[iii–iv]; 2 page reproduction in half-tone of a letter from W. B. Yeats
to the translator; Contents, pp. v–viii; Introduction by Yone Noguchi,
pp. ix–xxii; Translator's preface and notes, pp. xxiii–xxxiv; text of
translation, pp. 1–353; notes, pp. 355–410; Bibliography of W. B.
Yeats, pp. 411–416; Colophon, p. [417]; Advertisement, p. [418].

Issued in linen and paper, Irish style, paper label on spine.

I have not seen a copy of this book.

Akagisosho Dai 64 Hen | Uiriamu Batora Ieitsu Saku |
Kurihara Kojo Yaku | [Japanese characters] MABOROSHI
NO UMI (The Shadowy Waters, translated by Kojo
Kurihara.) 1914. 10. [October]

$6 \times 3\frac{11}{16}$; pp. 52: comprising introduction and translation.

I have not seen a copy of this book.

TRAGEDIE | IRLANDESI [in red] | DI | WILLIAM
BUTLER YEATS | VERSIONE PROEMIO E NOTE | DI | CARLO
LINATI | MILANO | STUDIO EDITORIALE LOMBARDO |
MDCCCCXIV

$8\frac{2}{5} \times 5\frac{1}{2}$; pp. xlviii, 140: comprising half-title, verso blank, pp. [i–ii]; title-page, Proprietà letteraria on verso, pp. [iii–iv]; list of plays under English titles, verso blank, pp. [v–vi]; fly-title, verso blank, pp. [vii–viii]; text, pp. ix–xxxix; p. [xl] blank; fly-title, verso blank, pp. [xli–xlii]; text, pp. xliii–xlviii; fly-title, quotation on verso, pp. [1–2]; dedication, list of characters on verso, pp. [3–4]; text, pp. 5–131; p. [132] blank; fly-title, verso blank, pp. [133–134]; list of contents, verso blank, pp. [135–136]; reservation of rights, verso blank, pp. [137–138]; imprint, Finito di stampare in Fabriano da Giuseppe Vedova coi tipi dello Studio Editoriale Lombardo de Milano XXI aprile MCMXIV p. [139]; p. [140] blank. There is a frontispiece portrait of the author by A. Mancini.

Issued in grey paper boards with white linen spine, lettered in red on spine; grey end-papers matching binding; all edges untrimmed. Published in 1914.

Contents

Proemio. William Butler Yeats, sua lirica, suoi drammi e la rinascenza celtico-irlandese. By Carlo Linati.
Bibliografia delle opere di W. B. Yeats
    (A footnote states that this is largely taken from my bibliography of 1908.)
Lady Cathleen (*The Countess Cathleen*)
Visiona di Maggio (*The Land of Heart's Desire*)
Sull'acque Tenebrose (*The Shadowy Waters*)
La Poverella (*Cathleen ni Houlihan*)
The translations are in prose.

ERZÄHLUNGEN UND ESSAYS | von | william butler yeats | übertragen und eingeleitet | von | friedrich eckstein | [swelled rule] | im insel-verlag zu leipzig | 1916

$8\frac{1}{10} \times 5\frac{1}{4}$; pp. 184.

Issued in slate-blue boards with white linen spine; lettered in red and black on front cover and in black on spine; white end-papers; top edges stained yellow, others trimmed. Published in 1916.

Contents

Einleitung des Übersetzers. Dated Wien, 1914.
Die Gesetzestafeln (*The Tables of the Law*)
Die Anbetung der heiligen drei Könige (*The Adoration of the Magi*)

Der Glücklichste unter den Dichtern (The Happiest of the Poets)
Die Philosophie in den Dichtungen Shelleys (The Philosophy of Shelley's
Poetry)
William Blake und die Phantasie (William Blake and the Imagination)
William Blake und seine Illustrationen zur "Göttlichen Komödie".
(William Blake and his illustrations to the "Divine Comedy")
Das keltische Element in der Literatur (The Celtic Element in Literature)
Zum Psalter Sprechen (Speaking to the Psaltery)
Der Leib des Vater Christian Rosenkreuz (The Body of the Father
Christian Rosencrux)

WILLIAM B. YEATS | [rule] | GREVINNAN CATHLEEN |
LEGEND I FEM SCENER | TILL SVENSKA AV | TERESIA EUREN |
[monogram] | STOCKHOLM | THURE WAHLEDOWS FÖRLAG

$8\frac{1}{2} \times 5$; pp. 88: comprising half-title, verso blank, pp. [1–2]; title,
imprint, below rule, Stockholm 1923 Tryckeriet Progress A.–B. on
verso, pp. [3–4]; list of characters, verso blank, pp. [5–6]; fly-title,
verso blank, pp. [7–8]; text, pp. [9]–88.

Issued in cream stiff paper covers, lettered in black and red on front
cover, lettered in black on spine; announcement of two forthcoming
books by W. B. Yeats on back cover; all edges untrimmed. Published
in 1923.

IRLÄNDSKA | DRAMER | AV | W. B. YEATS | [swelled
rule] | TILL SVENSKA AV | HUGO HULTENBERG | [publishers'
monogram] | STOCKHOLM | [rule] | P. A. NORSTEDT & SÖNERS |
FÖRLAG

$7\frac{4}{5} \times 5$; pp. 160: comprising half-title, verso blank, pp. [1–2]; title,
notice on verso that the versions are taken from *Plays in Prose and
Verse*, and, at foot, imprint, Stockholm 1923 Kungl. Boktryckeriet.
P. A. Norstedt & Söner 233280 pp. [3–4]; fly-title, verso blank, pp.
[5–6]; text, pp. 7–158; list of contents, p. [159]; p. [160] blank.

Issued in stiff white paper covers, lettering in red and black and design
in red on front cover, lettering in black between black double rules on
spine, advertisements on back cover; all edges untrimmed.

Issued also in green marbled paper boards with green linen spine,
design in gold on front cover, dark green panel lettered in gold between
two gold bars on spine; white end-papers; top edges stained green,
other edges trimmed. A leaf identical with the cover of the paper-
bound edition precedes the half-title. There is a frontispiece portrait
of W. B. Yeats from a photograph. Published in 1923.

Contents

Cathleen, Houlihans dotter
Soppkitteln (The Pot of Broth)
Timglaset. En moralitet (The Hour-Glass)
På Bailes strand
De mörka vattnen (The Shadowy Waters)

RÖDE HANRAHAN | AV | W. B. YEATS | [swelled rule] | ÖVERSÄTTNING | AV | MARGARETHA FRÖLICH | [publishers' monogram] | STOCKHOLM | [rule] | P. A. NORSTEDT & SÖNERS | FÖRLAG

7⅘×5; pp. iv, 168: comprising half-title, verso blank, pp. [i–ii]; title, on verso original title of book (in English) and, at foot, imprint Stockholm 1924 Kungl. Boktryckeriet. P. A. Norstedt & Söner 233892, pp. [iii–iv]; list of contents, verso blank, pp. [1–2]; fly-title, verso blank, pp. [3–4]; text, pp. 5–168.

Issued in two styles of binding as for *Irländska Dramer.* Published in 1924.

Contents

Berättelser om Röde Hanrahan. (6 stories.)
Längtans ros. (Poem and 7 stories.)
Rosa Alchemica.

BLAESTEN MELLEM SIVENE | DIGTE OG SKVESPIL | AF | W. B. YEATS | PAA DANSK VED | VALDEMAR RØRDAM | [publishers' monogram] | P. HAASE & SØNS FORLAG | KØBENHAVN | MCMXXIV

8×5¾; pp. xii, 228: comprising half-title, verso blank, pp. [i–ii]; title, imprint, Trykt hos. J. Jorgensen & Co. * Ivar Jantzen, on verso, pp. [iii–iv]; list of contents, verso blank, pp. [v–vi]; Preface, pp. [vii]–xi; p. [xii] blank; fly-title, verso blank, pp. [1–2]; text, pp. [3]–226; pp. [227–228] blank. Frontispiece portrait of the Author by J. B. Yeats.

Issued in orange paper covers, lettered in red and black and with design in green on front cover, lettered in black on spine; advertisements on back cover; all edges untrimmed. Published in 1924.

Contents

Preface by Valdemar Rørdam. Dated August 1924.
Af Ungdomsdigte (Early Poems) 1895
Comtesse Cathleen (1892–1912)

Af Blaesten Imellem Sivene (The Wind Among the Reeds) 1899
Dronning Maives Alderdom (The Old Age of Queen Maeve) 1903
Af I de Syv Skove (In the Seven Woods) 1904
Skyggernes Hav (The Shadowy Waters) 1906
Af Den Grønne Hjelm (From *The Green Helmet*) 1912
Af Ansvarligheder (Responsibilities) 1914
Af De Vilde Svaner ved Coole (The Wild Swans at Coole) 1919
Af Michael Robartes og Danserinden (Michael Robartes and the Dancer) 1921
Notes. Signed V.R.

ENHÖRNINGEN FRÅN | STJÄRNORNA | DROTT-
NINGEN | TVÅ SKÅDESPEL | AV | W. B. YEATS | BEMYNDIGAD
ÖVERSÄTTNING | [Publishers' monogram] | STOCKHOLM |
[rule] | P. A. NORSTEDT & SÖNERS | FÖRLAG

7⅘×5; pp. 152: comprising half-title, verso blank, pp. [1–2]; title,
original titles of plays on verso and, at foot, imprint, Stockholm 1924
Kungl. Boktryckeriet. P. A. Norstedt & Söner 240160, pp. [3–4];
fly-title, verso blank, pp. [5–6]; text, pp. 7–152.

Issued in two styles of binding as for *Irländska Dramer*. Published in
1924.

Contents

Enhörningen från Stjarnorna (The Unicorn from the Stars)
Drottningen (The Player Queen)

LÄNGTANS LAND | AV W. B. YEATS | TILL SVENSKA AV |
KARL ASPLUND | [publishers' monogram] | STOCKHOLM
P. A. NORSTEDT | & SÖNERS FORLAG

7⅞×4¹⁵⁄₁₆; pp. 44: comprising half-title, verso blank, pp. [1–2]; title,
original title *The Land of Heart's Desire* and, at foot, Stockholm.
1924. Kungl. Boktryckeriet P. A. Norstedt & Söner. 240561, on
verso, pp. [3–4]; dedication and, at foot of page, quotation, verso
blank, pp. [5–6]; Dramatis Personae, p. 7; Scene, p. 8; text, pp. 9–44.

Issued in paper covers only in style similar to *Irländska Dramer*.
Published in 1924.

SEKAI DOWA TAIKEI AIRURANDO HEN (TALES
AND LEGENDS OF THE WORLD, IRELAND). TRANSLATED BY
MAKOTO SANGU. ILLUSTRATED. KINDAISHA, TOKYO, APRIL,
1925.

A large volume of more than six hundred pages, in which is included the translation of a greater part of the tales in *Fairy and Folk Tales of the Irish Peasantry*, 1888. (No. 212.)

I have not seen a copy of this book.

GRÄFIN CATHLEEN | EIN DRAMA VON | W. B. YEATS |
HELLERAU | IM VERLAG VON JAKOB HEGNER | MCMXXV

$8 \times 4\frac{1}{2}$; pp. 100: comprising pp. [1–2] blank; half-title, verso blank, pp. [3–4]; title, on verso Berechtigte Übertragung von | Ernst E. Stein, and at foot of page, Für Bühnen Handschrift | Aufführungsrechte sind vom Verlag zu erwerben, pp. [5–6]; list of characters, verso blank, pp. [7–8]; text, pp. [9]–96; p. [97] blank; imprint, Gesetzt und gedruckt in Bessemer-Schriften von 1795 bei Jakob Hegner, Hellerau.

Printed on Japanese vellum and issued in light brown paper covers lettered in light brown on a black panel W. B. | YEATS | CATH | LEEN; lettered in black, longitudinally, on spine W. B. YEATS: GRÄFIN CATH-LEEN; all edges untrimmed. Also issued in green cloth, lettered in black inside two black rules on golden panel, lettered in gold, longitudinally, on spine; top edges stained red. The cloth bound volume measures $7\frac{3}{4} \times 4\frac{1}{2}$. Published in 1925.

Sekaimeishi-Sen (9) | [Japanese characters] IEITSU SHISHU Yoshikawa Norihiko Yaku | Buneido, Tokyo. 1925. 11 [November] | (Selected Poems of W. B. Yeats, translated by Norihiko Yoshikawa).

$5\frac{1}{4} \times 3\frac{3}{4}$; pp. xii, 152: comprising preface and contents, pp. [i–xii]; half-title, verso blank, pp. [1–2]; text, pp. 3–152.

I have not seen a copy of this book.

W. B. YEATS | DIE CHYMISCHE ROSE | [rule] | MCMXXVII |
BEI JAKOB HEGNER. HELLERAU

$7\frac{1}{2} \times 4\frac{4}{5}$; pp. 224.

Issued in pale green cloth, lettering in blue on front cover which has two thin lines in blue at edges, lettering in blue, and two thin blue lines at head and foot on spine, two thin blue lines at edges of back cover; white end-papers; top edges stained pale green, others trimmed. Published in 1927.

Contents

Geschichten von Rot Hanrahan
    6 stories

Die Geheime Rose
    Poem and 7 stories
Rosa Alchemica
    3 stories
A note on verso of title gives the translator's name Herberth E.
Herlitschka.

[Japanese characters] TWO PLAYS FOR DANCERS |
By W. B. Yeats | translated by | Jirō Nan'e 1928 Limited
No. V | Tokyo Shihaku Kyokai.

$8\frac{11}{16} \times 5\frac{15}{16}$; pp. xiv, 150. The translations are of 'At the Hawk's Well'
and 'The Only Jealousy of Emer.' There is a frontispiece portrait
of Yeats, and illustrations of the Musicians, The Old Man, The Young
Man, and The Guardian of the We . . . The translations are followed
by 'Yeats's Plays for Dancers: A Study,' by Jirō Nan'e.

I have not seen a copy of this book.

IEITSU SHISO (SELECT POEMS OF W. B. YEATS). TRANS-
LATED BY TSUNEYA KANASUGI. KEIMEISHA, TOKYO,
NOVEMBER, 1928.

$7\frac{2}{5} \times 4\frac{9}{10}$; pp. iv, 124: comprising half-title, verso blank, pp. [i–ii];
title, verso blank, pp. [iii–iv]; Contents, pp. 1–6; Translations of
poems, pp. 1–120; fly-leaf, pp. [121–122]; colophon, p. [123].

Issued in cloth, lettering in black ink on back and front cover.

Published in 1928.

I have not seen a copy of this book.

W. B. YEATS | HRABĚNKA | CATHLEENOVÁ | (1892–
1912) | DRAMA | O PĚTI VÝJEVECH | [rule] | ROZMĚREM
ORIGINÁLU PŘELOŽIL | JOS. J. DAVID | VPRAZLE | [rule] |
NOVÁ BIBLIOTÉKA SV. XV | M CM XXIX

7×5; pp. 88: comprising publishers' initials, verso blank, pp. [1–2];
title, verso blank, pp. [3–4]; quotation and dedication, verso blank,
pp. [5–6]; text, pp. 7–10; list of characters, verso blank, pp. [11–12];
text, pp. 13–83; p. [84] blank; list of contents, verso blank, pp. [85–
86]; colophon, Nová Bibliotéka | Svazek XXV | Pořádá Dr. Josef
Kopal | W. B. Yeats | HRABĚNKA CATHLEENOVÁ | Rozměrem originálu
přeložil Jos. J. David | Úprava a sbálka C. Bondy | Tiskl F. Obzina
ve Vyškově | Nakladatelé | Kvasnička a Hampl v Praze | 1929, p. [87];
p. [88] blank.

Issued in white stiff paper covers, lettering and design in gold and grey on front cover, lettering in black on spine; monogram on back cover; all edges untrimmed. Published in 1929.

w. b. yeats | ZEMĚ TOUHY | p | v. praze 1929 | [asterisk] | EDICE PHILOBIBLON | 8

9 × 5¾; pp. 32: comprising quotation from Blake within panel, verso blank, pp. [1–2]; title, verso blank, pp. [3–4]; illustration, verso blank, pp. [5–6]; list of characters, verso blank, pp. [7–8]; text, pp. 9–[29]; design, p. [30]; colophon, verso blank, pp. [31–32].

Issued in blue paper covers folded over card, label, lettered in black within panel, on front cover; all edges untrimmed. Published in 1929.

THE GAISFORD GREEK PRIZE | COMPOSITION FOR 1929 | BY | N. K. HUTTON | SCHOLAR OF UNIVERSITY COLLEGE, OXFORD | GLASGOW | JACKSON, WYLIE AND CO. | PUBLISHERS TO THE UNIVERSITY | 1929

10 × 6⅖; pp. 12: comprising title, verso blank, pp. [1–2]; acknowledgement to the Author and Messrs. Macmillan & Co. Ltd for permission to reprint *The Sad Shepherd*, p. [3]; Greek translation and English text of *The Sad Shepherd* on opposing pages, pp. [4]–11; p. [12] blank.

Issued in plum coloured stiff paper covers, lettered in black on front cover as on title; stitched; all edges trimmed. Published in 1929.

The British Museum copy was received on September 30, 1929.

WILLIAM B. YEATS [*in black*] | IRISCHE SCHAUBÜHNE [*in red*] | DEUTSCH VON HENRY VON HEISELER | [long rule in red] | PRIVATER DRUCK DER STIFTER UND FREUNDE · 1933

9⅘ × 6⁷⁄₁₀; pp. viii, 292: comprising pp. [i–ii] blank; half-title, verso blank, pp. [iii–iv]; title, Herausgegeben von Bernt von Heiseler on verso, pp. [v–vi]; text, pp. [vii]–286; list of contents and dates of the completion of the translations, p. [287]; p. [288] blank; ornament (in red) and imprint, Dieses Werk wurde als Privatausgabe einer Gesellschaft von Stiftern und Freunden bei Fritz Schmidberger, München in einer Auflage von 250 nummerierten Exemplaren gedruckt. Vorliegendes Buch trägt die Nummer (numbered in red ink), p. [289]; p. [290] blank.

Issued in yellow cloth, with label, printed in black, on spine; marbled yellow end-papers; all edges trimmed. Published in 1933.

Contents

Vorbemerkung des Herausgebers
Die Gräfin Cathleen
Das Wunschland des Herzens
Die Schattigen Wasser
Cathleen ni Houlihan
Das Stundenglas
An Baile's Strand
Des Königs Schwelle
Deirdre
Das Einhorn von den Sternen
Der Goldne Helm

The translations are in verse and prose, following the original.

The British Museum copy bears the date stamp May 30, 1933.

TAI O KUNDE ARUKU YOSEITACHI (THE TROOPING FAIRIES). ("IWANAMI BUNKO" SER.). TRANSLATED INTO JAPANESE BY MAKOTO SANGU. ILLUSTRATED. IWANAMI, TOKYO, MARCH, 1935 AND LATER.

$6\frac{1}{10} \times 4\frac{1}{5}$; pp. 244: comprising title, verso blank, pp. [1–2]; Preface, pp. 3–4; Contents, pp. 5–6; Translation of *The Trooping Fairies and other tales*, pp. 7–232; colophon, p. [233]; advertisements, pp. [234–244].

Issued in paper covers.

Published in 1935.

I have not seen a copy of this book.

YEATS | POESIE | MILANO MCMXXXIX

$4\frac{3}{4} \times 3$; pp. 28, unnumbered: comprising pp. [1–2] blank; title, verso blank, pp. [3–4]; text, pp. [5–25]; p. [26] blank; colophon on p. [27]; p. [28] blank.

Issued in red paper covers folded over end-papers, lettered in black, as on title-page, on front cover; all edges trimmed. Inside the folded covers is inserted loose a photograph of W. B. Yeats, on the back of which is printed:

Yeats | nato il 13 giugno 1865 | a Sandymount presso Dublino; | morto il 29 gennaio 1939 | a Roquebrune Cap-Martin.

The colophon reads:

"all' Insegna del Pesce d'Oro"

* * * * * * *

Di questo volumetto nella versione de Leone Traverso a cura di Giovanni Scheiwiller si sono stampati dalle Industrie Grafiche Pietro Vera di Milano il 7–9–1939–XVII, 220 esemplari su carta uso mano e 30 esemplari su carta "Japon" numerati da I a XXX per gli amici del libro.

Esemplare N.   . (numbered with stamping machine).

Published in September 1939.

Contents

Ephemera 1889
Morte di Signora 1919 (Poems I and IV of *Upon a Dying Lady*)
Gli Uccelli Bianchi 1893
I Cigni Selvaggi a Coole 1919
Navigando verso Bisanzio 1928
I Isola del Lago d'Innisfree 1893
Affanno d'Amore 1893
I Magi 1914
[*The Travail of Passion*] (no title given) 1899
[*The Valley of Lovers*] (no title given) 1899
[*Blood and the Moon* III] (no title given) 1933
Sogni Infranti 1919
Bisanzio 1930

DE BALLADE | VAN PRIESTER GILLIGAN | DOOR | JOHAN VAN DELDEN | [ornament]

$9\frac{1}{2} \times 7\frac{1}{4}$; pp. 8, unnumbered: comprising half-title, verso blank, pp. [1–2]; title, verso blank, pp. [3–4]; text, pp. [5–8].

Issued in stiff cream card covers, fastened with two metal staples; no lettering on cover; no end-papers; all edges trimmed.

40 copies were privately printed for Johan van Delden, Beerta, Holland, in 1941. No copies were supplied to the trade.

The translation first appeared in *De Gemeenschap*, a Dutch Roman Catholic literary monthly, December 1940.

WILLIAM BUTLER YEATS | DE GRAVIN CATELENE | VERTAALD DOOR A. ROLAND HOLST | 'THE SORROWFUL ARE DUMB FOR THEE' | (KLACHT VAN MORION SHENONE OVER | MISS MARY BOURKE) | A. A. M. STOLS, UITGEVER | 'S-GRAVEN-HAGE, 1941

$7\frac{3}{8} \times 4\frac{3}{4}$; pp. 64: comprising half-title, verso blank, pp. [1–2]; title, verso blank, pp. [3–4]; Personen, verso blank, pp. [5–6]; text, pp.

7–63; imprint, Gedrukte bij de firma Boosten & Stols | te Maastricht. Publisher's emblem printed below, p. [64]. Printed on yellow tinted paper.

Issued in yellow paper boards with yellow linen spine, publisher's emblem in gold on front cover, lettering in gold w. B. YEATS [asterisk] DE GRAVIN CATELENE on spine; off-white end-papers; all edges trimmed.

The translation first appeared in *De Gids*, Vol. I., pp. 163–198, 1931. There was a second impression in 1946.

WILLIAM BUTLER YEATS | LADY CATHLEEN | 1892 | L'ORIOLO A POLVERE | 1903 | ROSA E BALLO EDITORI MILANO 1944

$6\frac{1}{4} \times 4\frac{3}{4}$; pp. viii, 124: comprising pp. i–ii blank; half-title, English names of plays and translator's name on verso, pp. iii–iv; title, name of series and copyright notice on verso, pp. v–vi; fly-title, verso blank, pp. vii–viii; introduction, pp. 1–2; Personaggi, verso blank, pp. 3–4; text, pp. 5–118; fly-title, verso blank, pp. 119–120; index, verso blank, pp. 121–122; imprint, Finito di stampare il 30 ottobre 1944 | per conto di Rosa e Ballo Editori—Milano | Presso arti grafici astra—via Bertani 12, p. 123; p. 124 blank. Frontispiece portrait of W. B. Yeats by A. Mancini.

No. 19 of a series Teatro Moderno. Issued in stiff terra-cotta paper covers, lettered in black and white on front cover, number in series in black on spine; no end-papers; all edges trimmed.

Contents
Lady Cathleen
L'Oriolo a Polvere (*The Hour-Glass*)
Nota (containing brief bibliography)

The translations, which are in prose, are by Carlo Linati.

WILLIAM BUTLER YEATS | VISIONI DI MAGGIO | 1894 | SULL'ACQUE TENEBROSE | 1900 | LA POVERELLA | 1902 | ROSA E BALLO EDITORE MILANO 1945

$6\frac{1}{4} \times 4\frac{2}{3}$; pp. viii, 112: comprising pp. [i–ii] blank; half-title, English names of plays and translator's name on verso, pp. [iii–iv]; title, name of series and copyright notice on verso, pp. [v–vi]; fly-title, dedication on verso, pp. [vii–viii]; text, pp. 1–106; fly-title, verso blank, pp. [107–108]; index, verso blank, pp. [109–110]; imprint, Finito di stampare il 20 gennaio 1945 | per conto di Rosa e Ballo

editore—Milano | Presso arti grafiche astra—via Bertani 12 | p. [111];
p. [112] blank. Frontispiece portrait of W. B. Yeats by Augustus
John, R.A. facing title. Published in 1945.

No. 15 of a series Teatro Moderno. Issued in uniform style with the
previous entry. The title given on the cover is TRE ATTI UNICI.

Contents

Visioni di maggio (The Land of Heart's Desire)
Sull'acque tenebrose (The Shadowy Waters)
La Poverella (Cathleen ni Houlihan)
Nota (containing brief bibliography)

The translations are by Carlo Linati. *The Shadowy Waters* is in prose
and verse, the other two plays in prose.

IEITSU SHISO (SELECT POEMS OF W. B. YEATS). ("IWANAMI
BUNKO" SER.). TRANSLATED INTO JAPANESE BY MAKOTO
SANGU. IWANAMI, TOKYO, NOVEMBER, 1946.

$6 \times 4\frac{1}{8}$; pp. 168: comprising title, verso blank, pp. [1–2]; Contents,
pp. [3–6]; Translations of poems, pp. 7–95; Notes, pp. 97–112;
Appendices—*W. B. Yeats, a Critical Study* by M. Sangu, with Notes,
pp. 115–151; *An Hour with W. B. Yeats* by M. Sangu, with Notes,
pp. 153–163; Postscript, pp. 155–156; colophon, p. [167].

Issued in paper covers.

Published in 1946.

Contents

From *Crossways*
> The Song of the Happy Shepherd; The Sad Shepherd; The Cloak,
> the Boat, and the Shoes; The Indian upon God; The Falling of the
> Leaves; Ephemera; The Stolen Child; To an Isle in the Water; An
> Old Song Resung; The Meditation of the Old Fisherman.

From *The Rose*
> The Rose of the World; The Rose of Peace; A Fairy Song; The
> Lake Isle of Innisfree; The Sorrow of Love; When You are Old;
> The White Birds; The Two Trees; A Dream of Death.

From *The Wind Among the Reeds*
> The Hosting of the Sidhe; The Everlasting Voices; The Moods;
> The Lover tells of the Rose in his Heart; The Fish; Into the
> Twilight; The Song of Wandering Aengus; The Song of the Old
> Mother; The Heart of the Woman; The Lover mourns for the Loss

*of Love; He reproves the Curlew; He remembers Forgotten Beauty;
A Poet to his Beloved; He gives his Beloved Certain Rhymes; To
his Heart bidding it have No Fear; He hears the Cry of the Sedge;
The Lover pleads with his Friend for Old Friends; He wishes for
the Cloths of Heaven; The Fiddler of Dooney.*
From *In the Seven Woods*
    *The Old Men admiring Themselves in the Water; O do not love
too long.*
From *The Green Helmet and Other Poems*
    A Drinking Song; The Coming of Wisdom with Time; To a Poet.
From *Responsibilities*
    A Coat.
From *The Wild Swans at Coole*
    *The Wild Swans at Coole; Men Improve with the Years; The
Scholars; To a Young Girl.*
From *The Tower*
    The Wheel; Youth and Age.
From *The Winding Stair and Other Poems*
    Death; The Nineteenth Century and After.
Notes to Poems
Appendices:
    William Butler Yeats, a Critical Biography.
    Reminiscences of a Visit to W. B. Yeats.
Notes to Appendices
Postscript.
I have not seen a copy of this book.

CATALINA DE HOULIHAN. Dibujos de Luis Sevane;
traducción de Maria Elvira Fernández. [Buenos Aires]
Ediciones Botella al Mar [1947].

28 pp. illus. Cien ejemplares numerados. No. 34.

I have not seen a copy of this book.

WILLIAM BUTLER YEATS |	WILLIAM BUTLER YEATS |
POEMS [*in red*] | ENRICO	POESIE [*in red*] | ENRICO
CEDERNA | MILANO [*The*	CEDERNA | MILANO [*The*
whole enclosed within a single	*whole enclosed within a single*
red line frame]	*red line frame.*]

$8\frac{1}{8} \times 5\frac{1}{8}$; pp. 220: comprising pp. [1–3] blank; titles, pp. [4–5]; name
of translator and of the writer of the note, and copyright notice, p.

[6]; fly-title, verso blank, pp. [7–8]; fly-title, p. [9]; text, pp. 10–[199]; p. [200] blank; fly-title, verso blank, pp. [201–202]; text, pp. 203–[206]; pp. [207–208] blank; fly-title, verso blank, pp. [209–210]; index, pp. 211–[214]; pp. [215–216] blank; notice of limitation, p. [217]; imprint, Questo volume è stato impresso | nel mese di aprile 1949, per | conto dell'editore Enrico | Cederna nelle officine di Enrico Gualdoni, | stampatore in Milano. | Printed in Italy—Stampato in Italia, p. [218]; pp. [219–220] blank.

Issued in grey paper jacket folded over white paper cover, lettering in red and black on front cover and on spine of jacket; all edges untrimmed.

The edition limited to 1600 copies of which 100 were *fuori commercio*. Published in 1949.

Contents

Lyrical

    From *Crossways*
      Ephemera

    From *The Rose*
      The Lake Isle of Innisfree
      The Sorrow of Love
      The White Birds
      To Some I have Talked with by the Fire

    From *The Wind Among the Reeds*
      He bids his Beloved be at Peace
      He tells of a Valley full of Lovers

    From *The Green Helmet and other Poems*
      The Coming of Wisdom with Time

    From *Responsibilities*
      The Magi

    From *The Wild Swans at Coole*
      The Wild Swans at Coole
      The Living Beauty
      To a Young Girl
      Broken Dreams
      Upon a Dying Lady (6 poems).

    From *The Tower*
      Sailing to Byzantium
      Ancestral Houses
      The New Faces
      Two Songs from a Play
      Leda and the Swan

From *The Winding Stair and other Poems*
    A Dialogue of Self and Soul
    From *Blood and the Moon* III.
        Oil and Blood
        Byzantium
    From *Words for Music Perhaps*
        After Long Silence
  Narrative and Dramatic
    The Shadowy Waters
    The Gift of Harun-al-Rashid
Note

The English and Italian texts face one another on opposite pages throughout, the translation being by Leone Traverso and the note by Margherita Guidacci.

W. B. YEATS | L'ŒUF | DE HÉRON | TRADUIT DE L'ANGLAIS PAR ROGER GIROUX | "L'AGE D'OR" | TEXTES CONTEMPOR-AINS | PUBLIÉS SOUS LA DIRECTION DE HENRI PARISOT | AUX ÉDITIONS PREMIÈRES

$6\frac{3}{8} \times 5$; pp. 64: comprising pp. [1–2] blank; half-title, verso blank, pp. [3–4]; title, notice of limitation and of copyright on verso, pp. [5–6]; Personnages, verso blank, pp. [7–8]; text, pp. 9–61; imprint, Achevé d'imprimer sur les presses | de l'Imprimerie Maurice Dauer a Paris, | en mai mil neuf cent cinquante, pour le compte des Editions Premières, | 2 bis, rue des Ciseaux, a Paris (vi^e). p. 62; pp. 63–64 blank.

Issued in blue paper covers, lettering and design by Max Ernst in black on front cover, lettering in black on spine and on back cover; no end-papers; all edges untrimmed.

The edition consisted of 775 copies of which 25 were on Marais Crèvecœur, numbered 1 to 25, and 750 on Alfama, numbered 26 to 775; there were also some copies *hors commerce*, marked H.C.

Published in 1950.

[Japanese characters] TAKA NO IDO | Hoka Nihen | Ietsu | Makumura-Mine-Ko Yaku | [ornament] | Kadokawa Bunko | 685. (At the Hawk's Well and Other Two Plays by W. B. Yeats, translated by Mineko Matsumura. Kadokawa-Shoten, Tokyo, 1953.)

$5\frac{15}{16} \times 4\frac{5}{16}$; pp. 95.

Contains translations of 'Cathleen ni Hoolihan,' 'The Land of Heart's Desire,' and 'At the Hawk's Well.'

I have not seen a copy of this book.

[Japanese characters] NŌ NO TENKAI (The development of Noh.) By Jirō Nan'e. Tokyo: Hinoko Shoten. 1954.

Pp. 142: comprising two essays: The Revival of Masks and Introduction to Yeats's Plays, pp. 3–52; and translations of 'At the Hawk's Well' and 'The Only Jealousy of Emer,' pp. 53–142.

I have not seen a copy of this book.

THEATRE, traduit de l'anglais par Madeleine Gilbert. Paris, Éditions Denoël [1954]

Pp. [7]–234.

'Il a été tiré de cet ouvrage dix exemplaires sur vergé Johannot numeroté de l à 10 . . .'

Contents.—La comtesse Cathleen.—La terre du désir du coeur.—Les ombres sur la mer.—L'unique rivale d'Emer.—La mort de Cuchulainn. —Les mots sur la vitre.

I have not seen a copy of this book.

Collection Bilingue des Classiques Étrangers | YEATS | Poèmes choisis | traduction, préface et notes | par | M.-L. Cazamian | Aubier | Editions Montaigne

$7\frac{1}{8} \times 4\frac{9}{16}$; pp. 386: comprising cover, verso blank, pp. [1–2]; half-title and notice of English edition from which poems were selected, verso blank, pp. [3–4]; title, rights of reproduction notice on verso, pp. [5–6]; introduction, pp. 8–96; text, pp. [97]–363; p. [364] blank; notes, pp. 365–369; p. [370] blank; bibliography, pp. [371]–372; index des noms cités et des poèmes, pp. [373]–378; table des matières, pp. 379–[383]; imprint, achevé d'imprimer le 12 Novembre 1954 par l'imprimerie firmindidot pour F. Aubier (éditions Montaigne) a Paris, edition detail at foot of page, p. [384]; p. [385] blank; list of books in series, p. [386].

Issued in orange-coloured paper covers, lettered in black on front and back covers; no end-papers; all edges trimmed. The numbering begins with the front cover. Published November 12, 1954.

Contents

Friends
The Cold Heaven
The Magi

From *The Wild Swans at Coole* (1919)
The Wild Swans at Coole
In Memory of Major Robert Gregory
An Irish Airman Foresees his Death
Lines Written in Dejection
The Fisherman
The Scholars

From *The Dreaming of the Bones* (1921)
Why Does my Heart Beat So?
Why Should the Heart Take Fright?
At the Grey Round of the Hill

From *Michael Robartes and the Dancer* (1921)
Easter, 1916
Sixteen Dead Men
The Rose Tree
On a Political Prisoner
The Second Coming
A Prayer for my Daughter

From *The Tower* (1928)
Sailing to Byzantium
Meditations in Time of Civil War
The Wheel
A Prayer for my Son
Two Songs from a Play
Leda and the Swan
From 'Oedipus at Colonus'
Coole Park and Ballylee
Byzantium
Ribh at the Tomb of Baile and Aillinn
The Gyres
An Acre of Grass
What Then?
The Man and the Echo
Under Ben Bulben

VERZEN IN VERTALING van A Roland Holst. Amsterdam, De Beuk [1955]

30 pp.

I have not seen a copy of this book.

THE SELECT POEMS | OF | W. B. YEATS | SHORTER
LYRICS WITH JAPANESE TRANSLATIONS, | NOTES,
CRITICAL BIOGRAPHY, etc. | EDITED BY | MAKOTO SANGU |
[Japanese characters] | [engraved vignette of wolf-hound] |
TOKYO | AZUMA SHOBO | 1955
8¼ × 5¾; pp. 8, 236.

Issued in dark-green cloth; THE SELECT POEMS | OF | W. B. YEATS and
device of wolf-hound in gold on front cover, title in Japanese characters and device of shamrock leaves in gold on spine; white end-papers;
all edges trimmed. Illustrated with frontispiece photograph of W. B.
Yeats and four drawings.

English text, pp. 3–84; Japanese translations, pp. 85–174; notes.

Contents

From *Crossways* (1889)
The Song of the Happy Shepherd
The Sad Shepherd
The Cloak, the Boat, and the Shoes
The Indian upon God
The Falling of the Leaves
Ephemera
The Stolen Child
To an Isle in the Water
An Old Song Resung
The Meditation of the Old Fisherman
From *The Rose* (1893)
The Rose of the World
The Rose of Peace
A Faery Song
The Lake Isle of Innisfree
The Sorrow of Love
When You are Old
The White Birds
A Dream of Death
The Two Trees
From *The Wind Among the Reeds* (1899)
The Hosting of the Sidhe
The Everlasting Voices
The Moods
The Lover tells of the Rose in His Heart

POÈMES | DE | W. B. YEATS | Traduits par | Alliette Audra | préface de | Edmond Jaloux | de l'Académie Française | La Colombe | Editions du vieux Colombier | 5, rue Rousselet, 5 | Paris

$6\frac{3}{4} \times 4\frac{3}{8}$; pp. 98: comprising pp. [1–2] blank; half-title, verso blank, pp. [3–4]; title, notice of English edition from which poems were selected, notice of limitation, and copyright notice, pp. [5–6]; in memoriam page, verso blank, pp. [7–8]; preface, pp. 9–13; p. [14] blank; fly-title, p. [15]; text, pp. 16–91; p. [92] blank; table des poèmes, pp. 93–94; imprint, Imprimé en France, [rule], D.L. Nº463—4e Trimetre 1955 Imprimerie spéciale de La Colombe., verso blank, pp. [95–96]; pp. [97–98] blank.

Issued in dark-rust linen, lettered in gold on spine; end-papers mottled and white; all edges trimmed. Published in 1956.

Contents

The Lover tells of the Rose in his heart
The Lover asks forgiveness because of his many moods
The Lover speaks to his hearers of his songs in coming days
He Gives his Beloved certain Rhymes

The English and French texts face one another on opposite pages throughout. Many of the translations are in prose.

DAS EINHORN VON DEN STERNEN; ein tragisches Spiel in drei Akten. Deutsch von Herberth E. Herlitschka. Emsdetten, Verlag Lechte [1956]. 89 pp. (Dramen der Zeit, Bd. 14)

I have not seen a copy of this book.

POEMAS. Selección, versión y prólogo de Jaime Ferran. Madrid, Ediciones Rialp, 1957.

99 pp. port. (Adonais, 140)

I have not seen a copy of this book.

IRISCHE LEGENDE. Text zu einer Oper [von] Werner Egk, mit 5 Originallithographien von Oskar Kokoschka. Freiburg im Breisgau, Klemm [1957].

Free adaptation of the Irish Folk-tale, Countess Cathleen O'Shea, as told by W. B. Yeats, and of Yeats' play, Countess Cathleen.

I have not seen a copy of this book.

[Japanese characters] IEITSU SHISHU | Oshima-Shōtarō Yaku *Poems of Yeats,* translated by Shōtarō Oshima. Tokyo: Hokuseido.

$7\frac{1}{2} \times 5\frac{1}{8}$; pp. xviii, 342: comprising title, publisher's acknowledgement on verso, pp. [i–ii]; contents, pp. iii–xiii; p. [xiv] blank; preface, pp. xv–xviii; text, pp. [1]–296; interview with Yeats by the translator, pp. 297–309; p. [310] blank; notes, pp. 311–339; postscript, pp. 340–342. There are two frontispieces: the first a photograph of Yeats inscribed To S. Oshima from W. B. Yeats, Jan 1934; the second a holograph, signed W. B. Yeats, of Yeats's Poem 'Symbols.'

Issued in purple cloth, lettering in gold on spine, design in gold on front cover; off-white mottled end-papers; all edges trimmed. Published in 1958. A second edition, revised, was published in 1963.

Contents

From *A Full Moon in March*
　　Church and State
　　Ribh considers Christian Love insufficient
　　The Four Ages of Man
　　A Needle's Eye
　　Meru

From *Last Poems*
　　The Gyres
　　Lapis Lazuli
　　Imitated from the Japanese
　　Sweet Dancer
　　The Three Bushes
　　The Lady's First Song
　　The Lady's Second Song
　　The Lady's Third Song
　　The Chambermaid's First Song
　　The Chambermaid's Second Song
　　An Acre of Grass
　　Those Images
　　The Statues
　　Long-legged Fly
　　A Bronze Head
　　The Apparitions
　　Why should not Old Men be Mad?
　　The Statesman's Holiday
　　The Circus Animal's Desertion
　　Politics
　　The Man and the Echo
　　The Black Tower
　　Under Ben Bulben

BOOKS WITH INTRODUCTIONS BY YEATS

GITANJALI │ (OFFERTA DI CANTI) │ DI RABINDRA- │ NATH
TAGORE │ [ornament] │ CARABBA │ EDITORE │ LANCIANO
[*The last three lines printed between ornaments. The whole of
the above printed in black inside a decorative border in red.*]

$6\frac{7}{10} \times 4\frac{3}{10}$; pp. 8, 1–3, iv–xviii, 19–144.

Issued in buff ribbed cloth, ornament carrying the words SCRITTORI │
ITALIANI │ E │ STRANIERI stamped blind on front cover, lettering and
decoration in gold on spine; decorated end-papers green on white;
all edges trimmed. Printed in September 1914.

The translation by Arundel del Re includes translation of *Introduzione* by W. B. Yeats. Pp. 3–xv.

RABINDRANATH TAGORE. DE BRIEF VAN DEN KONING. VERTALING VAN HENRI BOREL. [VOORWOORD VAN W. B. YEATS.] UTRECHT, W. DE HAAN, [1916]

I have not seen a copy of this book.

2. TRANSLATIONS IN PERIODICALS

UNE EPITAPHE
(This is part of a selection of poems from *The Book of the Rhymers'
Club*, 1892, headed *Un Manifeste Littéraire Anglais* and signed
The Pilgrim. The English and French texts are printed on
opposite pages.)
Le Mercure de France, March 1892.

LA TRISTESSE DU BERGER. TROIS LÉGENDES POPULAIRES
D'IRELAND
The Sad Shepherd and *The Untiring Ones*.
(Translated by Henry D. Davray)
L'Hermitage, July 1896.

ROSA ALCHEMICA
(Translated by Henry D. Davray)
Le Mercure de France, October 1898.

L'HOMME QUI CONNUT EN SONGE LE PAYS DES FÉES
(Signed Yeats. No translator's name)
L'Humanité Nouvelle, September 1899.

POÈMES
*L'Ile d'Innisfree. La Rose du Monde. Chanson (Impetuous heart,
be still). Le vent (The wind blows over the gates of the day)*. (No
translator's name.)
L'Humanité Nouvelle, December 1899.

LES ERRANCES D'OISIN
*Chanson de Jeune Fille. Ephemera, une Idylle d'Automne.
Chanson Indienne. Kanva, l'Indien, sur Dieu*. (No translator's
name.)

LE CRÉPUSCULE CELTE
Les Inlassables. (Translated by René Philipon)

INNISFREE
(Translated by Laurence Jerrold)

Le Magazine Internationale. (I have been unable to trace the date.
It does not occur in the first four numbers, i.e. to November
1895, all that can be found in the Bibliothèque Nationale.)

CAITLÍN NÍ UALLACHÁIN

(Translated by Father Tomás ÓCeallaigh)
The United Irishman, February 11, 18 and 25, March 4 and 11, 1905.
Reprinted in pamphlet form, 1905.

TROIS POÈMES D'AMOUR

Les Chevaux de l'Ombre. Le Travail de la Passion. O'Sullivan Rua à Marie Lavell. (Translated by Stuart Merrill.)
Vers et Prose, March–May 1905.

HE WISHES FOR THE CLOTHS OF HEAVEN

(Translated by Hakuson Kuriyagawa)
Myōjō (The Morning Star), June 1905.

"MOOD" an extract from Ideas of Good and Evil

(Translated by Bin Ueda)
Myōjō (The Morning Star), November 1905.

THE HOUR-GLASS

(Translated by Kaoru Osani)
Kabuki (The Kabuki Drama), January, April, May 1909.

TO THE ROSE UPON THE ROOD OF TIME

(Translated by Homei Iwano)
Chūgaku sekai, dai-ni bungei gō (The middle school world: second literary issue), November 1909.

CATHLEEN NI HOOLIHAN

(Translated by Kaoru Osanai)
Taiyō (The Sun), Vol. XIV, No. 4, 1910.

THE LOVER MOURNS FOR THE LOSS OF LOVE. FALLING OF THE LEAVES. THE HEART OF THE WOMAN.

(Translated by Makoto Sangū)
Kōyūkai zasshi (The alumni Bulletin), June 1911.

THE SHADOWY WATERS

(Translated by Teiichi Nakagi)
Geki to shi (Dramas and Poems), November 1911.

THE WHITE BIRDS. THE SONG OF WANDERING AENGUS.
(Translated by Makoto Sangū)
Kōyūkai ʒasshi (The alumni Bulletin), December 1911.

FERGUS AND THE DRUID
(Translated by Makoto Sangū)
Kōyūkai ʒasshi (The alumni Bulletin), April 1912.

THE SORROW OF LOVE. THE MOODS.
(Translated by Makoto Sangū)
Kōyūkai ʒasshi (The alumni Bulletin), June 1912.

THE GREEN HELMET
(Translated by Teiichi Nakagi)
Geki to shi (Dramas and poems), November 1912.

ON BAILE'S STRAND
(Translated by Yaso Saijō)

THE WHITE BIRDS
(Translated by Konosuke Hinatsu)

THE POT OF BROTH
(Translated by Ryōshirō Matsuda)

THE HEART OF THE WOMAN. AEDH GIVES HIS BELOVED
CERTAIN RHYMES. THE SONG OF OLD MOTHER. BREASAL
THE FISHERMAN. HANRAHAN LAMENTS BECAUSE OF HIS
WANDERINGS.
(Translated by Yaso Saijō)

THE FALLING OF THE LEAVES
(Translated by Kōnosuke Hinatsu)
Sei hai (The holy grail), June 1913.

DEIRDRE
(Translated by Nijuichi Kayano)
Mita bungaku (Mita literature), January 1913.

THE SYMBOLISM OF POETRY. WILLIAM BLAKE AND THE
IMAGINATION.
(Translated by Makoto Sangū)
Mirai (The Future), Vol. II, February 1914.

WILLIAM BLAKE AND HIS ILLUSTRATIONS TO 'THE DIVINE
COMEDY'

(Translated by Makoto Sangū)
Mirai (The Future), Vol. II, 1914.

THE HEART OF THE SPRING

(Translated by Ryūnosuke Yanagawa)
Shin shichō (The new trend of thoughts), February 1914.

MAGIC

(Translated by Makoto Sangū)
Teikoku bungaku (Imperial literature), March 1914.

THEATRE

(Translated by Makoto Sangū)
Teikoku bungaku (Imperial literature), April 1914.

THE EATERS OF PRECIOUS STONES. THE THREE O'BYRNES AND
THE EVIL FAIRIES. REGINA, REGINA PIGMEORUM, VENI.

(Translated by Ryūnosuke Yanagawa)

THE AUTUMN OF THE BODY

(Translated by Makoto Sangū)
Shin shichō (The new trend of thoughts), April 1914.

A DREAM OF DEATH. THE WHITE BIRDS.

(Translated by Michihiro Matsubara)
Sōsaku (The creative writing), May 1914.

THE SORROW OF LOVE. THE LAKE ISLE OF INNISFREE. THE
FALLING OF THE LEAVES.

(Translated by Michihiro Matsubara)
Sōsaku (The creative writing), July 1914.

WHAT'S POPULAR POETRY

(Translated by Makoto Sangū)
Shin shichō (The new trend of thoughts), August 1914.

IRELAND AND THE ARTS

(Translated by Makoto Sangū)
Teikoku bungaku (Imperial literature), November 1914.

HE WISHES HIS BELOVED WERE DEAD. THE LOVER MOURNS
FOR THE LOSS OF LOVE. HE GIVES HIS BELOVED CERTAIN
RHYMES.

(Translated by Makoto Sangū)
Teikoku bungaku (Imperial literature), April 1915.

THE WHITE BIRDS

(Translated by Misao Kume (pseudonym of Hōjin Yano))
Gakusuikai ̣zasshi (Gakusuiki magazine), June 1915.

THE LAND OF HEART'S DESIRE

(Translated by Tetsujiro Enaka)
Arusu, 1915.

WHEN YOU ARE OLD. A DREAM OF DEATH.

(Translated by Makoto Sangū)
Eigo no Nippon (The Nippon), November 1916.

THE SONG OF WANDERING AENGUS. THE SORROW OF LOVE.

(Translated by Makoto Sangū)
Eigo no Nippon (The Nippon), December 1916.

L'ORIOLO A POLVERE. MORALITÀ

Ronda (Roma), November 1919.

THE HEART OF THE SPRING

(Translated by Ryūnosuke Akutagawa)
Kaihō (Liberation), October 1919. Reprinted in *Kagedōrō*
(Shadow-lantern), Tokyo, 1920.

AT THE HAWK'S WELL

(Translated with notes by Tokuboku Hirata)
Eigo bungaku (The Lamp), February, March, April 1920.

A PRAYER FOR MY DAUGHTER

(Translated by Tetsuzo Okada)
Eigo bungaku (The Lamp), March 1920.

HE REPROVES THE CURLEW. A POET TO HIS BELOVED. INTO
THE TWILIGHT.

(Translated by Hōjin Yano)
Suiyō (The Jar), May 1920.

THE LAKE ISLE OF INNISFREE. HE GIVES HIS BELOVED CERTAIN
RHYMES. THE LOVER TELLS OF THE ROSE IN HIS HEART.
THE SONG OF WANDERING AENGUS. THE VALLEY OF THE
BLACK PIG.

(Translated by Hōjin Yano)
Suiyō (The Jar), July 1920.
These poems in *Suiyō* were reprinted in *Geibun* (Art and Litera-
ture), April, June, July 1921.

DEIRDRE

(Translated by F. Roger-Cornaz)
Les Écrits Nouveaux, August–September 1921.

CALVARY

(Translated by Mineko Matsumura)
Geki to hyōron (Drama and criticism). The initial number, 1922.

LA SAGESSE DU ROI

(Translated by Claude Dravaine)
Revue Politique et Littéraire, October 7, 1923.

TRE DIKTER AV YEATS. INNISFREE. EN DRÖM OM EN SALIG
SJAL. HIMMELENS KLÄDEN.

(*Three Poems by Yeats. Innisfree. A Dream of a Blessed Spirit.
He Wishes for the Cloths of Heaven.* Translated by Karl Asplund.)
Svenska Dagbladet, November 15, 1923.

HISTOIRES DE HANRAHAN LE ROUGE

(Translated by Jeanne Lichnerowicz)
Hanrahan le Rouge
    Revue Politique et Littéraire, December 1, 1923.
La Tresse de la Corde
    ibid., December 15, 1923.
Hanrahan et Cathleen la Fille de Houlihan
La Malédiction d'Hanrahan le Rouge
    ibid., January 5, 1924.
La Mort d'Hanrahan le Rouge
    ibid., February 2, 1924.

THE REFORM OF THE THEATRE

(Translated by Shōtarō Oshima)
Gikyoku (The Drama), February 1924.

THE CRUCIFIXION OF THE OUTCAST
(Translated with notes by Shōtarō Oshima)
Masago (The Sand), March 1924.

LA TERRE DU DESIR DU CŒUR
(Translated by Jeanne Lichnerowicz)
Europe, June 1924.
In the National Library of Ireland, bound up with the foregoing, is a version of *The Shadowy Waters*, *Les Eaux d'Ombre*, by the same translator. I have not been able to discover in what revue this appeared.

L'ACTRICE REINE
(Translated by Cecil Georges-Bazile)
Annales politiques et littéraires, August 31 and September 7, 1924.

DEIRDRE
(Translated by W. van Maanen)
Onze Eeuw (*Our Century*), Vol. III., pp. 193–216. 1924.

THE OLD MEN OF THE TWILIGHT
(Translated by Shōtarō Oshima)
Eigo kenkyu (The Study of English), April 1926.

THE ADORATION OF THE MAGI
(Translated by Ensekiken)
Sabat (Sabbato), April 1926.

LA SAGESSE DU ROI
(Translated by Claude Dravaine)
Revue Politique et Littéraire, April 16, 1927.
(This is a revision of the translation which appeared in the same Revue, October 7, 1923.)

LE CŒUR DU PRINTEMPS
(Translated by Claude Dravaine)
Revue Politique et Littéraire, January 21, 1928.

VISION D'UN ESPRIT BIENHEUREUX. HISTOIRES DE HANRAHAN
LE ROUGE: LA MALEDICTION DE HANRAHAN. LES MUSICIENS
DEMANDENT UNE BÉNÉDICTION POUR LEUR PSALTERIONS
ET POUR EUX-MÊMES. A PROPOS D'ŒDIPE À COLONNE.
L'EMBARQUEMENT POUR BYZANCE.
(Translated, with a short introduction by André Malvil.)
Le Monde Nouveau, October 15, 1928.

GRAVIN CATHLEEN

(Translated by H. G. Heynen)
Roëping (Vocation), Vol. VIII., pp. 479–489 and pp. 565–575.
1930.

DE GRAVIN CATELENE

(Translated by A. Roland Holst)
De Gids (The Guide), Amsterdam, Vol. I., pp. 163–198. 1931.
Reprinted in volume form, 1941. Second edition, 1946.

CATHLEEN NI HOULIHAN

(Translated by Henry von Heiseler)
Corona (München), Vol. II., pp. 87–100. July, 1931.

LE CRÉPUSCULE CELTIQUE:

Regina, Regina Pigmeorum, Veni. Une Voix, 1902. *Terre, Feu
et Eau,* 1902. *L'Homme et ses Bottes. Les Sorciers.*
(Translated by Claude Dravaine)
Revue Politique et Littéraire, November 18, 1933.

DIT IS'T GEWOLKTE. GELEERDEN. VOLKSLEIDERS. LEDA EN
DE ZWAAN.

(*These are the Clouds. The Scholars. Leaders of the Crowd. Leda
and the Swan.* Translated by Johan de Molenaar.)
Helikon, Vol. III., pp. 17–20. 1933.

HE WISHES FOR THE CLOTHS OF HEAVEN. HE THINKS OF
THOSE WHO HAVE SPOKEN EVIL OF HIS BELOVED. HE
TELLS OF THE PERFECT BEAUTY. HE GIVES HIS BELOVED
CERTAIN RHYMES.

(Translated by Johan de Molenaar)
Helikon, Vol. IV., pp. 87–88. 1934.

DER STRAND VON BAILE

(Translated by E. E. Stein)
Die Neue Rundschau, November 1934.

DIE SCHWELLE DES KÖNIGS

(Translated by E. E. Stein)
Die Neue Rundschau, October 1935.

UN DISEUR DE CONTES

(Translated by Claude Dravaine)
Revue Politique et Littéraire, November 16, 1935.

AFTER LONG SILENCE. GIRL'S SONG.

(Translated by Gabriel Smit)
Gulden Winckel, Vol. VII. May 1937.

TO A FRIEND WHOSE WORK HAS COME TO NOTHING

Kroniek van Hedenhaagsche Kunst en Cultuur (*Chronicle of Contemporary Art and Culture*), Vol. IV., p. 101. 1938.

ZEE-KIEZEN NEAR BYZANTIUM

(Translated by P. N. van Eyck)
Groot Nederland, Vol. I., pp. 217–218. 1939.
Reprinted in *Benaderingen* (*Approach*), a collection of poems translated by P. N. van Eyck, published by A. A. M. Stols, Maastricht, 1940.

SULL'ACQUE TENEBROSE

Il Dramma (Turin), August 15, 1940.

VISIONI DI MAGGIO

(Translated by Carlo Linati)
Il Dramma (Turin), October 1, 1940.

LADY CATHLEEN

Il Dramma (Turin), December 1, 1940.

DE BALLADE VAN PRIESTER GILLIGAN

(Translated by Johan van Delden)
De Gemeenschap, December 1940.
Privately reprinted in an edition of 40 copies, 1941.

LA POVERELLA

(*Cathleen ni Houlihan*, translated by Carlo Linati)
Il Dramma, January 15, 1941.

L'UNICORNO DALLE STELLE

(Translated by Agar Pampanini)
Il Dramma, December 1, 1941.

RECONCILIATION

(Translated by A. Roland Holst)
De Gids (The Guide), 1942.

LA CLESSIDRA

(*The Hour-Glass*, translated by Agar Pampanini)

L'ATTRICE REGINA

(Translated by Michaela de Pastrovich Pampanini)

IL MIRACOLO

(*The Cat and the Moon*, translated by Agar Pampanini)
Il Dramma, October 1, 1943.

LE POT DE BOUILLON

(Translated by Claude Dravaine)
Jeux, Tréteaux et Personnages, November–December 1946.

A VAIN HOPE. THE FOUR AGES OF MAN.

(Translated by Shōtarō Oshima)
Waseda bungaku (Waseda literature), December 1946.

LE SABLIER

(Translated by Claude Dravaine)
Jeux, Tretéaux et Personnages, September–October, 1947.

GOLGOTHA

(*Calvary*, translated by Herberth E. Herlitschka)
Die Neue Rundschau, Zweites Heft, 1950.

AT THE HAWK'S WELL

(Translated by Mario Yokomichi)
No-gaku no yube (The eve of Noh plays), October 1950.

AFTER LONG SILENCE. THE ROSE TREE.

(Translated with notes by Shōtarō Oshima)
Keisei (Formation), Vol. I, No. 4 1953.

SUR UN CENTAURE NOIR, TABLEAU D'EDMOND DULAC

(Translated by Harry Goldgar and Yvonne Féron)
Western Review, Winter 1951.

THE SONG OF WANDERING AENGUS

The Study of English (Tokyo), April 1955.

THE ROSE OF PEACE

(Translated by Makoto Sangū)

BYZANTIUM

(Translated by Shōtarō Oshima)
Shi-kai (The poetic world), No. 50 1957.

THE HERNE'S EGG
   (Translated by Roger Giroux)

ON A BLACK CENTAUR BY EDMUND DULAC
   (Translated by Yves Bonnefoy)
   Cahiers Renaud-Barrault 37, February 1962.

PART V

JAPANESE PUBLICATIONS IN ENGLISH

JAPANESE PUBLICATIONS IN ENGLISH

The Yoyo-Juku Series No. 3 | [Japanese characters] THE | LAND OF HEART'S DESIRE | AND | TWO OTHER PLAYS | by | W. B. Yeats | Translated with Introduction and Notes | by | Okakura Yoshisabura | and | Takei Ryokichi | [ornament] | Tokyo | Kenkyūsha | 1925

$7 \times 4\frac{13}{16}$; pp. 99: comprising The Land of Heart's Desire. pp. 1–36; Cathleen ni Hoolihan, pp. 37–56; Deidre, pp. 57–99.

I have not seen a copy of this book.

SELECT POEMS OF WILLIAM BUTLER YEATS ("KENKYUSHA ENGLISH CLASSICS"). EDITED WITH INTRODUCTION AND NOTES BY KAZUMI YANO. TOKYO, KENKYUSHA, 1928.

$7\frac{1}{2} \times 5\frac{1}{8}$; pp. [14], xlvi, 246: comprising half-title, verso blank, pp. [1–2]; title and verso, pp. [3–4]; dedication, pp. [5–6]; preface in Japanese, pp. [7–9]; p. [10] blank; contents, pp. [11–13]; p. [14] blank; introduction in Japanese, pp. l–xlvi; poems, pp. 1–127; p. [128] blank; notes in Japanese and English, pp. 129–230; index to notes, pp. 231–240; index of titles, pp. 241–244; colophon, verso blank, pp. [245–246]. Two illustrations in collotype are inserted in the text.

Issued in red cloth, lettered in gold with design on spine and front cover.

As You Like It Series | [rule] No. 28 [in green] | W. B. YEATS | THE LAND OF | HEART'S DESIRE | [woodcut of flowers] | Sanseido.

$7\frac{11}{16} \times 5\frac{15}{16}$; pp. ii, 38: comprising half-title, persons in the play on verso, pp. i–ii; preface, pp. 1–2; text, pp. 3–33; note to the play by Yeats, p. 34; pp. 35–36, blank; list of As You Like It Series, p. 37; p. [38] blank.

Issued in paper covers. Published September 1929.

I have not seen a copy of this book.

POEMS OF W. B. YEATS ("THE KAIRYUDO TEXTS OF ENGLISH POETRY"). EDITED BY MAKOTO SANGU. KAIRYUDO, TOKYO, AUGUST, 1939.

$8\frac{7}{8} \times 6$; pp. viii, 48: comprising half-title, verso blank, pp. [i–ii]; Yeats's portrait, title, verso blank, pp. [iii–iv]; short biography of Yeats, verso blank, pp. [v–vi]; contents, pp. [vii–viii]; poems, pp. 1–45; p. [46] blank; colophon, verso blank, pp. [47–48].

Issued in paper covers.

I have not seen a copy of this book.

APPENDICES

THE CUALA PRESS, FIRST CALLED THE DUN EMER PRESS

A full and careful description of the publications of this Press may be found in *The Dun Emer Press and The Cuala Press* by Mr. William Maxwell, which was privately printed by him in an edition of thirty copies in 1932. This contained "a complete list of Books Pamphlets Leaflets and Broadsides printed by Miss Yeats with some Notes by the Compiler," and carried the record down to May 1932. Besides describing 47 books published by the Press the volume included mention of 20 Booklets and Pamphlets privately printed, and of 9 Books privately printed for their authors, and also noted the contents of the first series of *A Broadside*, issued monthly for six years, June 1908 to May 1915.

As a prospectus of November 1908 describes the books issued from the Press as being chosen and edited by W. B. Yeats I have thought it useful to append a list of these down to the beginning of 1939. I am able, in most cases, to add the date of publication of each book, an item of information not given in Mr. Maxwell's list. These dates are taken from a list issued by the Cuala Press in 1921; from October 1921 till October 1931 the records of the Press are unfortunately missing; I have therefore, for those years, supplied the dates—with one exception—on which copies were received by the British Museum Library, and have been able to confirm a number of these from the dated invoices received from the Press with my own copies; these must, I consider, approximate closely to the actual dates of publication. From 1932 onward the publication dates were kindly supplied me by Mrs. W. B. Yeats from the existing records.

THE DUN EMER PRESS

1 IN THE SEVEN WOODS by W. B. Yeats. 325 copies. Finished July 1903. Published August 1903.

2 THE NUTS OF KNOWLEDGE by A.E. 200 copies. Finished October 1903. Published December 1, 1903.

3 THE LOVE SONGS OF CONNACHT collected and translated by Douglas Hyde with preface by W. B. Yeats. 300 copies. Finished April 1904. Published July 4, 1904.

4   TWENTY-ONE POEMS by Lionel Johnson. Selected by W. B.
    Yeats. 220 copies. Finished October 1904. Published February
    21, 1905.

5   STORIES OF RED HANRAHAN by W. B. Yeats. 500
    copies. Finished October 1904. Published May 16, 1905.

6   SOME ESSAYS AND PASSAGES by John Eglinton. Selected
    by W. B. Yeats. 200 copies. Finished April 1905. Published
    August 25, 1905.

7   SIXTEEN POEMS by William Allingham. Selected by W. B.
    Yeats. 200 copies. Finished September 1905. Published Novem-
    ber 27, 1905.

8   A BOOK OF SAINTS AND WONDERS by Lady Gregory.
    200 copies. Finished August 1906. Published September 10,
    1906.

9   BY STILL WATERS: LYRICAL POEMS by A.E. 200 copies.
    Finished November 1906. Published December 14, 1906.

10 TWENTY ONE POEMS by Katharine Tynan. Selected by
    W. B. Yeats. 200 copies. Finished March 1907. Published
    August 6, 1907.

11 DISCOVERIES by W. B. Yeats. 200 copies. Finished Septem-
    ber 1907. Published December 15, 1907.

THE CUALA PRESS

12 POETRY AND IRELAND by W. B. Yeats and Lionel Johnson.
    250 copies. Finished October 1908. Published December 1,
    1908.

13 POEMS AND TRANSLATIONS by John M. Synge with
    preface by W. B. Yeats. 250 copies. Finished April 1909.
    Published July 5, 1909.

14 DEIRDRE OF THE SORROWS by John M. Synge with
    preface by W. B. Yeats. 250 copies. Finished May 1910.
    Published July 5, 1910.

15 THE GREEN HELMET AND OTHER POEMS by W. B.
    Yeats. 400 copies. Finished September 1910. Published
    December 1910.

16 SYNGE AND THE IRELAND OF HIS TIME by W. B.
    Yeats. With a Note concerning a walk through Connemara with

him by Jack B. Yeats. 350 copies. Finished May 1911. Published July 26, 1911.

17 SELECTIONS FROM THE WRITINGS OF LORD DUN-SANY with preface by W. B. Yeats. 250 copies. Finished August 1912. Published October 1912.

18 A SELECTION FROM THE LOVE POETRY OF W. B. YEATS. 300 copies. Finished May 1913. Published July 25, 1913.

18A POEMS WRITTEN IN DISCOURAGEMENT by W. B. Yeats 1912–1913. 50 copies, not for sale. Printed October 1913.

19 A WOMAN'S RELIQUARY edited by Edward Dowden. 300 copies. Finished September 1913. Published November 17, 1913.

[A note in a prospectus of 1914 states that "This book is not a part of the Cuala Series arranged by W. B. Yeats."]

19A THE HOUR GLASS by W. B. Yeats. 50 copies, not for sale. Printed January 1914.

20 RESPONSIBILITIES: POEMS AND A PLAY by W. B. Yeats. 400 copies. Finished May 1914. Published May 25, 1914.

21 THE POST OFFICE by Rabindranath Tagore, translated by Devabrata Mukerjea, with preface by W. B. Yeats. 400 copies. Finished June 1914. Published July 27, 1914.

22 JOHN M. SYNGE: A FEW PERSONAL RECOLLECTIONS by John Masefield. 350 copies. Finished April 1915. Published June 2, 1915.

23 REVERIES OVER CHILDHOOD AND YOUTH by W. B. Yeats. Issued with portfolio containing three illustrations. 425 copies. Finished October 1915. Published March 20, 1916.

24 CERTAIN NOBLE PLAYS OF JAPAN chosen from the manuscripts of Ernest Fenollosa by Ezra Pound, with an introduction by W. B. Yeats. 350 copies. Finished July 1916. Published September 16, 1916.

25 PASSAGES FROM THE LETTERS OF JOHN BUTLER YEATS selected by Ezra Pound. 400 copies. Finished February 1917. Published on May Eve, 1917.

26 THE WILD SWANS AT COOLE by W. B. Yeats. 400 copies. Finished October 1917. Published November 17, 1917.

27 THE KILTARTAN POETRY BOOK. Prose Translations
from the Irish by Lady Gregory. 400 copies. Finished August
1918. Published November 22, 1918.

28 TWO PLAYS FOR DANCERS by W. B. Yeats. 400 copies.
Finished January 1919. Published January 1919.

29 FURTHER LETTERS OF JOHN BUTLER YEATS selected
by Lennox Robinson. 400 copies. Finished January 1920.
British Museum copy received March 23, 1920.

30 MICHAEL ROBARTES AND THE DANCER by W. B. Yeats.
400 copies. Finished November 1920. Published February 1921.

31 FOUR YEARS by W. B. Yeats. 400 copies. Finished October
1921. British Museum copy received December 19, 1921.

32 SEVEN POEMS AND A FRAGMENT by W. B. Yeats. 500
copies. Finished April 1922. British Museum copy received
June 8, 1922.

33 EARLY MEMORIES by John Butler Yeats. 500 copies. Finished
July 1923. British Museum copy received September 17, 1923.

34 AN OFFERING OF SWANS by Oliver Gogarty, with preface
by W. B. Yeats. 300 copies. Finished October 1923. British
Museum copy received January 7, 1924.

35 THE CAT AND THE MOON by W. B. Yeats. 500 copies.
Finished May 1924. British Museum copy received June 25,
1924.

36 THE BOUNTY OF SWEDEN by W. B. Yeats. 400 copies.
Finished May 1925. British Museum copy received July 7, 1925.

37 LOVE'S BITTER SWEET. Translations from the Irish by
Robin Flower. 500 copies. Finished October 1925. British
Museum copy received December 28, 1925.

38 ESTRANGEMENT by W. B. Yeats. 300 copies. Finished
June 1926. British Museum copy received August 9, 1926.

39 POEMS by Thomas Parnell, selected by Lennox Robinson.
200 copies. Finished May 1927. British Museum copy received
June 24, 1927.

40 OCTOBER BLAST by W. B. Yeats. 350 copies. Finished
June 1927. British Museum copy received August 18, 1927.

41 THE DEATH OF SYNGE by W. B. Yeats. 400 copies.
Finished May 1928. British Museum copy received June 15,
1928.

42 A LITTLE ANTHOLOGY OF MODERN IRISH VERSE selected by Lennox Robinson. 300 copies. Finished September 1928. British Museum copy received November 28, 1928.

43 A PACKET FOR EZRA POUND by W. B. Yeats. 425 copies. Finished June 1929. British Museum copy received August 21, 1929.

44 LYRICS AND SATIRES FROM TOM MOORE selected by Sean O'Faolain, with five designs by Hilda Roberts. 130 copies. Finished November 1929.

45 WILD APPLES by Oliver Gogarty, with preface by W. B. Yeats. 250 copies. Finished February 1930. British Museum copy received April 4, 1930.

46 COOLE by Lady Gregory, with an introductory poem by W. B. Yeats. 250 copies. Finished May 1931. British Museum copy received July 9, 1931.

47 STORIES OF MICHAEL ROBARTES AND HIS FRIENDS by W. B. Yeats. 450 copies. Finished October 1931. Published March 1932.

48 THE WILD BIRD'S NEST. Poems from the Irish by Frank O'Connor. 250 copies. Published July 12, 1932.

49 WORDS FOR MUSIC PERHAPS by W. B. Yeats. 450 copies. Finished September 1932. Published November 14, 1932.

50 PILGRIMAGE IN THE WEST by Mario M. Rossi, translated by J. M. Hone. 300 copies. Finished June 1933. Published July 1933.

51 ARABLE HOLDINGS by F. R. Higgins. 300 copies. Finished October 1933. Published November 1933.

52 THE WORDS UPON THE WINDOW PANE by W. B. Yeats. 350 copies. Finished January 1934. Published April 1934.

53 THE KING OF THE GREAT CLOCK TOWER by W. B. Yeats. 400 copies. Finished October 1934. Published December 14, 1934.

54 DRAMATIS PERSONÆ by W. B. Yeats. 400 copies. Finished October 1935. Published December 9, 1935.

54A POEMS by William Butler Yeats. 30 copies, not for sale. Printed 1935.

55   BROADSIDES, a collection of old and new songs with coloured
      illustrations and music, edited by W. B. Yeats and F. R. Higgins
      with an introductory essay autographed by the editors. 100
      copies. December 1935.
      [This refers to the bound volumes of the second series of
      BROADSIDES.]

56   PASSAGES FROM THE LETTERS OF A.E. TO W. B.
      YEATS. 300 copies. Finished June 1936. Published August 18,
      1936.

57   ESSAYS 1931–1936 by W. B. Yeats. 300 copies. Finished
      October 1937. Published December 14, 1937.

58   BROADSIDES, a collection of new Irish and English songs
      with coloured illustrations and music, edited by W. B. Yeats
      and Dorothy Wellesley with an introductory essay autographed
      by the editors. 150 copies. December 1937.
      [This refers to the bound volumes of the third series of BROAD-
      SIDES.]

59   NEW POEMS by W. B. Yeats. 450 copies. Finished April 1938.
      Published May 18, 1938.

60   LORDS AND COMMONS, translations from the Irish by
      Frank O'Connor. 250 copies. Finished August 1938. Published
      October 25, 1938.

Illuminated Poems by W. B. Yeats have been issued by the Dun Emer
and the Cuala Press, as follows. For the dates of issue I am indebted
to Mr. P. S. O'Hegarty's *Notes*.

The Lake Isle of Innisfree.	1908
The Pity of Love.	1908
The Lover Tells of the Rose.	1908
Had I the Heavens' Embroidered Cloths.	1908
Into the Twilight.	1910
The Lover Pleads.	1910
From *The Celtic Twilight.*	1910
(A passage from the essay *Earth, Fire and Water* be- ginning "We can make our minds like still water.")	
The Fiddler of Dooney.	1928
With Picture by George Atkinson, R.H.A.	
Silver Apples.	1937

The Cuala Press has issued the following as Christmas cards:

Autumn Beauty. With Picture by Dorothy Blackham.   1937
A Cradle Song. With Picture by Jack B. Yeats.
The Magi. With Picture by Nano Reid.
Laugh Heart (from *Into the Twilight*). With Picture by E. C. Yeats.

APPENDIX II

SOME BOOKS ABOUT YEATS AND HIS WORK

In addition to the books dealing with Yeats's life and work already described in Part II (3) above, the following books have been published:

Some Critical Appreciations of William Butler Yeats as Poet, Orator and Dramatist. No publisher given. The closest approximation to a date is 1903; October of that year is the latest magazine excerpt. (Contains contributions from G. K. Chesterton, Richard Ashe King, William Sharp, Clement Shorter, and from various magazines.)

William Butler Yeats. By Horatio Sheafe Krans. New York: McClure Phillips & Co., 1904; London: Heinemann. 1905.

Irish Plays and Playwrights. By Cornelius Weygandt. Boston and New York: Houghton Mifflin Company. 1913.

W. B. Yeats. A critical study. By Forrest Reid. London: Secker. 1915.

William Butler Yeats. The Poet in Contemporary Ireland. By J. M. Hone. Dublin and London: Maunsel & Co. 1916.

The Early Poetry of W. B. Yeats. By Patty Gurd. Lancaster, Pa.: Press of the New Era Printing Company. 1916.

W. B. Yeats. A literary study. By C. L. Wrenn. Durham: Durham University Journal; London: T. Murby & Co. 1920.

Shin bungei (New Literature). Vol. I, No. 5. Yeats number. Tokyo: Shin Bungei Sha. 1921.
(Contains contributions from Yū Funabashi, Kiyoshi Satō, Takeshi Saito.)

Eigo seinen (The Rising Generation). Vol. L, Nos. 9–12. W. B. Yeats numbers. Tokyo: 1924.
February 1. (Contains contributions from Rintaro Fukuhara, Masujirō Honda, Yone Noguchi, Makoto Sangū, Junzō Satō, Sōfū Taketomo, Gisuke Tomita, Hōjin Yano.)
February 15. (Contains contributions from Yonejirō Noguchi, Makoto Sangū, Hōjin Yano.)
March 1. (Contains contributions from Makoto Sangū, Hōjin Yano.)

March 15. (Contains contributions from Makoto Sangū, Seiichi Uchida.)

Jeitsu Kenkyu. W. B. Yeats: A Study. By Shôtarô Oshima. Tokyo: Taibunsha. 1927.

Wesen der Dichtung und Aufgabe des Dichters bei William Butler Yeats. By Gerta Hüttemann. Bonn. 1929.

Kōsaku Yamada Gesammelte Werke. Vol. II. By Kōsaku Yamada. Tokyo: Shunju Sha. 1930.

(Contains Kōsaku Yamada's music for 'At the Hawk's Well'; his translation into Japanese of four songs from the same play; and his reminiscences of the writing of the music in New York in July 1918.)

Mysticism in A.E. and W. B. Yeats in relation to Oriental and American Thought. By Grace Emily Jackson. Ohio State University. 1932.

A Letter to W. B. Yeats. By L. A. G. Strong. London: Leonard and Virginia Woolf. 1932.

W. B. Yeats. By Shôtarô Oshima. Tokyo: Kenkyusha. 1934.

William Butler Yeats. By John H. Pollock. London: Duckworth & Co; Dublin: Talbot Press. 1935.

William Butler Yeats. Aetat 70. A pamphlet reprinted from *The Irish Times* of June 13, 1935.

(Contains contributions from Aodh De Blacam, Francis Hackett, Denis Johnston, Andrew Malone.)

Ad Multos Annos William Butler Yeats in his seventieth year. By Joyce Mayhew. A pamphlet. Five hundred copies printed by the Eucalyptus Press for Albert M. Bender September 1935. Mills College, California.

The Works of Morris and Yeats in relation to Early Saga Literature. By Agnes D. M. Hoare. Cambridge University Press, 1937.

The Time of Yeats. By Cornelius Weygandt. New York and London: D. Appleton-Century Company. 1937.

Sailing to Byzantium. A study in the development of the later style and symbolism in the poetry of W. B. Yeats. By J. P. O'Donnell. Cambridge, Mass.: Harvard University Press. 1939.

Poet Young and Old—W. B. Yeats. By Arthur J. M. Smith. University of Toronto Press. 1939.

Scattering Branches. Tributes to the Memory of W. B. Yeats. Edited by Stephen Gwynn. London: Macmillan & Co. 1940.

(Contains contributions from Stephen Gwynn, Maud Gonne, Sir William Rothenstein, Lennox Robinson, W. G. Fay, Edmund Dulac, F. R. Higgins, C. Day Lewis, L. A. G. Strong.)

Reissued under the title *William Butler Yeats Essays in Tribute.* Port Washington, New York: Kennikat Press. 1965.

Some Memories of W. B. Yeats. By John Masefield. Dublin: Cuala Press. 1940.

The Poetry of W. B. Yeats. By Louis MacNeice. Oxford University Press. 1941.

The Southern Review. Vol. VII, No. 3. William Butler Yeats Memorial Issue. Louisiana State University, Winter, 1941. (Contains contributions from R. P. Blackmur, L. C. Knights, T. S. Eliot, F. O. Matthiessen, Delmore Schwartz, Horace Gregory, Donald Davidson, John Crowe Ransom, Kenneth Burke, Morton Dauwen Zabel, Allen Tate, Arthur Mizener, Austin Warren, Howard Baker, Randall Jarrell.)

Poetry, Monads and Society. By Kabir Humayum. Calcutta: University of Calcutta Press. 1941.

The Development of W. B. Yeats. By V. K. Menon. Edinburgh and London: Oliver & Boyd. 1942.
Revised edition: Edinburgh, Oliver & Boyd, 1960; Philadelphia, Dufour Editions, 1961.

Three Mystic Poets: a study of W. B. Yeats, A. E., and Rabindranath Tagore. By Albinash Chandra Bose. Kolhapur: School and College Bookstall. 1945.

Towards a Mythology. Studies in the poetry of W. B. Yeats. By Peter Ure. University Press of Liverpool. 1946.

Trois Poëtes: Hopkins, Yeats, Eliot. By Georges Cattaui. Paris: Egloff. 1947.

The Golden Nightingale. Essays on Some Principles of Poetry in the Lyrics of William Butler Yeats. By Donald A. Stauffer. Macmillan. 1949.

The Permanence of Yeats. Selected criticism. Edited by James Hall and Martin Steinmann. New York: The Macmillan Company. 1950.
(Contains contributions from J. Middleton Murry, Edmund Wilson, R. P. Blackmur, Cleanth Brooks, Jr., J. C. Ransom, Allen Tate, David Daiches, Arthur Mizener, F. R. Leavis, Stephen Spender, D. S. Savage, Joseph Warren Beach, Austin Warren, Eric Bentley, Kenneth Burke, W. Y. Tindall, Donald Davidson, Elder Olson, A. Norman Jeffares, Delmore Schwartz T. S. Eliot, W. H. Auden, M. D. Zabel, W. E. Houghton.)
Published as a paperback by Collier Books in 1961. Collier Books BS 11.

The Darkling Plain. A study of the later fortunes of romanticism in English Poetry from George Darley to W. B. Yeats. By John F. A. Heath-Stubbs. London: Eyre & Spottiswoode Ltd. 1950. Toronto: Collins. 1950.

The Lonely Tower. Studies in the Poetry of W. B. Yeats. By T. R.

Henn. London: Methuen & Co. 1950. New York: Pellegrini & Cudahy. 1952.

A second edition, revised, was published in 1965. London: Methuen & Co. New York: Barnes & Noble.

W. B. Yeats: The Tragic Phase. A study of the Last Poems. By Vivienne Koch. London: Routledge and Kegan Paul Ltd. 1951.

The Interpretation of the Cuchulain Legend in the Works of W. B. Yeats. By B. Bjersby. Upsala: A.-B. Lundequistska Bokhandeln. Dublin: Hodges, Figgis and Company; Cambridge, Mass.: Harvard University Press. 1951.

W. B. Yeats Self Critic. A Study of His Early Verse. By Thomas Parkinson. Berkeley: University of California Press; London: Cambridge University Press. 1951.

Three Great Irishmen. Shaw, Yeats, Joyce. By Arland Ussher. London: Victor Gollancz Ltd. 1952.

W. B. Yeats. By G. S. Fraser. Published for The British Council and the National Book League by Longmans, Green & Co. 1954.

Stephens, Yeats, and Other Irish Concerns. By George Brandon Saul. New York: The New York Public Library. 1954.

Notable Images of Virtue Emily Brontë, George Meredith, W. B. Yeats. By C. Day Lewis. Toronto: The Ryerson Press. 1954.

A. E. Housman & W. B. Yeats. Two lectures by Richard Aldington. Hurst, Berkshire: The Peacock Press. 1955.

Emergence from Chaos. [Dylan Thomas, Whitman, Yeats, Rimbaud, Rilke, Eliot] By Stuart Holroyd. Boston: Houghton Mifflin Co. 1957. London: Victor Gollancz Ltd. 1957.

The Romantic Survival. [Yeats, Auden, Dylan Thomas] By John Bayley. London: Constable & Co. Ltd. 1957. Fair Lawn, New Jersey: Essential Books, 1957.

Prolegomena to the Study of Yeats's Poems. By George Brandon Saul. Philadelphia: University of Pennsylvania Press. 1957. London: Oxford University Press. 1957.

Romantic Image. By Frank Kermode. London: Routledge and Kegan Paul Ltd. 1957. New York: The Macmillan Company. 1957.

I, the Poet William Yeats. A photographic exhibition illustrating the life and work of W. B. Yeats. Reading: Department of English, University of Reading. 1957. [Typescript]

Yeats and the Belief in Life: An address at the University of New Hampshire, January 17, 1957. By Archibald Macleish. Durham: University of New Hampshire Press. 1958.

Prolegomena to the Study of Yeats's Plays. By George Brandon Saul. Philadelphia: University of Pennsylvania Press. 1958. London: Oxford University Press. 1958.

W. B. Yeats and Tradition. By F. A. C. Wilson. London: Victor Gollancz Ltd. 1958. New York: The Macmillan Company. 1958.

Yeats at the Municipal Gallery. With an Introduction by Arland Ussher. Dublin: The Dolmen Press. 1959. [A pamphlet.]

A Reader's Guide to William Butler Yeats. By John Unterecker. New York: Noonday Press. 1959. London: Thames and Hudson Ltd. 1959.

The Poet in the Poem. The Personae of Eliot, Yeats, and Pound. By George T. Wright. Berkeley and Los Angeles: University of California Press. 1960.

The Poetry of W. B. Yeats. By Yvor Winters. Denver: The Swallow Pamphlets, No. 10. 1960.

The Whole Mystery of Art; pattern into poetry in the work of W. B. Yeats. By George Melchiori. London: Routledge and Kegan Paul Ltd. 1960. New York: The Macmillan Company. 1961.

The Poetry of W. B. Yeats. By A. Norman Jeffares. London: Edward Arnold Ltd. 1961. Published in America as a paperback in Barron's Studies in English Literature Series.

W. B. Yeats: His Poetry and Thought. By A. G. Stock. Cambridge University Press. 1961.

William Butler Yeats. The Lyric of Tragedy. By B. L. Reid. Norman, Oklahoma: University of Oklahoma Press. 1961. Nottingham, England: W. S. Hall. 1961.

W. B. Yeats Images of a Poet. Edited by D. J. Gordon. Manchester: University of Manchester Press. 1961. New York: Barnes & Noble. 1962. [Expanded from I, the Poet William Yeats. 1957.]

Yeats's Early Contacts with French Poetry. By Edward Davis. Pretoria, South Africa: University of South Africa Press. 1961. [Paperback.]

Poets in the Flesh: Tagore, Yeats, Dunsany, Stephens, Drinkwater. By R. Rattray. Cambridge, England: Golden Head Press Ltd. 1961.

Dublin in the Age of William Butler Yeats and James Joyce. By Richard M. Kain. Norman, Oklahoma: University of Oklahoma Press. 1962. A volume in the Centers of Civilization series.

William Butler Yeats: The Poet as a Mythmaker. By Morton I. Seidan. East Lansing, Michigan: Michigan State University Press. 1962.

The Yeats Country. Compiled by Sheelah Kirby, edited by Patrick Gallagher, with drawings and maps by Ruth Brandt. Dublin: The Dolmen Press. 1962.

William Morris and W. B. Yeats. By Peter Faulkner. Dublin: The Dolmen Press. 1962.

The Poetry of W. B. Yeats. By Bhabatosh Chatterjee. Bombay: Orient Longmans. 1962.

W. B. Yeats. By B. P. Misra. Delhi: Kitab Mahal. 1962. [Paperback.]

Yeats the Playwright. A Commentary on Character and Design in the Major Plays. By Peter Ure. London: Routledge and Kegan Paul Ltd. 1963. New York: Barnes & Noble. 1963.

Yeats: A Collection of Critical Essays. Edited by John Unterecker. Englewood Cliffs, New Jersey: Prentice-Hall Inc. 1963. Issued in cloth- and paper-bound editions. A volume in the Twentieth Century Views series.

(Contains contributions from W. H. Auden, R. P. Blackmur, Curtis Bradford, T. S. Eliot, Richard Ellmann, D. J. Gordon, Ian Fletcher, Hugh Kenner, Frank Kermode, Giorgio Melchiori, A. G. Stock, Allan Tate, W. Y. Tindall, John Unterecker.)

A Review of English Literature. Vol. IV, No. 3. W. B. Yeats Issue. Longmans, Green & Company, London. July 1963.

(Contains contributions from S. B. Bushrui, Glenn O'Malley, Jon Stallworthy (2), W. B. Stanford, Donald T. Torchiana.)

The Irish Book. Vol. II, Nos. 3/4. Special Yeats Issue. The Dolmen Press, Dublin. Autumn 1963.

(Contains contributions from Russell K. Alspach, Peter Faulkner, Michaél Ó Haodha, Liam Miller, Ann Saddlemyer, Robin Skelton.)

The Drama of Chekhov, Synge, Yeats, and Pirandello. By Frank L. Lucas. London: Cassell. 1963.

La lotta con Proteo. By Glauco Cambon. Milano: Bompiani. 1963. (Studies of Faulkner, Joyce, Melville, Montale, Whitman, Yeats.)

Yeats. By Peter Ure. Edinburgh and London: Oliver and Boyd Ltd. 1963. New York: Grove Press Inc. 1964. A volume in the Writers and Critics series.

W. B. Yeats oder Der Dichter in der modernen Welt. By Johannes Kleinstuck. Hamburg: Leibniz-Verlag. 1963.

The Hidden God. By Cleanth Brooks. New Haven and London: Yale University Press. 1963. (Studies of Eliot, Faulkner, Hemingway, Warren, Yeats.)

The Vast Design. Patterns in W. B. Yeats's Aesthetic. By Edward Engelberg. Toronto: The University of Toronto Press. 1964.

The New Poetic. By C. K. Stead. London: Hutchison University Library. 1964.

Rilke, Valery and Yeats. The Domain of the Self. By Priscilla Washburn Shaw. New Brunswick, New Jersey: Rutgers University Press. 1964.

The Age of Yeats. Edited by George Brandon Saul. New York: Dell
Publishing Company Inc. 1964. Laurel Masterpieces of World
Literature, No. 0049. [Paperback.]

Modern Drama. Vol. VII, No. 3, Devoted to Yeats's Plays. Univer-
sity of Kansas, Lawrence, Kansas. December, 1964.
(Contains contributions from David R. Clark, Gabriel
Fallon, Marjorie J. Lightfoot, John R. Moore, Daniel J. Murphy,
Marilyn Gaddis Rose, Sister Aloyse Scanlon, John Unterecker,
Peter Ure, Helen Hennessy Vendler, Sidney Warschausky.)

W. B. Yeats and the Theatre of Desolate Reality. By David R. Clark.
Dublin: The Dolmen Press. 1965.

*William Butler Yeats 1865–1965 A Catalogue of his Works and Associ-
ated Items in Olin Library, Wesleyan University, together with
an Essay by David R. Clark '42.* Middletown 1965. Dublin:
The Dolmen Press. 1965.

Yeats's Verse-Plays: The Revisions 1900–1910. By S. B. Bushrui.
Oxford: Clarendon Press. 1965.

W. B. Yeats: A Critical Introduction. By Balachandra Rajan. London: Hutchinson & Co. Ltd. 1965. A volume in the Hutchinson
Universal Library.

The Tragic Drama of William Butler Yeats. Figures in a Dance. By
Leonard E. Nathan. New York and London: Columbia University Press. 1965.

Thoor Ballylee—Home of William Butler Yeats. Edited by Liam
Miller from a paper given by Mary Hanley to the Kiltartan
Society in 1961 with a foreword by T. R. Henn. Dublin: The
Dolmen Press. 1965.

In Excited Reverie. A centenary tribute to William Butler Yeats.
Edited by A. Norman Jeffares and K. G. W. Cross. London:
Macmillan & Co. Ltd. 1965. New York: St. Martin's Press. 1965.
(Contains contributions from Hazard Adams, Russell K. Als-
pach, S. B. Bushrui, David Daiches, Edward Engelberg, T. R.
Henn, A. D. Hope, Brendan Kennelly, Hugh MacDiarmuid,
Conor Cruse O'Brien, Lennox Robinson, W. R. Rodgers, Jon
Stallworthy, A. G. Stock, Randolph Stow, Donald T. Torchiana.)

Ireland Weekly Bulletin of the Department of External Affairs. No.
706. [Devoted to the life and work of Yeats.] Dublin, June 15,
1965.
(Contains an anomyous critical biography with nine illustrations.)

Yeats and Castiglione. Poet and Courtier. By Corinna Salvadori.
London: Allen Figgis. 1965. New York: Barnes & Noble.
1965.

The Dublin Magazine. Vol. 4, No. 2. W. B. Yeats Centenary Edition.
Dublin: New Square Publications. Summer, 1965.

(Contains contributions from Muriel C. Bradbrook, George Mills Harper, T. R. Henn, A. Norman Jeffares.)

Threshold. No. 19. The Theatre of W. B. Yeats Centenary 1965. Threshold Publications, Belfast, Autumn, 1965.
(Contains contributions from Ronald Ayling, Pronoti Baski, Austin Clarke, Ruby Cohn, John Jay, Frederick Kalister, Roger McHugh, Mary O'Malley, Shotaro Oshima, Raymond Warren.)

Poets of Reality. By J. Hillis Miller. Cambridge: Harvard University Press. 1965. (Studies of Conrad, Eliot, Wallace Stevens, Dylan Thomas, William Carlos Williams, Yeats.)

University Review. Vol. III, No. 8. Special Yeats Edition. Organ of the Graduates' Association of the University of Ireland, Dublin. [August 1965?]
(Contains contributions from Brian Coffey, Thomas Dillon, Denis Donoghue, James Liddy, Brian Lynch, Thomas Mac-Greevy, Robert O'Driscoll, John O'Meara, Lorna Reynolds.)

Tri-Quarterly. Vol. I, No. 4. W. B. Yeats Centenary Edition. Evanston, Illinois. Fall, 1965.
(Contains contributions from Padraic Colum, Richard Ellmann, William P. Fay, Colton Johnson, Patrick Kavanagh, John V. Kelleher, Thomas Kinsella, Roger McHugh, Conor Cruse O'Brien, Moody E. Prior, B. Rajan, W. D. Snodgrass, Stephen Spender, D. T. Torchiana.)

The Dolmen Press Yeats Centenary Papers. General Editor: Liam Miller. Dublin: The Dolmen Press. London: Oxford University Press. Chester Springs, Pennsylvania: Dufour Editions.

No. I. *Yeats and the Easter Rising.* By Edward Malins. 1965.

No. II. *Beulah to Byzantium. A Study of Parallels in the Works of W. B. Yeats, William Blake, Samuel Palmer and Edward Calvert.* By Raymond Lister. 1965.

No. III. *Yeats and Innisfree.* By Russell K. Alspach. 1965.

No. IV. *Yeats's Idea of the Gael.* By Giles W. Telfer. 1965.

No. V. *Yeats & the Irish Eighteenth Century.* By Peter Faulkner. 1965.

No. VI. *Yeats and the Noh: Types of Japanese Beauty and their Reflection in Yeats's Plays.* By Hiro Ishibashi. 1966. [See No. 363]

No. VII. *In . . . Luminous Wind.* By George Brandon Saul. 1966.

No. VIII. *Yeats's 'Last Poems' again.* By Curtis Bradford. 1966. [See No. 364]

No. IX. *Yeats's Quest for Eden.* By George Mills Harper. 1966.

No. X. *Yeats and Patrick McCarten A Fenian Friendship.* By John Unterecker. 1967. [See No. 366]

No. XI. *Yeats and Joyce.* By Richard Ellmann. 1967.

James Joyce Quarterly. Vol. 3, No. 2. Yeats Issue. The University
of Tulsa, Winter, 1965.
(Contains contributions from Russell K. Alspach, Robert Friend
III, Richard M. Kain, Bernard Levine, Thomas Parkinson.)
An Honored Guest. New Essays on W. B. Yeats. Edited by Denis
Donoghue and J. R. Mulryne. London: Edward Arnold Ltd.
1965. New York: St. Martin's Press. 1966.
(Contains contributions from Donald Davie, Denis Donoghue,
Ian Fletcher, Northrop Frye, T. R. Henn, John Holloway,
Graham Martin, J. R. Mulryne, Charles Tomlinson, Peter Ure.)
The Yeats Society of Japan Bulletin. No. 1. Tokyo: The Yeats Society
of Japan. April, 1966.
(Contains contributions from Tetsuro Sano, Mariko Kai; and an
essay 'The Establishment and Inauguration of The Yeats Society
of Japan.')

YEATS AND BROADCASTING

BY GEORGE WHALLEY

Broadcast materials, when not suitable for *verbatim* reproduction in print, are peculiarly evanescent. Through the accidents of war many scripts, recordings, and written details of production were lost or destroyed in London, Dublin, and Belfast. Of the dozen broadcasts in which Yeats took part, only one complete programme and extracts from four others are now preserved on recordings. Only three of Yeats's scripts have survived at Broadcasting House; but other scripts —most of them in draft form—are preserved in Dublin among the Yeats papers in the possession of Mrs Yeats.

An interview with Yeats on the occasion of his first broadcast was reported in the *Belfast News-Letter*, September 9, 1931. For an account, written by George Barnes, of Yeats's broadcasts in 1937, see Hone's *Life*, pp. 454–7. V. C. Clinton-Baddeley has also given some account of his work in these programmes in his *Words for Music*, Cambridge 1940; and in more circumstantial detail in a broadcast in December 1931 (see p. 417 below).

In addition to the broadcasts which Yeats gave or arranged, performances of his plays and recitals of his poems were broadcast from 1929 onwards. *An Irish Programme*, Dublin, March 18, 1929, included "extracts and recitations from W. B. Yeats and Lady Gregory" as well as Irish instrumental music and songs; among those taking part were Sara Allgood, Tyrone Guthrie, Fred O'Donovan, Mary O'Farrell, and Herbert Ross. It is difficult to imagine that Yeats himself had had no hand in the production; and this programme formed the model for three other broadcasts (2, 4 and 8) in which Yeats took an active part. On November 27, 1930 Sara Allgood gave a reading of Yeats poems, with a commentary by Desmond MacCarthy; and on July 12, 1937 Shelah Richards and Ian Aylmer read "a Selection of Poetry of W. B. Yeats and A.E." Up to the end of 1937 four of Yeats's plays had been broadcast: *The Pot of Broth* (September 20, 1929), *King Œdipus* (September 14, 1931), *The Land of Heart's Desire* (August 27, 1934), and *Words upon the Window Pane* (November 22, 1937).

The essay "I Became an Author", printed in *The Listener* of August 4, 1938, was commissioned for publication and was not broadcast.

1   ŒDIPUS THE KING. September 8, 1931: 7.15–7.30 p.m. BBC Belfast: North Ireland Programme only. Produced by H. W. McMullan.

This talk was advertised as "Mr. W. B. Yeats: On his Version for the Modern Stage of the Greek play, 'King Œdipus,' to be broadcast from the Belfast Studio by the Abbey Players on September 14."

SCRIPT. The BBC Belfast file copy was destroyed during the war. A typescript, entitled "Talk on 'Œdipus the King' to be broadcast from Belfast September 8", is among the Yeats papers.

2   READING OF POEMS. September 8, 1931: 9.10–9.25 p.m. BBC Belfast: National Programme and North Ireland Programme. Produced by H. W. McMullan.

Yeats's reading comprised the central section of *An Irish Programme*, in which Sara Allgood sang Irish ballads, and the Belfast Wireless Symphony Orchestra played Irish music.

POEMS READ.   *The Lake Isle of Innisfree*
               The Fiddler of Dooney
               The Song of Wandering Aengus
               In Memory of Eva Gore-Booth and Con Markiewicz
               For Anne Gregory
               Sailing to Byzantium [cancelled in script]

SCRIPT. The BBC Belfast file copy was destroyed during the war. A rough working typescript with many MS alterations and corrections is among the Yeats papers. Further revisions may have been made during production.

RECORDING. No recording of the original broadcast is preserved. A BBC disc (No 22145 front: duration 5.05), dated April 10, 1932, is marked "Extract from a Talk on Rhythm"—probably because the opening sentence is "I am going to read my poems with great emphasis upon their rhythm"—and contains the introduction to this programme and his reading of the first two poems. This disc is either dubbed from a recording of the original Belfast broadcast, or is a test reading recorded when Yeats was preparing Broadcast 3 in London. A copy of this recording is held by the Lamont Library, Harvard.

3   POEMS ABOUT WOMEN. April 10, 1932: 9.5–9.30 p.m. BBC London: National Programme.

The opening sentence reads: "I asked a great friend, a very old woman, what I should read tonight. She said, 'Read them poems about women.'" The friend was Olivia Shakespear (see *Letters*, p. 786). Yeats read the poems with a continuous commentary.

POEMS READ. *To an Isle in the Water*
Down by the Salley Gardens [possibly cancelled in script]
I am of Ireland
His Phoenix
The Folly of Being Comforted
He Wishes for the Cloths of Heaven
Upon a Dying Lady I, II, VII, V
On a Political Prisoner

SCRIPT. The BBC file copy was destroyed during the war. A MS and three typescripts successively revised are among the Yeats papers.

4 ST PATRICK'S NIGHT. March 17, 1934: 9.35–10.30 p.m. BBC Belfast: National Programme and North Ireland Programme.

This broadcast was announced as "A Programme of Irish Music and Humour, and Poetry by W. B. Yeats spoken by himself." Details of the rest of the programme are not preserved, but the recordings show that there were songs and fiddle tunes.

POEMS READ. *The Song of the Old Mother*
A Faery Song
The Fiddler of Dooney
Running to Paradise
The Fisherman
Down by the Salley Gardens (sung by an actor)

SCRIPT. The Belfast file copy was destroyed during the war. A typescript with final corrections in Yeats's hand is among the Yeats papers.

RECORDING. Two BBC discs (No 216B, 22145 back: duration about 8 min) include Yeats's introduction and his reading of the first poem, and extracts from other parts of the programme. A copy of this recording of the first poem and introduction to the second is held by the Lamont Library, Harvard.
Printed in *The Listener*, April 4, 1934, under the title 'The Growth of a Poet.'

5 THE IRISH LITERARY MOVEMENT. No date. Radio Eireann.

A dialogue between Yeats and an interviewer identified in the script as "D.McD." The interlocutor was perhaps Donagh McDonagh.

SCRIPT. A typescript is among the Yeats papers.

6 READING OF POEMS. June 13, 1935: 10.40–10.55 p.m. BBC London: National Programme.

The script was prepared by Yeats and a contract prepared for "W. B. Yeats reading his own poems". There is a MS note on the contract: "No longer reading these himself." The poems were read by Audrey Moran, the programme being announced as "Selection of W. B. Yeats's Favourite Lyrics, on the occasion of his 70th birthday."

POEMS READ. *The Song of the Happy Shepherd*
The Indian to His Love
The Sad Shepherd
To an Isle in the Water
The Lake Isle of Innisfree
Brown Penny
The Wild Swans at Coole
He Wishes for the Cloths of Heaven

SCRIPT. File copy at Broadcasting House.

7 MODERN POETRY. October 11, 1936: 9.5–9.50 p.m. The Eighteenth of the Broadcast National Lectures. BBC London: National Programme.

The substance of this talk is closely connected with the Introduction to the *Oxford Book of Modern Verse*, in which collection are printed all the passages of verse read except the lines from *Burnt Norton*. For Yeats's references to this talk, see *Letters*, pp. 859, 863, 866, 867, 868, 885.

POEMS READ. Lionel Johnson, *The Church of a Dream*
T. Sturge Moore, *The Dying Swan*
Michael Field, *Sweeter Far than the Harp*
If They Honoured Me
Paul Fort (*tr.* F. York Powell), *The Sailor and the Shark* (8 lines)
T. S. Eliot, *Preludes* (8 lines)
C. Day Lewis, 'I've heard them lilting' (2 stanzas)
Edith Sitwell, *Ass-face*
T. S. Eliot, *Burnt Norton* (6 lines)
Dorothy Wellesley, *Matrix* (20 lines)
W. J. Turner, *The Seven Days of the Sun* vii
O. St J. Gogarty, *Dedication*
Non Dolet

SCRIPT. The text was printed in *The Listener* of October 14, 1936, and as a separate BBC pamphlet of 26 pages, 1936. Also printed in *The Living Age*, December 1936, and in *Essays 1931 to 1936*, 1937. See p. 359 above.

RECORDING. A BBC disc (No 1235E, 2 sides: duration 4.05 + 4.22) preserves the opening section and the introductory remarks to Edith Sitwell's *Ass-face*. A copy of this record is held by the Lamont Library, Harvard.

8 ABBEY THEATRE BROADCAST. February 1, 1937. Radio Eireann.

This programme, recorded in the Abbey Theatre, consisted of songs, patter, and violin solos; poems by Yeats, James Stephens, and F. R. Higgins were also read. Though Yeats had much to do with the preparation of this programme (see *Letters*, pp. 875, 878–9), the only voices identifiable in the recording are those of John Stephenson and Miss Ria Mooney.

SCRIPT. No script is preserved.

RECORDING. Radio Eireann has a recording of this performance. It is reported to be "technically extremely bad", and was not used—as Yeats originally intended—for a rebroadcast from London.

9 IN THE POET'S PUB. April 2, 1937: 9.20–9.40 p.m. BBC London: National Programme. Produced by George Barnes.

The script was prepared and introduced by Yeats, the poems being read by V. C. Clinton-Baddeley after rehearsal under Yeats's direction. A second performance was planned for April 8, 1938, but was cancelled because Clinton-Baddeley was not able to take part.

POEMS READ. I. Hilaire Belloc, *Tarantella*
G. K. Chesterton, *The Rolling English Road* (omitting the last 2 stanzas)
Walter de la Mare, *Off the Ground* (read as patter)
II. Henry Newbolt, *Drake's Drum*
Sylvia Townsend Warner, *The Sailor*
Paul Fort (*tr*. F. York Powell), *The Sailor and the Shark*

The poems were read in two groups, each group being introduced by Yeats. Intervals between the poems, and sometimes between stanzas, were marked by drum-rolls to emphasise the rhythm and "to set the mind dreaming"; and towards the end of the last poem other voices joined in the refrain and the verse passed into an improvised song.

Yeats had originally chosen a poem each by Hardy, Kipling, and Edith Sitwell; but these were "sternly rejected" [? by George Barnes] in production. See Hone's *Life*, p. 456.

SCRIPT. File copy at Broadcasting House. A MS version of the introduction is among the Yeats papers.

RECORDING. BBC discs of the whole programme, 5 sides, are preserved at Broadcasting House (No. 14879, 14880, 14881A front: duration 18.58)

10   IN THE POET'S PARLOUR. April 22, 1937: 10.20–10.40 p.m. BBC London: National Programme. Produced by George Barnes.

The script was prepared and introduced by Yeats. The poems were read by V. C. Clinton-Baddeley and Margot Ruddock; Eva Towns also took part, apparently playing the bamboo pipe. Melodies and rhythms were devised by Imogen Holst to meet Yeats's wishes.

POEMS READ.   I. *Sweet Dancer* (spoken by Margot Ruddock)
'*I am of Ireland*' (spoken by Clinton-Baddeley, the refrain sung by Margot Ruddock)
'The Wicked Hawthorn Tree' from *The King of the Great Clock Tower* (sung by Clinton-Baddeley and Margot Ruddock)
II. J. E. Flecker, *Santorin* (spoken by Margot Ruddock)
Lionel Johnson, *To Morfydd* (spoken and chanted by Margot Ruddock)
F. R. Higgins, *Song for the Clatter Bones* (spoken by Clinton-Baddeley; with a variant in line 2 *proh pudore*)
The Pilgrim (spoken by Clinton-Baddeley)

The poems were read in two groups, each group being introduced by Yeats. Pipe tunes were played between the poems of the first section; the same tune being played before and after "*I am of Ireland*", and the tune "The Hawthorne Tree" played before the poem of the same name. An Irish cradlesong was played on the pipe before *To Morfydd*, the end of that poem being interrupted by drum and clatter-bones. The clatter-bones were also sounded after *Song for the Clatter Bones*.

The poems announced in the *Radio Times* were: Edith Sitwell's *The King of China's Daughter*, J. E. Flecker's *Santorin*, Lionel Johnson's *To Morfydd*, Yeats's *Sweet Dancer*, "*I am of Ireland*", *Poem from the Japanese*, and *The Wicked Hawthorn Tree*. This evidently represents an early version of the script. Clinton-Baddeley remembers rehearsing with Margot Ruddock *Poem from the Japanese*, but it appears not to have been broadcast. Clinton-Baddeley and Jill Balcon recorded this poem for Book IV of *The London Library of Recorded English* in about 1945.

SCRIPT. File copy at Broadcasting House. A MS of the introduction, fragmentary and almost indecipherable, is among the Yeats papers.

11 MY OWN POETRY. July 3, 1937: 10.0–10.20 p.m. BBC London: National Programme. Produced by George Barnes.

The script was prepared and introduced by Yeats. The poems were read by V. C. Clinton-Baddeley and Margot Ruddock, with music specially composed by Edmund Dulac (see *Letters*, pp. 888, 890–1). Olive Groves (singer) and Marie Goossens (harp) also took part.

POEMS READ.   I. *The Rose Tree* (spoken by Clinton-Baddeley)
An Irish Airman Foresees his Death (spoken by Clinton-Baddeley)
The Curse of Cromwell (spoken by Margot Ruddock)
II. *Mad as the Mist and Snow* (spoken by Clinton-Baddeley)
Sailing to Byzantium (spoken by Clinton-Baddeley: with a variant in the first line, see *Life*, p. 456)
He and She (sung by Olive Groves to a setting by Edmund Dulac)

The poems were read in two groups, each group being introduced by Yeats. There is no direction in the script for instrumental interludes between the poems, but the treatment was presumably similar to that used in Broadcast 10.

The poems announced in the *Radio Times* were: *In Memory of Eva Gore-Booth and Con Markiewicz, The Rose Tree, An Irish Airman, Mad as the Mist and Snow, Sailing to Byzantium, He and She, The Curse of Cromwell*. This evidently represents an early version of the script. Margot Ruddock rehearsed *In Memory of Eva Gore-Booth* but the poem was not broadcast.

SCRIPT. File copy at Broadcasting House. The MS draft is among the Yeats papers.

RECORDING. No recording of this programme is preserved. In 1945 V. C. Clinton-Baddeley recorded *Mad as the Mist and Snow* for Book IV of *The London Library of Recorded English*, reading the poem in the style evolved under Yeats's direction in this broadcast.

12 MY OWN POETRY AGAIN. October 29, 1937: 10.45–11.05 p.m. BBC London: National Programme. Produced by George Barnes.

This broadcast was announced as "A Programme introduced and read by W. B. Yeats assisted by Margot Ruddock". Unlike the other three broadcasts of 1937, but like Broadcast 3, the commentary ran continuously from one poem to another without instrumental interludes.

POEMS READ. *The Lake Isle of Innisfree*
The Fiddler of Dooney
The Happy Townland
Into the Twilight (sung by Margot Ruddock "to her own music without accompaniment")
The Countess Cathleen in Paradise (sung by Margot Ruddock)
Coole Park and Ballylee, 1931
The Old Men Admiring Themselves in the Water (spoken by Margot Ruddock)

SCRIPT. The BBC file copy was destroyed during the war. A typescript marked "My own copy" is among the Yeats papers; but it breaks off at the foot of a page at the end of the second stanza of *Coole Park*. The title of the final poem and other details of the production are supplied from notes made by George Barnes and V. C. Clinton-Baddeley in 1949–1950.

RECORDING. A BBC disc at Broadcasting House (No 22145 back: duration 2.27), dated October 28, 1937, records the introduction, the reading of *Innisfree*, and the 3rd and 4th stanzas of *Coole Park and Ballylee*. A copy of this disc is held by the Lamont Library, Harvard.

NOTE. In June 1937 Yeats proposed to James Stephens that they make a radio debate on the theme that "all arts are an expression of desire" and that "all arts must be united again"; they would work the discussion "into a kind of drama in which we will get very abusive". Stephens declined the suggestion; and although Edmund Dulac offered to take Stephens's place the broadcast was never made. See Hone's *Life*, p. 458.

SOME BROADCASTS ABOUT YEATS

AND HIS MANNER OF READING POETRY

A   W. B. YEATS—A DUBLIN PORTRAIT. June 5, 1949: 7.15–8.15 p.m. BBC London: Third Programme. Repeated June 10 and 21, 1949: Third Programme. Produced by Maurice Brown.

The script was prepared and edited by W. R. Rodgers, and narrated by Fred O'Donovan. The verse was spoken by Frank O'Connor. Other material was edited from interviews recorded by Maurice Brown and W. R. Rodgers in Dublin between 3 and 18 February 1949: the speakers were Richard Best, Austin Clarke, Alfred Hanna, W. K. Magee, Madame MacBride, Sean MacBride, Nora MacGuinness,

Brinsley Macnamara, Miss Macnie, Frank O'Connor, Sean O'Faolain, Lennox Robinson, Robert Smyllie, Mrs Iseult Stuart, Dossy Wright, Anne Yeats, Mrs W. B. Yeats.

The recording of Yeats reading *The Lake Isle of Innisfree* in Broadcast 12 was interpolated.

Frank O'Connor read from *All Souls' Night, Sailing to Byzantium, Beautiful Lofty Things, He Wishes for the Cloths of Heaven*, 'I am like the children' (from MS), *Nineteen Hundred and Nineteen, What Then?, The Tower, High Talk.*

SCRIPT. A file copy of the script is at Broadcasting House, transcribed from the recordings.

RECORDING. A recording of the whole programme is preserved on two BBC discs (No MX 13584–9). The unedited interviews with Madame MacBride and with Mrs Stuart are preserved separately (No 13843 back, 13844 back: duration 3.55+5.20. No 14881A back, 13843 front, 13844 front: duration 2.12+4.16+3.34). A third disc, recording the rest of the interview with Madame MacBride seems to have disappeared since I heard it at Broadcasting House in the summer of 1954.

B 1. BROADCASTING WITH W. B. YEATS. December 11, 1949: 10.40–11.00 p.m. BBC Bristol: West of England Home Service. Repeated June 25, 1950: Third Programme. Produced by Gilbert Phelps.

The script was prepared and spoken by V. C. Clinton-Baddeley: being an account of his preparation under Yeats's direction to speak poems in three of the 1937 broadcasts (Nos. 8, 9, 10), with illustrations of the way Yeats wanted certain poems read. Jill Balcon took part in the programme.

POEMS READ. *Poem from the Japanese* (spoken by Clinton-Baddeley, the refrain spoken by Jill Balcon)
Sweet Dancer (spoken by Jill Balcon)
'I am of Ireland' (spoken and sung by Clinton-Baddeley and Jill Balcon)
The Rose Tree (spoken by Clinton-Baddeley)
Mad as the Mist and Snow (spoken by Clinton-Baddeley)
The Curse of Cromwell (spoken by Jill Balcon)
Sailing to Byzantium (spoken by Clinton-Baddeley)

SCRIPT. There is a file copy at Broadcasting House. Mr Clinton-Baddeley has shown me his own marked copy.

This talk supplements and expands some details in George Barnes's account: particularly the incident of Yeats altering the opening line of *Sailing to Byzantium* in Broadcast 11, and the attempt to combine music and verse in Broadcast 10.

THE SHADOWY WATERS | A musical dramatic poem in one Act with a Prologue | based on the poem of W. B. Yeats | translated into Greek by Veta Pezopoulos | Retranslated into English by Geoffrey Dunn | who has used, wherever possible, Yeats's own wording | Music by Manolis Kalomiris | The first performance was given by the National Opera of Greece at | Athens on 4 January 1951 | The first performances in England: Friday, 23 October 1953, and | Monday, 26 October 1953. BBC Third Programme | with the following cast:|

Forgael (*tenor*)	Richard Lewis	
Dectora (*soprano*)	Jennifer Vyvyan	
Aibric (*baritone*)	John Cameron	
First Sailor (*bass*)	Norman Lumsden	
Second Sailor (*tenor*)	Alexander Young	
Third Sailor (*bass*)	Chorister	
The Prologue (*mezzo soprano*)	Marjorie Thomas	
Two bird voices 1. (*soprano*)	Margaret Ritchie	
2. (*mezzo soprano*)	Marion Lowe	

Chorus of sailors and women's voices |

The BBC Opera Chorus | The Philharmonia Orchestra | Conducted by: Alec Sherman | Producer: Geoffrey Dunn

7⅛× 4¾; pp. 16: comprising title, brief biographical sketch of Manolis Kalomiris and permission acknowledgement on verso, pp. [1–2]; text of libretto, pp. 3–[16]; imprint, Published by the British Broadcasting corporation, 35 Marylebone High Street, London, w. 1. Printed by the Broadwater Press Ltd, Welwyn Garden City, Herts. No. 2996 at foot of p. [16]. A correction slip is inserted loose: this is headed CORRECTION and reads 'for The Philharmonia Orchestra please read The New London Orchestra'

Issued in paper covers, lettered in blue-green and black on front cover, the whole within a frame of blue-green rules, lettered in black on back cover, within black rules. [Published in 1953?]

C WORDS FOR MUSIC PERHAPS. August 4, 1957: 9.00–9.30, 10.25–10.40 p.m. BBC London: Third Programme. Repeated August 8, 1957. Produced by D. S. Carne-Ross.

The script was prepared and narrated by George Whalley. Other speakers were L. A. G. Strong, Allan MacLelland, V. C. Clinton-Baddeley, and Denis McCarthy. Timpanist, James Blades.

Recordings of Yeats reading part of *Coole Park and Ballylee* (from No. 12), and extracts from the National Lecture (No. 7) and from *In the Poet's Pub* (No. 9) were interpolated into the Introduction.

POEMS READ. I *Mad as the Mist and Snow* (spoken by V. C. Clinton-
        Baddeley)
      The Fisherman (spoken by L. A. G. Strong)
  II (spoken by Allan MacLelland)
      Easter, 1916
      The Second Coming
      Leda and the Swan
      Sailing to Byzantium
      The Man and the Echo
      High Talk

The programme was presented in two parts: an introductory discussion and exposition of Yeats's views on reading poetry (30 minutes), followed after an interval by 15 minutes of poetry reading, the six poems being read in two groups. With a view to extending the method used by Yeats in Broadcasts 9 and 10, interludes with timpani and percussion were played between the poems.

INDEX

H H2

I I